P9-EDY-063

DATE DUE

DEMCO 38-296

THE AMERICAN MARKETPLACE

THE AMERICAN MARKETPLACE

Demographics and Spending Patterns

EDITED BY JANET HESLOP

New Strategist Publications, Inc.
Ithaca, New York

Riverside Community College
Library
4800 Magnolia Avenue
Riverside, California 92506

HA214 .A6 1997
The American marketplace :
demographics and spending
patterns

4851

607/273-0913

Copyright 1997. NEW STRATEGIST PUBLICATIONS, INC.

All rights reserved.

No part of this book may be reproduced, stored in a retrieval system, or transmitted in any form or by any means, electronic, mechanical, photocopying, microfilming, recording, or otherwise without written permission from the Publisher.

ISBN 1-885070-07-1

Printed in the United States of America

Dedicated to teaching my daughters
Laura
Amber
Emily
the importance of hard work and perseverance,
as my father taught me.

Table of Contents

Chapter 3. Income Trends

Chapter 4. Labor Trends

Chapter 5. Living Arrangement Trends

Chapter 6. Population Trends

Chapter 7. Spending Trends

Chapter 8. Wealth Trends

List of Tables

Chapter 3. Income Trends

Chapter 4. Labor Trends

Chapter 5. Living Arrangement Trends

Chapter 6. Population Trends

Chapter 7. Spending Trends

Chapter 8. Wealth Trends

Introduction

If there is one thing Americans have in abundance, it is numbers. At any time, billions of statistics await our perusal just a mouse-click away. It is easier than ever to become overwhelmed with data and miss the story.

The American Marketplace: Demographics & Spending Patterns cuts through the statistical clutter and tells you the American story—now and in the future. It examines American lifestyles in rich detail, from the proportion of immigrants who settle in California to the proportion of babies born out of wedlock, from the net worth of baby boomers to the amount of money people spend on entertainment. It also looks into the future, with projections of populations, households, workers, and industries.

Since we published the first edition of *The American Marketplace* in 1992 (when it had the title of *The Official Guide to the American Marketplace*), dramatic technological change has reshaped the demographic reference industry. The government's detailed demographic data, once widely available to all in printed reports, is now accessible only to Internet users or in unpublished tables obtained by calling the appropriate government agency with a specific request. The government's web sites, which house enormous spreadsheets of data, are of great value to researchers with the time and skills to first download and then extract the important nuggets of information. The shift from printed reports to web sites—while convenient for number-crunchers—has made demographic analysis a bigger chore. For many researchers, it is more time-consuming than ever to get no-nonsense answers to your questions about the demographic characteristics of Americans.

The American Marketplace has the answers. It has the numbers and the stories behind them. Thumbing through its pages, you can gain more insight into the consumer marketplace than you could by spending all afternoon surfing databases on the Internet. By having it on your bookshelf, you can get the answers to your questions even faster than you could with the fastest modem.

How to Use This Book

The American Marketplace is designed for easy use. It is divided into eight topic areas, organized alphabetically: Education, Health, Income, Labor Force, Living Arrangements, Population, Spending, and Wealth.

Most of the tables in this book are based on data collected by the federal government, in particular the Census Bureau, the Bureau of Labor Statistics, the

National Center for Education Statistics, and the National Center for Health Statistics. The federal government continues to be the best source of up-to-date, reliable information on the changing characteristics of Americans. When government data are not available about an important topic, we have included data from other surveys and studies.

While the data in this book are produced by the government, we are not simply reprinting the government's spreadsheets—as do many reference books. Each table is individually compiled and created by New Strategist, with calculations performed by our statisticians to reveal the trends. A page of text accompanies most of the tables, analyzing the data and highlighting future trends. If you want more information than the tables and text provide, you can locate the original source of the data, which is listed at the bottom of each table.

The book contains a lengthy table list to help you locate the information you need. For a more detailed search, use the index in the back of the book. Also in the back of the book is the glossary, which defines many of the terms commonly used in the tables and text. A list of telephone contacts also appears at the end of the book, allowing researchers to access government specialists by topic.

We hope *The American Marketplace* will help you cut through the clutter and track the trends. Use it and prosper.

1

Education Trends

♦ **The U.S. has the best-educated population in the world.**
One in four men and one in five women are college graduates.

♦ **Blacks are closing the gap with whites in educational attainment.**
More than 80 percent of whites aged 25 or older are high school graduates, compared with 73 percent of blacks and 53 percent of Hispanics.

♦ **School enrollments are on the rise.**
Between 1996 and 2006, enrollment in the nation's elementary and secondary schools will rise by 6 percent, with the biggest increase occurring at the secondary level.

♦ **The SAT scores of minority groups have been rising since 1975-76.**
Among blacks, verbal scores were up by 24 points between 1975-76 and 1994-95, while math scores rose 34 points.

♦ **As family income rises, children are more likely to go to college.**
Among families with incomes of $75,000 or more who have children aged 18 to 24, 64 percent have a child in college full-time.

♦ **College enrollment rates have increased for whites, blacks, and Hispanics in the past two decades.**
The rate grew from 49 to 63 percent for whites between 1976 and 1995, from 42 to 51 percent for blacks, and from 49 to 55 percent for Hispanics.

♦ **Women earn over half of bachelor's and master's degrees and will earn half of doctorates by 2006.**
As a growing share of women gain educational credentials in the years ahead, women's earnings will rise, narrowing the gap between men's and women's incomes.

Americans Are Increasingly Well-Educated

The United States has the best-educated population in the world. One in four men and one in five women are college graduates.

The educational attainment of Americans has increased dramatically over the past three decades. Just 30 years ago, over half of Americans had not even graduated from high school. Then the parents of the baby-boom generation encouraged their children to finish high school and go to college. The well-educated baby-boom generation has lifted the educational level of the population as a whole.

Overall, 82 percent of men aged 25 or older are high school graduates. The proportion ranges from 64 percent among men aged 65 or older to 88 percent among men aged 35 to 44. The share of men with at least a college degree peaks among those aged 45 to 54, with 33 percent having a bachelor's degree. Only 17 percent of men aged 65 or older are college graduates.

The proportion of women with a high school diploma is identical to that of men, at 82 percent. The proportion ranges from 64 percent among women aged 65 or older to 89 percent among women aged 35 to 44. Women are less likely than men to be college graduates. Only 20 percent of women hold a bachelor's degree. Those most likely to have completed a college education are women aged 35 to 44, at 25 percent. Women aged 25 to 34 are slightly more likely than their male counterparts to have a bachelor's degree.

♦ Young adults are somewhat less educated than baby boomers, but they may catch up as they get older because many will go back to school.

♦ The educational level of Americans aged 65 or older will rise sharply as baby boomers reach old age. This will increase the sophistication of older consumers, changing the ways businesses market to this segment of the population.

Educational Attainment by Sex and Age, 1995

(number and percent distribution of persons aged 25 or older by sex, age, and educational attainment, 1995; numbers in thousands)

	total	not a high school graduate	high school graduate or more	high school graduate only	some college, no degree	associate's degree	bachelor's degree or more				
							total	bachelor's degree	master's degree	professional degree	doctoral degree
Total men, number	79,463	14,520	64,942	25,378	13,795	5,138	20,631	13,132	4,591	1,713	1,195
Aged 25 to 34	20,589	2,867	17,623	7,176	3,824	1,549	5,174	3,935	849	271	119
Aged 35 to 44	20,972	2,592	18,378	6,872	3,972	1,659	5,875	3,784	1,284	517	290
Aged 45 to 54	15,022	2,086	12,934	4,351	2,564	1,110	4,909	2,766	1,323	448	372
Aged 55 to 64	9,878	2,231	7,647	3,181	1,548	480	2,438	1,336	641	237	224
Aged 65 or older	13,003	4,744	8,262	3,799	1,886	341	2,237	1,310	494	239	192
Total men, percent	100.0%	18.3%	81.7%	31.9%	17.4%	6.5%	26.0%	16.5%	5.8%	2.2%	1.5%
Aged 25 to 34	100.0	13.9	85.6	34.9	18.6	7.5	25.1	19.1	4.1	1.3	0.6
Aged 35 to 44	100.0	12.4	87.6	32.8	18.9	7.9	28.0	18.0	6.1	2.5	1.4
Aged 45 to 54	100.0	13.9	86.1	29.0	17.1	7.4	32.7	18.4	8.8	3.0	2.5
Aged 55 to 64	100.0	22.6	77.4	32.2	15.7	4.9	24.7	13.5	6.5	2.4	2.3
Aged 65 or older	100.0	36.5	63.5	29.2	14.5	2.6	17.2	10.1	3.8	1.8	1.5

(continued)

(continued from previous page)

	total	not a high school graduate	high school graduate or more	high school graduate only	some college, no degree	associate's degree	bachelor's degree or more				
							total	bachelor's degree	master's degree	professional degree	doctoral degree
Total women, number	86,975	15,992	70,983	31,072	15,561	6,756	17,594	12,181	4,226	715	472
Aged 25 to 34	20,800	2,459	18,341	6,885	4,271	2,015	5,170	4,125	779	201	65
Aged 35 to 44	21,363	2,335	19,028	7,230	4,265	2,135	5,398	3,604	1,359	276	159
Aged 45 to 54	15,671	2,134	13,538	5,617	2,967	1,256	3,698	2,265	1,167	122	144
Aged 55 to 64	10,878	2,499	8,381	4,564	1,696	608	1,513	931	467	60	55
Aged 65 or older	18,264	6,565	11,699	6,776	2,363	743	1,817	1,255	454	58	51
Total women, percent	100.0%	18.4%	81.6%	35.7%	17.9%	7.8%	20.2%	14.0%	4.9%	0.8%	0.5%
Aged 25 to 34	100.0	11.8	88.2	33.1	20.5	9.7	24.9	19.8	3.7	1.0	0.3
Aged 35 to 44	100.0	10.9	89.1	33.8	20.0	10.0	25.3	16.9	6.4	1.3	0.7
Aged 45 to 54	100.0	13.6	86.4	35.8	18.9	8.0	23.6	14.5	7.4	0.8	0.9
Aged 55 to 64	100.0	23.0	77.0	42.0	15.6	5.6	13.9	8.6	4.3	0.6	0.5
Aged 65 or older	100.0	35.9	64.1	37.1	12.9	4.1	9.9	6.9	2.5	0.3	0.3

Source: Bureau of the Census, Educational Attainment in the United States: March 1995, Current Population Reports, P20-489, 1996; calculations by New Strategist

Whites Better Educated Than Blacks or Hispanics

More than 80 percent of whites aged 25 or older are high school graduates, compared with 73 percent of blacks and 53 percent of Hispanics.

The educational gap between whites and blacks is greatest in the older age groups. Whites and blacks under age 40 are almost equally likely to be high school graduates. But dramatic differences exist among the older generations. Sixty-six percent of white men aged 65 or older have a high school diploma. Only 35 percent of their black counterparts are high school graduates. Among Hispanics, even young adults are poorly educated. Only 53 percent of Hispanic men and 54 percent of Hispanic women aged 25 or older are high school graduates.

At the college level, the gap widens between blacks and whites. While one in four white men aged 25 or older has a college degree, only 13 percent of black men are college graduates. A similar gap occurs among women, with 21 percent of white women aged 25 or older holding a college degree compared with 13 percent of black women. Only 10 percent of Hispanic men and 8 percent of Hispanic women have college degrees.

♦ The rapidly rising cost of college may make it more difficult for blacks to close the education gap with whites.

♦ A lack of schooling among Hispanic immigrants is behind the low level of educational attainment for all Hispanics. If the massive immigration of Hispanics into the U.S. continues, expect to see few gains in the educational attainment of this segment of the population.

Educational Attainment by Age, Race, and Hispanic Origin, 1995

(percent of persons aged 25 or older who are high school or college graduates, by sex, age, race, and Hispanic origin, 1995)

	high school graduate or more				bachelor's degree or more			
	total	white	black	Hispanic	total	white	black	Hispanic
Total men	81.7%	83.0%	73.4%	52.9%	26.0%	27.2%	13.6%	10.1%
Aged 25 to 29	86.3	86.6	88.1	55.7	24.5	25.4	17.2	7.8
Aged 30 to 34	85.9	86.5	84.1	55.0	25.7	27.0	14.8	10.5
Aged 35 to 39	87.8	88.2	86.1	62.1	26.6	27.8	14.2	10.6
Aged 40 to 44	87.4	89.2	77.1	59.0	29.6	31.0	16.4	12.5
Aged 45 to 49	87.7	89.5	76.5	54.5	35.0	37.0	15.2	12.6
Aged 50 to 54	84.0	86.0	69.5	46.3	29.6	30.8	16.7	9.2
Aged 55 to 59	79.9	81.6	56.5	46.2	25.4	26.8	11.7	12.8
Aged 60 to 64	74.7	77.6	49.6	38.5	23.8	25.7	6.6	8.1
Aged 65 or older	63.5	66.2	35.1	32.2	17.2	18.3	4.8	7.9
Total women	81.6	83.0	74.1	53.8	20.2	21.0	12.9	8.4
Aged 25 to 29	87.4	88.2	85.1	58.7	24.9	26.6	13.6	10.1
Aged 30 to 34	88.9	90.0	84.4	64.2	24.8	26.5	13.3	9.9
Aged 35 to 39	88.9	89.8	87.6	61.1	24.5	25.7	15.6	9.8
Aged 40 to 44	89.3	90.8	83.3	62.5	26.1	27.0	16.6	10.0
Aged 45 to 49	88.4	90.1	78.3	53.4	25.5	26.9	14.7	7.7
Aged 50 to 54	83.8	85.5	75.0	50.6	21.2	21.5	15.7	8.6
Aged 55 to 59	79.8	81.9	67.7	43.1	15.4	16.2	8.9	4.0
Aged 60 to 64	74.1	76.3	57.0	35.5	12.3	12.4	9.6	5.9
Aged 65 or older	64.1	67.0	38.2	27.5	10.0	10.3	6.6	4.0

Source: Bureau of the Census, Educational Attainment in the United States: 1995, *Current Population Reports, P20-489, 1996*

More Than 4 Million First Graders

Nearly all Americans between the ages of 5 and 18 are in school, and the share of the youngest and oldest in school is rising.

The baby boomlet of the late 1980s is increasing school enrollment. More than 4 million children were in first grade in 1994. No other grade had more than 4 million students.

The proportion of Americans who are in school has grown dramatically since 1970 at both the younger and older ages. The proportion of 3- and 4-year-olds enrolled in nursery school more than doubled between 1970 and 1994, from 21 to 47 percent. The proportion of 18- and 19-year-olds in school, most of them in college, has grown from 48 to 60 percent.

Kindergarten enrollment is likely to remain around 4 million during the next few years because the children born during the birth peak (which occurred from 1989 through the early 1990s) will enter kindergarten. As this baby boomlet advances, enrollments in higher grades will also expand, straining the budgets of local school districts.

♦ With more parents using nursery school as day care, and with education increasingly important to earnings, the percentage of younger and older Americans enrolled in school will continue to rise in the years ahead.

School Enrollment by Grade Level, 1994

(number and percent distribution of students enrolled in elementary and secondary schools by grade, fall 1994; numbers in thousands)

	number	percent
Total students	49,991	100.0%
Total elementary	35,375	70.8
Kindergarten	3,863	7.7
1st grade	4,341	8.7
2nd grade	3,962	7.9
3rd grade	3,779	7.6
4th grade	3,917	7.8
5th grade	3,917	7.8
6th grade	3,952	7.9
7th grade	3,920	7.8
8th grade	3,724	7.4
Total secondary	14,616	29.2
9th grade	3,830	7.7
10th grade	3,742	7.5
11th grade	3,450	6.9
12th grade	3,594	7.2

Source: Bureau of the Census, School Enrollment—Social and Economic Characteristics of Students: October 1994, *Current Population Reports, P20-487, 1996*

School Enrollment Projected to Rise Steadily

As most local school districts already know, school enrollments are on the rise.

Between 1996 and 2006, enrollment in the nation's elementary and secondary schools will rise by 6 percent, with the biggest increase occurring at the secondary level.

Enrollment in kindergarten through 8th grade is projected to rise by 2 percent between 1996 and 2006 as the baby boomlet of the late 1980s and early 1990s enters school. Enrollment in secondary school is projected to increase much faster, up by 15 percent between 1996 and 2006. Secondary-school enrollments will increase more than elementary because the baby-boomlet generation will replace the small baby-bust generation now in high school.

♦ Because births will remain close to 4 million through the 1990s and beyond, the current rise in school enrollments is not a short-term problem that can be solved by squeezing a few more children into each classroom. Instead, enrollments are rising to a higher level and stabilizing there. This will mean new schools, more teachers, and possibly higher taxes.

Projected Enrollment in Kindergarten Through 12th Grade, 1996 to 2006

(number of students enrolled in public and private schools, fall 1996 to fall 2006; percent change, 1996-2006; numbers in thousands)

	enrollment in public and private schools		
	total	*K-8th*	*9th-12th*
1996	51,683	37,330	14,353
1997	52,400	37,772	14,628
1998	52,921	38,109	14,811
1999	53,342	38,303	15,039
2000	53,668	38,484	15,184
2001	53,933	38,686	15,248
2002	54,168	38,764	15,404
2003	54,312	38,726	15,586
2004	54,449	38,519	15,930
2005	54,587	38,289	16,299
2006	54,615	38,092	16,523

Percent change

| 1996 to 2006 | 5.7% | 2.0% | 15.1% |

Source: National Center for Education Statistics, Projections of Education Statistics to 2006, *Internet web site, http://www.ed.gov/NCES; calculations by New Strategist*

Private School Enrollment Will Rise

Enrollment in private elementary and secondary schools will rise at about the same rate as total school enrollment.

Among the 51 million students enrolled in the nation's elementary and secondary schools, just 5.8 million, or 11 percent, attend private schools. Private school enrollment is projected to rise to 6.1 million by 2006, with secondary enrollment growing faster than elementary as the larger baby-boomlet generation replaces the smaller baby-bust generation in the secondary grades.

Of the children attending private schools, most attend religious institutions. Fifty-one percent go to Catholic schools, while another 34 percent attend other religious schools. Only 16 percent of private school students attend nonsectarian schools.

♦ These projections assume that the percentage of children who attend private schools by grade remains unchanged. But if Americans' perception of the quality of education in public schools does not improve, private school enrollments may surge. Baby-boom parents are accustomed to paying for day care, and they may not find the costs of private school too much of a burden.

Private School Enrollment, 1996 to 2006

(number of students enrolled in public and private schools, and private school enrollment by grade level, fall 1996 to fall 2006; percent change, 1996-2006; numbers in thousands)

| | total enrollment | enrollment in private schools | | |
		total	K-8th	9th-12th
1996	51,683	5,798	4,493	1,304
1997	52,400	5,876	4,547	1,329
1998	52,921	5,933	4,587	1,346
1999	53,342	5,977	4,610	1,367
2000	53,668	6,012	4,632	1,380
2001	53,933	6,042	4,656	1,386
2002	54,168	6,066	4,666	1,400
2003	54,312	6,078	4,661	1,416
2004	54,449	6,084	4,636	1,448
2005	54,587	6,090	4,609	1,481
2006	54,615	6,086	4,585	1,501
Percent change				
1996 to 2006	5.7%	5.0%	2.0%	15.1%

Source: National Center for Education Statistics, Projections of Education Statistics to 2006, *Internet web site,* http://www.ed.gov/NCES; *calculations by New Strategist*

Fewer High School Dropouts

As education becomes the route to prosperity, dropouts are gambling with their future. High school dropout rates have tumbled for both whites and blacks in the past decade.

Among 16-to-24-year-olds in 1994, only 11.5 percent were not high school graduates or not currently enrolled in school, down from 14 percent in 1974. Dropout rates have fallen for both men and women, with women's dropout rate now below that of men.

Dropout rates remain stubbornly high for Hispanics. While just 8 percent of whites and 13 percent of blacks aged 16 to 24 were dropouts in 1994, fully 30 percent of Hispanics in that age group were dropouts. For Hispanic men, the dropout rate has increased since 1984. Nearly one in three Hispanic men aged 16 to 24 was a high school dropout in 1994.

♦ The immigration of poorly educated Hispanics to the U.S. during the 1980s explains the rise in the dropout rate for Hispanic men. This rate is likely to remain high as long as recent immigrants make up a large proportion of the Hispanic population.

High School Dropouts by Sex, Race, and Hispanic Origin, 1974, 1984, and 1994

(percent of persons aged 16 to 24 who were not enrolled in school or high school graduates by sex, race, and Hispanic origin, 1974, 1984, and 1994; percentage point change, 1974-1994)

	1994	1984	1974	percentage point change 1974-94
Total	11.5%	13.1%	14.3%	-2.8
White, non-Hispanic	7.7	11.0	11.9	-4.2
Black, non-Hispanic	12.6	15.5	21.2	-8.6
Hispanic	30.0	29.8	33.0	-3.0
Total men	12.3	14.0	14.2	-1.9
White, non-Hispanic	8.0	12.0	12.0	-4.0
Black, non-Hispanic	14.1	16.8	20.1	-6.0
Hispanic	31.6	30.6	33.8	-2.2
Total women	10.6	12.3	14.4	-3.8
White, non-Hispanic	7.5	10.1	11.8	-4.3
Black, non-Hispanic	11.3	14.3	22.1	-10.8
Hispanic	28.1	29.0	32.2	-4.1

Source: National Center for Education Statistics, Digest of Education Statistics 1996, *NCES 96-133; calculations by New Strategist*

A Boom in High School Diplomas

The number of people graduating from high school will climb by 17 percent between 1996 and 2006.

As the small baby-bust generation is replaced in the nation's high schools by the larger baby-boomlet generation, the number of high school graduates will climb from 2.6 million in 1996 to 3 million in 2006. The annual crop of graduates, which has been shrinking for years, began a steady rise in 1993.

♦ Since more than 4 million babies were born each year from 1989 through 1993, the number of high school graduates should remain at record levels through 2011.

Projections of High School Graduates, 1996 to 2006

(number of persons graduating from high school, 1996 to 2006, and percent change 1996-2006; numbers in thousands)

	high school graduates
1996	2,588
1997	2,612
1998	2,734
1999	2,828
2000	2,873
2001	2,933
2002	2,961
2003	2,981
2004	3,054
2005	3,051
2006	3,022

Percent change

1996 to 2006	16.8%

Source: National Center for Education Statistics, Projections of Education Statistics to 2006, *Internet web site,* http://www.ed.gov/NCES; *calculations by New Strategist*

SAT Scores Rising for All Minority Groups

The much-talked-about decline in SAT scores over the past few decades is a more complex story than it seems. For many test takers, scores are rising.

The growing diversity of test takers has been driving down average scores. In 1994-95, more than 1 million prospective college students took the Scholastic Aptitude Test (SAT), up from just 11,000 in 1941 when the test was first administered. As increasing numbers of students took the test, average scores were pushed down. But a closer look reveals rising scores for most groups.

The SAT scores of minority groups have been rising since 1975-76. Among blacks, verbal scores were up by 24 points between 1975-76 and 1994-95, while math scores were 34 points higher. Whites are the only racial group whose scores have declined—and only on the verbal section of the exam.

♦ Overall, SAT scores are likely to show slow improvement in the years ahead as minority scores continue to rise.

SAT Scores by Race and Ethnicity, 1975-76 and 1994-95

(average SAT scores and change in scores by race and ethnicity of student, 1975-76 and 1994-95)

	1994-95	1975-76	change
Verbal SAT			
Total students	428	431	-3
White	448	451	-3
Black	356	332	24
Mexican-American	376	371	5
Puerto Rican	372	364	8
Asian-American	418	414	4
American Indian	403	388	15
Other	432	410	22
Mathematical SAT			
Total students	482	472	10
White	498	493	5
Black	388	354	34
Mexican-American	426	410	16
Puerto Rican	411	401	10
Asian-American	538	518	20
American Indian	447	420	27
Other	486	458	28

Source: National Center for Education Statistics, Digest of Education Statistics *1996, NCES 96-133; calculations by New Strategist*

Among Affluent, Most Children Go to College

As family income rises, children are more likely to go to college.

It's no suprise that family income is one of the best predictors of whether children have the opportunity to go to college. Among all families with children aged 18 to 24, 40 percent have a child in college full-time. This proportion rises steadily with income, to a 64 percent majority among families with incomes of $75,000 or more.

Among families with children aged 18 to 24 whose incomes are below $20,000, just 23 percent have a child in college full-time.

♦ Children of the affluent can devote full attention to their studies because their parents are paying the bills. Many children from less affluent families must attend school part-time because they have to work.

Families with Children in College, 1994

(total number of families, number with children aged 18 to 24, and number and percent with children aged 18 to 24 attending college full-time by household income, 1994; numbers in thousands)

			with one or more children attending college full-time		
	total	with children aged 18-24	number	percent of total families	percent of families with children 18-24
Total families	69,743	10,404	4,160	6.0%	40.0%
Under $20,000	17,627	2,166	489	2.8	22.6
$20,000 to $29,999	10,291	1,247	384	3.7	30.8
$30,000 to $39,999	9,734	1,412	462	4.7	32.7
$40,000 to $49,999	7,023	1,134	482	6.9	42.5
$50,000 to $74,999	10,968	1,984	988	9.0	49.8
$75,000 or more	8,066	1,589	1,013	12.6	63.8

Source: Bureau of the Census, School Enrollment—Social and Economic Characteristics of Students: October 1994, *Current Population Reports, P20-487, 1996; calculations by New Strategist*

College Enrollment Rates Have Soared

Rates are up because Americans are trying to better their lives.

The rate at which high school graduates enroll in college has soared over the past few decades, despite the rising cost of attending college. Once a privilege reserved for the nation's elite, the college experience now belongs to a majority of young adults.

Among women aged 16 to 24 who graduated from high school in 1995, 61 percent enrolled in college within 12 months. This figure is up sharply from just 38 percent in 1960. Among men, rates increased from 54 to 63 percent between 1960 and 1995.

College enrollment rates have increased for whites, blacks, and Hispanics in the past two decades. For whites, the rate has grown from 49 percent in 1976 to 63 percent in 1995. For blacks, the rate increased from 42 to 51 percent during those years. The Hispanic rate has also grown, from 49 percent in 1976 to 55 percent in 1994.

♦ Many of those who start college never finish—which is why fewer than half of the nation's young adults have a college diploma although more than half enroll in college. Because even a few years of college can make a big difference in earning power, however, the rise in enrollment rates is good news.

College Enrollment Rates by Sex, 1960 to 1995

(percent of persons aged 16 to 24 who graduated from high school in the previous 12 months and were enrolled in college as of October of each year, by sex; percentage point difference in enrollment rates of women and men; selected years, 1960-95)

	women	men	percentage point difference
1995	61.4%	62.6%	-1.2
1994	63.2	60.6	2.6
1993	65.4	59.7	5.7
1992	63.8	59.6	4.2
1991	67.1	57.6	9.5
1990	62.0	57.8	4.2
1989	61.6	57.6	4.0
1988	60.8	57.0	3.8
1987	55.3	58.4	-3.1
1986	51.9	55.9	-4.0
1985	56.9	58.6	-1.7
1980	51.8	46.7	5.1
1975	49.0	52.6	-3.6
1970	48.5	55.2	-6.7
1965	45.3	57.3	-12.0
1960	37.9	54.0	-16.1

Source: National Center for Education Statistics, Digest of Education Statistics 1996, *NCES 96-133; calculations by New Strategist*

College Enrollment Rates by Race and Hispanic Origin, 1976 to 1995

(percent of persons aged 16 to 24 who graduated from high school in the previous 12 months and were enrolled in college as of October of each year, by race and Hispanic origin, selected years, 1976-95)

	white	black	Hispanic*
1995	62.6%	51.4%	-
1994	63.6	50.9	55.1%
1993	62.8	55.6	55.4
1992	63.4	47.9	58.1
1991	64.6	45.6	53.1
1990	61.5	46.3	53.3
1989	60.4	52.8	53.2
1988	60.7	45.0	48.6
1987	56.6	51.9	45.0
1986	56.0	36.5	43.0
1985	59.4	42.3	46.6
1980	49.9	41.8	49.9
1976	48.9	41.9	48.9

* Three-year rolling average due to small sample size.
Source: National Center for Education Statistics, Digest of Education Statistics 1996, *NCES 96-133*

One in Five College Students Is a Minority

Among the nation's 14 million college students, over 3 million are black, Hispanic, Asian, or another minority.

Non-Hispanic whites accounted for 73 percent of college students in 1994, according to the National Center for Education Statistics. Non-Hispanic blacks were just over 10 percent of college students, slightly lower than the black share of the total population. Seven percent of college students were Hispanic, while just over 5 percent were Asian. Foreign students (called nonresident aliens) accounted for 3 percent of college students but were a much larger share of those earning graduate-level degrees.

Non-Hispanic whites were awarded 80 percent of all bachelor's degrees in 1993-94. Blacks earned 7 percent and Hispanics 4 percent. The non-Hispanic white share of degrees falls sharply at the master's and doctoral level—not because minorities are better represented, but because foreign students make up a large share of those earning degrees. At the master's level, nonresident aliens accounted for 12 percent of degrees awarded in 1993-94. At the doctoral level, they accounted for 27 percent of degrees.

♦ Because blacks and Hispanics receive a much smaller share of bachelor's and higher degrees than their share of the population, their educational level relative to whites is not likely to rise much in the foreseeable future.

College Enrollment by Race, Ethnicity, and Sex, 1994

(number and percent distribution of students in institutions of higher education by race, ethnicity, and sex, fall 1994; numbers in thousands)

	number	percent
Total	14,279	100.0%
White, non-Hispanic	10,427	73.0
Total minority	3,396	23.8
Black, non-Hispanic	1,449	10.1
Hispanic	1,046	7.3
Asian or Pacific Islander	774	5.4
American Indian/Alaskan Nativ	127	0.9
Nonresident alien	456	3.2
Total men	6,372	44.6
White, non-Hispanic	4,651	32.6
Total minority	1,452	10.2
Black, non-Hispanic	550	3.8
Hispanic	464	3.2
Asian or Pacific Islander	385	2.7
American Indian/Alaskan Nativ	53	0.4
Nonresident alien	270	1.9
Total women	7,907	55.4
White, non-Hispanic	5,776	40.5
Total minority	1,944	13.6
Black, non-Hispanic	899	6.3
Hispanic	582	4.1
Asian or Pacific Islander	389	2.7
American Indian/Alaskan Nativ	74	0.5
Nonresident alien	186	1.3

Source: National Center for Education Statistics, Digest of Education Statistics 1996, NCES 96-133

Degrees Conferred by Race, Ethnicity, and Level of Degree, 1993-94

(number and percent distribution of degrees conferred by level of degree, race, and ethnicity of degree holder, 1993-94)

	associate's		bachelor's		master's		doctoral		first-professional	
	number	*percent*	*number*	*percent*	*number*	*percent*	*number*	*percent*	*number*	*percent*
Total	540,923	100.0%	1,165,973	100.0%	385,419	100.0%	43,149	100.0%	75,418	100.0%
White, non-Hispanic	428,273	79.2	936,227	80.3	288,288	74.8	27,156	62.9	60,140	79.7
Black, non-Hispanic	46,451	8.6	83,576	7.2	21,937	5.7	1,393	3.2	4,444	5.9
Hispanic	32,438	6.0	50,241	4.3	11,913	3.1	903	2.1	3,134	4.2
Asian	18,659	3.4	55,660	4.8	15,267	4.0	2,025	4.7	5,892	7.8
Native American	4,975	0.9	6,189	0.5	1,697	0.4	134	0.3	371	0.5
Nonresident alien	10,127	1.9	34,080	2.9	46,317	12.0	11,538	26.7	1,437	1.9

Source: National Center for Education Statistics, Digest of Education Statistics 1996, NCES 96-133

College Enrollment Will Rise

As the children of baby boomers reach college age, the number of college students will climb.

By 2006, the number of people enrolled in college will top 16 million. Women already account for over half of all college students, and their share should increase, according to the National Center for Education Statistics. The number of students attending college full-time is projected to climb by 21 percent over the ten-year period of 1996 to 2006, accounting for 61 percent of all college students. Seventy-eight percent of college students attend public institutions. Assuming this proportion remains the same, public institutions will enroll nearly 13 million students in 2006, while private schools will enroll 3.6 million.

◆ College enrollments will rise well into the next century. The children born during the peak of the baby boomlet, from 1989 through the early 1990s, will reach college age beginning in 2007.

◆ Because of their lower cost, public institutions could see enrollments grow much more rapidly than is shown in these projections. Private colleges could experience slower growth because of their higher cost.

Projections of College Enrollment, 1996 to 2006

(number of persons enrolled in college by sex, attendance status, and control of institution; 1996 to 2006; percent change, 1996-2006; numbers in thousands)

	total	men	women	attendance status full-time	attendance status part-time	control public	control private
1996	14,398	6,470	7,928	8,224	6,175	11,254	3,145
1997	14,596	6,549	8,047	8,396	6,200	11,405	3,191
1998	14,886	6,681	8,205	8,655	6,231	11,627	3,259
1999	15,228	6,866	8,362	8,939	6,289	11,886	3,342
2000	15,497	6,985	8,512	9,171	6,325	12,091	3,406
2001	15,671	7,079	8,592	9,318	6,353	12,225	3,446
2002	15,798	7,137	8,660	9,433	6,364	12,319	3,479
2003	15,932	7,194	8,738	9,555	6,377	12,420	3,512
2004	16,078	7,251	8,827	9,681	6,397	12,531	3,547
2005	16,229	7,304	8,925	9,800	6,428	12,646	3,582
2006	16,389	7,375	9,014	9,943	6,446	12,768	3,621

Percent change

1996 to 2006	13.8%	14.0%	13.7%	20.9%	4.4%	13.5%	15.1%

Source: National Center for Education Statistics, Projections of Education Statistics to 2006, *Internet web site,* http://www.ed.gov/NCES; *calculations by New Strategist*

More College Students Aged 18 to 21

The number of college students aged 18 to 21 is expected to rise in the next decade, while the number of older students will decline.

After years of rapid growth, the number of older students should decline between 1994 and 2006 as the small baby-bust generation enters the 25-to-34 age group. In contrast, the number of students of traditional college age, 18 to 21, is projected to increase as the larger baby-boomlet generation reaches this age group.

The share of college students aged 25 or older will fall from 45 percent in 1994 to 40 percent in 2006. The proportion of students aged 18 to 21 will climb from 37 to 41 percent. Because most students today spend more than four years getting a college degree, the "traditional" college ages are expanding into the 22-to-24 age group. But between 1994 and 2006, the share of students aged 22 to 24 is expected to remain about the same, at just over 17 percent.

♦ The children born during the peak of the baby boomlet, from 1989 through the early 1990s, will reach college age beginning in 2007. Consequently, the share of college students in the 18-to-21 age group should continue to expand well beyond the year 2006.

Projections of College Enrollment
by Age and Sex, 1994 and 2006

(number and percent distribution of college students by age and sex, 1994 and 2006; percent change in number, 1994-2006; numbers in thousands)

	1994		2006		percent change 1994-2006
	number	percent	number	percent	
Total	14,082	100.0%	16,389	100.0%	16.4%
Aged 14 to 17	159	1.1	201	1.2	26.4
Aged 18 and 19	2,702	19.2	3,574	21.8	32.3
Aged 20 and 21	2,491	17.7	3,221	19.7	29.3
Aged 22 to 24	2,450	17.4	2,890	17.6	18.0
Aged 25 to 29	1,914	13.6	2,082	12.7	8.8
Aged 30 to 34	1,394	9.9	1,181	7.2	-15.3
Aged 35 or older	2,972	21.1	3,241	19.8	9.1
Total men	6,328	100.0	7,375	100.0	16.5
Aged 14 to 17	66	1.0	91	1.2	37.9
Aged 18 and 19	1,250	19.8	1,638	22.2	31.0
Aged 20 and 21	1,182	18.7	1,520	20.6	28.6
Aged 22 to 24	1,273	20.1	1,432	19.4	12.5
Aged 25 to 29	881	13.9	901	12.2	2.3
Aged 30 to 34	600	9.5	511	6.9	-14.8
Aged 35 or older	1,076	17.0	1,282	17.4	19.1
Total women	7,754	100.0	9,014	100.0	16.2
Aged 14 to 17	93	1.2	110	1.2	18.3
Aged 18 and 19	1,453	18.7	1,936	21.5	33.2
Aged 20 and 21	1,309	16.9	1,701	18.9	29.9
Aged 22 to 24	1,177	15.2	1,458	16.2	23.9
Aged 25 to 29	1,033	13.3	1,181	13.1	14.3
Aged 30 to 34	794	10.2	669	7.4	-15.7
Aged 35 or older	1,896	24.5	1,960	21.7	3.4

Source: National Center for Education Statistics, Projections of Education Statistics to 2006, *Internet web site,* http://www.ed.gov/NCES; *calculations by New Strategist*

Women Earn Most Degrees

Women already earn over half of bachelor's and master's degrees. They will earn half of all doctorates by 2006.

As women pursue careers, they are eager for credentials commanding a premium wage. Women are now a significant presence in all degree programs and fields of study. Their percentage is smallest in engineering, where they earned only about 15 percent of bachelor's and master's degrees in 1993-94. But in other traditionally male fields, such as mathematics, women earned 46 percent of bachelor's degrees and 38 percent of master's degrees.

Women earned 39 percent of all doctorates in 1993-94, a proportion that is projected to rise to 50 percent by 2006. While they earned only 11 percent of doctorates awarded in engineering and just 22 percent of those in mathematics, they earned a majority of doctoral degrees in foreign languages, health professions and related sciences, psychology, and library science.

Women earned 41 percent of all professional degrees in 1993-94, a share that is projected to remain fairly constant. They earned fully 67 percent of degrees in pharmacy, 38 percent of degrees in medicine, and 43 percent of law degrees.

♦ The proportion of doctors, lawyers, and other professionals who are women should expand rapidly in the next few decades as the young women now earning degrees replace older men who are retiring from these professions.

♦ As a growing share of women gain educational credentials in the years ahead, women's earnings will rise, narrowing the gap in men's and women's incomes.

Degrees Conferred by Level of Degree and Sex, 1996 to 2006

(number and percent distribution of degrees conferred by level of degree and sex of student, 1996 and 2006; percent change in number, 1996-2006)

| | 1996 | | 2006 | | percent change |
	number	percent	number	percent	1996-2006
Associate's degree	534,000	100.0%	584,000	100.0%	9.4%
Men	212,000	39.7	224,000	38.4	5.7
Women	323,000	60.5	360,000	61.6	11.5
Bachelor's degree	1,195,000	100.0	1,316,000	100.0	10.1
Men	533,000	44.6	591,000	44.9	10.9
Women	663,000	55.5	725,000	55.1	9.4
Master's degree	409,000	100.0	462,000	100.0	13.0
Men	199,000	48.7	212,000	45.9	6.5
Women	210,000	51.3	250,000	54.1	19.0
Doctoral degree	43,300	100.0	43,200	100.0	-0.2
Men	26,500	61.2	21,800	50.5	-17.7
Women	16,800	38.8	21,400	49.5	27.4
First-professional degree	78,000	100.0	91,700	100.0	17.6
Men	45,900	58.8	55,200	60.2	20.3
Women	32,100	41.2	36,500	39.8	13.7

Source: National Center for Education Statistics, Projections of Education Statistics to 2006, *Internet web site,* http://www.ed.gov/NCES; *calculations by New Strategist*

Bachelor's Degrees Conferred by Sex and Field of Study, 1993-94

(number of bachelor's degrees conferred by sex of student and field of study, and percent conferred to women, 1993-1994)

	total	men	women	percent women
All fields	1,169,275	532,422	636,853	54.5%
Agriculture and natural resources	18,070	11,748	6,322	35.0
Architecture and related programs	8,975	5,764	3,211	35.8
Area, ethnic, and cultural studies	5,573	1,958	3,615	64.9
Biological sciences/life sciences	51383	25,050	26,333	51.2
Business and management	246,654	129,161	117493	47.6
Communications	51,827	21,359	30,468	58.8
Computer and information sciences	24,200	17,317	6,883	28.4
Education	107,600	24,450	83,150	77.3
Engineering	78,225	66,597	11,628	14.9
English language and literature	53,924	18,425	35,499	65.8
Foreign languages	14,378	4,304	10,074	70.1
Health professions and related sciences	74,421	13,062	61,359	82.4
Home economics	15,522	1,933	13,589	87.5
Law and legal studies	2,171	648	1,523	70.2
Liberal/general studies	33,397	13,117	20,280	60.7
Library sciences	62	5	57	91.9
Mathematics	14,396	7,735	6,661	46.3
Multi-disciplinary studies	25,167	9,058	16,109	64.0
Parks and recreation	11,470	5,823	5,647	49.2
Philosophy and religion	7,546	4,844	2,702	35.8
Physical sciences	18,400	12,223	6,177	33.6
Protective services	23,009	14,169	8,840	38.4
Psychology	69,259	18,642	50,617	73.1
Public administration and services	17,815	3,919	13,896	78.0
Social sciences and history	133,680	72,006	61,674	46.1
Theological studies	5,434	4,125	1,309	24.1
Visual and performing arts	49,053	19,538	29,515	60.2

Source: National Center for Education Statistics, Digest of Education Statistics 1996, *NCES 96-133; calculations by New Strategist*

Master's Degrees Conferred by Sex and Field of Study, 1993-94

(number of master's degrees conferred by sex of student and field of study, and percent conferred to women, 1993-1994)

	total	men	women	percent women
All fields	387,050	176,085	210,985	54.5%
Agriculture and natural resources	4,119	2,515	1,604	38.9
Architecture and related programs	3,943	2,428	1,515	38.4
Area, ethnic, and cultural studies	1,633	768	865	53.0
Biological sciences/life sciences	5,196	2,465	2,731	52.6
Business and management	93,437	59,335	34,102	36.5
Communications	5,419	2,098	3,321	61.3
Computer and information sciences	10,416	7,724	2,692	25.8
Education	98,938	23,008	75,930	76.7
Engineering	29,754	25,154	4,600	15.5
English language and literature	7,885	2,712	5,173	65.6
Foreign languages	3,288	1,087	2,201	66.9
Health professions and related sciences	28,025	5,814	22,211	79.3
Home economics	2,421	405	2,016	83.3
Law and legal studies	2,432	1,608	824	33.9
Liberal/general studies	2,496	913	1,583	63.4
Library sciences	5,116	1,040	4,076	79.7
Mathematics	4,100	2,536	1,564	38.1
Multi-disciplinary studies	2,464	1,194	1,270	51.5
Parks and recreation	1,625	845	780	48.0
Philosophy and religion	1,350	837	513	38.0
Physical sciences	5,679	4,018	1,661	29.2
Protective services	1,437	902	535	37.2
Psychology	12,181	3,401	8,780	72.1
Public administration and services	21,833	6,406	15,427	70.7
Social sciences and history	14,561	8,152	6,409	44.0
Theological studies	4,956	3,034	1,922	38.8
Visual and performing arts	9,925	4,229	5,696	57.4

Source: National Center for Education Statistics, Digest of Education Statistics 1996, *NCES 96-133; calculations by New Strategist*

Doctoral Degrees Conferred by Sex and Field of Study, 1993-94

(number of doctoral degrees conferred by sex of student and field of study, and percent conferred to women, 1993-1994)

	total	men	women	percent women
All fields	43,185	26,552	16,633	38.5%
Agriculture and natural resources	1,278	982	296	23.2
Architecture and related programs	161	111	50	31.1
Area, ethnic, and cultural studies	155	75	80	51.6
Biological sciences/life sciences	4,534	2,690	1,844	40.7
Business and management	1,364	980	384	28.2
Communications	345	174	171	49.6
Computer and information sciences	810	685	125	15.4
Education	6,908	2,706	4,202	60.8
Engineering	5,979	5,315	664	11.1
English language and literature	1,344	568	776	57.7
Foreign languages	886	355	531	59.9
Health professions and related sciences	1,902	789	1,113	58.5
Home economics	365	93	272	74.5
Law and legal studies	79	63	16	20.3
Liberal/general studies	80	46	34	42.5
Library sciences	45	14	31	68.9
Mathematics	1,157	904	253	21.9
Multi-disciplinary studies	227	151	76	33.5
Parks and recreation	116	70	46	39.7
Philosophy and religion	528	383	145	27.5
Physical sciences	4,650	3,642	1,008	21.7
Protective services	25	14	11	44.0
Psychology	3,563	1,346	2,217	62.2
Public administration and services	519	238	281	54.1
Social sciences and history	3,627	2,317	1,310	36.1
Theological studies	1,448	1,235	213	14.7
Visual and performing arts	1,054	585	469	44.5

Source: National Center for Education Statistics, Digest of Education Statistics 1996, *NCES 96-133; calculations by New Strategist*

First-Professional Degrees Conferred
by Sex and Field of Study, 1993-94

(number of first-professional degrees conferred by sex of student and field of study, and percent conferred to women, 1993-1994)

	total	men	women	percent women
Total	75,418	44,707	30,711	40.7%
Dentistry (D.D.S. or D.M.D.)	3,787	2,330	1,457	38.5
Medicine (M.D.)	15,368	9,544	5,824	37.9
Optometry (O.D.)	1,103	554	549	49.8
Osteopathic medicine (D.O.)	1,798	1,165	633	35.2
Pharmacy (Pharm.D.)	1,936	643	1,293	66.8
Podiatry (Pod.D., D.P. or D.P.M.)	465	330	135	29.0
Veterinary medicine (D.V.M.)	2,089	798	1,291	61.8
Chiropractic (D.C. or D.C.M.)	2,806	2,010	796	28.4
Law (LL.B. or J.D.)	40,044	22,826	17,218	43.0
Theology (M. Div., M.H.L., B.D., or Ord.)	5,967	4,486	1,481	24.8

Source: National Center for Education Statistics, Digest of Education Statistics 1996, *NCES 96-133; calculations by New Strategist*

Most Couples Alike in Education

Over half of the nation's 55 million married couples have the same level of educational attainment.

When comparing the educational level of husbands and wives, the largest single group is husbands and wives who have graduated from high school but have not gone to college. This group accounts for 19 percent of all couples. The second-largest group is husbands and wives who both have bachelor's degrees or higher levels of education, accounting for 15 percent of all couples. Couples in which both husband and wife are high school dropouts account for slightly more than 9 percent of couples. For another 11 percent of couples, both husband and wife have been to college but do not have a bachelor's degree.

In most cases, husbands are better-educated than wives. Overall, 27 percent of husbands have a bachelor's degree, compared with 22 percent of wives. Only 7 percent of wives have a bachelor's degree while their husbands do not.

◆ As the well-educated baby-boom generation ages, the educational level of married couples will rise. The proportion of couples in which both husband and wife have bachelor's degrees will increase sharply, as will the share of married couples in which the wife is better-educated than the husband.

Education of Husband by Education of Wife, 1995

(number and percent distribution of husbands and wives aged 18 or older by education of husband and wife, 1995; numbers in thousands)

	total wives	not a high school graduate	high school graduate only	some college or associate's degree	bachelor's degree or more
Total husbands, number	54,934	8,011	20,399	14,686	11,839
Not a high school graduate	9,259	5,055	3,136	879	189
High school graduate only	17,372	2,083	10,292	3,758	1,239
Some college/assoc. degree	13,366	707	4,449	6,129	2,081
Bachelor's degree or more	14,938	165	2,523	3,920	8,330
Total husbands, percent	100.0%	14.6%	37.1%	26.7%	21.6%
Not a high school graduate	16.9	9.2	5.7	1.6	0.3
High school graduate only	31.6	3.8	18.7	6.8	2.3
Some college/assoc. degree	24.3	1.3	8.1	11.2	3.8
Bachelor's degree or more	27.2	0.3	4.6	7.1	15.2

Source: Bureau of the Census, Educational Attainment in the United States: March 1995, *Current Population Reports, P20-489, 1996; calculations by New Strategist*

White-Collar Workers Are Well-Educated

Professional specialty workers are the best-educated in the U.S. More than 80 percent have a college degree.

Professional specialty occupations, which include law and medicine, often require years of education beyond the bachelor's degree level. Those employed in executive, administrative, and managerial occupations are the second-best-educated workers. Over half of men and one-third of women in these occupations hold at least a bachelor's degree.

The least-educated workers are those in farming, forestry, and fishing as well as handlers, equipment cleaners, helpers, and laborers. More than one in four of these workers does not have a high school diploma.

♦ As the value of an education continues to grow in our increasingly technological society, the educational level of the work force will rise. Even the blue-collar work force will become more educated as younger, better-educated workers replace those who are older and less-educated.

Occupation by Educational Attainment, 1995

(percent of employed persons aged 25 to 64 who are high school or college graduates by occupation and sex, 1995)

	men		women	
	high school graduates	college graduates	high school graduates	college graduates
Total employed	88.5%	30.5%	91.3%	27.1%
Executive, administrative, and managerial	97.5	55.0	97.5	41.0
Professional specialty	99.4	81.5	99.2	72.2
Technicians and related support	98.0	34.8	99.1	27.7
Sales	95.9	37.4	91.9	19.7
Administrative support, including clerical	94.6	23.9	96.9	12.1
Private household	-	-	61.3	5.6
Other service	83.1	12.2	79.2	5.9
Farming, forestry, and fishing	67.9	12.1	78.2	12.4
Precision production, craft, and repair	83.8	6.7	81.8	6.1
Machine operators, assemblers, inspectors	75.7	4.2	67.5	3.2
Transportation and material moving	79.4	6.0	83.2	4.5
Handlers, equipment cleaners, helpers, laborers	73.8	5.1	71.4	4.3

Note: (-) means number in sample is too small to make a reliable estimate.
Source: Bureau of the Census, Educational Attainment in the United States: March 1995, *Current Population Reports, P20-489, 1996*

Educational Attainment Varies Widely by State

The best-educated states include Alaska, Colorado, and Washington. Those with the least-educated populations include West Virginia, South Carolina, and Alabama.

The proportion of residents aged 25 or older who have a high school diploma ranges from a low of 73 percent in West Virginia to a high of 92 percent in Alaska, a difference of nearly 20 percentage points. The proportion of residents with a college degree is also lowest in West Virginia, at 13 percent. Sixteen states have more than twice as many college graduates, with Colorado, Connecticut, Massachusetts, and Vermont exceeding 30 percent. It is no surprise that the states with the least-educated populations are also some of the poorest, while those with the best-educated populations are some of the richest. Educated people typically make much more money than those with less education.

♦ The educational level of the work force is one factor behind business location decisions. Better-educated populations attract business investment, increasing the employment opportunities for people who live there.

Educational Attainment by State, 1995

(percent of persons aged 25 or older who are high school or college graduates, by state, 1995)

	high school graduate	college graduate		high school graduate	college graduate
U.S.total	81.7%	23.0%	Missouri	82.2%	21.9%
Alabama	74.4	17.3	Montana	84.7	22.1
Alaska	92.1	25.2	Nebraska	89.1	24.1
Arizona	82.3	19.1	Nevada	85.3	17.4
Arkansas	76.2	14.2	New Hampshire	86.8	25.8
California	79.6	24.2	New Jersey	85.4	27.9
Colorado	91.3	33.3	New Mexico	80.0	21.4
Connecticut	85.6	32.7	New York	82.5	26.3
Delaware	81.4	22.9	North Carolina	76.3	20.6
District of Columbia	78.9	38.2	North Dakota	81.6	19.8
Florida	82.8	22.1	Ohio	83.4	19.7
Georgia	78.2	22.7	Oklahoma	82.6	19.1
Hawaii	84.1	22.6	Oregon	85.1	23.0
Idaho	86.4	22.1	Pennsylvania	81.4	20.5
Illinois	82.3	24.6	Rhode Island	78.9	27.9
Indiana	81.6	16.9	South Carolina	74.3	18.2
Iowa	84.7	19.7	South Dakota	83.7	18.9
Kansas	86.5	25.8	Tennessee	77.4	17.8
Kentucky	76.7	19.3	Texas	76.2	22.0
Louisiana	75.8	20.1	Utah	90.2	24.0
Maine	86.2	21.5	Vermont	87.6	30.3
Maryland	82.0	26.4	Virginia	82.7	26.0
Massachusetts	85.8	32.6	Washington	91.4	26.5
Michigan	83.7	20.7	West Virginia	72.7	12.7
Minnesota	88.4	26.5	Wisconsin	86.6	20.6
Mississippi	76.4	17.6	Wyoming	89.3	21.2

Source: Bureau of the Census, Educational Attainment in the United States: March 1995, *Current Population Reports, P20-489, 1996*

Education Varies by Metropolitan Area

The residents of some of the nation's largest metropolitan areas are far better educated than are Americans as a whole.

The best-educated Americans are those living in Boston, where 40 percent of residents have at least a bachelor's degree. In many other large metropolitan areas, including San Francisco and Seattle, more than one-third of the population have a college degree.

Among large metropolitan areas, those with the smallest proportion of college-educated residents are Pittsburgh and San Antonio. In both metros, fewer than 19 percent of residents have a degree.

♦ As well-educated younger generations of Americans replace older, less-educated people, education levels will rise in most of the nation's metropolitan areas.

Educational Attainment by Metropolitan Area, 1995

(percent of persons aged 25 or older in the nation's largest metropolitan statistical areas who are high school or college graduates, ranked alphabetically, 1995)

	high school graduates	college graduates
Total U.S.	81.7%	23.0%
Altanta, GA	88.0	34.3
Baltimore, MD	80.4	22.2
Boston, MA	88.8	40.2
Buffalo-Niagara Falls, NY	81.2	21.3
Charlotte-Gastonia-Rock Hill, NC-SC	80.9	31.5
Chicago, IL	82.6	29.0
Cincinnati, OH-KY-IN	80.9	24.8
Cleveland, OH	75.2	21.3
Columbus, OH	82.7	21.4
Dallas, TX	78.5	24.4
Fort Worth-Arlington, TX	82.3	23.0
Denver, CO	93.2	34.4
Detroit, MI	80.6	22.3
Hartford-New Britain-Middletown, CT	80.1	26.7
Houston, TX	82.7	27.9
Indianapolis, IN	82.9	30.8
Kansas City, MO-KS	87.0	31.5
Los Angeles-Long Beach, CA	73.0	22.0
Anaheim-Santa Ana, CA	83.9	28.9
Riverside-San Bernardino, CA	79.4	24.1
Miami-Hialeah, FL	80.1	24.8
Fort Lauderdale-Hollywood-Pompano Beach, FL	89.0	20.8
Milwaukee, WI	86.6	28.2
Minneapolis-St. Paul, MN-WI	85.8	28.1
New Orleans, LA	84.3	24.3
New York, NY	78.5	26.8
Nassau-Suffolk, NY	89.4	31.7
Newark, NJ	86.1	31.5
Bergen-Passaic, NJ	84.7	29.4
Norfolk-Virginia Beach-Newport News, VA	89.3	23.3
Philadelphia, PA-NJ	85.1	32.7
Phoenix, AZ	84.1	22.1

(continued)

(continued from previous page)

	high school graduates	college graduates
Pittsburgh, PA	81.9%	18.8%
Portland, OR	88.3	24.2
Providence-Pawtucket-Fall River, RI-MA	78.8	23.6
Sacramento, CA	83.0	25.9
St. Louis, MO-IL	82.2	23.9
Salt Lake City-Ogden, UT	91.2	24.6
San Antonio, TX	71.8	17.2
San Diego, CA	82.9	25.1
Oakland, CA	88.7	33.1
San Francisco, CA	88.6	37.0
San Jose, CA	85.9	31.2
Seattle, WA	94.9	37.0
Tampa-St. Petersburg-Clearwater, FL	83.1	21.0
Washington, DC-MD-VA	85.7	33.4

Source: Bureau of the Census, Educational Attainment in the United States: March 1995, *Current Population Reports, P20-489, 1996*

2

Health Trends

♦ **The food preferences of Americans have changed dramatically over the past two decades.**
Americans are eating more yogurt, poultry, broccoli, and cheese, and less beef, eggs, sugar, and whole milk.

♦ **The number of births peaked in 1990.**
The 4,158,000 babies born in 1990 was the largest number since the last of the baby-boom generation was being born in the early 1960s.

♦ **Those most likely to exercise frequently are aged 55 or older.**
Americans' most popular recreational activities include basketball, bowling, fresh-water fishing, and fitness walking.

♦ **Most Americans have health insurance, but millions do not.**
Only 1 percent of the nation's elderly are without health care coverage, compared with 14 percent of children.

♦ **Americans are less likely to smoke, drink, or use drugs today than a few decades ago.**
Among 18-to-25-year-olds, the use of illicit drugs has dropped from an enormous 37 percent in 1979 to just 13 percent in 1994.

♦ **More than 24,000 Americans were murdered in 1994, and nearly half were black.**
Among the 8,013 people aged 15 to 24 who were murdered in 1994, 53 percent were black males.

♦ **Americans born in 1995 can expect to live to age 75.8.**
Most of the gains in life expectancy during this century have been due to declining death rates among infants and children.

Most Americans Feel Good

Most Americans rate their health as excellent or very good, according to the National Center for Health Statistics.

The proportion of Americans who rate their health as excellent declines with age. But even among people aged 65 or older, fewer than one-third rate their health as fair or poor, while nearly 40 percent rate their health as very good or excellent.

The higher their income, the better people feel. Nearly 50 percent of people in households with incomes of $35,000 or more rate their health as excellent, compared with just 26 percent of people in households with incomes below $10,000. There are several reasons for the relationship between income and health. Older Americans are most likely to report poor health, and many also have low incomes because they are retired. Another reason is that people in poor health often do not have as much earning power as the healthy.

♦ As the population ages, the proportion of Americans who feel excellent is likely to decline somewhat, while the proportion who feel only fair or poor could grow.

Health Status of the Population, 1994

(percent distribution of self-assessed or parent-assessed health status of the population by age, sex, and household income, 1994)

	total	excellent	very good	good	fair	poor
Total	100.0%	37.9%	28.5%	23.4%	7.3%	2.9%
Under age 5	100.0	53.4	27.3	16.4	2.5	0.4
Aged 5 to 17	100.0	51.2	27.3	18.4	2.6	0.4
Aged 18 to 24	100.0	43.0	31.5	21.1	3.7	0.6
Aged 25 to 44	100.0	38.8	31.1	22.6	5.7	1.8
Aged 45 to 64	100.0	28.4	27.7	27.3	11.4	5.2
Aged 65 or older	100.0	15.7	23.0	33.4	18.4	9.6
Sex						
Male	100.0	40.8	28.3	21.7	6.4	2.7
Female	100.0	35.2	28.7	25.0	8.1	3.0
Household income						
Less than $10,000	100.0	25.5	23.6	29.0	14.1	7.8
$10,000 to $19,999	100.0	28.4	26.1	29.4	11.2	4.9
$20,000 to $34,999	100.0	35.3	29.9	25.5	7.1	2.2
$35,000 or more	100.0	47.9	30.2	17.5	3.5	0.9

Source: National Center for Health Statistics, Current Estimates From the National Health Interview Survey, 1994, *Series 10, No. 193, 1995*

Changing Tastes

The food preferences of Americans have changed dramatically over the past two decades, for better and for worse.

In 1994, Americans ate more yogurt, poultry, broccoli, cheese, and low-fat milk than they did in 1970. They ate less beef, eggs, sugar, and whole milk. They drank 40 percent fewer gallons of distilled spirits and more bottled water.

These changes in eating habits are partly due to the deluge of nutritional advice directed at Americans over the past couple of decades. Food consumption trends also reflect changing tastes. A growing preference for spicy foods, for example, boosted consumption of onions by 61 percent.

Many eating trends of the past two decades run counter to the advice of nutritionists. Americans drink 115 percent more soft drinks now than they did in 1970. Although they ate less sugar in 1994 than in 1970, their consumption of corn sweeteners soared. Americans are eating more fresh fruits and vegetables, but also more fats and oils.

♦ The trend away from red meat and high-fat food is likely to continue as medical research confirms the health benefits of a low-fat diet.

Food and Beverage Consumption, 1970 to 1994

(number of pounds of selected foods and gallons of selected beverages consumed per capita, 1970 and 1994; percent change in consumption,1970-94)

	1994	1970	percent change 1970-1994
Red meat	114.8	131.7	-12.8%
Beef	63.6	79.6	-20.1
Pork	49.5	48.0	3.1
Fish and shellfish	15.1	11.7	29.1
Poultry	63.7	33.8	88.5
Chicken	49.5	27.4	80.7
Turkey	14.2	6.4	121.9
Eggs (number)	237.6	308.9	-23.1
Yogurt	4.7	0.8	487.5
Cheese	26.8	11.4	135.1
Ice cream	16.1	17.8	-9.6
Fats and oils	66.9	52.6	27.2
Butter	4.8	5.4	-11.1
Margarine	9.9	10.8	-8.3
Salad, cooking oil	24.3	15.4	57.8
Flour and cereal products	198.7	135.3	46.9
Sweeteners	147.6	122.9	20.1
Sugar	65.0	101.8	-36.1
Corn sweeteners	81.3	19.6	314.8
Fresh fruits	126.7	79.6	59.2
Bananas	28.1	17.4	61.5
Apples	19.5	17.0	14.7
Oranges	13.1	16.2	-19.1
Melons	26.1	21.6	20.8
Fresh vegetables	113.9	85.6	33.1
Broccoli	2.8	0.5	460.0
Carrots	7.9	6.0	31.7
Iceberg lettuce	22.5	22.4	0.4
Onions	16.3	10.1	61.4
Tomatoes	15.7	12.1	29.8
Potatoes	141.0	121.7	15.9
Nonalcoholic beverages	130.4	95.8	36.1
Whole milk	9.1	25.5	-64.3
Lowfat milk	12.2	4.4	177.3

(continued)

(continued from previous page)

	1994	1970	percent change 1970-1994
Coffee	21.1	33.4	-36.8%
Bottled water	10.5	2.4*	337.5
Soft drinks	52.2	24.3	114.8
Fruit juices	8.6	5.7	50.9
Alcoholic beverages	36.4	35.7	2.0
Beer	32.0	30.6	4.6
Wine	2.5	2.2	13.6
Distilled spirits	1.8	3.0	-40.0

* Data for 1980.
Source: Bureau of the Census, Statistical Abstract of the United States: 1996; *calculations by New Strategist*

Births to Remain Below 4 Million Until 2005

Births peaked in 1990, at nearly 4.2 million.

Baby-boom parents boosted births to 4,158,000 in 1990. This was the largest number since the last of the boomers themselves were being born in the early 1960s.

The children born in 1990 entered first grade in 1996, boosting the U.S. elementary and secondary school population to a record high of 51.7 million. The school-aged population is expected to expand by another 3 million by 2006 as the children of boomers fill the elementary and secondary grades.

After peaking in 1990, the annual number of births has slowly declined, falling to 3.9 million by 1997. The Census Bureau projects that the annual number of births will remain at about this level through the turn of the century, before rising again as the children of baby boomers have children.

◆ Many of the nation's schools, already crowded by the birth boom of the late 1980s and early 1990s, should budget for expansion. The number of students entering elementary school is not projected to decline significantly in the foreseeable future.

Number of Births, 1990 to 2050

(annual number of births, 1990 to 1997, and projected to 2050; numbers in thousands)

year	births
1990	4,158
1991	4,111
1992	4,065
1993	4,000
1994	3,953
1995	3,900
1996	3,921
1997	3,907
1998	3,899
1999	3,896
2000	3,899
2005	4,001
2010	4,243
2015	4,450
2020	4,579
2025	4,679
2030	4,822
2035	5,022
2040	5,248
2045	5,465
2050	5,672

Source: National Center for Health Statistics, Advance Report of Final Natality Statistics, 1994, *Monthly Vital Statistics Report, Vol. 44, No. 11 Supplement, 1996; and Bureau of the Census,* Population Projections of the United States by Age, Sex, Race and Hispanic Origin: 1995 to 2050, *Current Population Reports, P25-1130, 1996*

Nation's Newborns Are Highly Diverse

The nation's newborns are far more diverse than the population as a whole.

An astonishing 33 percent of babies were born to unmarried women in 1994. The proportion of babies born out of wedlock has surged in the past two decades, up from just 11 percent in 1970. Among blacks, fully 70 percent of babies are born out of wedlock, while the share among Hispanics is 43 percent, and 25 percent among whites.

Only 80 percent of the 3.9 million babies born in 1995 were white. Counted as white births are many Hispanic newborns, since Hispanics may be of any race and most are white. Minority births account for a growing share of all births partly because black and Hispanic women have higher fertility rates than non-Hispanic white women.

♦ As the nation's highly diverse population of children grows up, the minority share of Americans will rise sharply.

♦ The rising share of births to unmarried women reflects women's growing economic independence and men's declining economic fortunes. As women earn higher incomes, they have less need to marry before having children.

Births by Age, Race, and Hispanic Origin of Mother, 1995

(number and percent distribution of births by age, race, and Hispanic origin of mother, 1995)

	total births	white	black	Asian	Native American	Hispanic
Total number	3,900,089	3,105,315	598,558	158,447	37,769	671,849
Under age 15	12,318	5,911	5,910	289	209	3,209
Aged 15 to 19	500,744	350,999	132,846	9,069	7,830	117,907
Aged 20 to 24	967,591	745,822	182,644	27,023	12,102	206,430
Aged 25 to 29	1,064,984	876,074	132,389	47,806	8,714	175,962
Aged 30 to 34	904,143	755,955	95,059	47,210	5,920	113,085
Aged 35 to 39	381,455	314,962	41,941	22,066	2,486	45,887
Aged 40 to 44	66,195	53,447	7,530	4,724	494	9,004
Aged 45 to 49	2,660	2,147	240	260	14	365
Percent distribution by age						
Total	100.0%	79.6%	15.3%	4.1%	1.0%	17.2%
Under age 15	100.0	48.0	48.0	2.3	1.7	26.1
Aged 15 to 19	100.0	70.1	26.5	1.8	1.6	23.5
Aged 20 to 24	100.0	77.1	18.9	2.8	1.3	21.3
Aged 25 to 29	100.0	82.3	12.4	4.5	0.8	16.5
Aged 30 to 34	100.0	83.6	10.5	5.2	0.7	12.5
Aged 35 to 39	100.0	82.6	11.0	5.8	0.7	12.0
Aged 40 to 44	100.0	80.7	11.4	7.1	0.7	13.6
Aged 45 to 49	100.0	80.7	9.0	9.8	0.5	13.7
Percent distribution by race and Hispanic origin						
Total	100.0%	100.0%	100.0%	100.0%	100.0%	100.0%
Under age 15	0.3	0.2	1.0	0.2	0.6	0.5
Aged 15 to 19	12.8	11.3	22.2	5.7	20.7	17.5
Aged 20 to 24	24.8	24.0	30.5	17.1	32.0	30.7
Aged 25 to 29	27.3	28.2	22.1	30.2	23.1	26.2
Aged 30 to 34	23.2	24.3	15.9	29.8	15.7	16.8
Aged 35 to 39	9.8	10.1	7.0	13.9	6.6	6.8
Aged 40 to 44	1.7	1.7	1.3	3.0	1.3	1.3
Aged 45 to 49	0.1	0.1	0.0	0.2	0.0	0.1

Note: Births by race and Hispanic origin will not add to total because Hispanics may be of any race and "not stated" is not included.
Source: National Center for Health Statistics, Births and Deaths: United States, 1995, Monthly Vital Statistics Report, Vol. 45, No. 3, Supplement 2, 1996; calculations by New Strategist

Births by Age and Marital Status of Mother, 1994

(total number of births and number and percent to unmarried women, by age, race and Hispanic origin of mother, 1994)

	total births	births to unmarried women	
		number	percent
Total	3,952,767	1,289,592	32.6%
Under age 15	12,901	12,186	94.5
Aged 15 to 19	505,488	381,499	75.5
Aged 20 to 24	1,001,418	449,246	44.9
Aged 25 to 29	1,088,845	237,636	21.8
Aged 30 to 34	906,498	136,991	15.1
Aged 35 to 39	371,608	59,701	16.1
Aged 40 or older	66,009	12,333	18.7
White	3,121,004	794,261	25.4
Under age 15	5,978	5,407	90.4
Aged 15 to 19	348,081	235,263	67.6
Aged 20 to 24	764,085	277,364	36.3
Aged 25 to 29	889,581	146,527	16.5
Aged 30 to 34	754,871	83,870	11.1
Aged 35 to 39	305,291	37,594	12.3
Aged 40 or older	53,117	8,236	15.5
Black	636,391	448,315	70.4
Under age 15	6,465	6,404	99.1
Aged 15 to 19	140,968	134,371	95.3
Aged 20 to 24	197,841	156,304	79.0
Aged 25 to 29	142,355	81,599	57.3
Aged 30 to 34	99,155	47,044	47.4
Aged 35 to 39	42,029	19,242	45.8
Aged 40 or older	7,578	3,351	44.2
Hispanic	665,026	286,469	43.1
Under age 15	3,147	2,805	89.1
Aged 15 to 19	115,232	80,319	69.7
Aged 20 to 24	205,732	96,594	47.0
Aged 25 to 29	176,031	58,474	33.2
Aged 30 to 34	111,461	31,899	28.6
Aged 35 to 39	44,370	13,437	30.3
Aged 40 or older	9,053	2,941	32.5

Source: National Center for Health Statistics, Advance Report of Final Natality Statistics, 1994, *Vol. 44, No. 11 Supplement, 1996; calculations by New Strategist*

Exercise Not Just for the Young

Those most likely to exercise frequently are Americans aged 55 or older.

While children and young adults are most likely to be involved in regular sports activities, older Americans are the fitness fanatics. Twenty-eight percent of Americans aged 55 or older frequently take part in fitness activities, the highest share among all age groups. Interestingly, 35-to-44-year-olds are those least likely to take part frequently in fitness activities—despite all the hype about baby boomers staying fit. In fact, this age group is too busy with demanding careers and young children to bother with regular exercise.

Americans' most popular recreational activities include basketball, bowling, freshwater fishing, and fitness walking. More than 35 million Americans aged 6 or older took part in each of these activities in 1995. Other popular recreational activities include bicycling, free weights, running, and golf.

♦ The aging population will boost the popularity of some fitness activities, while making others less popular. A big gainer is likely to be fitness walking.

Sports and Fitness Participation by Age, 1995

(percent of people aged 6 or older frequently participating in sports and fitness activities combined, and percent participating frequently in fitness activities, by age, 1995)

	sports and fitness	fitness only
Aged 6 to 11	48.1%	12.8%
Aged 12 to 17	62.5	24.2
Aged 18 to 24	38.5	21.4
Aged 25 to 34	35.9	23.0
Aged 35 to 44	29.0	20.4
Aged 45 to 54	35.4	26.7
Aged 55 or older	32.3	28.2

Note: Frequent participation in sports activities ranges from 15 to 100 days/year depending on the activity, while frequent participation in fitness activities is 100 or more days/year.
Source: Fitness Products Council, North Palm Beach, Florida, 1996

Sports and Fitness Participation, 1990 and 1995

(number of people aged 6 or older participating in selected sports or fitness activities at least once in the past 12 months, 1990 and 1995; percent change 1990-95; numbers in thousands)

	1995	1990	percent change 1990-1995
Aerobics (high impact)	10,506	12,359	-15.0%
Aerobics (low impact)	13,737	15,950	-13.9
Basketball	46,474	39,808	16.7
Bicycling (fitness)	28,604	28,182	1.5
Bowling	53,130	53,537	-0.8
Fitness walking	35,621	31,952	11.5
Free weights	39,701	29,052	36.7
Freshwater fishing	48,747	50,673	-3.8
Golf	24,572	24,530	0.2
Mountain biking	9,399	4,146	126.7
Rollerskating (in-line)	22,508	4,307	422.6
Running/jogging	32,534	31,612	2.9
Skiing (cross-country)	4,625	6,180	-25.2
Skiing (downhill)	13,016	14,226	-8.5
Snowboarding	3,396	1,793	89.4
Stair-climbing machines	20,258	12,271	65.1
Swimming (fitness)	24,715	24,385	1.4
Tennis	18,479	21,742	-15.0
Treadmill exercise	29,615	11,484	157.9

Source: Sports Participation Index, 1995, *prepared for the Sporting Goods Manufacturers Association, North Palm Beach, Florida, by American Sports Data, Inc., Hartsdale, New York, 1996*

Over 15 Percent of Americans Are Uninsured

The majority of Americans have health insurance, but millions do not.

Young adults are most likely to be without health insurance. Among the 41 million Americans without health insurance, one in five is aged 18 to 24. Within this age group, 28 percent are without health insurance. Among people aged 25 to 34, 23 percent do not have health insurance.

Because Medicare covers the elderly, those most likely to have health insurance are Americans aged 65 or older. Only 1 percent of the elderly are without health care coverage. In contrast, 14 percent of the nation's children do not have health insurance.

One-third of Hispanics and one-fifth of blacks do not have health insurance. Among whites, only 13 percent are without health insurance. One in four persons living in households with incomes below $25,000 is uninsured.

♦ The proportion of Americans who lack health insurance has been rising because an increasing share work for businesses that do not offer coverage.

Health Insurance Coverage, 1995

(number and percent of persons by sex, age, race, Hispanic origin, household income, and health insurance coverage status, 1995)

	total persons	with health insurance		without health insurance	
		number	percent	number	percent
Total	264,315	223,733	84.6%	40,582	15.4%
Sex					
Male	129,144	107,496	83.2	21,648	16.8
Female	135,171	116,237	86.0	18,934	14.0
Age					
Under age 18	71,148	61,353	86.2	9,795	13.8
Aged 18 to 24	24,843	17,847	71.8	6,996	28.2
Aged 25 to 34	40,919	31,561	77.1	9,358	22.9
Aged 35 to 44	43,078	35,946	83.4	7,132	16.6
Aged 45 to 64	52,668	45,668	86.7	7,000	13.3
Aged 65 or older	31,658	31,358	99.1	300	0.9
Race and Hispanic origin					
White	218,443	187,338	85.8	31,105	14.2
Black	33,889	26,782	79.0	7,107	21.0
Hispanic	28,438	18,964	66.7	9,474	33.3
Household income					
Less than $25,000	78,435	59,722	76.1	18,713	23.9
$25,000 to $49,999	84,459	70,762	83.8	13,697	16.2
$50,000 to $74,999	54,453	48,479	90.7	4,974	9.3
$75,000 or more	47,967	44,770	93.3	31,197	6.7

Note: Numbers by race and Hispanic origin will not add to total because Hispanics may be of any race and not all races are shown.
Source: U.S. Census Bureau, unpublished tables from the 1996 Current Population Survey

Vices on the Decline

Americans are less likely to smoke, drink, or use drugs today than a few decades ago.

The proportion of Americans who smoke cigarettes fell by 17 percentage points between 1965 and 1993, from 42 to 25 percent. In 1993, 28 percent of men and 23 percent of women smoked.

A far higher proportion of Americans drink. In 1994, 69 percent said they drink at least occasionally, while 31 percent said they abstain. Drinking is greatest among young adults and declines with age. Fully 81 percent of people aged 18 to 29 say they drink, compared with fewer than half of Americans aged 70 or older.

Although the media have focused attention on the small rise in drug use over the past few years, the proportion of Americans who use drugs is down sharply from 1979. Among 18-to-25-year-olds, the use of illicit drugs has dropped from an enormous 37 percent in 1979 to just 13 percent in 1994.

♦ The proportion of people who smoke cigarettes, drink alcohol, or use drugs should continue to decline as the population ages.

Cigarette Smoking by Sex and Age, 1965 and 1993

(percent of persons aged 18 or older who currently smoke cigarettes by sex and age, 1965, 1990, and 1993; percentage point change, 1990-93 and 1965-93)

	1993	1990	1965	percentage point change 1990-1993	percentage point change 1965-1993
Total	25.0%	25.5%	42.4%	-0.5	-17.4
Men	27.7	28.4	51.9	-0.7	-24.2
Aged 18 to 24	28.8	26.6	54.1	2.2	-25.3
Aged 25 to 34	30.2	31.6	60.7	-1.4	-30.5
Aged 35 to 44	32.0	34.5	58.2	-2.5	-26.2
Aged 45 to 64	29.2	29.3	51.9	-0.1	-22.7
Aged 65 or older	13.5	14.6	28.5	-1.1	-15.0
Women	22.5	22.8	33.9	-0.3	-11.4
Aged 18 to 24	22.9	22.5	38.1	0.4	-15.2
Aged 25 to 34	27.3	28.2	43.7	-0.9	-16.4
Aged 35 to 44	27.4	24.8	43.7	2.6	-16.3
Aged 45 to 64	23.0	24.8	32.0	-1.8	-9.0
Aged 65 or older	10.5	11.5	9.6	-1.0	0.9

Source: National Center for Health Statistics, Health United States 1995, *(PHS)96-1232, 1996; calculations by New Strategist*

Alcohol Consumption by Age, 1994

"Do you ever have occasion to use any alcoholic beverages such as liquor, wine, or beer, or are you a total abstainer?"

(percent of persons aged 18 or older who currently drink alcohol or abstain, by age, 1994)

	currently use	abstain
Total	69.1%	30.9%
Aged 18 to 29	80.6	19.4
Aged 30 to 39	79.6	20.4
Aged 40 to 49	67.4	32.6
Aged 50 to 59	63.5	36.5
Aged 60 to 69	67.3	32.7
Aged 70 to 79	43.1	56.9
Aged 80 or older	40.0	60.0

Source: 1994 General Social Survey, National Opinion Research Center, University of Chicago

Drug Use Trends by Age and Type of Drug, 1979 to 1994

(percent of persons aged 12 or older reporting any illicit drug use in the past month by age and type of drug, 1979 and 1994; percentage point change, 1979-94)

	1994	1979	percentage point change 1979-1994
Total	5.8%	13.7%	-7.9
Aged 12 to 17	9.5	18.5	-9.0
Aged 18 to 25	13.2	37.4	-24.2
Aged 26 to 34	7.8	18.4	-10.6
Aged 35 or older	2.9	2.6	0.3
Type of drug			
Marijuana or hashish	4.7	12.8	-8.1
Cocaine	0.6	2.4	-1.8
Crack	0.2	-	-
Inhalants	0.7	1.4	-0.7
Hallucinogens	0.3	1.2	-0.9
Heroin	0.1	0.1	0.0
Stimulants*	0.1	1.1	-1.0
Sedatives*	0.1	0.9	-0.8
Tranquilizers*	0.2	0.7	-0.5

Note: Illicit drug use is defined as the nonmedical use of marijuana or hashish, cocaine (including crack), inhalants, hallucinogens (including PCP, heroin or psychotherapeutics) at least once.
* Nonmedical use of any prescription stimulant, sedative, or tranquilizer; does not include over-the-counter drugs.
Source: Substance Abuse and Mental Health Services Administration, Preliminary Estimates From the 1994 National Household Survey on Drug Abuse, *Advance Report Number 10, 1995; calculations by New Strategist*

Colds and Flu Are the Most Common Illnesses

Americans suffered from more than 65 million colds and more than 90 million bouts with the flu in 1994.

Each year, about 25 percent of Americans come down with a cold that sends them to a doctor or makes them stay in bed for at least one day. An even larger 35 percent are bedridden by the flu.

The incidence of most acute illnesses declines with age. While 69 percent of children under age 5 catch a cold each year that sends them to the doctor or to bed, only 12 percent of people aged 65 or older are so afflicted. Not only do older people have more immunities than children, but they are less likely to be around others who are sick.

In contrast to acute illnesses, the prevalence of chronic conditions increases with age. The most common chronic conditions among the elderly are arthritis, hearing impairments, heart conditions, and high blood pressure. Nearly half of people aged 65 or older have arthritis.

♦ As the baby-boom generation enters its 50s and 60s during the next decades, chronic conditions will receive increasing attention—particularly arthritis, heart conditions, and hearing impairments.

Acute Health Conditions by Age, 1994

(number and rate per 100 persons of selected acute conditions by age and type of condition, 1994; numbers in thousands)

	common cold	influenza	digestive problems	injuries
Total	65,968	90,447	15,863	61,887
Under age 5	14,020	7,645	2,155	5,246
Aged 5 to 17	14,574	22,921	4,110	12,904
Aged 18 to 24	6,590	9,783	1,866	8,267
Aged 25 to 44	18,591	31,351	3,918	20,726
Aged 45 to 64	8,372	13,058	2,084	8,659
Aged 65 or older	3,822	5,688	1,729	6,086
Rate per 100 persons				
Total	25.4	34.8	6.1	23.8
Under age 5	68.5	37.3	10.5	25.6
Aged 5 to 17	29.4	46.3	8.3	26.0
Aged 18 to 24	26.1	38.7	7.4	32.7
Aged 25 to 44	22.4	37.8	4.7	25.0
Aged 45 to 64	16.6	25.9	4.1	17.2
Aged 65 or older	12.3	18.3	5.6	19.6

Note: An acute condition is an illness or injury that lasts less than three months and which was medically attended or caused at least one day of restricted activity.
Source: National Center for Health Statistics, Current Estimates from the National Health Interview Survey, 1994, Vital and Health Statistics, 1994, Series 10, No. 193, 1995

Chronic Health Conditions by Age, 1994

(number and percent distribution of persons with selected chronic conditions by type of condition and age, 1994; numbers in thousands)

	total	under 18	18 to 44	45 to 64	65 to 74	75 or older
Number						
Arthritis	33,446	187	5,656	12,045	8,704	6,854
Visual impairments	8,601	609	3,168	2,273	1,122	1,428
Cataracts	6,473	96	347	872	2,062	3,096
Hearing impairments	22,400	1,224	5,339	6,952	4,282	4,603
Orthopedic impairments	31,068	1,961	15,400	8,570	2,812	2,326
Diabetes	7,766	97	1,346	3,182	1,855	1,287
Heart condition	22,279	1,265	4,097	6,838	5,133	4,946
High blood pressure	28,236	189	5,549	11,206	6,338	4,955
Hay fever	26,146	4,236	13,339	6,089	1,581	900
Chronic sinusitis	34,902	4,562	16,586	9,067	2,739	1,948
Percent distribution						
Arthritis	100.0%	0.6%	16.9%	36.0%	26.0%	20.5%
Visual impairments	100.0	7.1	36.8	26.4	13.0	16.6
Cataracts	100.0	1.5	5.4	13.5	31.9	47.8
Hearing impairments	100.0	5.5	23.8	31.0	19.1	20.5
Orthopedic impairments	100.0	6.3	49.6	27.6	9.1	7.5
Diabetes	100.0	1.2	17.3	41.0	23.9	16.6
Heart condition	100.0	5.7	18.4	30.7	23.0	22.2
High blood pressure	100.0	0.7	19.7	39.7	22.4	17.5
Hay fever	100.0	16.2	51.0	23.3	6.0	3.4
Chronic sinusitis	100.0	13.1	47.5	26.0	7.8	5.6

Note: Chronic conditions are those that last at least three months or belong to a group of conditions that are considered to be chronic regardless of when they began.
Source: National Center for Health Statistics, Current Estimates From the National Health Interview Survey, 1994, *Series 10, No. 193, 1995*

Many Americans Have a Work Disability

One in three persons with a work disability is aged 45 or older.

Seventeen million Americans between the ages of 16 and 64 have a work disability, or 10 percent of the working-age population. Fifty-one percent of those with a work disability are women. The Census Bureau collects work disability data by asking people whether there is anyone in the household with a condition that limits the kind or amount of work they can do at a job. Those with work disabilities may be limited in the kind or amount of work they can do, or they may be unable to work at all.

Overall, 11 million people with work disabilities (64 percent of disabled workers) are severely disabled, while another 6 million do not have severe disabilities. This proportion is much the same in every age group and for both men and women.

♦ As the enormous baby-boom generation ages, the number of Americans with work disabilities is likely to grow rapidly, even if the proportion who are disabled remains the same. Expect the disabled to become increasingly vocal as boomers join their ranks.

Persons with a Work Disability by Sex and Age, 1996

(total number of persons aged 16 to 64, and number and percent with a work disability, by sex, age, and severity, 1996; numbers in thousands)

| | | with a work disability | | | | | |
| | | total | | not severe | | severe | |
	total	number	percent	number	percent	number	percent
Total	168,266	17,016	10.1%	6,144	3.7%	10,872	6.5%
16 to 24	32,264	1,371	4.2	559	1.7	812	2.5
25 to 34	40,563	2,567	6.3	1,033	2.5	1,534	3.8
35 to 44	42,812	4,065	9.5	1,521	3.6	2,544	5.9
45 to 54	31,546	4,162	13.2	1,481	4.7	2,680	8.5
55 to 64	21,081	4,851	23.0	1,549	7.3	3,302	15.7
Men	82,606	8,164	9.9	2,984	3.6	5,181	6.3
16 to 24	16,154	672	4.2	277	1.7	395	2.4
25 to 34	20,053	1,160	5.8	429	2.1	731	3.6
35 to 44	21,022	2,013	9.6	725	3.4	1,287	6.1
45 to 54	15,287	2,054	13.4	755	4.9	1,300	8.5
55 to 64	10,090	2,266	22.5	799	7.9	1,467	14.5
Women	85,660	8,852	10.3	3,160	3.7	5,692	6.6
16 to 24	16,110	699	4.3	283	1.8	417	2.6
25 to 34	20,510	1,408	6.9	605	2.9	803	3.9
35 to 44	21,790	2,053	9.4	796	3.7	1,257	5.8
45 to 54	16,259	2,107	13.0	727	4.5	1,380	8.5
55 to 64	10,991	2,585	23.5	750	6.8	1,835	16.7

Source: Bureau of the Census, Internet web site, http://www.census.gov

Doctor Visits Number in the Millions

Americans visited doctors more than 680 million times in 1994.

The average American visits a doctor 2.6 times a year. Women see doctors more often than men—3.1 times a year versus men's 2.2. Overall, women account for 60 percent of all doctor visits.

Boys under age 15 visit a doctor more often than girls, but at all other ages women see doctors more often than men. Pregnancy is one reason for women's higher rates of physician visits. Women of childbearing age—25 to 44—account for the largest share of doctor visits. Americans aged 75 or older see a doctor much more frequently than younger people, an average of six visits a year, compared with only one to two for young adults.

◆ As the population ages, doctor visits will increase. The future cost of medical care will rise significantly unless less-expensive practitioners such as nurses and physician's assistants provide more of this care.

Physician Visits by Sex and Age, 1994

(number and percent distribution of office visits to physicians and number of visits per person, by sex and age, 1994)

	number (in 000s)	percent distribution	visits per person
Total	681,457	100.0%	2.6
Female, total	408,049	59.9	3.1
Under age 15	57,606	8.5	2.0
Aged 15 to 24	39,890	5.9	2.2
Aged 25 to 44	122,194	17.9	2.9
Aged 45 to 64	90,644	13.3	3.5
Aged 65 to 74	51,079	7.5	5.0
Aged 75 or older	46,637	6.8	5.9
Male, total	273,409	40.1	2.2
Under age 15	66,815	9.8	2.2
Aged 15 to 24	20,832	3.1	1.1
Aged 25 to 44	61,948	9.1	1.5
Aged 45 to 64	58,394	8.6	2.4
Aged 65 to 74	36,382	5.3	4.5
Aged 75 or older	29,038	4.3	6.0

Source: National Center for Health Statistics, National Ambulatory Medical Care Survey: 1994 Summary, Advance Data, No. 273, 1996

Hospital Stays Becoming Shorter

The average hospital stay was 5.9 days in 1994, down from 6.4 days in 1991.

As insurance companies try to cut costs, hospital stays have shortened—but only for women. In 1994, women's hospital stays averaged 5.1 days, down from 6.0 days in 1991. Men's hospitals stays averaged 7.0 days in both years.

Drive-through deliveries account for only part of the drop in average hospital stays for women, since the decline occurred in older age groups as well. Among women aged 65 or older, for example, the average hospital stay fell from 8.8 to 7.3 days. Among men in this age group there was no change in the average hospital stay.

America's hospitals discharged more than 27 million patients (excluding newborns) in 1994, most of them women. People aged 65 or older account for the largest share of hospital discharges among men, while the 18-to-44 age group accounts for the largest share among women due to childbirth.

♦ As the average length of a hospital stay falls, the public is beginning to resist. The average length of a hospital stay may stabilize in the next few years as the government steps in to regulate the insurers.

Hospital Care by Age and Sex, 1994

(number of inpatients discharged from short-stay, non-federal hospitals, in thousands, and average length of stay in days, by age and sex, 1994)

	total	men	women
Discharges, total	27,400	11,059	13,641
Under age 18	3,068	1,535	1,534
Aged 18 to 44	9,848	2,785	7,064
Aged 45 to 64	6,142	2,986	3,156
Aged 65 or older	8,341	3,754	4,587
Length of stay, total	5.9	7.0	5.1
Under age 18	5.8	6.4	5.0
Aged 18 to 44	4.1	6.4	3.6
Aged 45 to 64	5.8	6.3	5.4
Aged 65 or older	7.8	8.3	7.3

Source: National Center for Health Statistics, Current Estimates from the National Health Interview Survey, 1994, *Series 10, No. 193, 1995*

Home Health and Hospice Care

The number of Americans receiving home health care is up 53 percent since 1992.

More than 1.8 million Americans received home health care in 1994, up from 1.2 million in 1992. Home health care can be less expensive than hospital care, which is why it is growing so rapidly. Nearly three out of four people receiving home health care are aged 65 or older.

The number of Americans being cared for in hospices reached 61,000 in 1994, up from 47,200 in 1992. Hospices are home-like places where terminally ill patients spend their final days in more comfortable surroundings. As with home health care, most patients in hospices are aged 65 or older—69 percent in 1994.

♦ If the costs of home health care and hospices can be controlled, these alternatives to hospital care are likely to expand greatly over the next few decades.

Home Health and Hospice Care by Age and Sex, 1994

(number and percent distribution of persons receiving home health or hospice care by age and sex, 1994)

	home health care		hospice care	
	number	*percent*	*number*	*percent*
Total	1,889,400	100.0%	61,000	100.0%
Under age 45	236,000	12.5	5,200	8.6
Aged 45 to 54	86,300	4.6	4,100	6.8
Aged 55 to 64	187,300	9.9	9,500	15.6
Aged 65 or older	1,367,900	72.4	41,900	68.8
Aged 65 to 69	176,000	9.3	5,800	9.5
Aged 70 to 74	237,800	12.6	8,400	13.8
Aged 75 to 79	283,700	15.0	7,500	12.3
Aged 80 to 84	299,900	15.9	10,000	16.5
Aged 85 or older	370,600	19.6	10,100	16.6
Sex				
Male	613,400	32.5	27,200	44.7
Female	1,276,000	67.5	33,700	55.3

Note: Numbers by age will not add to total because persons of unknown age are not shown.
Source: National Center for Health Statistics, Overview of Home Health and Hospice Care Patients, *Advance Data, No. 274, 1996*

AIDS Cases Number Over One-Half Million

Of all persons with AIDS, more than 62 percent have died.

Since 1993, the number of new AIDS cases reported annually has fallen. The demographic characteristics of persons testing positive for HIV is shifting from whites to minorities, and especially to blacks. Through 1995, non-Hispanic blacks accounted for 34 percent of cumulative AIDS cases—much larger than the black share of the total population. Among preschoolers with AIDS, 61 percent are non-Hispanic black. Hispanics account for 18 percent of cumulative AIDS cases, with the largest Hispanic share among children and teens.

Of the half-million cumulative AIDS cases, over 200,000 (45 percent) were first reported among people in their 30s. Fully 85 percent of persons diagnosed with AIDS are men.

♦ Because of the manner in which HIV is acquired, and because of the long incubation period, AIDS will continue to be a disease that affects adults primarily in the 25-to-44 age group.

AIDS Cases by Age and Sex Through 1995

(cumulative number and percent distribution of AIDS cases by age at diagnosis and sex, through 1995)

	both sexes		male		female	
	number	*percent*	*number*	*percent*	*number*	*percent*
Total	513,486	100.0%	438,294	100.0%	75,191	100.0%
Under age 5	5,526	1.1	2,763	0.6	2,763	3.7
Aged 5 to 12	1,422	0.3	812	0.2	610	0.8
Aged 13 to 19	2,354	0.5	1,534	0.3	820	1.1
Aged 20 to 24	18,955	3.7	14,396	3.3	4,559	6.1
Aged 25 to 29	73,973	14.4	61,674	14.1	12,299	16.4
Aged 30 to 34	118,898	23.2	101,309	23.1	17,589	23.4
Aged 35 to 39	114,377	22.3	98,758	22.5	15,619	20.8
Aged 40 to 44	81,000	15.8	71,200	16.2	9,800	13.0
Aged 45 to 49	44,883	8.7	40,265	9.2	4,618	6.1
Aged 50 to 54	24,031	4.7	21,514	4.9	2,517	3.3
Aged 55 to 59	13,575	2.6	11,997	2.7	1,578	2.1
Aged 60 to 64	7,720	1.5	6,709	1.5	1,011	1.3
Aged 65 or older	6,771	1.3	5,363	1.2	1,408	1.9

Source: U.S. Department of Health and Human Services, Centers for Disease Control and Prevention, HIV/AIDS Surveillance Report, Vol. 7, No. 2, 1996

AIDS Cases by Age, Race, and Hispanic Origin Through 1995

(cumulative number and percent distribution of AIDS cases by age at diagnosis, race, and Hispanic origin, through 1995)

| | | non-Hispanic | | |
	total	*white*	*black*	*Hispanic*
Total, number	513,486	243,107	174,714	90,031
Under age 5	5,526	846	3,357	1,268
Aged 5 to 12	1,422	424	617	361
Aged 13 to 19	2,354	838	1,040	437
Aged 20 to 24	18,955	7,423	7,384	3,926
Aged 25 to 29	73,973	34,328	24,476	14,355
Aged 30 to 34	118,898	57,136	38,726	21,755
Aged 35 to 39	114,377	53,814	39,723	19,634
Aged 40 to 44	81,000	38,589	28,317	13,193
Aged 45 to 49	44,883	22,712	14,576	7,097
Aged 50 to 54	24,031	12,232	7,782	3,752
Aged 55 to 59	13,575	6,905	4,322	2,180
Aged 60 to 64	7,720	4,047	2,413	1,179
Aged 65 or older	6,771	3,813	1,981	894
Total, percent	100.0%	47.3%	34.0%	17.5%
Under age 5	100.0	15.3	60.7	22.9
Aged 5 to 12	100.0	29.8	43.4	25.4
Aged 13 to 19	100.0	35.6	44.2	18.6
Aged 20 to 24	100.0	39.2	39.0	20.7
Aged 25 to 29	100.0	46.4	33.1	19.4
Aged 30 to 34	100.0	48.1	32.6	18.3
Aged 35 to 39	100.0	47.0	34.7	17.2
Aged 40 to 44	100.0	47.6	35.0	16.3
Aged 45 to 49	100.0	50.6	32.5	15.8
Aged 50 to 54	100.0	50.9	32.4	15.6
Aged 55 to 59	100.0	50.9	31.8	16.1
Aged 60 to 64	100.0	52.4	31.3	15.3
Aged 65 or older	100.0	56.3	29.3	13.2

Note: Numbers by race and Hispanic origin will not add to total because not all races are shown.
Source: U.S. Department of Health and Human Services, Centers for Disease Control and Prevention,
HIV/AIDS Surveillance Report, *Vol. 7, No. 2, 1996*

Homicide Is a Top Killer of Black Men

More than 24,000 Americans were murdered in 1994, and nearly half were black.

Black men account for 40 percent of the nation's murder victims, although they are just 6 percent of the United States population. The statistics are even worse for black men aged 15 to 24. Among the 8,013 people aged 15 to 24 who were murdered in 1994, 53 percent were black males. Fully 56 percent of black men aged 15 to 24 who died in 1994 were murdered. Among white men aged 15 to 24, only 14 percent of those who died were murdered.

Black women are far more likely to be murdered than white women, although their homicide rate is below that of black men. Twenty-six percent of black women aged 15 to 24 who died in 1994 were murdered, compared with only 9 percent of white women in that age group.

♦ The shockingly high murder rate among blacks, especially young adults, will continue to spur the American public to take action against crime. Expect to see increasingly strident demands for stricter gun-control laws and stiffer penalties for violent criminals.

Homicides by Race and Sex, 1994

(number and percent distribution of homicides by race and sex, and homicides as a percent of all deaths by race and sex; for the total population and the 15-to-24 age group, 1994)

	total population			population aged 15 to 24		
	deaths by homicide	percent distribution of deaths by homicide	homicides as a percent of all deaths	deaths by homicide	percent distribution of deaths by homicide	homicides as a percent of all deaths in age group
Total	24,547	100.0%	1.1%	8,013	100.0%	22.7%
Men	19,342	78.8	1.7	6,923	86.4	25.9
Women	5,205	21.2	0.5	1,090	13.6	12.8
White	11,718	47.7	0.6	3,057	38.2	12.5
Men	8,810	35.9	0.9	2,508	31.3	13.7
Women	2,908	11.8	0.3	549	6.9	8.9
Black	12,092	49.3	4.3	4,720	58.9	50.0
Men	9,969	40.6	6.5	4,214	52.6	56.3
Women	2,123	8.6	1.6	506	6.3	25.9

Note: Numbers will not add to total because not all races are shown.
Source: National Center for Health Statistics, Advance Report of Final Mortality Statistics, 1994, *Monthly Vital Statistics Report, Vol. 45, No. 3 Supplement, 1996 and internet site,* http://www.cdc.gov; *calculations by New Strategist*

Heart Disease and Cancer Are Biggest Killers

In 1995 more than half of all deaths in the United States were caused by heart disease or cancer.

Heart disease and cancer each kill more than half a million Americans every year. Chronic diseases such as these are by far the leading causes of death among Americans. Accidents are responsible for just 4 percent of deaths in the United States, with motor vehicle accidents accounting for fewer than half of all accidental deaths. The causes of death that often make headlines—AIDS and suicide—rank 8th and 9th as causes of death. Together, they accounted for only 3 percent of all deaths in 1995. AIDS entered the top ten list in 1990.

♦ Although medical science has made considerable progress in combating heart disease, it remains by far the leading killer of Americans. It will continue to hold this position into the foreseeable future.

Ten Leading Causes of Death in the U.S., 1995

(number and percent distribution of deaths for the ten leading causes of death for all persons, 1995)

	number	percent
All causes	2,312,203	100.0%
1. Heart diseases	738,781	32.0
2. Cancer	537,969	23.3
3. Cerebrovascular diseases	158,061	6.8
4. Chronic obstructive pulmonary diseases	104,756	4.5
5. Accidents and adverse effects	89,703	3.9
Motor vehicle accidents	41,786	1.8
All other accidents and adverse effects	47,916	2.1
6. Pneumonia and influenza	83,528	3.6
7. Diabetes mellitus	59,085	2.6
8. Human immunodeficiency virus infection	42,506	1.8
9. Suicide	30,893	1.3
10. Chronic liver disease and cirrhosis	24,848	1.1
All other causes	442,073	19.1

Source: National Center for Health Statistics, Births and Deaths: United States, 1995, *Monthly Vital Statistics Report, Vol. 45, No. 3, Supplement 2, 1996; calculations by New Strategist*

Life Expectancy Continues to Rise

Americans born in 1995 can expect to live to age 75.8.

Since 1900, life expectancy at birth has climbed by 60 percent, from 47 years to more than 75 years. Life expectancy for males has climbed by nearly 57 percent since 1900. For females the gain has been an even higher 63 percent. At the turn of the century, newborn girls could expect to outlive newborn boys by just two years. Today, female life expectancy exceeds that of males by more than six years. Although some claim job stress causes this gender gap, most research points to biological rather than social causes.

Most of the gains in life expectancy during this century have been due to declining death rates among infants and children. But life expectancy has grown even at older ages as medical science combats heart disease and other chronic ailments. Life expectancy at age 65 has grown by 46 percent since 1900, from 12 to 17 years.

Black life expectancy is below that of whites, but blacks are gaining faster. The life expectancy of black males and females has more than doubled since the turn of the century.

♦ The costs of extending life at very old ages are enormous, raising ethical questions about the equitable distribution of society's medical resources. These questions will have to be answered as the baby-boom generation ages.

Life Expectancy by Race and Sex, 1900 to 1995

(years of life remaining at birth and at age 65, by race and sex; percent change in years of life remaining, 1900-95)

	total			white			black		
	total	males	females	total	males	females	total	males	females
At birth									
1995	75.8	72.6	78.9	76.5	73.4	79.6	69.8	65.4	74.0
1990	75.4	71.8	78.8	76.1	72.7	79.4	69.1	64.5	73.6
1980	73.7	70.0	77.4	74.4	70.7	78.1	68.1	63.8	72.5
1970	70.8	67.1	74.7	71.7	68.0	75.6	64.1	60.0	68.3
1960	69.7	66.6	73.1	70.6	67.4	74.1	63.2	60.7	65.9
1950	68.2	65.6	71.1	69.1	66.5	72.2	60.7	58.9	62.7
1900	47.3	46.3	48.3	47.6	46.6	48.7	33.0	32.5	33.5
Percent change									
1900 to 1995	60.3%	56.8%	63.4%	60.7%	57.5%	63.4%	111.5%	101.2%	120.9%
At age 65									
1995	17.4	15.6	18.9	17.5	15.7	19.0	15.7	13.7	17.2
1990	17.2	15.1	18.9	17.3	15.2	19.1	15.4	13.2	17.2
1980	16.4	14.1	18.3	16.5	14.2	18.4	15.1	13.0	16.8
1970	15.2	13.1	17.0	15.2	13.1	17.1	14.2	12.5	15.7
1960	14.3	12.8	15.8	14.4	12.9	15.9	13.9	12.7	15.1
1950	13.9	12.8	15.0	-	12.8	15.1	13.9	12.9	14.9
1900	11.9	11.5	12.2	-	11.5	12.2	-	10.4	11.4
Percent change									
1900 to 1995	46.2%	35.7%	54.9%	-	36.5%	55.7%	-	31.7%	50.9%

Note: (-) means data are not available.
Source: National Center for Health Statistics, Births and Deaths: United States, 1995, Monthly Vital Statistics Report, Vol. 45, No. 3, Supplement 2, 1996; calculations by New Strategist

3

Income Trends

♦ **One in three households has an income of $50,000 or more.**
The U.S. is likely to see record levels of affluence by the end of the 1990s as the baby-boom generation enters its peak-earning years.

♦ **Americans' economic fortunes are closely tied to their living arrangements.**
Since 1990, married couples and female-headed families have been gaining ground while other types of households have been losing out to inflation.

♦ **The median income of householders with a bachelor's degree was $58,052 in 1995.**
The higher the educational degree, the greater the financial rewards—nearly 40 percent of householders with professional degrees had a household income of $100,000 or more.

♦ **Since 1980, men's median income has fallen by 3 percent, while women's has grown by 33 percent, after adjusting for inflation.**
Women are benefiting from growth in the service sector of the economy, while men are hurt by the loss of well-paying manufacturing jobs.

♦ **The median income of white men fell by 3 percent between 1980 and 1995, after adjusting for inflation.**
Hispanic men saw their incomes fall by 17 percent during those years, while the incomes of black men rose by 8 percent.

♦ **Whites account for most of the nation's 36 million poor.**
Childhood poverty will remain a chronic problem until single-parent families begin to decline as a share of all families.

Household Affluence Nears Record High

One in three households has an income of $50,000 or more.

The share of households earning $50,000 or more is slightly below the record level set in 1989. But it is up slightly from the level of the early 1990s. The share of households with incomes of $100,000 or more reached an all-time high of 7.1 percent in 1994 It remained at that level in 1995.

At the other end of the income scale, the share of households with incomes below $25,000 stood at 37 percent in 1995, below the 39 percent of 1980. This figure had fallen as low as 35 percent in 1989. The middle class—if defined as households with incomes between $25,000 and $50,000—really did shrink over the past 15 years, from 34 percent of households in 1980 to 31 percent in 1995.

Although the recession of the early 1990s cut into Americans' incomes, an economic recovery is apparent in the 1995 statistics. The share of households with incomes of $50,000 or more should continue to rise.

◆ The United States is likely to see record levels of affluence by the end of the 1990s as the baby-boom generation enters its peak-earning years.

◆ The proportion of households with incomes of $25,000 to $50,000 should stabilize during the 1990s as those leaving the middle class for affluence are replaced by those achieving middle-class status as paychecks grow.

Distribution of Households by Income, 1980 to 1995

(number and percent distribution of households by income, 1980 to 1995; in 1995 dollars; households in thousands as of the following year)

	total households	total	under $15,000	$15,000-$24,999	$25,000-$34,999	$35,000-$49,999	$50,000-$74,999	$75,000-$99,999	$100,000 or more
1995	99,627	100.0%	21.0%	15.9%	14.2%	16.9%	17.1%	7.7%	7.1%
1994	98,990	100.0	22.1	16.3	14.1	16.3	16.7	7.5	7.1
1993	97,107	100.0	22.2	16.0	14.7	16.2	16.7	7.4	6.7
1992	96,426	100.0	22.2	16.0	14.5	16.8	17.1	7.2	6.2
1991	95,699	100.0	21.5	16.0	14.6	17.1	17.2	7.4	6.3
1990	94,312	100.0	20.6	15.5	14.4	17.7	17.6	7.6	6.6
1989	93,347	100.0	20.2	15.4	13.8	17.6	18.0	8.0	7.0
1988	92,830	100.0	20.5	15.6	14.0	17.4	18.1	7.8	6.7
1987	91,124	100.0	20.9	15.3	14.2	17.5	17.8	7.9	6.4
1986	89,479	100.0	21.1	15.5	14.2	17.4	18.1	7.5	6.2
1985	88,458	100.0	21.7	16.0	14.5	18.1	17.4	7.1	5.3
1984	86,789	100.0	22.0	16.4	14.4	18.1	17.3	6.8	5.1
1983	85,290	100.0	22.2	17.1	14.8	18.1	16.8	6.4	4.6
1982	83,918	100.0	22.6	16.8	15.0	18.6	16.5	6.3	4.3
1981	83,527	100.0	22.1	17.3	14.8	18.4	17.1	6.4	3.9
1980	82,368	100.0	22.0	16.5	14.6	19.3	17.4	6.3	4.0

Source: Bureau of the Census, Money Income in the United States: 1995, *Current Population Reports, P60-193, 1996*

Richer or Poorer?

The poorest households receive a smaller share of income today than they did in 1980. The richest households receive much more.

If you add up all the money going to American households, including earnings, interest, dividends, Social Security benefits, and so on, the result is called "aggregate household income." Year-to-year changes in how this aggregate is divided among the nation's households can reveal trends in income inequality. The numbers on the next page show how much aggregate income is received by each fifth of households, from poorest to richest. They also show how much accrues to the 5 percent of households with the highest incomes.

Since 1980, incomes have become more unequal, but this trend may have ended by the mid-1990s. The percentage of aggregate income received by the richest 5 percent of households rose from 15.8 percent in 1980 to a peak of 21.2 percent in 1994, then fell slightly in 1995. The percentage received by the bottom fifth of households fell from 4.3 percent to a low of 3.6 percent in 1994, then rose slightly to 3.7 percent in 1995.

♦ A rise or fall in the amount of income accruing to each fifth of households reveals trends in the distribution of income among households, not the economic well-being of individual households. Households headed by young adults typically start out at the bottom, for example, then rise through the distribution as entry-level workers gain job experience and earn more.

Distribution of Aggregate Household Income, 1980 to 1995

(total number of households, and percent of income received by each fifth and top 5 percent of households, 1980-95; households in thousands as of the following year)

	total households	total	bottom fifth	second fifth	third fifth	fourth fifth	top fifth	top 5 percent
1995	99,627	100.0%	3.7%	9.1%	15.2%	23.3%	48.7%	21.0%
1994	98,990	100.0	3.6	8.9	15.0	23.4	49.1	21.2
1993	97,107	100.0	3.6	9.0	15.1	23.5	48.9	21.0
1992	96,426	100.0	3.8	9.4	15.8	24.2	46.9	18.6
1991	95,699	100.0	3.8	9.6	15.9	24.2	46.5	18.1
1990	94,312	100.0	3.9	9.6	15.9	24.0	46.6	18.6
1989	93,347	100.0	3.8	9.5	15.8	24.0	46.8	18.9
1988	92,830	100.0	3.8	9.6	16.0	24.3	46.3	18.3
1987	91,124	100.0	3.8	9.6	16.1	24.3	46.2	18.2
1986	89,479	100.0	3.9	9.7	16.2	24.5	45.7	17.5
1985	88,458	100.0	4.0	9.7	16.3	24.6	45.3	17.0
1984	86,789	100.0	4.1	9.9	16.4	24.7	44.9	16.5
1983	85,290	100.0	4.1	10.0	16.5	24.7	44.7	16.4
1982	83,918	100.0	4.1	10.1	16.6	24.7	44.5	16.2
1981	83,527	100.0	4.2	10.2	16.8	25.0	43.8	15.6
1980	82,368	100.0	4.3	10.3	16.9	24.9	43.7	15.8

Source: Bureau of the Census, Money Income in the United States: 1995, *Current Population Reports, P60-193, 1996*

Incomes of the Young Have Fallen the Most

Since 1980, the incomes of householders under age 25 have fallen by 11 percent, after adjusting for inflation.

The fortunes of younger and older householders have diverged sharply since 1980. The median incomes of households headed by people under age 45 have dropped after adjusting for inflation, while those headed by people aged 45 or older have increased. Young adults have been hit the worst as entry-level wages fell and single-parent families increased. Median income of the youngest householders declined 11 percent between 1980 and 1995. In sharp contrast, median income of households headed by people aged 65 or older gained 17 percent over the same period.

In 1990, household incomes began to fall for the oldest age group as interest rates declined. And in what may be an important shift, household incomes for young adults fell less than those for most older age groups. The only householders to gain ground since 1990 are those aged 55 to 64, with a small 0.9 percent increase in median household income.

♦ The changing economy of the past 15 years has curtailed the earning power of young adults. While their incomes are likely to grow as they gain more experience on the job, they may never do as well as older generations.

♦ The incomes of the elderly have grown as recent retirees with generous pensions and other benefits replace the less affluent elderly. These gains are likely to continue for another decade before the trend reverses as baby boomers retire.

Median Household Income by Age of Householder, 1980 to 1995

(median household income by age of householder, 1980-95; percent change for selected years; in 1995 dollars)

	total households	under 25	25 to 34	35 to 44	45 to 54	55 to 64	65 or older
1995	$34,076	$20,979	$34,701	$43,465	$48,058	$38,077	$19,096
1994	33,178	19,888	34,090	42,848	48,600	36,230	18,608
1993	32,949	20,390	32,991	43,096	48,733	35,304	18,721
1992	33,278	19,186	33,933	43,290	48,268	36,925	18,613
1991	33,709	20,491	34,510	44,029	48,955	37,265	18,994
1990	34,914	20,991	35,399	44,963	48,882	37,739	19,653
1989	35,526	22,937	36,653	46,255	51,033	37,878	19,383
1988	35,073	21,952	36,597	47,091	49,228	37,234	19,225
1987	34,962	22,064	36,176	47,202	49,912	36,973	19,376
1986	34,620	21,289	36,011	45,591	49,586	37,232	19,252
1985	33,452	21,315	35,529	44,001	47,056	36,198	18,772
1984	32,878	20,576	34,814	43,687	46,228	35,341	18,774
1983	31,957	20,507	33,274	42,352	46,442	34,853	17,930
1982	32,155	22,025	33,925	42,038	44,612	35,191	17,601
1981	32,263	22,398	34,697	42,936	45,744	35,590	16,750
1980	32,795	23,538	35,808	43,752	46,518	36,196	16,260

Percent change

	total households	under 25	25 to 34	35 to 44	45 to 54	55 to 64	65 or older
1990-1995	-2.4%	-0.1%	-2.0%	-3.3%	-1.7%	0.9%	-2.8%
1980-1995	3.9	-10.9	-3.1	-0.7	3.3	5.2	17.4

Source: Bureau of the Census, Internet web site, http://www.census.gov; *calculations by New Strategist*

Household Income Winners and Losers

Americans' economic fortunes are closely tied to their living arrangements.

Since 1980, the incomes of married couples have grown more than those of male- or female-headed families. Couples saw their median income rise by 10 percent between 1980 and 1995, after adjusting for inflation. The median income of female-headed families rose by 6 percent during those years.

Nonfamily households—including both people who live alone and those living with roommates or partners—have seen their median income grow by 14 percent since 1980, after adjusting for inflation. In contrast, male-headed families have lost ground, with a 4 percent decline in their median income in the past 15 years.

Since 1990, married couples and female-headed families have been gaining ground while other households have been losing out to inflation. The median income of male-headed families fell by 9 percent between 1990 and 1995, while the median income of nonfamily households was down 3 percent. Declining interest rates are behind the drop in the median income of nonfamily households. Many nonfamily householders are older people who live alone, dependent on interest earned from savings for part of their income.

♦ The incomes of married couples are likely to grow faster than those of other household types during the 1990s as women's earnings rise and as a growing proportion of married couples include two earners.

Median Household Income by Type of Household, 1980 to 1995

(median household income by type of household, 1980-1995; percent change for selected years; in 1995 dollars)

	total households	family households				nonfamily households
		total	married couples	female hh, no spouse present	male hh, no spouse present	
1995	$34,076	$41,224	$47,129	$21,348	$33,534	$19,929
1994	33,178	40,506	46,317	20,435	31,336	19,484
1993	32,949	39,533	45,487	19,559	31,481	19,912
1992	33,278	40,181	45,585	19,950	32,924	19,259
1991	33,710	40,733	45,961	20,102	34,698	19,893
1990	34,914	41,635	46,636	21,069	36,791	20,627
1989	35,526	42,565	47,519	21,364	37,284	21,035
1988	35,073	41,857	46,939	20,678	36,898	20,803
1987	34,962	41,919	46,891	20,767	35,826	19,921
1986	34,620	41,358	45,714	19,936	36,573	19,674
1985	33,452	39,689	44,135	20,277	34,494	19,543
1984	32,878	39,092	43,543	19,762	36,011	19,049
1983	31,957	37,921	41,817	18,727	35,012	18,377
1982	32,155	37,644	41,554	18,943	33,821	18,205
1981	32,263	38,146	42,466	19,352	34,746	17,566
1980	32,795	39,187	42,924	20,055	34,767	17,510
Percent change						
1990-1995	-2.4%	-1.0%	1.1%	1.3%	-8.9%	-3.4%
1980-1995	3.9	5.2	9.8	6.4	-3.5	13.8

Source: Bureau of the Census, Internet web site, http://www.census.gov; *calculations by New Strategist*

Black Incomes Are Growing the Fastest

The median income of black households rose by 3 percent between 1990 and 1995, after adjusting for inflation.

Although black incomes rose slightly, the median income of white and Hispanic households fell. Since 1980, the median income of black households has increased by 12 percent, much more than the 3 percent gain for white households, after adjusting for inflation. The median income of Hispanic households fell by 10 percent between 1980 and 1995.

Despite the rise in the incomes of blacks, their household median is just 63 percent of that for whites. This is up from 58 percent in 1980, however. The median income of Hispanic households fell relative to the white median, from 73 to 64 percent.

◆ The gap between black and white median household incomes is largely due to the difference in the composition of black and white households. Black households are much less likely to be headed by married couples—the most affluent household type—than are white households.

◆ Hispanic household income has been falling because of the influx of Hispanic immigrants, most with low earnings.

Median Household Income by Race and Hispanic Origin, 1980 to 1995

(median household income by race and Hispanic origin of householder, 1980-95; percent change for selected years; in 1995 dollars)

	total households	white	black	Hispanic
1995	$34,076	$35,766	$22,393	$22,860
1994	33,178	34,992	21,623	24,085
1993	32,949	34,762	20,601	24,137
1992	33,278	34,987	20,373	24,546
1991	33,709	35,324	21,044	25,390
1990	34,914	36,416	21,777	26,037
1989	35,526	37,370	22,225	26,942
1988	35,073	37,077	21,136	26,227
1987	34,962	36,836	21,025	25,940
1986	34,620	36,397	20,969	25,519
1985	33,452	35,279	20,989	24,737
1984	32,878	34,685	19,759	24,924
1983	32,160	33,716	19,085	24,167
1982	32,155	33,664	19,079	24,196
1981	32,263	34,088	19,129	25,879
1980	32,795	34,598	19,932	25,278
Percent change				
1990-1995	-2.4%	-1.8%	2.8%	-12.2%
1980-1995	3.9	3.4	12.3	-9.6

Source: Bureau of the Census, Money Income in the United States: 1995, *Current Population Reports, P60-193, 1996; calculations by New Strategist*

Householders Aged 45 to 54
Have the Highest Incomes

Household incomes peak at $48,058 in the 45-to-54 age group.

Incomes are greatest for householders aged 45 to 54 because workers typically are at the height of their careers at that age. More than one in seven householders aged 45 to 54 had an income of $100,000 or more in 1995. Householders aged 75 or older had the lowest incomes, just $15,342 in 1995.

The median income of householders under age 25 was only $20,979 in 1995. This was less than that of householders aged 65 to 74, at $23,031. The low incomes of young householders make it difficult for them to save money for a down payment on a home. This is one reason for the decline in homeownership rates among young adults.

♦ The baby-boom generation is now filling the 45-to-54 age group, when incomes peak. The number of affluent households should increase sharply.

♦ Today's 65-to-74-year-olds are the most affluent older generation in history, with generous Social Security and pension benefits. It's unlikely that future generations of elderly will be as fortunate.

Household Income by Age of Householder, 1995

(number and percent distribution of households by household income and age of householder, 1995; households in thousands as of 1996)

	total	under 25	25 to 34	35 to 44	45 to 54	55 to 64	65 to 74	75 or older
Total	99,627	5,282	19,225	23,226	18,008	12,401	11,908	9,578
Under $25,000	36,754	3,110	6,394	5,789	4,086	4,075	6,372	6,930
$25,000 to $49,999	31,044	1,645	7,364	7,656	5,290	3,703	3,509	1,876
$50,000 to $74,999	17,038	415	3,458	5,455	3,943	2,189	1,125	453
$75,000 to $99,999	7,677	77	1,197	2,353	2,295	1,201	385	170
$100,000 or more	7,114	36	811	1,974	2,394	1,234	518	148
Median income	$34,076	$20,979	$34,701	$43,465	$48,058	$38,077	$23,031	$15,342
Percent distribution								
Total	100.0%	100.0%	100.0%	100.0%	100.0%	100.0%	100.0%	100.0%
Under $25,000	36.9	58.9	33.3	24.9	22.7	32.9	53.5	72.4
$25,000 to $49,999	31.2	31.1	38.3	33.0	29.4	29.9	29.5	19.6
$50,000 to $74,999	17.1	7.9	18.0	23.5	21.9	17.7	9.4	4.7
$75,000 to $99,999	7.7	1.5	6.2	10.1	12.7	9.7	3.2	1.8
$100,000 or more	7.1	0.7	4.2	8.5	13.3	10.0	4.4	1.5

Source: Bureau of the Census, Money Income in the United States: 1995, *Current Population Reports, P60-193, 1996; calculations by New Strategist*

Income Peaks in Middle-Age for Whites, Blacks, and Hispanics

Median household income peaks at ages 45 to 54 for all racial and ethnic groups.

Among whites, the median income of householders aged 45 to 54 was more than $50,000 in 1995. One in ten white householders in this age group has an income of $100,000 or more. Among blacks, median household income peaks at $30,210 in the 45-to-54 age group. Only 5 percent of black householders aged 45 to 54 have incomes of $100,000 or more. Incomes peak for Hispanics at just $29,441 among 45-to-54-year-olds, and only 4 percent of householders in this age group have an income of $100,000 or more.

The median income of black households is far below that of whites because white households are much more likely to be headed by married couples—the most affluent household type. Hispanic household incomes are low because many are recent immigrants with low earnings.

♦ The poorest householders among whites, blacks, and Hispanics are those aged 75 or older. Black householders in this age group had a median income of just $9,866 in 1995.

♦ With the enormous baby-boom generation now in the peak-earning age groups, the proportion of households with affluent incomes should rise within each racial and ethnic group.

Income of White Households by Age, 1995

(number and percent distribution of white households by household income and age of householder, 1995; households in thousands as of 1996)

	total	under 25	25 to 34	35 to 44	45 to 54	55 to 64	65 to 74	75 or older
Total	84,511	4,254	15,730	19,373	15,214	10,614	10,583	8,743
Under $25,000	29,214	2,406	4,635	4,186	3,055	3,173	5,518	6,245
$25,000 to $49,999	26,732	1,391	6,252	6,429	4,452	3,234	3,203	1,771
$50,000 to $74,999	15,092	351	3,021	4,818	3,453	1,983	1,046	422
$75,000 to $99,999	6,940	71	1,098	2,128	2,055	1,085	339	161
$100,000 or more	6,533	35	724	1,813	2,200	1,138	479	144
Median income	$35,766	$22,203	$36,912	$45,924	$50,607	$40,150	$23,816	$15,807
Percent distribution								
Total	100.0%	100.0%	100.0%	100.0%	100.0%	100.0%	100.0%	100.0%
Under $25,000	34.6	56.6	29.5	21.6	20.1	29.9	52.1	71.4
$25,000 to $49,999	31.6	32.7	39.7	33.2	29.3	30.5	30.3	20.3
$50,000 to $74,999	17.9	8.3	19.2	24.9	22.7	18.7	9.9	4.8
$75,000 to $99,999	8.2	1.7	7.0	11.0	13.5	10.2	3.2	1.8
$100,000 or more	7.7	0.8	4.6	9.4	14.5	10.7	4.5	1.6

Source: Bureau of the Census, unpublished data from the 1996 Current Population Survey; calculations by New Strategist

Income of Black Households by Age, 1995

(number and percent distribution of black households by household income and age of householder, 1995; households in thousands as of 1996)

	total	under 25	25 to 34	35 to 44	45 to 54	55 to 64	65 to 74	75 or older
Total	11,577	774	2,633	2,889	2,118	1,385	1,064	713
Under $25,000	6,297	569	1,456	1,304	881	766	722	600
$25,000 to $49,999	3,263	165	820	944	641	376	233	84
$50,000 to $74,999	1,298	37	269	464	324	123	57	24
$75,000 to $99,999	460	5	60	122	170	64	33	5
$100,000 or more	259	-	26	56	102	56	19	-
Median income	$22,393	$12,825	$21,871	$28,097	$30,210	$21,843	$15,925	$9,866
Percent distribution								
Total	100.0%	100.0%	100.0%	100.0%	100.0%	100.0%	100.0%	100.0%
Under $25,000	54.4	73.5	55.3	45.1	41.6	55.3	67.9	84.2
$25,000 to $49,999	28.2	21.3	31.1	32.7	30.3	27.1	21.9	11.8
$50,000 to $74,999	11.2	4.8	10.2	16.1	15.3	8.9	5.4	3.4
$75,000 to $99,999	4.0	0.6	2.3	4.2	8.0	4.6	3.1	0.7
$100,000 or more	2.2	-	1.0	1.9	4.8	4.0	1.8	-

Note: (-) means sample is too small to make a reliable estimate.
Source: Bureau of the Census, unpublished data from the 1996 Current Population Survey; calculations by New Strategist

Income of Hispanic Households by Age, 1995

(number and percent distribution of Hispanic households by household income and age of householder, 1995; households in thousands as of 1996)

	total	under 25	25 to 34	35 to 44	45 to 54	55 to 64	65 to 74	75 or older
Total	7,939	749	2,195	2,109	1,181	808	609	289
Under $25,000	4,257	503	1,160	994	512	424	430	234
$25,000 to $49,999	2,281	190	672	674	358	220	120	47
$50,000 to $74,999	917	35	248	302	191	98	37	5
$75,000 to $99,999	292	11	69	81	73	41	12	3
$100,000 or more	193	11	45	58	46	25	9	-
Median income	$22,860	$16,854	$23,187	$26,492	$29,441	$22,859	$14,561	$12,277
Percent distribution								
Total	100.0%	100.0%	100.0%	100.0%	100.0%	100.0%	100.0%	100.0%
Under $25,000	53.6	67.2	52.8	47.1	43.4	52.5	70.6	81.0
$25,000 to $49,999	28.7	25.4	30.6	32.0	30.3	27.2	19.7	16.3
$50,000 to $74,999	11.6	4.7	11.3	14.3	16.2	12.1	6.1	1.7
$75,000 to $99,999	3.7	1.5	3.1	3.8	6.2	5.1	2.0	1.0
$100,000 or more	2.4	1.5	2.1	2.8	3.9	3.1	1.5	-

Note: (-) means sample is too small to make a reliable estimate.
Source: Bureau of the Census, unpublished data from the 1996 Current Population Survey; calculations by New Strategist

Incomes of Black Couples Close to White

Black married couples have a median income nearly twice as high as that of the average black household.

Median income of all black households is only 63 percent that of white households. But the median income of black couples is 87 percent that of their white counterparts. Black couples had a median household income of $41,362 in 1995, versus $47,608 for white couples. The median income of all black households is much lower ($22,393) because so many black households are female-headed families.

Female-headed families have low incomes regardless of race or Hispanic origin. Among these households, however, blacks and Hispanics have much lower incomes than whites. Black female-headed families had a median income of $15,589 in 1995. Hispanic female-headed families had an even lower income of $14,755, while white female-headed families had a significantly higher income of $24,431.

Within each racial and ethnic group, women who live alone have the lowest household incomes. Hispanic women who live alone have the lowest median income of all—just $8,908 in 1995.

♦ Within each racial and ethnic group, the household types that have been growing the fastest are also the ones with the lowest incomes—female-headed families and women living alone. The rapid growth of the poorest households has limited overall household income growth.

Median Household Income by Type of Household, Race, and Hispanic Origin, 1995

(median household income by type of household, race, and Hispanic origin of householder, 1995)

	total	white	black	Hispanic
Total	$34,076	$35,766	$22,393	$22,860
Family households	41,224	43,265	26,838	25,491
Married couples	47,129	47,608	41,362	30,195
Female householder, no spouse present	21,348	24,431	15,589	14,755
Male householder, no spouse present	33,534	35,129	27,071	25,053
Nonfamily households	19,929	20,585	15,007	13,780
Female householder	15,892	16,325	11,872	10,196
Living alone	14,331	14,667	10,958	8,908
Male householder	26,023	26,898	19,172	17,339
Living alone	22,586	23,552	17,017	14,181

Source: Bureau of the Census, Money Income in the United States: 1995, *Current Population Reports, P60-193, 1996*

Median Income of Married Couples Exceeds $47,000

Married couples are by far the most affluent household type.

Many married couples are dual earners, which accounts for their higher incomes. More than one in ten couples had an income of $100,000 or more in 1995. Nearly one in four had an income of $75,000 or more.

Married couples are the only household type whose median income is above the all-household average of $34,076. Female-headed families have a median income of $21,348, while male-headed families have an income of $33,534.

Women who live alone had the lowest household incomes, a median of just over $14,331 in 1995. Most women who live alone are older widows, which accounts for their low incomes. Men who live alone have much higher incomes than their female counterparts—a median of $22,586. That's because most men who live alone are under age 45 and in the labor force.

♦ The incomes of women who live alone are likely to rise in the decades ahead as baby-boom women with pensions of their own become widows in old age.

Household Income by Household Type, 1995:
Total Households

(number and percent distribution of households by household income and type of household, 1995; households in thousands as of 1996)

		family households			
	total households	total	married couples	female hh, no spouse present	male hh, no spouse present
Total	99,627	69,594	53,567	12,514	3,513
Under $25,000	36,754	19,089	10,750	7,084	1,254
$25,000 to $49,999	31,044	22,900	17,738	3,854	1,310
$50,000 to $74,999	17,038	14,432	12,751	1,106	576
$75,000 to $99,999	7,677	6,803	6,295	289	221
$100,000 or more	7,114	6,370	6,033	183	154
Median income	$34,076	$41,224	$47,129	$21,348	$33,534
Percent distribution					
Total	100.0%	100.0%	100.0%	100.0%	100.0%
Under $25,000	36.9	27.4	20.1	56.6	35.7
$25,000 to $49,999	31.2	32.9	33.1	30.8	37.3
$50,000 to $74,999	17.1	20.7	23.8	8.8	16.4
$75,000 to $99,999	7.7	9.8	11.8	2.3	6.3
$100,000 or more	7.1	9.2	11.3	1.5	4.4

		nonfamily households			
		female householders		male householders	
	total	total	living alone	total	living alone
Total	30,033	16,685	14,612	13,348	10,288
Under $25,000	17,667	11,273	10,683	6,395	5,580
$25,000 to $49,999	8,123	3,829	3,025	4,314	3,218
$50,000 to $74,999	2,606	1,061	645	1,545	903
$75,000 to $99,999	874	297	159	577	303
$100,000 or more	744	227	99	517	283
Median income	$19,929	$15,892	$14,331	$26,023	$22,586
Percent distribution					
Total	100.0%	100.0%	100.0%	100.0%	100.0%
Under $25,000	58.8	67.6	73.1	47.9	54.2
$25,000 to $49,999	27.0	22.9	20.7	32.3	31.3
$50,000 to $74,999	8.7	6.4	4.4	11.6	8.8
$75,000 to $99,999	2.9	1.8	1.1	4.3	2.9
$100,000 or more	2.5	1.4	0.7	3.9	2.8

Source: Bureau of the Census, unpublished tables from the 1996 Current Population Survey; calculations by New Strategist

At Every Age, Incomes Vary by Household Type

Regardless of age, married couples have the highest incomes, while female-headed families and women who live alone have the lowest.

Fewer than one-third of households headed by people under age 25 are married couples, which is one reason for the low incomes of this age group. Forty-one percent of householders under age 25 are people who live alone or women who head families without a spouse.

In contrast, households headed by 45-to-54-year-olds have the highest incomes, partly because most are married couples. Households headed by couples aged 45 to 54 are among the nation's income elite. In 1995, the median income of these couples surpassed $62,000. This age group is now filling with baby boomers.

♦ Record levels of affluence are virtually assured by the end of the 1990s as millions of baby boomers inflate the number of dual-earner married couples in their peak earning years.

Household Income by Household Type, 1995: Householders Under Age 25

(number and percent distribution of households headed by householders under age 25, by household income and type of household, 1995; households in thousands as of 1996)

| | total households | family households | | | |
		total	married couples	female hh, no spouse present	male hh, no spouse present
Total	5,282	3,016	1,528	1,093	395
Under $25,000	3,110	1,764	706	846	212
$25,000 to $49,999	1,645	981	660	195	128
$50,000 to $74,999	415	224	142	42	39
$75,000 to $99,999	76	28	15	8	5
$100,000 or more	36	20	4	4	12
Median income	$20,979	$21,025	$26,433	$11,179	$21,912
Percent distribution					
Total	100.0%	100.0%	100.0%	100.0%	100.0%
Under $25,000	58.9	58.5	46.2	77.4	53.7
$25,000 to $49,999	31.1	32.5	43.2	17.8	32.4
$50,000 to $74,999	7.9	7.4	9.3	3.8	9.9
$75,000 to $99,999	1.4	0.9	1.0	0.7	1.3
$100,000 or more	0.7	0.7	0.3	0.4	3.0

| | nonfamily households | | | | |
| | | female householders | | male householders | |
	total	total	living alone	total	living alone
Total	2,266	1,110	498	1,156	574
Under $25,000	1,346	669	426	676	445
$25,000 to $49,999	663	328	66	337	102
$50,000 to $74,999	192	87	5	104	22
$75,000 to $99,999	50	13	-	36	4
$100,000 or more	16	12	1	3	-
Median income	$20,935	$20,443	$13,616	$21,411	$15,718
Percent distribution					
Total	100.0%	100.0%	100.0%	100.0%	100.0%
Under $25,000	59.4	60.3	85.5	58.5	77.5
$25,000 to $49,999	29.3	29.5	13.3	29.2	17.8
$50,000 to $74,999	8.5	7.8	1.0	9.0	3.8
$75,000 to $99,999	2.2	1.2	-	3.1	0.7
$100,000 or more	0.7	1.1	0.2	0.3	-

Note: (-) means sample is too small to make a reliable estimate.
Source: Bureau of the Census, unpublished tables from the 1996 Current Population Survey; calculations by New Strategist

Household Income by Household Type, 1995:
Householders Aged 25 to 34

(number and percent distribution of households headed by householders aged 25 to 34, by household income and type of household, 1995; households in thousands as of 1996)

		family households			
	total households	*total*	*married couples*	*female hh, no spouse present*	*male hh, no spouse present*
Total	19,225	13,727	9,960	2,904	862
Under $25,000	6,394	4,256	1,845	2,093	318
$25,000 to $49,999	7,364	5,140	4,177	608	354
$50,000 to $74,999	3,458	2,725	2,450	152	122
$75,000 to $99,999	1,197	969	905	27	37
$100,000 or more	811	635	581	24	30
Median income	$34,701	$37,188	$43,800	$14,867	$30,546
Percent distribution					
Total	100.0%	100.0%	100.0%	100.0%	100.0%
Under $25,000	33.3	31.0	18.5	72.1	36.9
$25,000 to $49,999	38.3	37.4	41.9	20.9	41.1
$50,000 to $74,999	18.0	19.9	24.6	5.2	14.2
$75,000 to $99,999	6.2	7.1	9.1	0.9	4.3
$100,000 or more	4.2	4.6	5.8	0.8	3.5

		nonfamily households			
		female householders		male householders	
	total	*total*	*living alone*	*total*	*living alone*
Total	5,498	2,124	1,487	3,374	2,249
Under $25,000	2,137	845	744	1,291	1,051
$25,000 to $49,999	2,225	874	606	1,350	918
$50,000 to $74,999	735	300	113	435	182
$75,000 to $99,999	227	59	13	169	55
$100,000 or more	176	47	11	129	42
Median income	$30,190	$29,784	$24,970	$30,402	$26,185
Percent distribution					
Total	100.0%	100.0%	100.0%	100.0%	100.0%
Under $25,000	38.9	39.8	50.0	38.3	46.7
$25,000 to $49,999	40.5	41.1	40.8	40.0	40.8
$50,000 to $74,999	13.4	14.1	7.6	12.9	8.1
$75,000 to $99,999	4.1	2.8	0.9	5.0	2.4
$100,000 or more	3.2	2.2	0.7	3.8	1.9

Source: Bureau of the Census, unpublished tables from the 1996 Current Population Survey; calculations by New Strategist

Household Income by Household Type, 1995:
Householders Aged 35 to 44

(number and percent distribution of households headed by householders aged 35 to 44, by household income and type of household, 1995; households in thousands as of 1996)

| | | family households | | | |
	total households	total	married couples	female hh, no spouse present	male hh, no spouse present
Total	23,226	18,504	13,897	3,660	947
Under $25,000	5,789	3,998	1,773	1,926	299
$25,000 to $49,999	7,656	5,844	4,249	1,231	365
$50,000 to $74,999	5,454	4,774	4,228	380	167
$75,000 to $99,999	2,352	2,096	1,958	72	68
$100,000 or more	1,974	1,791	1,690	54	47
Median income	$43,465	$47,246	$54,515	$23,481	$36,571
Percent distribution					
Total	100.0%	100.0%	100.0%	100.0%	100.0%
Under $25,000	24.9	21.6	12.8	52.6	31.6
$25,000 to $49,999	33.0	31.6	30.6	33.6	38.5
$50,000 to $74,999	23.5	25.8	30.4	10.4	17.6
$75,000 to $99,999	10.1	11.3	14.1	2.0	7.2
$100,000 or more	8.5	9.7	12.2	1.5	5.0

| | | nonfamily households | | | |
| | | female householders | | male householders | |
	total	total	living alone	total	living alone
Total	4,723	1,742	1,485	2,981	2,318
Under $25,000	1,791	674	638	1,117	971
$25,000 to $49,999	1,812	709	615	1,103	890
$50,000 to $74,999	680	215	152	464	297
$75,000 to $99,999	255	93	56	163	90
$100,000 or more	183	51	23	132	69
Median income	$30,791	$29,738	$27,343	$31,409	$28,737
Percent distribution					
Total	100.0%	100.0%	100.0%	100.0%	100.0%
Under $25,000	37.9	38.7	43.0	37.5	41.9
$25,000 to $49,999	38.4	40.7	41.4	37.0	38.4
$50,000 to $74,999	14.4	12.3	10.2	15.6	12.8
$75,000 to $99,999	5.4	5.3	3.8	5.5	3.9
$100,000 or more	3.9	2.9	1.5	4.4	3.0

Source: Bureau of the Census, unpublished tables from the 1996 Current Population Survey; calculations by New Strategist

Household Income by Household Type, 1995: Householders Aged 45 to 54

(number and percent distribution of households headed by householders aged 45 to 54, by household income and type of household, 1995; households in thousands as of 1996)

	total households	family households			
		total	married couples	female hh, no spouse present	male hh, no spouse present
Total	18,008	13,908	11,161	2,116	632
Under $25,000	4,085	2,157	1,122	868	167
$25,000 to $49,999	5,289	3,944	2,857	845	240
$50,000 to $74,999	3,944	3,479	3,089	256	133
$75,000 to $99,999	2,295	2,111	1,962	91	59
$100,000 or more	2,394	2,218	2,130	57	32
Median income	$48,058	$55,461	$62,576	$30,349	$40,903
Percent distribution					
Total	100.0%	100.0%	100.0%	100.0%	100.0%
Under $25,000	22.7	15.5	10.1	41.0	26.4
$25,000 to $49,999	29.4	28.4	25.6	39.9	38.0
$50,000 to $74,999	21.9	25.0	27.7	12.1	21.0
$75,000 to $99,999	12.7	15.2	17.6	4.3	9.3
$100,000 or more	13.3	15.9	19.1	2.7	5.1

	nonfamily households				
		female householders		male householders	
	total	total	living alone	total	living alone
Total	4,099	2,009	1,756	2,090	1,750
Under $25,000	1,930	1,079	1,012	850	766
$25,000 to $49,999	1,345	605	541	740	633
$50,000 to $74,999	464	193	147	272	193
$75,000 to $99,999	184	64	36	119	83
$100,000 or more	176	67	24	108	77
Median income	$26,536	$23,186	$21,545	$30,656	$27,956
Percent distribution					
Total	100.0%	100.0%	100.0%	100.0%	100.0%
Under $25,000	47.1	53.7	57.6	40.7	43.8
$25,000 to $49,999	32.8	30.1	30.8	35.4	36.2
$50,000 to $74,999	11.3	9.6	8.4	13.0	11.0
$75,000 to $99,999	4.5	3.2	2.1	5.7	4.7
$100,000 or more	4.3	3.3	1.4	5.2	4.4

Source: Bureau of the Census, unpublished data from the 1996 Current Population Survey; calculations by New Strategist

Household Income by Household Type, 1995:
Householders Aged 55 to 64

(number and percent distribution of households headed by householders aged 55 to 64, by household income and type of household, 1995; households in thousands as of 1996)

		family households			
	total households	total	married couples	female hh, no spouse present	male hh, no spouse present
Total	12,401	9,134	7,741	1,111	283
Under $25,000	4,075	2,137	1,512	520	104
$25,000 to $49,999	3,702	2,864	2,366	419	79
$50,000 to $74,999	2,188	1,909	1,755	103	53
$75,000 to $99,999	1,201	1,098	1,023	50	22
$100,000 or more	1,234	1,127	1,084	19	23
Median income	$38,077	$45,419	$49,898	$26,919	$35,836
Percent distribution					
Total	100.0%	100.0%	100.0%	100.0%	100.0%
Under $25,000	32.9	23.4	19.5	46.8	36.7
$25,000 to $49,999	29.9	31.4	30.6	37.7	27.9
$50,000 to $74,999	17.6	20.9	22.7	9.3	18.7
$75,000 to $99,999	9.7	12.0	13.2	4.5	7.8
$100,000 or more	10.0	12.3	14.0	1.7	8.1

		nonfamily households			
		female householders		male householders	
	total	total	living alone	total	living alone
Total	3,267	1,967	1,852	1,299	1,089
Under $25,000	1,937	1,303	1,255	634	585
$25,000 to $49,999	839	484	445	357	289
$50,000 to $74,999	280	125	110	156	110
$75,000 to $99,999	104	43	31	62	50
$100,000 or more	107	15	12	92	56
Median income	$19,427	$16,879	$16,164	$25,917	$22,062
Percent distribution					
Total	100.0%	100.0%	100.0%	100.0%	100.0%
Under $25,000	59.3	66.2	67.8	48.8	53.7
$25,000 to $49,999	25.7	24.6	24.0	27.5	26.5
$50,000 to $74,999	8.6	6.4	5.9	12.0	10.1
$75,000 to $99,999	3.2	2.2	1.7	4.8	4.6
$100,000 or more	3.3	0.8	0.6	7.1	5.1

Source: Bureau of the Census, unpublished data from the 1996 Current Population Survey; calculations by New Strategist

Household Income by Household Type, 1995:
Householders Aged 65 to 74

(number and percent distribution of households headed by householders aged 65 to 74, by household income and type of household, 1995; households in thousands as of 1996)

		family households			
	total households	*total*	*married couples*	*female hh, no spouse present*	*male hh, no spouse present*
Total	11,908	7,340	6,177	914	249
Under $25,000	6,373	2,754	2,181	474	101
$25,000 to $49,999	3,509	2,786	2,390	302	94
$50,000 to $74,999	1,125	974	836	105	34
$75,000 to $99,999	385	356	324	15	17
$100,000 or more	518	469	444	19	6
Median income	$23,031	$30,647	$31,614	$24,386	$31,289
Percent distribution					
Total	100.0%	100.0%	100.0%	100.0%	100.0%
Under $25,000	53.5	37.5	35.3	51.9	40.6
$25,000 to $49,999	29.5	38.0	38.7	33.0	37.8
$50,000 to $74,999	9.4	13.3	13.5	11.5	13.7
$75,000 to $99,999	3.2	4.9	5.2	1.6	6.8
$100,000 or more	4.4	6.4	7.2	2.1	2.4

		nonfamily households			
		female householders		male householders	
	total	*total*	*living alone*	*total*	*living alone*
Total	4,568	3,240	3,137	1,328	1,240
Under $25,000	3,617	2,685	2,645	934	901
$25,000 to $49,999	724	460	412	263	237
$50,000 to $74,999	148	65	51	83	72
$75,000 to $99,999	29	15	15	13	7
$100,000 or more	49	14	13	36	24
Median income	$13,298	$12,435	$12,149	$16,159	$15,443
Percent distribution					
Total	100.0%	100.0%	100.0%	100.0%	100.0%
Under $25,000	79.2	82.9	84.3	70.3	72.7
$25,000 to $49,999	15.8	14.2	13.1	19.8	19.1
$50,000 to $74,999	3.2	2.0	1.6	6.3	5.8
$75,000 to $99,999	0.6	0.5	0.5	1.0	0.6
$100,000 or more	1.1	0.4	0.4	2.7	1.9

Source: Bureau of the Census, unpublished data from the 1996 Current Population Survey; calculations by New Strategist

Household Income by Household Type, 1995:
Householders Aged 75 or Older

(number and percent distribution of households headed by householders aged 75 or older, by household income and type of household, 1995; households in thousands as of 1996)

	total households	family households			
		total	married couples	female hh, no spouse present	male hh, no spouse present
Total	9,578	3,966	3,104	717	145
Under $25,000	6,930	2,021	1,610	360	52
$25,000 to $49,999	1,876	1,342	1,040	256	49
$50,000 to $74,999	454	347	249	69	28
$75,000 to $99,999	169	144	106	26	12
$100,000 or more	148	111	100	7	4
Median income	$15,342	$24,660	$24,381	$24,897	$33,992
Percent distribution					
Total	100.0%	100.0%	100.0%	100.0%	100.0%
Under $25,000	72.4	51.0	51.9	50.2	35.9
$25,000 to $49,999	19.6	33.8	33.5	35.7	33.8
$50,000 to $74,999	4.7	8.7	8.0	9.6	19.3
$75,000 to $99,999	1.8	3.6	3.4	3.6	8.3
$100,000 or more	1.5	2.8	3.2	1.0	2.8

	total	nonfamily households			
		female householders		male householders	
		total	living alone	total	living alone
Total	5,612	4,493	4,397	1,119	1,067
Under $25,000	4,908	4,018	3,966	891	861
$25,000 to $49,999	532	369	339	164	148
$50,000 to $74,999	107	76	68	31	29
$75,000 to $99,999	26	10	9	16	13
$100,000 or more	38	21	16	17	15
Median income	$11,325	$10,774	$10,619	$14,018	$13,607
Percent distribution					
Total	100.0%	100.0%	100.0%	100.0%	100.0%
Under $25,000	87.5	89.4	90.2	79.6	80.7
$25,000 to $49,999	9.5	8.2	7.7	14.7	13.9
$50,000 to $74,999	1.9	1.7	1.5	2.8	2.7
$75,000 to $99,999	0.5	0.2	0.2	1.4	1.2
$100,000 or more	0.7	0.5	0.4	1.5	1.4

Source: Bureau of the Census, unpublished data from the 1996 Current Population Survey; calculations by New Strategist

Dual-Earner Couples Are Income Elite

Dual-earner couples had a median household income of $64,283 in 1995.

The median income of dual-earner couples in which both husband and wife work full-time is nearly double the all-household median of $34,076. Twenty-nine percent of the nation's married couples are dual earners who work full-time.

Among all married couples, those with school-aged children have the highest incomes, a median of $54,547 in 1995. These couples are likely to be in their peak earning years. Couples without children at home have the lowest incomes because many are older and retired.

Among dual-earner couples, those without children at home have the highest incomes—a median of $67,418 in 1995. Forty percent have incomes of $75,000 or more. Many are empty-nesters still in their peak earning years. Nearly half of dual-earner couples do not have children at home.

◆ The proportion of married couples in which both husband and wife work full-time will rise as the baby boom's children grow up and more baby-boom women take on full-time jobs.

◆ The rising number of dual-earner married couples in their peak earning years will be a powerful boost to the economy, causing record levels of affluence by the turn of the century.

Household Income of Married Couples, 1995

(number and percent distribution of married-couple households by income, and presence and age of related children under age 18 at home, 1995; households in thousands as of 1996)

	total couples	no children	total	all under 6	some under 6 some 6 to 17	all 6 to 17
					with one or more children	
Total	53,570	27,537	26,034	6,770	5,828	13,436
Under $25,000	10,800	6,516	4,284	1,359	1,113	1,813
$25,000 to $49,999	17,746	9,002	8,742	2,469	2,167	4,106
$50,000 to $74,999	12,750	5,885	6,865	1,598	1,408	3,856
$75,000 to $99,999	6,276	3,060	3,215	693	578	1,945
$100,000 or more	5,999	3,072	2,927	650	561	1,716
Median income	$47,062	$44,316	$49,969	$45,543	$45,223	$54,547
Percent distribution						
Total	100.0%	100.0%	100.0%	100.0%	100.0%	100.0%
Under $25,000	20.2	23.7	16.5	20.1	19.1	13.5
$25,000 to $49,999	33.1	32.7	33.6	36.5	37.2	30.6
$50,000 to $74,999	23.8	21.4	26.4	23.6	24.2	28.7
$75,000 to $99,999	11.7	11.1	12.3	10.2	9.9	14.5
$100,000 or more	11.2	11.2	11.2	9.6	9.6	12.8

Source: Bureau of the Census, Money Income in the United States: 1995, *Current Population Reports, P60-193, 1996; calculations by New Strategist*

Household Income of Dual-Earner Married Couples, 1995

(number and percent distribution of married-couple households in which both husband and wife work full-time, year-round by income, presence and age of related children under age 18 at home, 1995; households in thousands as of 1996)

	total couples	no children	with one or more children			
			total	all under 6	some under 6 some 6 to 17	all 6 to 17
Total	15,359	7,212	8,148	1,884	1,395	4,869
Under $25,000	452	175	278	50	41	184
$25,000 to $49,999	4,089	1,794	2,294	611	484	1,200
$50,000 to $74,999	5,123	2,313	2,809	636	470	1,703
$75,000 to $99,999	2,998	1,470	1,527	320	213	991
$100,000 or more	2,697	1,458	1,239	265	185	789
Median income	$64,283	$67,418	$61,857	$58,486	$57,178	$64,204
Percent distribution						
Total	100.0%	100.0%	100.0%	100.0%	100.0%	100.0%
Under $25,000	2.9	2.4	3.4	2.7	2.9	3.8
$25,000 to $49,999	26.6	24.9	28.2	32.4	34.7	24.6
$50,000 to $74,999	33.4	32.1	34.5	33.8	33.7	35.0
$75,000 to $99,999	19.5	20.4	18.7	17.0	15.3	20.4
$100,000 or more	17.6	20.2	15.2	14.1	13.3	16.2

Source: Bureau of the Census, Money Income in the United States: 1995, *Current Population Reports, P60-193, 1996; calculations by New Strategist*

Female-Headed Families Have Varying Incomes

Households headed by single women with children have the lowest incomes among female- and male-headed households.

Only two-thirds of families headed by men or women without a spouse are single parents with children under age 18. The other one-third are a variety of family types such as sisters sharing an apartment or middle-aged sons living with their mothers.

The incomes of these families are as wide-ranging as their living arrangements. The poorest are single-parent families headed by women. Their median income was just $16,235 in 1995.

Female-headed families that do not include children had a much higher median income of $28,488 in 1995. Many of these households include at least two adults with earnings, boosting their incomes.

♦ Families headed by women are likely to see their incomes grow in the years ahead as women's earnings rise.

Household Income of Female- and Male-Headed Families, 1995

(number and percent distribution of female- and male-headed families with no spouse present, by household income and presence of related children under age 18 at home, 1995; families in thousands as of 1996)

	female-headed families			male-headed families		
	total	no children	one or more children	total	no children	one or more children
Total	12,514	3,763	8,751	3,513	1,579	1,934
Under $25,000	7,552	1,618	5,936	1,410	529	881
$25,000 to $49,999	3,648	1,482	2,165	1,276	605	671
$50,000 to $74,999	937	462	476	518	267	220
$75,000 to $99,999	234	147	86	182	107	75
$100,000 or more	143	54	89	127	71	56
Median income	$19,691	$28,488	$16,235	$30,358	$34,710	$26,990
Percent distribution						
Total	100.0%	100.0%	100.0%	100.0%	100.0%	100.0%
Under $25,000	60.3	43.0	67.8	40.1	33.5	45.6
$25,000 to $49,999	29.2	39.4	24.7	36.3	38.3	34.7
$50,000 to $74,999	7.5	12.3	5.4	14.7	16.9	11.4
$75,000 to $99,999	1.9	3.9	1.0	5.2	6.8	3.9
$100,000 or more	1.1	1.4	1.0	3.6	4.5	2.9

Source: Bureau of the Census, unpublished tables from the 1996 Current Population Survey; calculations by New Strategist

Older Women Who Live Alone Have Low Incomes

Women who live alone have very low incomes because many are older widows.

Among the nation's 25 million single-person households, 59 percent are headed by women. The median income of these households was just $14,331 in 1995. Men who live alone had a higher median income of $22,586. This income difference can be explained almost entirely by the differing ages of men and women who live alone. Most women who live alone are elderly widows with low incomes. Most men who live alone are under age 45 and in the work force.

Within age groups, men and women who live alone have similar incomes. The median income of women aged 25 to 34 who live alone was $24,970 in 1995, close to the $26,185 median of their male counterparts. Similarly, the median income of men aged 35 to 44 who live alone ($28,737) was only $1,400 higher than that of their female counterparts ($27,343).

♦ The incomes of men and women who live alone will continue to converge as women's incomes grow.

♦ The incomes of elderly men and women who live alone should rise as the poorer elderly population is replaced by the more affluent elderly now entering its 60s.

Household Income of Men Who Live Alone, 1995

(number and percent distribution of male-headed single-person households by household income and age of householder, 1995; households in thousands as of 1996)

	total	15 to 24	25 to 34	35 to 44	45 to 54	55 to 64	65 to 74	75 or older
Total	10,288	574	2,249	2,318	1,750	1,089	1,240	1,067
Under $25,000	5,580	445	1,051	971	766	585	901	861
$25,000 to $49,999	3,218	102	918	890	633	289	237	148
$50,000 to $74,999	903	22	182	297	193	110	72	29
$75,000 to $99,999	303	4	55	90	83	50	7	13
$100,000 or more	283	-	42	69	77	56	24	15
Median income	$22,586	$15,718	$26,185	$28,737	$27,956	$22,062	$15,443	$13,607
Percent distribution								
Total	100.0%	100.0%	100.0%	100.0%	100.0%	100.0%	100.0%	100.0%
Under $25,000	54.2	77.5	46.7	41.9	43.8	53.7	72.7	80.7
$25,000 to $49,999	31.3	17.8	40.8	38.4	36.2	26.5	19.1	13.9
$50,000 to $74,999	8.8	3.8	8.1	12.8	11.0	10.1	5.8	2.7
$75,000 to $99,999	2.9	0.7	2.4	3.9	4.7	4.6	0.6	1.2
$100,000 or more	2.8	-	1.9	3.0	4.4	5.1	1.9	1.4

Note: (-) means sample is too small to make a reliable estimate.
Source: Bureau of the Census, unpublished tables from the 1996 Current Population Survey; calculations by New Strategist

Household Income of Women Who Live Alone, 1995

(number and percent distribution of female-headed single-person households by household income and age of householder, 1995; households in thousands as of 1996)

	total	15 to 24	25 to 34	35 to 44	45 to 54	55 to 64	65 to 74	75 or older
Total	14,612	498	1,487	1,485	1,756	1,852	3,137	4,397
Under $25,000	10,683	426	744	638	1,012	1,255	2,645	3,966
$25,000 to $49,999	3,025	66	606	615	541	445	412	339
$50,000 to $74,999	645	5	113	152	147	110	51	68
$75,000 to $99,999	159	-	13	56	36	31	15	9
$100,000 or more	99	1	11	23	24	12	13	16
Median income	$14,331	$13,616	$24,970	$27,343	$21,545	$16,164	$12,149	$10,619
Percent distribution								
Total	100.0%	100.0%	100.0%	100.0%	100.0%	100.0%	100.0%	100.0%
Under $25,000	73.1	85.5	50.0	43.0	57.6	67.8	84.3	90.2
$25,000 to $49,999	20.7	13.3	40.8	41.4	30.8	24.0	13.1	7.7
$50,000 to $74,999	4.4	1.0	7.6	10.2	8.4	5.9	1.6	1.5
$75,000 to $99,999	1.1	-	0.9	3.8	2.1	1.7	0.5	0.2
$100,000 or more	0.7	0.2	0.7	1.5	1.4	0.6	0.4	0.4

Note: (-) means sample is too small to make a reliable estimate.
Source: Bureau of the Census, unpublished tables from the 1996 Current Population Survey; calculations by New Strategist

College-Educated Householders Earn Top Dollar

The median income of householders with a bachelor's degree was $58,052 in 1995.

The higher the educational degree, the greater the financial reward. At the top are householders with professional degrees, such as doctors or lawyers. Their median household income was $82,010 in 1995. Nearly 40 percent of this group had a household income of $100,000 or more.

Overall, the median income of householders with a bachelor's degree was 50 percent greater than the all-household average of $35,235. In contrast, those who went no further than high school had a below-average household income of $31,376. The median income of householders who did not graduate from high school was less than $20,000.

♦ The financial rewards accruing to college graduates will lift baby-boom incomes in the years ahead, particularly as the generation enters its peak earning years.

Household Income by Education of Householder, 1995

(number and percent distribution of householders aged 25 or older by household income and educational attainment of householder, 1995; households in thousands as of 1996)

	total	less than 9th grade	9th to 12th grade, no diploma	high school graduate	some college, no degree	assoc. degree	bachelor's degree or more				
							total	bachelor's degree	master's degree	prof. degree	doctoral degree
Total	94,346	8,062	9,683	29,507	16,951	6,719	23,424	14,871	5,706	1,641	1,206
Under $25,000	33,646	5,794	6,172	11,426	5,311	1,677	3,267	2,430	589	153	93
$25,000 to $49,999	29,398	1,656	2,459	10,547	5,929	2,353	6,454	4,490	1,405	328	231
$50,000 to $74,999	16,623	448	731	4,975	3,374	1,649	5,446	3,557	1,386	263	241
$75,000 to $99,999	7,600	97	220	1,619	1,353	625	3,685	2,185	1,020	253	227
$100,000 or more	7,078	68	99	940	983	416	4,572	2,209	1,306	643	414
Median income	$35,235	$15,043	$18,298	$31,376	$37,156	$42,118	$58,052	$52,857	$64,960	$82,010	$80,005
Percent distribution											
Total	100.0%	100.0%	100.0%	100.0%	100.0%	100.0%	100.0%	100.0%	100.0%	100.0%	100.0%
Under $25,000	35.7	71.9	63.7	38.7	31.3	25.0	13.9	16.3	10.3	9.3	7.7
$25,000 to $49,999	31.2	20.5	25.4	35.7	35.0	35.0	27.6	30.2	24.6	20.0	19.2
$50,000 to $74,999	17.6	5.6	7.5	16.9	19.9	24.5	23.2	23.9	24.3	16.0	20.0
$75,000 to $99,999	8.1	1.2	2.3	5.5	8.0	9.3	15.7	14.7	17.9	15.4	18.8
$100,000 or more	7.5	0.8	1.0	3.2	5.8	6.2	19.5	14.9	22.9	39.2	34.3

Source: Bureau of the Census, Money Income in the United States: 1995, Current Population Reports, P60-193, 1996; calculations by New Strategist

Women Gain, Men Lose

Since 1980, men's median income has fallen by 3 percent, while women's has grown by 33 percent, after adjusting for inflation.

One reason for the divergent patterns in men's and women's incomes is the changing nature of the economy. Women are benefiting from growth in the service sector of the economy, while men are hurt by the loss of well-paying manufacturing jobs. Men's income peaked in 1989, then fell during the recession of the early 1990s. Now they are slightly below their 1980 level, after adjusting for inflation. In contrast, women's incomes grew steadily between 1980 and 1989 and were barely touched by the recession of the early 1990s.

Men's incomes are far higher than women's because men are more likely to work full-time. Even so, most men don't make a lot of money. Incomes peak among men aged 45 to 54 at $35,586. Incomes peak among women (including both full- and part-time workers) in the 35-to-44 age group at $17,397. Women aged 45 to 54 saw their incomes grow the most since 1980, up by 50 percent, after adjusting for inflation.

♦ The declining incomes of men, who traditionally are the family breadwinners, is behind Americans' economic insecurity. Until men's incomes stabilize, this insecurity will continue.

Median Income of Men by Age, 1980 to 1995

(number of men aged 15 or older with income and median income of those with income, by age, 1980-1995; in 1995 dollars; men in thousands as of the following year)

	number with income	total	under 25	25 to 34	35 to 44	45 to 54	55 to 64	65 or older
1995	92,066	$22,562	$6,913	$23,609	$31,420	$35,586	$28,980	$16,484
1994	91,254	22,336	7,248	23,247	31,577	35,923	27,842	15,682
1993	90,194	22,256	6,780	23,126	32,001	34,967	26,513	15,802
1992	90,175	22,219	6,840	23,351	32,034	34,956	27,824	15,856
1991	88,653	22,904	7,028	24,164	32,786	35,559	28,488	16,065
1990	88,220	23,662	7,368	24,945	34,716	36,155	28,922	16,538
1989	87,454	24,449	7,759	26,261	36,179	38,053	30,022	16,109
1988	86,584	24,358	7,527	26,772	36,773	38,104	29,175	16,066
1987	85,713	23,861	7,321	26,733	36,278	38,217	29,357	16,001
1986	84,471	23,797	7,346	26,645	36,392	38,595	29,248	16,052
1985	83,631	23,102	7,075	26,432	35,916	36,606	28,691	15,438
1984	82,183	22,882	6,907	26,539	36,033	36,067	28,642	15,328
1983	80,909	22,387	6,555	25,714	34,336	35,369	28,604	14,906
1982	79,722	22,238	7,057	26,169	34,512	34,343	28,420	14,647
1981	79,688	22,789	5,196	27,219	35,718	35,558	29,372	13,765
1980	78,661	23,203	8,513	28,850	37,104	36,987	29,469	13,590

Percent change

1980 to 1995	–	-2.8%	-18.8%	-18.2%	-15.3%	-3.8%	-1.7%	21.3%

Source: Bureau of the Census, Internet web site, http://www.census.gov; *calculations by New Strategist*

Median Income of Women by Age, 1980 to 1995

(number of women aged 15 or older with income and median income of those with income, by age, 1980-1995; in 1995 dollars; women in thousands as of the following year)

	number with income	total	under 25	25 to 34	35 to 44	45 to 54	55 to 64	65 or older
1995	96,007	$12,130	$5,310	$15,557	$17,397	$17,723	$12,381	$9,355
1994	95,147	11,791	5,664	15,306	16,648	17,534	11,175	9,204
1993	94,417	11,650	5,644	14,753	16,710	17,216	11,421	8,964
1992	93,517	11,638	5,616	14,807	16,747	17,219	11,007	8,889
1991	92,569	11,722	5,815	14,506	16,924	16,475	11,080	9,163
1990	92,245	11,742	5,716	14,679	16,912	16,593	10,961	9,380
1989	91,399	11,828	5,824	15,032	16,967	16,153	11,262	9,408
1988	90,593	11,445	5,778	14,899	16,162	15,485	10,792	9,150
1987	89,661	11,128	5,914	14,729	16,092	15,110	10,117	9,251
1986	87,822	10,582	5,623	14,336	15,385	14,434	10,258	8,934
1985	86,531	10,222	5,369	13,992	14,553	13,624	10,160	8,941
1984	85,555	10,074	5,294	13,776	14,024	13,059	10,028	8,830
1983	83,830	9,669	5,290	13,011	13,557	12,555	9,378	8,567
1982	82,505	9,385	5,344	12,709	12,516	11,959	9,417	8,553
1981	82,139	9,232	3,376	12,852	12,459	11,891	9,092	7,960
1980	80,826	9,111	5,785	12,912	11,972	11,857	9,122	7,826

Percent change

1980 to 1995	-	33.1%	-8.2%	20.5%	45.3%	49.5%	35.7%	19.5%

Source: Bureau of the Census, Internet web site, http://www.census.gov; *calculations by New Strategist*

Men's and Women's Incomes Peak in Middle-Age

Men's income-peak is almost twice as high as women's.

Men's incomes peak in the 45-to-54 age group, with a median of $35,586 in 1995. Women's incomes peak in the same age group, with a much lower median of $17,723. The gap between women's and men's incomes is very large because these statistics include both full- and part-time workers, and women are much more likely than men to work part-time.

Over 12 percent of men aged 45 to 54 had an income of $75,000 or more in 1995, as did 11 percent of those aged 55 to 64. Incomes are lowest for men under age 25, with a median of just $6,913 in 1995. Many of these men are college students who work part-time.

Women are much less likely to have high incomes than men. Only 2 percent of women aged 45 to 54 had an income of $75,000 or more. But a significant 8 percent of women in this age group had an income of $50,000 or more. Older women have much lower incomes than their male counterparts because fewer of them are covered by pensions. Women aged 65 to 74 had a median income of just $9,277 in 1995, versus a median of $18,347 for men.

◆ As baby boomers move into the peak-earning years, the number of affluent men and women will increase for years to come.

◆ The income gap between older men and women should narrow as working women with their own pensions replace older women with no work experience.

Income of Men by Age, 1995

(number and percent distribution of men aged 15 or older by income and age, and median income of those with income, 1995; men in thousands as of 1996)

	total	under 25	25 to 34	35 to 44	45 to 54	55 to 64	65 to 74	75 or older
Total, number	98,593	18,254	20,390	21,273	15,324	10,092	8,213	5,047
With income	92,066	13,802	19,617	20,773	14,920	9,863	8,131	4,960
Under $15,000	30,564	10,469	5,303	3,954	2,576	2,399	3,192	2,671
$15,000 to $24,999	19,018	2,279	5,091	3,940	2,264	1,847	2,268	1,329
$25,000 to $49,999	27,289	934	7,173	7,928	5,588	3,230	1,772	664
$50,000 to $74,999	9,383	83	1,463	3,159	2,662	1,336	498	182
$75,000 or more	5,811	36	587	1,791	1,831	1,051	402	114
Median income	$22,562	$6,913	$23,609	$31,420	$35,586	$28,980	$18,347	$14,160
Total with income, percent	100.0%	100.0%	100.0%	100.0%	100.0%	100.0%	100.0%	100.0%
Under $15,000	33.2	75.9	27.0	19.0	17.3	24.3	39.3	53.9
$15,000 to $24,999	20.7	16.5	26.0	19.0	15.2	18.7	27.9	26.8
$25,000 to $49,999	29.6	6.8	36.6	38.2	37.5	32.7	21.8	13.4
$50,000 to $74,999	10.2	0.6	7.5	15.2	17.8	13.5	6.1	3.7
$75,000 or more	6.3	0.3	3.0	8.6	12.3	10.7	4.9	2.3

Source: Bureau of the Census, Money Income in the United States: 1995, *Current Population Reports, P60-193, 1996; calculations by New Strategist*

Income of Women by Age, 1995

(number and percent distribution of women aged 15 or older by income and age, and median income of those with income, 1995; women in thousands as of 1996)

	total	under 25	25 to 34	35 to 44	45 to 54	55 to 64	65 to 74	75 or older
Total, number	106,031	18,047	20,528	21,805	16,260	10,992	10,057	8,341
With income	96,007	13,550	18,856	20,458	15,139	10,014	9,826	8,163
Under $15,000	55,055	11,400	9,084	9,049	6,391	5,720	7,128	6,282
$15,000 to $24,999	18,775	1,572	4,772	4,426	3,381	1,875	1,593	1,156
$25,000 to $49,999	17,790	513	4,310	5,489	4,171	1,845	896	568
$50,000 to $74,999	3,136	43	529	1,074	857	378	150	106
$75,000 or more	1,252	22	163	421	339	198	59	51
Median income	$12,130	$5,310	$15,557	$17,397	$17,723	$12,381	$9,277	$9,427
Total with income, percent	100.0%	100.0%	100.0%	100.0%	100.0%	100.0%	100.0%	100.0%
Under $15,000	57.3	84.1	48.2	44.2	42.2	57.1	72.5	77.0
$15,000 to $24,999	19.6	11.6	25.3	21.6	22.3	18.7	16.2	14.2
$25,000 to $49,999	18.5	3.8	22.9	26.8	27.6	18.4	9.1	7.0
$50,000 to $74,999	3.3	0.3	2.8	5.2	5.7	3.8	1.5	1.3
$75,000 or more	1.3	0.2	0.9	2.1	2.2	2.0	0.6	0.6

Source: Bureau of the Census, Money Income in the United States: 1995, *Current Population Reports, P60-193, 1996; calculations by New Strategist*

Incomes Decline for White and Hispanic Men

The median income of white men fell by 3 percent between 1980 and 1995, after adjusting for inflation.

Hispanic men saw their incomes fall by 17 percent between 1980 and 1995. In contrast, the incomes of black men rose by 8 percent during those years, after adjusting for inflation.

Black, white, and Hispanic women saw their incomes grow between 1980 and 1995, after adjusting for inflation. Among white women, median income rose by 34 percent during those years. Among blacks it was up by 29 percent, and among Hispanics by 10 percent. Still, women's median income remains far below that of men, in part because women are more likely than men to work part-time.

The median income of white women was just 52 percent that of white men in 1995. Among blacks, the ratio was 68 percent and among Hispanics 60 percent. Although women's incomes are low relative to men's, they have gained ground since 1980. In that year, Hispanic women had a median income only 46 percent that of Hispanic men.

◆ Hispanic men and women have fared worse than whites or blacks because of the enormous Hispanic immigration of the 1980s. Many Hispanic immigrants have low incomes, depressing the income statistics for all Hispanics.

Median Income of Men by Race and Hispanic Origin, 1980 to 1995

(median income of men aged 15 or older with income, by race and Hispanic origin; percent change, 1980-95; in 1995 dollars)

	total	white	black	Hispanic
1995	$22,562	$23,895	$16,006	$14,840
1994	22,336	23,311	15,407	14,911
1993	22,256	23,183	15,403	14,437
1992	22,219	23,252	14,191	14,564
1991	22,904	23,940	14,504	15,462
1990	23,662	24,685	15,004	15,706
1989	24,449	25,641	15,497	16,469
1988	24,358	25,712	15,516	16,786
1987	23,861	25,362	15,045	16,407
1986	23,797	25,113	15,048	16,035
1985	23,102	24,235	15,251	16,195
1984	22,882	24,154	13,858	16,283
1983	22,433	23,601	13,802	16,588
1982	22,238	23,510	14,089	16,692
1981	22,789	24,181	14,379	17,258
1980	23,203	24,680	14,831	17,886
Percent change				
1980 to 1995	-2.8%	-3.2%	7.9%	-17.0%

Source: Bureau of the Census, Money Income in the United States: 1995, *Current Population Reports, P60-193, 1996; calculations by New Strategist*

Median Income of Women by Race and Hispanic Origin, 1980 to 1995

(median income of women aged 15 or older with income, by race and Hispanic origin; percent change, 1980-95; in 1995 dollars)

	total	white	black	Hispanic
1995	$12,130	$12,316	$10,961	$8,928
1994	11,791	11,960	10,843	8,857
1993	11,650	11,882	10,028	8,543
1992	11,638	11,908	9,653	9,025
1991	11,722	11,996	9,865	8,966
1990	11,742	12,030	9,711	8,783
1989	11,828	12,059	9,679	9,398
1988	11,445	11,727	9,467	9,005
1987	11,128	11,413	9,322	8,894
1986	10,582	10,790	9,130	8,813
1985	10,222	10,420	8,890	8,526
1984	10,074	10,193	9,041	8,551
1983	9,800	9,972	8,521	8,218
1982	9,385	9,512	8,390	8,194
1981	9,232	9,335	8,293	8,559
1980	9,111	9,161	8,481	8,157
Percent change				
1980 to 1995	33.1%	34.4%	29.2%	9.5%

Source: Bureau of the Census, Money Income in the United States: 1995, Current Population Reports, P60-193, 1996; calculations by New Strategist

The 73.8-Cent Dollar

The "59-cent dollar" has been replaced by the "73.8-cent dollar" as women's incomes grow faster than men's.

The "59-cent dollar" has long been used to symbolize women's low earnings relative to men's. But women are catching up. Among full-time workers, women's incomes are now 73.8 percent those of men's.

Women who worked full-time, year-round had a median income of $23,777 in 1995. Men who worked full-time, year-round had a median income of $32,199. Younger women earn much higher incomes relative to men than do older women. The ratio is higher because young women and men are educational equals and also have about the same number of years on the job. Not only are older women less educated than older men, but most have less job experience because they were not likely to work when their children were young.

♦ The "73.8-cent dollar" will grow over the next decade as the well-educated and career-oriented women of the baby-boom generation replace older, "just-a-job" women.

Median Income of Full-Time Workers by Age and Sex, 1995

(median income of persons aged 15 or older working year-round, full-time by age and sex, and ratio of women's income to men's, 1995)

	men	women	ratio of women's income to men's
Total	$32,199	$23,777	73.8
Under age 25	16,659	15,141	90.9
Aged 25 to 34	27,415	22,567	82.3
Aged 35 to 44	36,125	26,121	72.3
Aged 45 to 54	41,062	26,143	63.7
Aged 55 to 64	38,713	24,121	62.3
Aged 65 or older	41,259	26,606	64.5

Note: The ratio is calculated by dividing women's median income by men's median income and multiplying by 100.
Source: Bureau of the Census, unpublished tables from the 1996 Current Population Survey; calculations by New Strategist

Education Boosts Earnings

Although college costs have soared in recent years, the rewards are worth the expense. Earnings rise in lock-step with education.

Men with bachelor's degrees earned a median of $43,325 in 1995. Those who went no further than high school earned just $25,257. Women with bachelor's degrees earned a median of $28,252 in 1995, compared with just $15,017 earned by those who went no further than high school. Women's earnings are much lower than men's because these statistics include both full- and part-time workers, and women are much more likely than men to work part-time.

The highest-paid men are those with professional degrees, such as doctors or lawyers. Their personal earnings amounted to more than $67,000 in 1995. One-third earned over $100,000. The highest-paid women are also those with professional degrees, earning a median of $38,896 in 1995.

♦ Educational credentials will become more important in the years ahead as the economy continues to reward highly trained workers. A master's degree may be a necessity for a middle-class lifestyle in the 21st century.

♦ Because people tend to marry those with similar experiences, highly educated couples will continue to dominate the nation's affluent.

Earnings of Men by Education, 1995

(number and percent distribution of men aged 25 or older with earnings, by earnings and educational attainment, 1995; men in thousands as of 1996)

	total	less than 9th grade	9th to 12th grade, no diploma	high school graduate	some college, no degree	assoc. degree	bachelor's degree or more				
							total	bachelor's degree	master's degree	prof. degree	doctoral degree
Total	80,339	6,604	7,931	25,649	13,998	5,303	20,855	13,219	4,812	1,671	1,152
Without earnings	17,932	3,470	2,934	5,683	2,527	605	2,713	1,733	613	238	128
With earnings	62,407	3,134	4,996	19,966	11,470	4,698	18,142	11,486	4,199	1,433	1,024
Under $25,000	26,044	2,565	3,426	9,829	4,659	1,651	3,914	2,903	721	155	136
$25,000 to $49,999	23,370	493	1,329	7,940	4,906	2,192	6,509	4,492	1,460	292	265
$50,000 to $74,999	8,357	64	169	1,749	1,381	651	4,344	2,591	1,141	329	281
$75,000 to $99,999	2,238	6	38	245	315	114	1,518	754	434	183	148
$100,000 or more	2,397	6	35	200	208	90	1,858	747	444	473	194
Median earnings	$29,160	$13,804	$17,973	$25,257	$29,099	$31,324	$43,325	$40,067	$47,900	$67,505	$56,917
Percent distribution											
Total with earnings	100.0%	100.0%	100.0%	100.0%	100.0%	100.0%	100.0%	100.0%	100.0%	100.0%	100.0%
Under $25,000	41.7	81.8	68.6	49.2	40.6	35.1	21.6	25.3	17.2	10.8	13.3
$25,000 to $49,999	37.4	15.7	26.6	39.8	42.8	46.7	35.9	39.1	34.8	20.4	25.9
$50,000 to $74,999	13.4	2.0	3.4	8.8	12.0	13.9	23.9	22.6	27.2	23.0	27.4
$75,000 to $99,999	3.6	0.2	0.8	1.2	2.7	2.4	8.4	6.6	10.3	12.8	14.5
$100,000 or more	3.8	0.2	0.7	1.0	1.8	1.9	10.2	6.5	10.6	33.0	18.9

Source: Bureau of the Census, Educational Attainment in the United States: 1995, Current Population Reports, P20-489, 1996; calculations by New Strategist

Earnings of Women by Education, 1995

(number and percent distribution of women aged 25 or older with earnings, by earnings and educational attainment, 1995; women in thousands as of 1996)

	total	less than 9th grade	9th to 12th grade no diploma	high school graduate	some college no degree	assoc. degree	bachelor's degree or more				
							total	bachelor's degree	master's degree	prof. degree	doctoral degree
Total	87,984	7,019	9,171	30,911	15,203	6,868	18,813	13,321	4,288	745	459
Without earnings	33,735	5,376	5,555	12,553	4,602	1,516	4,134	3,177	770	119	68
With earnings	54,249	1,643	3,616	18,357	10,601	5,352	14,679	10,144	3,519	626	391
Under $25,000	36,478	1,566	3,304	14,712	7,535	3,248	6,114	4,808	1,044	174	87
$25,000 to $49,999	14,619	72	286	3,312	2,713	1,818	6,420	4,226	1,794	217	183
$50,000 to $74,999	2,384	4	18	258	281	239	1,583	883	516	112	72
$75,000 to $99,999	466	-	6	33	31	30	367	155	122	61	29
$100,000 or more	302	1	2	42	42	19	196	72	41	61	22
Median income	$17,630	$9,327	$9,838	$15,017	$17,430	$20,835	$28,252	$25,800	$34,148	$38,896	$38,357
Percent distribution											
Total with earnings	100.0%	100.0%	100.0%	100.0%	100.0%	100.0%	100.0%	100.0%	100.0%	100.0%	100.0%
Under $25,000	67.2	95.3	91.4	80.1	71.1	60.7	41.7	47.4	29.7	27.8	22.3
$25,000 to $49,999	26.9	4.4	7.9	18.0	25.6	34.0	43.7	41.7	51.0	34.7	46.8
$50,000 to $74,999	4.4	0.2	0.5	1.4	2.7	4.5	10.8	8.7	14.7	17.9	18.4
$75,000 to $99,999	0.9	-	0.2	0.2	0.3	0.6	2.5	1.5	3.5	9.7	7.4
$100,000 or more	0.6	0.1	0.1	0.2	0.4	0.4	1.3	0.7	1.2	9.7	5.6

Note: (-) means sample is too small to make a reliable estimate.
Source: Bureau of the Census, Educational Attainment in the United States: 1995, Current Population Reports, P20-489, 1996; calculations by New Strategist

Women's Weekly Pay Close to Men's

Among therapists, women earn 97 percent as much as men.

Men who work full-time have median weekly earnings of $538, while women earn $406. Although a substantial gap exists between men's and women's earnings, women have been closing the gap. In many occupations, women now make almost as much as men.

Women engineers make 86 percent as much as their male counterparts, while women psychologists and computer programmers make 89 percent as much as men. Other occupations in which women earn close to what men earn include registered nurses; social, recreation, and religious workers; secretaries; and food preparation workers.

Occupations where the biggest earnings gap remains include financial managers, marketing managers, physicians, and sales workers.

◆ One reason for the earnings gap is that the average male worker has been on the job longer than the average female worker. As women gain job experience, the earnings gap will shrink.

Median Weekly Earnings by Sex, 1995

(median weekly earnings of full-time wage and salary workers aged 16 or older by selected occupation and sex, and ratio of women's earnings to men's, 1995)

	men	women	ratio of women's earnings to men's
Total	$538	$406	75.5
Managerial and professional specialty	829	605	73.0
Executive, administrative, and managerial	833	570	68.4
Public administration officials and administrators	829	652	78.6
Financial managers	942	635	67.4
Personnel and labor relations managers	-	646	-
Purchasing managers	963	-	-
Marketing, advertising, and public relations managers	1,063	631	59.4
Education and related fields administrators	952	674	70.8
Medicine and health managers	838	580	69.2
Property and real estate managers	614	464	75.6
Professional specialty	827	632	76.4
Architects	741	-	-
Engineers	935	806	86.2
Mathematical and computer scientists	895	754	84.2
Natural scientists	794	663	83.5
Physicians	1,241	806	64.9
Registered nurses	715	693	96.9
Pharmacists	1,057	-	-
Dietitians	-	486	-
Therapists	685	665	97.1
Teachers, college and university	941	735	78.1
Teachers, except college and university	696	601	86.4
Librarians, archivists, and curators	-	597	-
Economists	928	666	71.8
Psychologists	658	586	89.1
Social, recreation, and religious workers	516	479	92.8
Lawyers and judges	1,229	944	76.8
Writers, artists, entertainers, and athletes	647	522	80.7
Technical, sales, and administrative support	556	383	68.9
Health technologists and technicians	555	451	81.3
Engineering and related technologists and technicians	613	519	84.7
Science technicians	605	439	72.6
Technicians, except health, engineering, and science	748	591	79.0

(continued)

(continued from previous page)

	men	women	ratio of women's earnings to men's
Airplane pilots and navigators	$960	-	-
Computer programmers	762	$681	89.4
Legal assistants	582	501	86.1
Sales occupations	579	330	57.0
Supervisors and proprietors	591	389	65.8
Finance and business services sales representatives	721	499	69.2
Commodities, except retail, sales representatives	703	568	80.8
Retail and personal services sales workers	365	253	69.3
Administrative support, including clerical	489	384	78.5
Supervisors	649	488	75.2
Computer equipment operators	524	393	75.0
Secretaries, stenographers, and typists	441	395	89.6
Information clerks	403	336	83.4
Records processing occupations, except financial	424	380	89.6
Financial records processing	445	382	85.8
Service occupations	357	264	73.9
Private household	-	193	-
Firefighting and fire prevention	629	-	-
Police and detectives	785	-	-
Food preparation and service occupations	273	246	90.1
Health service occupation	335	282	84.2
Cleaning and building service occupations	315	255	81.0
Personal service occupations	359	269	74.9
Precision production, craft, and repair	534	371	69.5
Mechanics and repairers	538	550	102.2
Construction trades	507	400	78.9
Precision production occupations	567	344	60.7
Operators, fabricators, and laborers	413	297	71.9
Machine operators, assemblers, and inspectors	421	296	70.3
Transportation and material moving occupations	482	354	73.4
Truck drivers	484	345	71.3
Bus drivers	497	331	66.6
Taxi-cab drivers and chauffeurs	362	-	-
Handlers, equipment cleaners, helpers, and laborers	328	284	86.6
Farming, forestry, and fishing	294	249	84.7

Note: The ratio is calculated by dividing women's median weekly earnings by men's median weekly earnings and multiplying by 100. (-) means sample is too small to make a reliable estimate.
Source: Bureau of Labor Statistics, Employment and Earnings, *January 1996; calculations by New Strategist*

Incomes Highest in the Northeast

Metropolitan residents have higher incomes than nonmetropolitan residents.

Suburban households in the nation's largest metropolitan areas have the highest incomes, a median of $44,073 in 1995—29 percent higher than the national median. Many suburban householders are middle-aged married couples in their peak earning years. Nonmetropolitan households have the lowest incomes, a median of $27,776, or just 82 percent of the national average. The elderly—many of them with low incomes because they are retired—head a larger share of households in nonmetropolitan areas. But cost of living differences between urban and rural areas make it difficult to measure people's standard of living by income alone.

Households in the Northeast, Midwest, and West have above-average incomes, while those in the South are below-average. Among the 50 states, Alaska has the highest household income, a median of $47,954 in 1995. But the cost of living in Alaska is also high, making it doubtful whether households there are actually any better off than those elsewhere in the United States. West Virginia has the lowest median household income, just $24,880 in 1995.

◆ The changing structure of the economy may result in smaller income differences by region and metropolitan residence. Because of increased telecommuting, place of residence may not determine income levels in the future as much as it does today.

Median Income by Metropolitan Status and Region of Residence, 1995

(number of households and median household income by metropolitan status and region of residence, 1995; households in thousands as of 1996)

	number of households	median income
Total households	99,627	$34,076
Residence status		
Inside metropolitan areas	79,875	36,079
1 million or more	53,007	37,903
Inside central cities	19,792	28,633
Outside central cities	33,215	44,073
Under 1 million	26,868	32,643
Inside central cities	11,193	29,478
Outside central cities	15,674	35,422
Outside metropolitan areas	19,753	27,776
Region		
Northeast	19,695	36,111
Midwest	23,707	35,839
South	35,143	30,942
West	21,082	35,979

Source: Bureau of the Census, Money Income in the United States: 1995, *Current Population Reports, P60-193, 1996*

Median Income of Households by State, 1995

(median income of households by state, 1995)

	median income		median income
Alabama	$25,991	Missouri	$34,825
Alaska	47,954	Montana	27,757
Arizona	30,863	Nebraska	32,929
Arkansas	25,814	Nevada	36,084
California	37,009	New Hampshire	39,171
Colorado	40,706	New Jersey	43,924
Connecticut	40,243	New Mexico	25,991
Delaware	34,928	New York	33,028
District of Columbia	30,748	North Carolina	31,979
Florida	29,745	North Dakota	29,089
Georgia	34,099	Ohio	34,941
Hawaii	42,851	Oklahoma	26,311
Idaho	32,676	Oregon	36,374
Illinois	38,071	Pennsylvania	34,524
Indiana	33,385	Rhode Island	35,359
Iowa	35,519	South Carolina	29,071
Kansas	30,341	South Dakota	29,578
Kentucky	29,810	Tennessee	29,015
Louisiana	27,949	Texas	32,039
Maine	33,858	Utah	36,480
Maryland	41,041	Vermont	33,824
Massachusetts	38,574	Virginia	36,222
Michigan	36,426	Washington	35,568
Minnesota	37,933	West Virginia	24,880
Mississippi	26,538	Wisconsin	40,955
Wyoming	31,529		

Source: Bureau of the Census, Internet web site, http://www.census.gov

Wages and Salaries Rank Number One

Wages and salaries are the most important source of income for the largest proportion of Americans.

Among the 157 million Americans of working age who had income in 1995, fully 82 percent earned money from wages or salaries. Among those with wage and salary income, the average amount received was $26,151.

For Americans aged 65 or older, the most important source of income is Social Security. Ninety-two percent of the elderly receive Social Security checks, averaging $7,972 per person in 1995.

Interest income is another widely received source of money. More than 100 million people received interest income in 1995, although the average amount received is small. Americans with interest income received an average of $1,436. Interest is a larger source of income for the elderly, who received an average of $3,114 in 1995.

♦ The nation's elderly are dependent on a variety of sources of income, including pensions, Social Security, and interest from savings. Retiring baby boomers will also have to depend on a variety of sources of income.

Sources of Income, 1995

(number of persons with income and average income for those with income, by selected sources of income and age, 1995; persons in thousands as of 1996)

	aged 15 or older		under age 65		aged 65 or older	
	number with income	average income	number with income	average income	number with income	average income
Total	188,073	$24,211	156,991	$25,519	31,081	$17,604
Wages and salary	132,588	25,935	128,674	26,151	4,181	19,304
Nonfarm self-employment	11,601	17,240	10,715	17,231	886	17,342
Social Security	37,534	7,656	8,795	6,626	28,739	7,972
Public assistance	4,989	3,674	4,907	3,707	81	1,706
Veterans' benefits	2,549	6,347	1,394	7,158	1,155	5,369
Disability benefits	1,620	8,739	1,387	8,567	233	9,768
Pensions	14,417	11,188	4,441	14,768	9,977	9,595
Interest	107,881	1,436	87,186	1,038	20,695	3,114
Dividends	29,700	2,112	23,630	1,763	6,070	3,471
Rents, royalties, estates or trusts	13,094	3,155	9,846	3,063	3,248	3,434
Education	7,692	3,539	7,671	3,545	21	1,382
Child support	5,190	3,335	5,179	3,340	11	915

Source: Bureau of the Census, Money Income in the United States: 1995, *Current Population Reports, P60-193, 1996*

Most Poor Americans Are White

Although blacks are more likely than whites to live in poverty, whites account for most of the nation's 36 million poor.

Only 11 percent of whites are poor, versus 29 percent of blacks and 30 percent of Hispanics. Within each racial and ethnic group, children are more likely to be poor than any other age group. Overall, 21 percent of the nation's children are poor. But among blacks, the figure is 42 percent. Among Hispanics, 40 percent of children under age 18 are poor.

Nearly 8 million families in the United States are poor. Again, white families account for a majority of all poor families. Single-parent families have the highest poverty rates. Over half of those headed by black or Hispanic women are poor, compared with 36 percent of single-parent families headed by whites.

◆ Childhood poverty will remain a chronic problem until single-parent families begin to decline as a share of all families.

Persons in Poverty by Race and Hispanic Origin, 1995

(number and percent of persons in poverty by age, race, and Hispanic origin, 1995; persons in thousands as of 1996)

	total		white		black		Hispanic	
	number	percent	number	percent	number	percent	number	percent
Total	36,425	13.8%	24,423	11.2%	9,872	29.3%	8,574	30.3%
Under age 18	14,665	20.8	8,981	16.2	4,761	41.9	4,080	40.0
Aged 18 to 24	4,553	18.3	3,156	15.9	1,117	30.5	1,097	30.6
Aged 25 to 34	5,196	12.7	3,601	10.8	1,304	24.4	1,325	24.7
Aged 35 to 44	4,096	9.4	2,812	7.9	995	18.8	942	23.2
Aged 45 to 54	2,470	7.8	1,683	6.3	630	18.2	429	19.7
Aged 55 to 59	1,163	10.3	840	8.7	246	21.4	186	23.0
Aged 60 to 64	996	10.2	777	9.2	191	19.5	174	25.4
Aged 65 or older	3,318	10.5	2,572	9.0	629	25.4	342	23.5

Note: Numbers will not add to total because Hispanics may be of any race and not all races are shown.
Source: Bureau of the Census, Poverty in the United States: 1995, *Current Population Reports, P60-194, 1996*

Families in Poverty by Race and Hispanic Origin, 1995

(number and percent of families in poverty by type of family, presence of related children under age 18, race, and Hispanic origin, 1995; families in thousands as of 1996)

	total		white		black		Hispanic	
	number	*percent*	*number*	*percent*	*number*	*percent*	*number*	*percent*
Total families	7,532	10.8%	4,994	8.5%	2,127	26.4%	1,695	27.0%
With children <18	5,976	16.3	3,839	12.9	1,821	34.1	1,470	33.2
Married couples	2,982	5.6	2,443	5.1	314	8.5	803	18.9
With children <18	1,961	7.5	1,583	7.0	209	9.9	657	22.6
Female householders,								
no spouse present	4,057	32.4	2,200	26.6	1,701	45.1	792	49.4
With children <18	3,634	41.5	1,980	35.6	1,533	53.2	735	57.3
Male householders,								
no spouse present	493	14.0	351	12.9	112	19.5	100	22.9
With children <18	381	19.7	276	18.4	79	23.4	78	32.9

Note: Numbers will not add to total because Hispanics may be of any race and because other races are not shown.
Source: Bureau of the Census, Poverty in the United States: 1995, *Current Population Reports, P60-194, 1996*

4

Labor Trends

♦ **Sixty-six percent of Americans aged 16 or older are in the labor force, up from 59 percent in 1960.**
Behind this increase is the rise of working women, whose labor force participation rate grew by more than 20 percentage points between 1960 and 1995.

♦ **Sixty-seven percent of married women with children under age 18 were in the labor force in 1995.**
The proportion of married mothers who do not work—traditional housewives—has fallen from 49 to 30 percent in the past 25 years.

♦ **More than one-fourth of working men and women are managers or professionals.**
Overall, 47 percent of men and 71 percent of women are white collar workers.

♦ **Nearly 9 million Americans, most of them men, were self-employed in 1995.**
Self-employment rises with age, from about 2 percent of workers under age 25 to one in four workers aged 65 or older.

♦ **Fifty percent of students aged 16 to 24 have jobs.**
Most working students have part-time jobs, but 12 percent of younger ones and one-third of older ones work full-time.

♦ **Non-Hispanic white men will decline as a proportion of all workers.**
By 2005, non-Hispanic white men will account for only 38 percent of workers, down from 41 percent in 1994.

♦ **Health care jobs account for six of the ten occupations projected to grow the fastest between 1994 and 2005.**
Home health aides is the occupation projected to grow the fastest—up 119 percent.

Two-Thirds of Americans Work

Sixty-six percent of Americans aged 16 or older are in the labor force, up from 59 percent in 1960. Behind this increase is the rise of working women.

In 1960, only 38 percent of women aged 16 or older were working or looking for work. By 1995, the figure had grown to 59 percent. During those years, the proportion of men aged 16 or older in the labor force fell from 83 to 75 percent. Early retirement is the major reason for the decline in men's labor force participation rates since 1960.

The unemployment rate stood at 5.6 percent in 1995, slightly higher than the 5.5 percent of 1990. Men and women are equally likely to be unemployed.

♦ Women's labor force participation rates will rise slowly in the years ahead as younger, career-oriented women replace older homemakers.

♦ Men's labor force participation rates are likely to stabilize because fewer employers can afford generous early retirement plans for their older workers.

Employment Status by Sex and Age, 1995

(employment status of the civilian noninstitutional population aged 16 or older, by sex and age, 1995; numbers in thousands)

| | in civilian labor force | | | | | not in labor force | |
| | total | percent of population | number employed | unemployed | | total | percent of population |
				number	percent		
Total persons	132,304	66.6%	124,900	7,404	5.6%	66,280	33.4%
Aged 16 to 19	7,765	53.5	6,419	1,346	17.3	6,746	46.5
Aged 20 to 24	13,688	76.6	12,443	1,244	9.1	4,176	23.4
Aged 25 to 34	34,198	83.8	32,356	1,841	5.4	6,600	16.2
Aged 35 to 44	35,751	84.6	34,202	1,549	4.3	6,503	15.4
Aged 45 to 54	25,223	81.4	24,378	844	3.3	5,751	18.6
Aged 55 to 64	11,860	57.2	11,435	425	3.6	8,875	42.8
Aged 65 or older	3,819	12.1	3,666	153	4.0	27,628	87.9
Total men	71,360	75.0	67,377	3,983	5.6	23,818	25.0
Aged 16 to 19	4,036	54.8	3,292	744	18.4	3,331	45.2
Aged 20 to 24	7,338	83.1	6,665	673	9.2	1,497	16.9
Aged 25 to 34	18,670	93.0	17,709	961	5.1	1,409	7.0
Aged 35 to 44	19,189	92.3	18,374	815	4.2	1,611	7.7
Aged 45 to 54	13,421	88.8	12,958	464	3.5	1,690	11.2
Aged 55 to 64	6,504	66.0	6,272	233	3.6	3,352	34.0
Aged 65 or older	2,201	16.8	2,108	94	4.3	10,929	83.2
Total women	60,944	58.9	57,523	3,421	5.6	42,462	41.1
Aged 16 to 19	3,729	52.2	3,127	602	16.1	3,415	47.8
Aged 20 to 24	6,349	70.3	5,779	571	9.0	2,680	29.7
Aged 25 to 34	15,528	74.9	14,647	880	5.7	5,191	25.1
Aged 35 to 44	16,562	77.2	15,828	735	4.4	4,891	22.8
Aged 45 to 54	11,801	74.4	11,421	381	3.2	4,061	25.6
Aged 55 to 64	5,356	49.2	5,163	193	3.6	5,524	50.8
Aged 65 or older	1,618	8.8	1,558	60	3.7	16,699	91.2

Note: The civilian labor force equals the number employed plus the number unemployed. The civilian population equals the number in the labor force plus the number not in the labor force.
Source: Bureau of Labor Statistics, Employment and Earnings, *January 1996; calculations by New Strategist*

Women Up, Men Down

Men's and women's labor force participation rates have gone in opposite directions over the past three decades.

Women's labor force participation rate has grown by more than 20 percentage points between 1960 and 1995, from 38 to 59 percent. At the same time, the rate for men has fallen by 8 percentage points, from 83 to 75 percent.

Women's labor force participation rates have increased in all but the oldest age group since 1960. The biggest gain has been among women aged 35 to 44. In 1960, just 36 percent of women in this age group were in the labor force. By 1995, the proportion reached 75 percent as mothers with young children went to work. Overall, three out of four women aged 20 to 54 are in the labor force.

Among men, labor force participation rates have fallen in every age group, with the biggest drop (21 percentage points) among men aged 55 to 64. In 1960, nearly nine out of ten men in this age group were in the labor force. By 1995, just two out of three were working as more men took early retirement. Among younger men, the decline in labor force participation can be attributed to working women. With most wives earning a paycheck, men can afford to go back to school or stay home and care for children.

◆ Expect little change in labor force participation rates over the next decade. The rise in women's labor force participation rate will slow because so many women are already at work. The decline in men's participation rate will halt or even reverse because fewer employers will offer early retirement incentives.

Labor Force Participation by Sex and Age, 1960 to 1995

(civilian labor force participation rates for persons aged 16 or older by sex and age, 1960-1995)

	1995	*1990*	*1980*	*1970*	*1960*
Total men	75.0%	76.1%	77.4%	79.7%	83.3%
Aged 16 to 19	54.8	55.7	60.5	56.1	55.0
Aged 20 to 24	83.1	84.3	85.9	83.3	88.1
Aged 25 to 34	93.0	94.2	95.2	96.4	97.5
Aged 35 to 44	92.3	94.4	95.5	96.9	97.7
Aged 45 to 54	88.8	90.7	91.2	94.3	95.7
Aged 55 to 64	66.0	67.7	72.1	83.0	86.8
Aged 65 or older	16.8	16.4	19.0	26.8	33.1
Total women	58.9	57.5	51.5	43.3	37.7
Aged 16 to 19	52.2	51.8	52.9	44.0	39.3
Aged 20 to 24	70.3	71.6	68.9	57.7	46.1
Aged 25 to 34	74.9	73.6	65.5	45.0	36.0
Aged 35 to 44	77.2	76.5	65.5	51.1	43.4
Aged 45 to 54	74.4	71.2	59.9	54.4	49.8
Aged 55 to 64	49.2	45.3	41.3	43.0	37.2
Aged 65 or older	8.8	8.7	8.1	9.7	10.8

Source: Bureau of Labor Statistics, Employment and Earnings, *selected years*

Most Blacks, Hispanics, and Whites Work

Participation rates range from a high of 76 percent for white men to a low of 53 percent for Hispanic women.

Black and white women have similar labor force participation rates, except in the youngest age groups. Black men, in contrast, have significantly lower labor force participation rates than white men in all age groups. Only 40 percent of black men aged 16 to 19 are in the labor force, versus 59 percent of white men in that age group. Black men are about twice likely as white men to be unemployed. Fully 37 percent of black men aged 16 to 19 could not find a job in 1995, versus 16 percent of white men in that age group.

Among Hispanics, labor force participation rates vary significantly depending on country of origin. Because Mexicans are by far the largest Hispanic group in the United States, their labor force participation rates determine the labor force pattern for Hispanics overall. Mexican Hispanics are much more likely to be in the labor force than are Puerto Rican or Cuban Hispanics. A majority of both Mexican and Cuban Hispanic women work. Fewer than half of Hispanic women of Puerto Rican origin are in the labor force.

♦ Unemployment rates are likely to remain high for young blacks because many live in central cities, where jobs are scarce.

Employment Status by Race, Sex, and Age, 1995

(employment status of the civilian nonistitutional population aged 16 or older by race, sex, and age, 1995; numbers in thousands)

| | | in civilian labor force | | | | not in labor force | |
| | total | percent of population | number employed | unemployed | | | |
				number	percent	number	percent
White men							
Aged 16 or older	61,146	75.7%	58,146	2,999	4.9%	19,587	24.3%
Aged 16 to 19	3,427	58.5	2,892	535	15.6	2,427	41.5
Aged 20 to 24	6,096	85.1	5,613	483	7.9	1,067	14.9
Aged 25 to 34	15,669	94.1	14,958	711	4.5	984	5.9
Aged 35 to 44	16,414	93.4	15,793	621	3.8	1,153	6.6
Aged 45 to 54	11,730	90.0	11,359	371	3.2	1,298	10.0
Aged 55 to 64	5,809	67.1	5,609	200	3.4	2,843	32.9
Aged 65 or older	2,000	16.9	1,921	79	4.0	9,815	83.1
White women							
Aged 16 or older	50,804	59.0	48,344	2,460	4.8	35,377	41.0
Aged 16 to 19	3,118	55.5	2,701	418	13.4	2,496	44.5
Aged 20 to 24	5,170	72.3	4,787	384	7.4	1,979	27.7
Aged 25 to 34	12,656	75.8	12,056	600	4.7	4,046	24.2
Aged 35 to 44	13,697	77.6	13,157	540	3.9	3,957	22.4
Aged 45 to 54	10,074	75.2	9,768	306	3.0	3,316	24.8
Aged 55 to 64	4,622	49.5	4,461	162	3.5	4,711	50.5
Aged 65 or older	1,466	9.0	1,415	52	3.5	14,871	91.0

(continued)

(continued from previous page)

		in civilian labor force				not in labor force	
				unemployed			
	total	percent of population	number employed	number	percent	number	percent
Black men							
Aged 16 or older	7,183	69.0%	6,422	762	10.6%	3,228	31.0%
Aged 16 to 19	453	40.1	285	168	37.1	677	59.9
Aged 20 to 24	866	74.6	714	153	17.6	295	25.4
Aged 25 to 34	2,089	87.5	1,895	195	9.3	299	12.5
Aged 35 to 44	1,987	84.1	1,836	150	7.6	375	15.9
Aged 45 to 54	1,148	78.5	1,085	63	5.5	314	21.5
Aged 55 to 64	490	54.4	468	21	4.4	411	45.6
Aged 65 or older	150	14.9	138	11	7.6	857	85.2
Black women							
Aged 16 or older	7,634	59.5	6,857	777	10.2	5,201	40.5
Aged 16 to 19	458	39.8	301	157	34.3	695	60.3
Aged 20 to 24	887	63.7	729	158	17.8	505	36.3
Aged 25 to 34	2,177	73.9	1,949	228	10.5	771	26.2
Aged 35 to 44	2,178	77.3	2,025	153	7.0	638	22.7
Aged 45 to 54	1,256	70.5	1,202	53	4.2	527	29.6
Aged 55 to 64	556	47.2	536	20	3.6	623	52.9
Aged 65 or older	121	7.7	114	7	5.6	1,443	92.2

Note: The civilian labor force equals the number employed plus the number unemployed. The civilian population equals the number in the labor force plus the number not in the labor force.
Source: Bureau of Labor Statistics, Employment and Earnings, *January 1996; calculations by New Strategist*

Employment Status of Hispanics by Sex, 1995

(employment status of the Hispanic civilian noninstitutional population aged 16 or older by sex and selected countries of origin, 1995; numbers in thousands)

| | | in civilian labor force | | | | not in labor force | |
| | | | | unemployed | | | |
	total	percent of population	employed	number	percent	number	percent
Total Hispanic men	7,376	79.1%	6,725	651	8.8%	1,952	20.9%
Mexican	4,862	80.9	4,427	436	9.0	1,147	19.1
Puerto Rican	605	70.6	535	69	11.4	252	29.4
Cuban	350	69.7	324	27	7.6	151	30.1
Total Hispanic women	4,891	52.6	4,403	488	10.0	4,409	47.4
Mexican	2,903	51.8	2,589	314	10.8	2,697	48.2
Puerto Rican	493	47.4	439	54	11.0	546	52.6
Cuban	263	50.8	244	18	7.0	255	49.2

Note: Includes Hispanics from countries of origin not shown separately. The civilian labor force equals the number employed plus the number unemployed. The civilian population equals the number in the labor force plus the number not in the labor force.
Source: Bureau of Labor Statistics, Employment and Earnings, *January 1996; calculations by New Strategist*

More Part-Time Workers

The number of Americans who work part-time has grown by 36 percent since 1980, approaching 25 million in 1995.

One in four working women worked part-time in 1995. This proportion has barely changed since 1980, increasing by less than 1 percentage point. Because the population of women has expanded during those years, however, the number of women who work part-time has grown by over 4 million.

Eleven percent of men work part-time, up by about 1 percentage point since 1980. The number of men who work part-time rose by over 2 million between 1980 and 1995. One reason for the rise in the share of men who work part-time is the increase in working wives. As more women go to work, more men can cut back on their work hours to pursue other activities, such as going to school or caring for children.

◆ If health care and other benefits were widely available to part-time workers, the proportion of people who work part-time would expand. But in today's economy, employer benefits are not likely to become more generous without a government mandate.

Full-Time and Part-Time Workers, 1980 to 1995

(number and percent of persons aged 16 or older in the civilian labor force by sex and full- and part-time status, 1980-1995; numbers in thousands)

	total	usually work full-time		usually work part-time	
		total	percent of labor force	total	percent of labor force
Total					
1995	132,303	107,588	81.3%	24,715	18.7%
1990	124,788	103,535	83.0	21,252	17.0
1980	106,940	88,831	83.1	18,109	16.9
Men					
1995	71,360	63,310	88.7	8,050	11.3
1990	68,233	61,246	89.8	6,987	10.2
1980	61,454	55,420	90.2	6,034	9.8
Women					
1995	60,943	44,278	72.7	16,665	27.3
1990	56,553	42,288	74.8	14,265	25.2
1980	45,485	33,409	73.5	12,076	26.5

Note: The unemployed are distributed by full- or part-time work depending on whether they are looking for full- or part-time work. Part-time employment is less than 35 hours per week.
Source: Bureau of Labor Statistics, Employment and Earnings, *January 1996; calculations by New Strategist*

A Surge in Working Mothers

Sixty-seven percent of married women with children under age 18 were in the labor force in 1995, up from 51 percent in 1970.

The proportion of married mothers who do not work (traditional housewives) has fallen from 49 to 30 percent in the past 25 years.

Most working women work full-time. The proportion of married mothers who work full-time has climbed from just 16 percent in 1970 to 46 percent in 1995—surpassing the proportion who are housewives. The proportion who work part-time has fallen from 35 percent in 1970 to 21 percent in 1995.

Labor force participation rates are higher for married mothers with school-aged children than for those with preschoolers. Fully 73 percent of mothers with school-aged children are in the labor force; 53 percent are full-time workers. Among married mothers with children under age 6, 60 percent are in the labor force. Women with young children are more likely to work part-time than full-time, but the proportion who work full-time has nearly quadrupled since 1970—from 10 to 39 percent.

♦ The rapid growth in the labor force participation rates of married women with children is now over. With nearly 70 percent already in the labor force, participation rates are likely to rise slowly or stabilize over the next few years.

♦ Because the economy now demands two earners to achieve a middle-class lifestyle, these trends are not likely to reverse. Working women—and working mothers—are here to stay.

Labor Force Participation of Married Women with Children, 1970 and 1995

(employment status of married women with spouse present by age of children, in percent, 1970 and 1995; percentage point change, 1970-95)

	1995	1970	percentage point change, 1970-95
Married women with children <18			
Worked during year	66.9%	51.3%	15.6
Worked full-time, year-round	46.2	16.4	29.8
Worked part-time or part-year	20.7	34.9	-14.2
Did not work	30.0	48.7	-18.7
Married women with children 6 to 17, none younger			
Worked during year	73.3	57.7	15.6
Worked full-time, year-round	52.6	22.8	29.8
Worked part-time or part-year	20.7	34.9	-14.2
Did not work	23.8	42.3	-18.5
Married women with children <6			
Worked during year	59.9	44.4	15.5
Worked full-time, year-round	39.3	9.6	29.7
Worked part-time or part-year	20.7	34.8	-14.1
Did not work	36.8	55.6	-18.8

Source: Bureau of Labor Statistics, unpublished data from the 1996 Current Population Survey; and Monthly Labor Review, *June 1994; calculations by New Strategist*

New Mothers Are Back at Work

Among women with infants, 53 percent are back at work before their baby celebrates a first birthday.

Older mothers and women with higher levels of education are most likely to work within a year of giving birth. Many have specialized skills and much to lose by dropping out of the labor force.

Fifty-seven percent of women aged 30 to 44 are back at work within a year of giving birth, versus 51 percent of women aged 20 to 24. Only 34 percent of women who did not graduate from high school are back at work within a year of giving birth, compared with 70 percent of college graduates. Some women who return to work soon after having a baby may prefer to spend more time out of the labor force, but the economic and professional sacrifice is too great.

Fifty-nine percent of first-time mothers worked during their child's first year of life, compared with just under half of women having a second or higher-order birth. With one child, it's much easier to coordinate day care, household tasks, and a job. With two children, the management of multiple roles becomes more difficult, making it more appealing to give up the extra income and stay home—at least for a while.

◆ Since two incomes are now needed for a middle-class standard of living, the labor force participation rates of new mothers will remain high.

Labor Force Participation of Women with Newborns, 1982 and 1994

(number and labor force participation rates of women aged 15 to 44 who had a child in the previous year by selected characteristics, 1982 and 1994; numbers in thousands)

	1994		1982	
	number	*percent in labor force*	number	*percent in labor force*
Total	3,890	53.1%	3,433	43.9%
Age				
15 to 19	397	39.3	1,306*	39.6
20 to 24	938	51.0		
25 to 29	1,054	54.5	1,139	45.9
30 to 44	1,501	57.1	988	47.4
Education				
Less than high school	832	33.5	690	27.0
High school, 4 years	1,303	48.1	1,597	44.3
College, 1 or more years	1,754	66.2	1,147	53.6
Bachelor's degree or more	773	69.7	518**	52.6
Birth order				
First birth	1,647	59.0	1,263	50.5
Second or higher-order birth	2,242	48.9	2,171	40.1
Marital status				
Married, husband present	2,798	54.5	2,743	43.4
Widowed, divorced, or separated	199	52.0	273	49.6
Never married	892	49.0	418	43.8

* Women aged 18 to 24.
** Four or more years of college.
Source: Bureau of the Census, Internet web site, http://www.census.gov; *and* Fertility of American Women: June 1992, *Current Population Reports, P20-470, 1993*

Job Tenure Falls for Men

Women's job tenure remains high.

The number of years workers have been with their current employer is on the decline—at least for men, according to the Employee Benefit Research Institute (EBRI).

Since 1983, when job tenure peaked for all but the youngest men, the sharpest declines in job tenure have been among the oldest male workers. Men aged 55 to 64 had been with their current employer a median of 17 years in 1983. By 1996, job tenure for this age group had fallen to 12 years—a 29 percent drop. Job tenure fell by more than three years for men aged 45 to 54, and by nearly two years for men aged 25 to 34.

In contrast to men, job tenure has changed little for women since 1983. This stability is due to women's increasing attachment to the labor force. Women are less likely to quit working after having children, boosting their years on the job.

♦ Job tenure declines when workers voluntarily switch jobs and when they are laid off and forced to find new jobs. The decline in job tenure among men is due to a combination of these factors, but its concentration among older men points toward involuntary lay-offs as the biggest factor.

♦ Current levels of job tenure among men are equivalent to those seen in the 1950s and 1960s, according to EBRI.

Job Tenure by Sex and Age, 1983 to 1996

(median number of years workers aged 25 to 64 have been with their current employer by sex and age, selected years, 1983 to 1996; and change in years, 1983-96)

	1996	1991	1987	1983	change 1983-96
Men					
Aged 25 to 34	3.0	3.7	3.7	3.4	-0.4
Aged 35 to 44	6.0	7.2	7.6	7.7	-1.7
Aged 45 to 54	10.0	12.2	12.3	13.4	-3.4
Aged 55 to 64	12.0	15.5	15.7	17.0	-5.0
Women					
Aged 25 to 34	2.7	3.2	3.1	3.1	-0.4
Aged 35 to 44	5.0	5.0	4.9	4.6	0.4
Aged 45 to 54	7.0	7.3	7.3	6.9	0.1
Aged 55 to 64	10.0	10.4	10.3	10.5	-0.5

Source: Employee Benefit Research Institute, 1996 Data on the Mobility of American Workers, 1997; calculations by New Strategist

White-Collar Workers Dominate Labor Force

More than one-fourth of working men and women are managers or professionals.

Overall, 47 percent of men are white-collar workers (a category that includes mangers and professionals, and technical, sales, and administrative support workers). Another 39 percent of men are blue-collar workers (a category that includes precision production, craft, and repair workers; and operators, fabricators, and laborers). Ten percent of men are service workers, while 4 percent are in farming, forestry, or fishing.

Among women, 71 percent are white-collar workers, 10 percent are in blue-collar employment, and 18 percent are service workers. One percent are in farming, forestry, or fishing.

Among both women and men, the largest share of workers by industry and occupation are managers or professionals in the service industries—20 percent of working women and 13 percent of working men. The service industries are wide-ranging and include hotels and motels, beauty shops, advertising agencies, computer businesses, repair shops, amusement parks, health clubs, hospitals, law firms, public and private schools, social agencies, and accounting firms.

◆ The distribution of working women by occupation and industry could change significantly as women become less concentrated in stereotypically female occupations such as nursing and teaching.

Workers by Occupation and Sex, 1995

(total number and percent distribution of employed persons aged 16 or older in the civilian labor force, by occupation and sex, 1995; numbers in thousands)

	total	*men*	*women*
Total employed, number	124,900	67,377	57,523
Total employed, percent	100.0%	100.0%	100.0%
Managerial and professional specialty	28.3	27.3	29.4
Executive, administrative, and managerial	13.8	14.6	12.8
Professional specialty	14.5	12.7	16.7
Technical, sales, and administrative support	30.0	19.8	41.9
Technicians and related support	3.1	2.8	3.5
Sales occupations	12.1	11.3	13.0
Administrative support, including clerical	14.7	5.6	25.4
Service occupations	13.6	10.1	17.7
Private household	0.7	0.1	1.4
Protective service	1.8	2.8	0.6
Service, exc. private household & protective	11.1	7.2	15.7
Precision production, craft, and repair	10.8	18.3	2.1
Operators, fabricators, and laborers	14.5	20.3	7.6
Machine operators, assemblers, inspectors	6.3	7.4	5.1
Transportation/material moving occupations	4.1	6.9	0.9
Handlers, equip. cleaners, helpers, laborers	4.0	6.0	1.7
Farming, forestry, and fishing	2.9	4.3	1.3

Source: Bureau of Labor Statistics, Employment and Earnings, *January 1996; calculations by New Strategist*

Employment of Men by Industry and Occupation, 1995

(number and percent distribution of employed men aged 16 or older by industry and occupation, 1995; numbers in thousands)

	total employed	managerial and prof. specialty	technical, sales, admin. support	service	precision prod., craft & repair	operators, fabricators, laborers	farming, forestry, fishing
Total men, number	67,377	18,379	13,311	6,775	12,323	13,677	2,915
Agriculture	2,559	125	30	8	34	70	2,292
Mining	543	130	37	3	222	150	1
Construction	6,906	1,052	135	24	4,265	1,414	17
Manufacturing	14,020	3,358	1,667	219	3,216	5,451	109
Transportation & public utilities	6,195	1,109	1,354	127	1,151	2,443	11
Wholesale/retail trade	13,759	1,604	5,899	2,241	1,227	2,744	44
Finance, insurance, real estate	3,332	1,247	1,626	182	174	38	65
Services	16,732	8,507	2,104	2,682	1,817	1,266	357
Public administration	3,331	1,247	459	1,289	217	101	19

(continued)

(continued from previous page)

Percent distribution by occupation

	total employed	managerial and prof. specialty	technical, sales, admin. support	service	precision prod., craft & repair	operators, fabricators, laborers	farming, forestry, fishing
Total men	100.0%	100.0%	100.0%	100.0%	100.0%	100.0%	100.0%
Agriculture	3.8	0.7	0.2	0.1	0.3	0.5	78.6
Mining	0.8	0.7	0.3	0.0	1.8	1.1	0.0
Construction	10.2	5.7	1.0	0.4	34.6	10.3	0.6
Manufacturing	20.8	18.3	12.5	3.2	26.1	39.9	3.7
Transportation & public utilities	9.2	6.0	10.2	1.9	9.3	17.9	0.4
Wholesale/retail trade	20.4	8.7	44.3	33.1	10.0	20.1	1.5
Finance, insurance, real estate	4.9	6.8	12.2	2.7	1.4	0.3	2.2
Services	24.8	46.3	15.8	39.6	14.7	9.3	12.2
Public administration	4.9	6.8	3.4	19.0	1.8	0.7	0.7

Percent distribution by industry

	total employed	managerial and prof. specialty	technical, sales, admin. support	service	precision prod., craft & repair	operators, fabricators, laborers	farming, forestry, fishing
Total men	100.0	27.3	19.8	10.1	18.3	20.3	4.3
Agriculture	100.0	4.9	1.2	0.3	1.3	2.7	89.6
Mining	100.0	23.9	6.8	0.6	40.9	27.6	0.2
Construction	100.0	15.2	2.0	0.3	61.8	20.5	0.2
Manufacturing	100.0	24.0	11.9	1.6	22.9	38.9	0.8
Transportation & public utilities	100.0	17.9	21.9	2.1	18.6	39.4	0.2
Wholesale/retail trade	100.0	11.7	42.9	16.3	8.9	19.9	0.3
Finance, insurance, real estate	100.0	37.4	48.8	5.5	5.2	1.1	2.0
Services	100.0	50.8	12.6	16.0	10.9	7.6	2.1
Public administration	100.0	37.4	13.8	38.7	6.5	3.0	0.6

Source: Bureau of Labor Statistics, Employment and Earnings, January 1996; calculations by New Strategist

Employment of Women by Industry and Occupation, 1995

(number and percent distribution of employed women aged 16 or older by industry and occupation, 1995; numbers in thousands)

	total employed	managerial and prof. specialty	technical, sales, admin. support	service	precision prod., craft & repair	operators, fabricators, laborers	farming, forestry, fishing
Total women, number	57,522	16,937	24,109	10,156	1,200	4,393	726
Agriculture	881	71	175	8	1	12	615
Mining	84	30	42	1	6	4	1
Construction	762	209	404	9	97	42	1
Manufacturing	6,473	1,233	1,812	75	621	2,731	2
Transportation & public utilities	2,513	525	1,552	120	72	243	–
Wholesale/retail trade	12,312	1,223	7,510	2,640	192	695	51
Finance, insurance, real estate	4,651	1,279	3,264	87	9	9	3
Services	27,220	11,277	8,137	6,928	190	640	48
Public administration	2,626	1,090	1,213	288	12	17	5

(continued)

(continued from previous page)

Percent distribution by occupation

	total employed	managerial and prof. specialty	technical, sales, admin. support	service	precision prod., craft & repair	operators, fabricators, laborers	farming, forestry, fishing
Total women	100.0%	100.0%	100.0%	100.0%	100.0%	100.0%	100.0%
Agriculture	1.5	0.4	0.7	0.1	0.1	0.3	84.7
Mining	0.1	0.2	0.2	0.0	0.5	0.1	0.1
Construction	1.3	1.2	1.7	0.1	8.1	1.0	0.1
Manufacturing	11.3	7.3	7.5	0.7	51.7	62.2	0.3
Transportation & public utilities	4.4	3.1	6.4	1.2	6.0	5.5	-
Wholesale/retail trade	21.4	7.2	31.2	26.0	16.0	15.8	7.0
Finance, insurance, real estate	8.1	7.6	13.5	0.9	0.8	0.2	0.4
Services	47.3	66.6	33.8	68.2	15.8	14.6	6.6
Public administration	4.6	6.4	5.0	2.8	1.0	0.4	0.7

Percent distribution by industry

	total employed	managerial and prof. specialty	technical, sales, admin. support	service	precision prod., craft & repair	operators, fabricators, laborers	farming, forestry, fishing
Total women	100.0	29.4	41.9	17.7	2.1	7.6	1.3
Agriculture	100.0	8.1	19.9	0.9	0.1	1.4	69.8
Mining	100.0	35.7	50.0	1.2	7.1	4.8	1.2
Construction	100.0	27.4	53.0	1.2	12.7	5.5	0.1
Manufacturing	100.0	19.0	28.0	1.2	9.6	42.2	0.0
Transportation & public utilities	100.0	20.9	61.8	4.8	2.9	9.7	-
Wholesale/retail trade	100.0	9.9	61.0	21.4	1.6	5.6	0.4
Finance, insurance, real estate	100.0	27.5	70.2	1.9	0.2	0.2	0.1
Services	100.0	41.4	29.9	25.5	0.7	2.4	0.2
Public administration	100.0	41.5	46.2	11.0	0.5	0.6	0.2

Note: (-) means sample is too small to make a reliable estimate.
Source: Bureau of Labor Statistics, Employment and Earnings, January 1996; calculations by New Strategist

Women Are Nearly Half of all Workers

Women accounted for 46 percent of workers in 1995, up from 44 percent in 1983.

Women hold 48 percent of managerial and professional specialty jobs and 64 percent of technical, sales, and administrative support jobs. Women are a majority of personnel managers, librarians, psychologists, and legal assistants. But they account for only 9 percent of precision production, craft, and repair workers. Women are only 8 percent of engineers, 13 percent of dentists, and 3 percent of airplane pilots and firefighters.

Between 1983 and 1995, women's share of workers increased in most occupations. Women's share of personnel and labor relations managers rose by 15 percentage points, from 44 to 59 percent. Their share of health care managers rose by 23 percentage points, from 57 to 80 percent. But some occupations already heavily dominated by women saw a decline in women's share of employment. Among nurses, women's share fell from 96 to 93 percent. Among sales workers, it fell from 70 to 66 percent.

♦ In the years ahead, women's share of workers will grow substantially among physicians, pharmacists, lawyers, technicians, and other professional white-collar workers. Women's share of blue-collar occupations is not likely to expand much since those jobs are disappearing.

Women Workers by Occupation, 1983 and 1995

(women as a percent of total employed persons aged 16 or older in selected occupations, 1983 and 1995, and percentage point change, 1983-1995)

	1995	1983	percentage point change 1983-1995
TOTAL EMPLOYED	46.1%	43.7%	2.4
Managerial and professional specialty	48.0	40.9	7.1
Executive, administrative, and managerial	42.7	32.4	10.3
Public administration officials and administrators	49.8	38.5	11.3
Financial managers	50.3	38.6	11.7
Personnel and labor relations managers	58.5	43.9	14.6
Purchasing managers	41.5	23.6	17.9
Marketing, advertising and public relations managers	35.7	21.8	13.9
Education and related fields administrators	58.7	41.4	17.3
Medicine and health managers	79.9	57.0	22.9
Property and real estate managers	49.8	42.8	7.0
Professional specialty	52.9	48.1	4.8
Architects	19.8	12.7	7.1
Engineers	8.4	5.8	2.6
Mathematical and computer scientists	32.0	29.6	2.4
Natural scientists	27.3	20.5	6.8
Physicians	24.4	15.8	8.6
Dentists	13.4	6.7	6.7
Registered nurses	93.1	95.8	-2.7
Pharmacists	36.2	26.7	9.5
Dietitians	93.2	90.8	2.4
Therapists	75.1	76.3	-1.2
Teachers, college and university	45.2	39.3	5.9
Teachers, except college and university	74.7	70.9	3.8
Librarians, archivists, and curators	83.2	84.4	-1.2
Economists	50.3	37.9	12.4
Psychologists	59.2	57.1	2.1
Social, recreation, and religious workers	52.5	43.1	9.4
Lawyers and judges	26.2	15.8	10.4
Writers, artists, entertainers, and athletes	49.4	42.7	6.7
Technical, sales and administrative support	64.4	64.6	-0.2
Health technologists and technicians	79.7	84.3	-4.6
Engineering and related technologists and technicians	17.8	18.4	-0.6

(continued)

(continued from previous page)

	1995	1983	percentage point change 1983-1995
Science technicians	35.5%	29.1%	6.4
Technicians, except health, engineering and science	39.9	35.3	4.6
Airplane pilots and navigators	3.4	2.1	1.3
Computer programmers	29.5	32.5	-3.0
Legal assistants	80.0	74.0	6.0
Sales occupations	49.5	47.5	2.0
Supervisors and proprietors	38.9	28.4	10.5
Finance and business services sales representatives	42.1	37.2	4.9
Commodities, except retail, sales representatives	21.2	15.1	6.1
Retail and personal services sales workers	65.6	69.7	-4.1
Administrative support, including clerical	79.5	79.9	-0.4
Supervisors, administrative support	60.0	53.4	6.6
Computer equipment operators	60.4	63.9	-3.5
Sercretaries, stenographers, and typists	97.8	98.2	-0.4
Information clerks	88.0	88.9	-0.9
Records processing occupations, except financial	79.4	82.4	-3.0
Financial records processing	92.4	89.4	3.0
Service occupations	60.0	60.1	-0.1
Private household	95.5	96.1	-0.6
Firefighting and fire prevention	2.7	1.0	1.7
Police and detectives	13.5	9.4	4.1
Food preparation and service occupations	58.3	63.3	-5.0
Health service occupations	88.2	89.2	-1.0
Cleaning and building service occupations	44.9	38.8	6.1
Personal service occupations	80.7	79.2	1.5
Precision production, craft and repair	8.9	8.1	0.8
Mechanics and repairers	3.9	3.0	0.9
Construction trades	2.3	1.8	0.5
Precision production occupations	23.3	21.5	1.8
Operators, fabricators and laborers	24.3	26.6	-2.3
Machine operators, assemblers, and inspectors	37.3	42.1	-4.8
Transportation and material moving occupations	9.5	7.8	1.7
Truck drivers	4.5	3.1	1.4
Bus drivers	46.4	45.5	0.9
Taxicab drivers and chauffeurs	10.5	10.4	0.1
Handlers, equipment cleaners, helpers, and laborers	19.1	16.8	2.3
Farming, forestry, and fishing	19.9	16.0	3.9

Source: Bureau of Labor Statistics, Employment and Earnings, *January 1996; calculations by New Strategist*

Whites, Blacks, and Hispanics on the Job

Regardless of race or ethnicity, the largest share of Americans hold technical, sales, and administrative support jobs.

Technical, sales, and administrative support jobs include secretaries, sales people, office clerks, mail carriers, and bank tellers. Among employed whites, 30 percent hold technical, sales, and administrative support positions. Among blacks, the figure is 29 percent, and among Hispanics, 24 percent. The similarity in the occupational distribution of whites, blacks, and Hispanics ends there.

The second most common occupational group among whites is managerial and professional specialty. Among blacks, service occupations rank second—such as police, waiters, and hairdressers. Among Hispanics, the second most common occupational group is the blue-collar category—operators, fabricators, and laborers. Whites are about twice as likely as blacks to have executive, administrative, or managerial jobs. Fifteen percent of whites hold these jobs, compared with 9 percent of blacks and 7 percent of Hispanics. Another 15 percent of white workers are in professional specialty jobs, such as teachers, nurses, or lawyers. Among blacks, the proportion in these positions is nearly 11 percent, while among Hispanics it is 7 percent.

◆ Although blacks and Hispanics lag behind whites in upper-level white-collar jobs, they are catching up. Blacks accounted for 7 percent of executives, administrators, and managers in 1995, up from 5 percent in 1983. Hispanics were 5 percent of all executives, administrators, and managers in 1995, up from 3 percent in 1983.

Workers by Occupation, Race, and Hispanic Origin, 1995

(total number and percent distribution of employed persons aged 16 or older in the civilian labor force, by occupation, race, and Hispanic origin, 1995; numbers in thousands)

	total	white	black	Hispanic
Total employed, number	124,900	106,490	13,279	11,127
Total employed, percent	100.0%	100.0%	100.0%	100.0%
Managerial and professional specialty	28.3	29.4	20.0	13.9
Executive, administrative, and managerial	13.8	14.5	9.3	7.4
Professional specialty	14.5	15.0	10.7	6.5
Technical, sales, and administrative support	30.0	30.2	28.7	24.4
Technicians and related support	3.1	3.2	2.8	2.2
Sales occupations	12.1	12.6	8.9	9.4
Administrative support, including clerical	14.7	14.5	16.9	12.9
Service occupations	13.6	12.4	21.7	19.7
Private household	0.7	0.6	1.0	1.8
Protective service	1.8	1.7	3.1	1.5
Service, except private household and protective	11.1	10.1	17.6	16.4
Precision production, craft, and repair	10.8	11.2	8.1	12.9
Operators, fabricators, and laborers	14.5	13.6	20.4	23.2
Machine operators, assemblers, and inspectors	6.3	5.8	9.2	11.2
Transportation and material moving occupations	4.1	4.0	5.7	4.6
Handlers, equipment cleaners, helpers, and laborers	4.0	3.8	5.5	7.3
Farming, forestry, and fishing	2.9	3.1	1.2	5.9

Note: Numbers will not add to total because Hispanics may be of any race and not all races are shown.
Source: Bureau of Labor Statistics, Employment and Earnings, *January 1996*

Black and Hispanic Workers by Occupation, 1983 and 1995

(blacks and Hispanics as a percent of total employed persons aged 16 or older in selected occupations, 1983 and 1995)

	black		Hispanic	
	1995	1983	1995	1983
TOTAL EMPLOYED	10.6%	9.3%	8.9%	5.3%
Managerial and professional specialty	7.5	5.6	4.4	2.6
Executive, administrative, and managerial	7.2	4.7	4.8	2.8
Public administration officials and administrators	13.6	8.3	4.7	3.8
Financial managers	6.3	3.5	5.7	3.1
Personnel and labor relations managers	15.8	4.9	3.4	2.6
Purchasing managers	6.6	5.1	3.1	1.4
Marketing, advertising, and public relations managers	2.2	2.7	3.3	1.7
Education and related fields administrators	11.2	11.3	4.7	2.4
Medicine and health managers	9.0	5.0	5.1	2.0
Properties and real estate managers	6.8	5.5	7.1	5.2
Professional specialty	7.8	6.4	4.0	2.5
Architects	2.5	1.6	5.8	1.5
Engineers	4.7	2.7	3.3	2.2
Mathematical and computer scientists	7.2	5.4	2.8	2.6
Natural scientists	3.9	2.6	2.6	2.1
Physicians	4.9	3.2	4.3	4.5
Dentists	1.9	2.4	2.6	1.0
Registered nurses	8.4	6.7	2.6	1.8
Pharmacists	4.3	3.8	1.8	2.6
Dietitians	18.4	21.0	7.5	3.7
Therapists	9.2	7.6	4.6	2.7
Teachers, college and university	6.2	4.4	3.6	1.8
Teachers, except college and university	9.3	9.1	4.4	2.7
Librarians, archivists, and curators	7.5	7.8	2.3	1.6
Economists	5.0	6.3	7.9	2.7
Psychologists	10.2	8.6	3.4	1.1
Social, recreation, and religious workers	16.8	12.1	6.4	3.8
Lawyers and judges	3.6	2.7	3.1	1.0
Writers, artists, entertainers, and athletes	6.2	4.8	4.8	2.9
Technical, sales, and administrative support	10.2	7.6	7.3	4.3
Health technologists and technicians	12.9	12.7	6.6	3.1
Engineering and related technologists and technicians	8.0	6.1	6.2	3.5

(continued)

(continued from previous page)

	black		Hispanic	
	1995	*1983*	*1995*	*1983*
Science technicians	8.9%	6.6%	7.3%	2.8%
Technicians, except health, engineering, and science	6.3	5.0	5.2	2.7
Airplane pilots and navigators	1.2	-	3.9	1.6
Computer programmers	6.5	4.4	4.8	2.1
Legal assistants	6.8	4.3	6.9	3.6
Sales occupations	7.8	4.7	6.9	3.7
Supervisors and proprietors	5.6	3.6	5.6	3.4
Finance and business services sales representatives	5.5	2.7	5.1	2.2
Commodities, except retail, sales representatives	2.7	2.1	4.9	2.2
Retail and personal services sales workers	11.4	6.7	8.9	4.8
Administrative support occupations, including clerical	12.2	9.6	7.8	5.0
Supervisors, administrative support	14.6	9.3	6.3	5.0
Computer equipment operators	15.5	12.5	8.9	6.0
Secretaries, stenographers, and typists	10.0	7.3	6.6	4.5
Information clerks	10.0	8.5	8.0	5.5
Records processing, except financial	15.4	13.9	7.7	4.8
Financial records processing	6.1	4.6	5.3	3.7
Service occupations	17.0	16.6	13.0	6.8
Private household	16.7	27.8	24.8	8.5
Firefighting and fire prevention	15.1	6.7	5.1	4.1
Police and detectives	16.9	13.1	7.4	4.0
Food preparation and service occupations	11.6	10.5	14.2	6.8
Health service occupations	27.6	23.5	8.4	4.8
Cleaning and building service occupations	21.9	24.4	19.0	9.2
Personal service occupations	13.5	11.1	8.8	6.0
Precision production, craft, and repair	7.9	6.8	10.6	6.2
Mechanics and repairers	8.3	6.8	8.3	5.3
Construction trades	7.1	6.6	11.4	6.0
Precision production occupations	8.8	7.3	12.3	7.4
Operators, fabricators, and laborers	15.0	14.0	14.3	8.3
Machine operators, assemblers, and inspectors	15.4	14.0	15.8	9.4
Transportation and material moving occupations	14.7	13.0	9.9	5.9
Truck drivers	12.6	12.3	10.4	5.7
Bus drivers	27.9	22.2	8.0	7.0
Taxicab drivers and chauffeurs	22.8	19.6	12.3	8.6
Handlers, equipment cleaners, helpers, and laborers	14.7	15.1	16.4	8.6
Farming, forestry, and fishing	4.2	7.5	18.1	8.2

Note: (-) means less than 0.5 percent.
Source: Bureau of Labor Statistics, Employment and Earnings, *January 1996*

Small Firms Offer Fewer Benefits

Small companies are less likely than large companies to offer health insurance, retirement plans, and paid vacations.

Sixty-six percent of small firms—defined by the Bureau of Labor Statistics as those with fewer than 100 workers—offer health insurance for their full-time employees. Among medium and large companies—those with 100 or more workers—82 percent offer health insurance. Fifty-six percent of medium and large companies have defined-benefit pension plans, compared with only 15 percent of small companies. And while virtually all big companies offer paid vacations, the proportion falls to 88 percent among small companies.

The only benefit found more frequently at small companies than larger ones are nonproduction bonuses. Forty-seven percent of small companies offer these, compared with 38 percent of medium and large companies. Smaller companies may offer bonuses to make up for the lack of other benefits.

◆ Because employee benefits are a large and growing expense for employers, the percentage of firms offering more than the basics is likely to shrink in the years ahead.

◆ Some benefits will become more common because they are relatively inexpensive to provide, including flexible benefit plans, unpaid family leave, eldercare, and childcare benefits.

Employee Benefits by Size of Firm, 1993-1994

(percent of full-time employees in private, nonfarm industries participating in selected employee benefit programs*; data for small firms are for 1994 and include those employing fewer than 100 workers; data for medium and large firms are for 1993 and include those employing 100 or more workers)

	medium and large firms	small firms
Paid		
Holidays	91%	82%
Vacations	97	88
Personal leave	21	13
Sick leave	65	50
Maternity leave	3	-
Paternity leave	1	-
Family leave	-	2
Unpaid		
Maternity leave	60	-
Paternity leave	53	-
Family leave	-	47
Insurance plans		
Medical insurance	82	66
Dental care	62	28
Vision care	26	10
Retirement plans		
Defined benefit pensions	56	15
Defined contribution	49	34
Other benefits		
Educational assistance	72	37
Recreation facilities	27	5
Nonproduction bonuses	38	47
Child care	7	1
Flexible benefits plans	12	3
Eldercare	31	33
Wellness programs	37	6

* Data are for benefits for which the employer pays part or all of the premium or expenses involved except unpaid parental and family leave.
Note: (-) means data not available.
Source: Bureau of Labor Statistics, Employee Benefits in Medium and Large Private Establishments, 1993, *Bulletin 2456; and* Employee Benefits in Small Private Establishments, 1994, *Bulletin 2475*

Men More Likely to Be Self-Employed

Nearly 9 million Americans, most of them men, were self-employed in 1995.

Of the 112 million Americans employed in nonagricultural industries, only 9 million are self-employed—or 8 percent. This figure underestimates the number of people who work for themselves because it excludes those with a business on the side if it is not their primary source of income. It also excludes any sole proprietorships that are incorporated.

Self-employment rises with age, from about 2 percent of workers under age 25 to one in four workers aged 65 or older. Many older self-employed workers are retired from a career and have started a business of their own to supplement their retirement income.

Men account for 61 percent of the self-employed. At every age, men are more likely to be self-employed than women.

♦ Self-employment is likely to become more common in the years ahead as the baby-boom generation ages, and as technology allows people to do more on their own.

Self-Employed Workers by Sex and Age, 1995

(total number of workers aged 16 or older employed in nonagricultural industries, number and percent who are self-employed, and percent distribution of self-employed by sex and age, 1995; numbers in thousands)

	total workers in nonagricultural industries	self-employed		
		number	percent of total workers	percent distribution
Total	112,448	8,902	7.9%	100.0%
Aged 16 to 19	6,024	108	1.8	1.2
Aged 20 to 24	11,846	267	2.3	3.0
Aged 25 to 34	29,877	1,718	5.8	19.3
Aged 35 to 44	30,699	2,697	8.8	30.3
Aged 45 to 54	21,585	2,209	10.2	24.8
Aged 55 to 64	9,758	1,262	12.9	14.2
Aged 65 or older	2,657	640	24.1	7.2
Men	59,332	5,461	9.2	100.0
Aged 16 to 19	3,005	57	1.9	1.0
Aged 20 to 24	6,239	155	2.5	2.8
Aged 25 to 34	16,137	1,002	6.2	18.3
Aged 35 to 44	16,170	1,658	10.3	30.4
Aged 45 to 54	11,205	1,364	12.2	25.0
Aged 55 to 64	5,177	804	15.5	14.7
Aged 65 or older	1,399	422	30.2	7.7
Women	53,115	3,440	6.5	100.0
Aged 16 to 19	3,019	51	1.7	1.5
Aged 20 to 24	5,607	112	2.0	3.3
Aged 25 to 34	13,740	716	5.2	20.8
Aged 35 to 44	14,529	1,039	7.2	30.2
Aged 45 to 54	10,381	846	8.1	24.6
Aged 55 to 64	4,581	458	10.0	13.3
Aged 65 or older	1,258	219	17.4	6.4

Source: Bureau of Labor Statistics, Employment and Earnings, *January 1996; calculations by New Strategist*

Twelve Million Alternative Workers

Ten percent of employed Americans aren't in traditional jobs.

In the first survey of what it terms "alternative" work arrangements, the Bureau of Labor Statistics finds one in ten workers in nontraditional jobs. Nontraditional workers are defined as independent contractors, on-call workers, workers for temporary-help agencies, or workers provided by contract firms. These workers are considered alternative because they are not employees of the organization for whom they perform their services, nor do they necessarily work standard schedules.

Two out of three alternative workers are independent contractors—freelancers, consultants, and others who obtain customers on their own for whom they provide a product or service. The likelihood of being an independent contractor increases with age, to a peak of 20 percent among working men aged 65 or older. The likelihood of being an on-call worker, such as a substitute teacher or construction worker, is greatest among the youngest and oldest workers. Temp work is also greatest among the young, while working for a contract firm varies little by age.

Most alternative workers—particularly independent contractors—are happy with their work arrangement, the survey finds.

◆ Although many people think the number of alternative workers is increasing, trend data to support this claim will not be available until the bureau again surveys alternative workers.

Workers in Alternative Work Arrangements by Sex and Age, 1995

(total number and percent of workers aged 16 or older employed in alternative work arrangements, by sex and age, 1995; numbers in thousands)

	total alternative workers	independent contractors	on-call workers	temporary-help agency workers	workers provided by contract firms
Total, number	12,110	8,309	1,968	1,181	652
Total, percent	9.8%	6.7%	1.6%	1.0%	0.5%
Aged 16 to 19	6.3	2.2	2.7	1.1	0.3
Aged 20 to 24	6.0	1.6	1.8	1.9	0.7
Aged 25 to 34	8.8	5.1	1.6	1.3	0.8
Aged 35 to 44	9.9	7.5	1.3	0.7	0.4
Aged 45 to 54	11.0	8.8	1.3	0.6	0.3
Aged 55 to 64	12.6	9.9	1.7	0.6	0.4
Aged 65 or older	20.8	15.7	3.7	0.6	0.8
Total men, percent	11.3	8.4	1.4	0.8	0.7
Aged 16 to 19	6.7	2.5	2.7	1.2	0.3
Aged 20 to 24	6.6	2.0	2.0	2.0	0.6
Aged 25 to 34	9.7	6.0	1.5	1.1	1.1
Aged 35 to 44	11.9	9.5	1.2	0.5	0.7
Aged 45 to 54	12.6	10.9	1.0	0.4	0.3
Aged 55 to 64	15.0	12.8	1.2	0.5	0.5
Aged 65 or older	25.0	19.7	3.4	0.6	1.3
Total women, percent	8.0	4.8	1.8	1.1	0.3
Aged 16 to 19	5.8	1.9	2.7	1.0	0.2
Aged 20 to 24	5.1	1.1	1.6	1.7	0.7
Aged 25 to 34	7.6	4.1	1.7	1.4	0.4
Aged 35 to 44	7.8	5.1	1.5	1.0	0.2
Aged 45 to 54	9.1	6.3	1.6	0.8	0.4
Aged 55 to 64	9.6	6.5	2.2	0.7	0.2
Aged 65 or older	15.0	10.1	4.3	0.6	-

Note: Independent contractors are wage and salary workers who obtain customers on their own to provide a product or service. On-call workers are in a pool of workers who are called to work only as needed, such as substitute teachers and construction workers supplied by a union hiring hall. Temporary help agency workers are those who said they are paid by a temporary help agency. Workers provided by contract firms are those employed by a company that provides employees or their services to others under contract, such as security, landscaping and computer programming.
Source: Bureau of Labor Statistics, Monthly Labor Review, *October 1996*

Many Students Juggle School and Work

Millions of students aged 16 to 24 have more than homework to do after classes.

Fifty percent of students aged 16 to 24 have jobs. Forty-one percent of high school students and 59 percent of college students hold jobs. Most working students have part-time jobs, but 12 percent of younger students and one-third of older ones work full-time. Labor force participation rates are similar for both men and women.

The students most likely to work, and to work full-time, are those attending college part-time. Fully 86 percent of part-time college students work, with 59 percent of workers holding full-time jobs. Fifty-three percent of students attending college full-time work, but only 19 percent of the workers have full-time jobs.

◆ With college expenses rising faster than the cost of living, a growing number of students will be juggling classes and jobs.

Employment by School Enrollment Status, 1995

(employment status of the civilian noninstitutional population aged 16 to 24 enrolled in school by sex, age, and enrollment level, 1995; number in thousands)

	total enrolled	civilian labor force		full-time		part-time	
		total	percent of population	number	percent	number	percent
Total, aged 16 to 24	14,298	7,097	49.6%	1,505	21.2%	5,593	78.8%
Aged 16 to 19	9,499	4,199	44.2	510	12.1	3,689	87.9
Aged 20 to 24	4,799	2,898	60.4	995	34.3	1,903	65.7
High school	7,307	2,987	40.9	280	9.4	2,708	90.7
College	6,991	4,110	58.8	1,225	29.8	2,885	70.2
Full-time students	5,724	3,022	52.8	582	19.3	2,439	80.7
Part-time students	1,267	1,088	85.9	643	59.1	445	40.9
Men, aged 16 to 24	7,127	3,465	48.6	817	23.6	2,648	76.4
Aged 16 to 19	4,836	2,087	43.2	290	13.9	1,797	86.1
Aged 20 to 24	2,291	1,378	60.1	527	38.2	851	61.8
High school	3,859	1,565	40.6	171	10.9	1,393	89.0
College	3,268	1,900	58.1	646	34.0	1,255	66.1
Full-time students	2,704	1,400	51.8	328	23.4	1,072	76.6
Part-time students	564	500	88.7	317	63.4	182	36.4
Women, aged 16 to 24	7,171	3,632	50.7	687	18.9	2,945	81.1
Aged 16 to 19	4,662	2,112	45.3	220	10.4	1,891	89.5
Aged 20 to 24	2,508	1,521	60.6	468	30.8	1,054	69.3
High school	3,448	1,422	41.2	107	7.5	1,314	92.4
College	3,723	2,210	59.4	580	26.2	1,631	73.8
Full-time students	3,019	1,622	53.7	254	15.7	1,368	84.3
Part-time students	703	589	83.7	326	55.3	263	44.7

Note: The unemployed are distributed under full- or part-time work depending on whether they are looking for full- or part-time work. Part-time employment is less than 35 hours per week. The civilian labor force equals the number employed plus the number unemployed. The civilian population equals the number in the labor force plus the number not in the labor force.
Source: Bureau of Labor Statistics, Employment and Earnings, *January 1996*

Many Working Americans Are Disabled

Only one in three disabled Americans aged 16 or older is in the labor force.

Among the 17 million Americans with a work disability, only 32 percent are in the labor force. Of these disabled workers, 18 percent work full-time.

The Census Bureau collects data on work disability by asking people whether they have a condition that limits the kind or amount of work they can do at a job. Those with work disabilities may be limited in the work they can do, or they may be unable to work at all. Among disabled men, 35 percent are in the labor force and 22 percent are full-time workers. Among disabled women, 29 percent are in the labor force and 14 percent work full-time.

With increasing age, the labor force participation rates of disabled Americans drop. Among disabled men and women, those most likely to work are aged 25 to 34—46 percent of men and 39 percent of women.

♦ As the enormous baby-boom generation ages, the number of Americans with work disabilities will grow, even if the proportion who have disabilities remains the same. Businesses not already serving and hiring the disabled should prepare to do so or face legal action.

Employment Status of Persons with a Work Disability, 1996

(number of persons aged 16 to 64 with a work disability, percent in labor force, and percent employed full-time, by sex and age, 1996; numbers in thousands)

	number	in labor force	employed full-time
Total	17,016	31.8%	17.7%
Aged 16 to 24	1,371	41.4	13.8
Aged 25 to 34	2,567	42.2	22.8
Aged 35 to 44	4,065	37.8	22.7
Aged 45 to 54	4,162	32.2	19.9
Aged 55 to 64	4,851	18.3	9.8
Men	8,164	35.3	21.7
Aged 16 to 24	672	44.3	14.6
Aged 25 to 34	1,160	46.2	27.3
Aged 35 to 44	2,013	41.4	26.6
Aged 45 to 54	2,054	35.6	25.9
Aged 55 to 64	2,266	21.4	12.9
Women	8,852	28.6	13.9
Aged 16 to 24	699	38.6	13.0
Aged 25 to 34	1,408	39.0	19.1
Aged 35 to 44	2,053	34.2	18.9
Aged 45 to 54	2,107	28.9	14.1
Aged 55 to 64	2,585	15.7	7.2

Source: Bureau of the Census, Internet web site, http://www.census.gov

Early Retirement Trend to End

The labor force participation rate of men aged 55 to 64 will rise between 1994 and 2005, ending the early retirement trend.

Among men aged 55 to 64, labor force paticipation rates will rise from 65.5 to 65.6 percent between 1994 and 2005, according to projections by the Bureau of Labor Statistics. The implications of this tiny rise are far larger than its fractional increase, because it means the decades-old trend toward ever-earlier retirement has come to an end. With the nation's businesses trimming costs, generous early retirement incentives will no longer be available to older workers—keeping many on the job longer.

Labor force participation rates among women will continue to rise in all but the youngest age group during the next few years. Rates are projected to decline among women under age 20 as more become full-time college students.

The number of older workers is projected to expand sharply because the baby-boom generation is now entering its 50s. The number of working women aged 45 to 54 should rise by 50 percent between 1994 and 2005, while the number aged 55 to 64 should rise by 63 percent. Among working men, the number aged 45 to 54 should increase by 36 percent, while the number in the 55-to-64 age group will grow by 43 percent.

♦ Although some people claim women will return to the home, a reversal in women's labor force participation rates is not likely. As their children grow up, baby-boom women will gain a renewed interest in their careers, driving labor force participation rates up.

Labor Force Projections by Sex and Age, 1994 to 2005

(number of persons aged 16 or older in the civilian labor force, percent change in number, and labor force participation rates, by sex and age, 1994 and 2005; numbers in thousands)

	1994	2005	percent change 1994-2005	participation rate 1994	participation rate 2005
Total	131,056	147,106	12.2%	66.6%	67.1%
Total men	70,817	76,842	8.5	75.1	72.9
Aged 16 to 19	3,896	4,457	14.4	54.1	52.0
Aged 20 to 24	7,540	8,167	8.3	83.1	81.9
Aged 25 to 34	18,854	16,279	-13.7	92.6	91.5
Aged 35 to 44	18,966	18,787	-0.9	92.8	91.4
Aged 45 to 54	12,962	17,616	35.9	89.1	87.7
Aged 55 to 64	6,423	9,150	42.5	65.5	65.6
Aged 65 or older	2,177	2,386	9.6	16.9	16.5
Total women	60,239	70,263	16.6	58.8	61.7
Aged 16 to 19	3,585	4,211	17.5	51.3	50.7
Aged 20 to 24	6,592	7,149	8.5	71.0	70.7
Aged 25 to 34	15,499	14,186	-8.5	74.0	76.4
Aged 35 to 44	16,259	17,078	5.0	77.1	80.0
Aged 45 to 54	11,357	17,070	50.3	74.6	80.7
Aged 55 to 64	5,289	8,613	62.8	48.9	56.6
Aged 65 or older	1,658	1,956	18.0	9.2	10.2

Source: Bureau of Labor Statistics, Monthly Labor Review, *November 1995*

Workers to Become More Diverse

Non-Hispanic white men will decline as a proportion of all workers.

By 2005, non-Hispanic white men will account for only 38 percent of workers, down from 41 percent in 1994, according to projections by the Bureau of Labor Statistics. As older workers retire, nearly half of those leaving the labor force between 1994 and 2005 will be non-Hispanic white men.

Overall, just 33 percent of workers entering the labor force between 1994 and 2005 will be non-Hispanic white men. Twelve percent will be non-Hispanic blacks, 16 percent will be Hispanics, and 6 percent will be Asians. Thirty-three percent of new workers will be non-Hispanic white women.

Women will account for 48 percent of the white and black labor force by 2005, and for 46 percent of Asian workers. Among Hispanics, only 40 percent of workers will be women in 2005 because Hispanic women are less likely to work than other women.

♦ Businesses that have not already done so need to prepare for a diverse workplace. Especially important will be recruiting and retaining women and minority workers.

Workers Entering and Leaving the Labor Force, 1994 to 2005

(number of persons aged 16 or older in the civilian labor force and number to enter and leave, by race, Hispanic origin, and sex, 1994 and 2005; numbers in thousands)

	total labor force, 1994	entrants 1994-2005	leavers 1994-2005	total labor force, 2005
TOTAL, NUMBER	131,051	39,343	23,289	147,106
Men	70,814	19,720	13,691	76,842
Women	60,238	19,624	9,598	70,263
White, non-Hispanic	100,463	26,058	18,177	108,345
Men	54,306	12,937	10,814	56,429
Women	46,157	13,122	7,363	51,916
Black, non-Hispanic	14,304	4,871	2,783	16,392
Men	6,981	2,314	1,512	7,783
Women	7,323	2,557	1,271	8,609
Hispanic	11,974	6,085	1,729	16,330
Men	7,210	3,321	1,039	9,492
Women	4,764	2,765	690	6,838
Asian and other, non-Hispanic	4,310	2,329	600	6,039
Men	2,317	1,148	326	3,139
Women	1,994	1,180	274	2,900
TOTAL, PERCENT	100.0%	100.0%	100.0%	100.0%
Men	54.0	50.1	58.8	52.2
Women	46.0	49.9	41.2	47.8
White, non-Hispanic	76.7	66.2	78.0	73.7
Men	41.4	32.9	46.4	38.4
Women	35.2	33.4	31.6	35.3
Black, non-Hispanic	10.9	12.4	12.0	11.1
Men	5.3	5.9	6.5	5.3
Women	5.6	6.5	5.5	5.9
Hispanic	9.1	15.5	7.4	11.1
Men	5.5	8.4	4.5	6.5
Women	3.6	7.0	3.0	4.6
Asian and other, non-Hispanic	3.3	5.9	2.6	4.1
Men	1.8	2.9	1.4	2.1
Women	1.5	3.0	1.2	2.0

Source: Bureau of Labor Statistics, Monthly Labor Review, *November 1995*

Health Care to Post Big Job Gains

Health care jobs account for six of the ten occupations projected to grow the fastest between 1994 and 2005.

The aging population will boost demand for health care workers. The occupation projected to grow the fastest is home health aides—up by 119 percent between 1994 and 2005.

A look at the occupations projected to grow or decline the fastest reveals the story of our economy. Most fast-growing occupations are in businesses now expanding rapidly, such as computing, law, crime prevention, and entertainment. In contrast, many of the occupations projected to lose jobs are in sectors of the economy being transformed by technology or losing out to global competition, such as mainframe computing, farming, and the telephone industry.

The occupations expected to gain the most jobs between 1994 and 2005 tell a different story. Most are low-paying service jobs—cashiers, janitors, retail salespersons, office clerks, nursing aides, and waiters. The United States needs an enormous number of support workers to run efficiently.

♦ One problem for the future service economy is how to fill the many low-paying service jobs that will go begging for workers. One potential source of workers is immigration.

Fastest-Growing Occupations, 1994 to 2005

(number of persons aged 16 or older employed in occupations with the largest projected percent increase in employment, 1994-2005; numerical and percent change in employment, 1994-2005; ranked by percent change; numbers in thousands)

	1994	2005	change, 1994-2005 number	change, 1994-2005 percent
Personal and home care aides	179	391	212	119%
Home health aides	420	848	428	102
Systems analysts	483	928	445	92
Computer engineers	195	372	177	90
Physical and corrective therapy assistants	78	142	64	83
Electronic pagination systems workers	18	33	15	83
Occupational therapy assistants and aides	16	29	13	82
Physical therapists	102	183	81	80
Residential counselors	165	290	125	76
Human services workers	168	293	125	75
Occupational therapists	54	93	39	72
Manicurists	38	64	26	69
Medical assistants	206	327	121	59
Paralegals	110	175	64	58
Medical records technicians	81	126	45	56
Teachers, special education	388	593	206	53
Amusement and recreation attendants	267	406	139	52
Correction officers	310	468	158	51
Operations research analysts	44	67	22	50
Guards	867	1282	415	48
Speech-language pathologists and audiologists	85	125	39	46
Detectives, except public	55	79	24	44
Surgical technologists	46	65	19	43
Dental hygienists	127	180	53	42
Dental assistants	190	269	79	42
Adjustment clerks	373	521	148	40
Teacher aides and educational assistants	932	1296	364	39
Data processing equipment repairers	75	104	29	38
Nursery and greenhouse managers	19	26	7	37
Securities and financial services sales workers	246	335	90	37

Source: Bureau of Labor Statistics, Monthly Labor Review, *November 1995*

Occupations with Largest Job Growth, 1994 to 2005

(number of persons aged 16 or older employed in occupations with the largest projected job gains, 1994-2005; numerical and percent change in employment, 1994-2005; ranked by numerical change; numbers in thousands)

	1994	2005	change, 1994-2005	
			number	percent
Cashiers	3,005	3,567	562	19%
Janitors and cleaners, including maids	3,043	3,602	559	18
Salespersons, retail	3,842	4,374	532	14
Waiters and waitresses	1,847	2,326	479	26
Registered nurses	1,906	2,379	473	25
General manager and top executives	3,046	3,512	466	15
System analysts	483	928	445	92
Home health aides	420	848	428	102
Guards	867	1,282	415	48
Nursing aides, orderlies, and attendants	1,265	1,652	387	31
Teachers, secondary school	1,340	1,726	386	29
Marketing and sales worker supervisors	2,293	2,673	380	17
Teacher aides and educational assistants	932	1,296	364	39
Receptionists and information clerks	1,019	1,337	318	31
Truck drivers, light and heavy	2,565	2,837	271	11
Secretaries, except legal and medical	2,842	3,109	267	9
Clerical supervisors and managers	1,340	1,600	261	19
Child-care workers	757	1,005	248	33
Maintenance repairers, general utility	1,273	1,505	231	18
Teachers, elementary	1,419	1,639	220	16
Personal and home care aides	179	391	212	119
Teachers, special education	388	593	206	53
Licensed practical nurses	702	899	197	28
Food service and lodging managers	579	771	192	33
Food preparation workers	1,190	1,378	187	16
Social workers	557	744	187	34
Lawyers	656	839	183	28
Financial managers	768	950	182	24
Computer engineers	195	372	177	90
Hand packers and packagers	942	1,102	160	17

Source: Bureau of Labor Statistics, Monthly Labor Review, *November 1995*

Occupations with Largest Job Losses, 1994 to 2005

(number of persons aged 16 or older employed in occupations with the largest projected job losses, 1994-2005; numerical and percent change in employment, 1994-2005; ranked by numerical loss; numbers in thousands)

	1994	2005	change, 1994-2005	
			number	percent
Farmers	1,276	1,003	-273	-21%
Typists and word processors	646	434	-212	-33
Bookkeeping, accounting, and auditing clerks	2,181	2,003	-178	-8
Bank tellers	559	407	-152	-27
Sewing machine operators, garment	531	391	-140	-26
Cleaners and servants, private household	496	387	-108	-22
Computer operators, except peripheral equipment	259	162	-98	-38
Billing, posting, and calculating machine operators	96	32	-64	-67
Duplicating, mail, and other office machine operators	222	166	-56	-25
Textile draw-out and winding machine operators	190	143	-47	-25
File clerks	278	236	-42	-15
Freight, stock, and material movers	765	728	-36	-5
Farm workers	906	870	-36	-4
Machine tool cutting operators & tenders, metal/plastic	119	85	-34	-29
Central office operators	48	14	-34	-70
Central office and PBX installers and repairers	84	51	-33	-39
Electrical and electronic assemblers	212	182	-30	-14
Station installers and repairers, telephone	37	11	-26	-70
Personnel clerks, except payroll and timekeeping	123	98	-26	-21
Data entry keyers, except composing	395	370	-25	-6
Bartenders	373	347	-25	-7
Inspectors, testers, and graders, precision	654	629	-25	-4
Directory assistance operators	33	10	-24	-70
Lathe, turning machine tool setters, metal/plastic	71	50	-22	-31
Custom tailors and sewers	84	63	-21	-25
Machine feeders and offbearers	262	242	-20	-8
Machinists	369	349	-20	-5
Service station attendants	167	148	-20	-12
Machine forming operators & tenders, metal/plastic	171	151	-19	-11
Communication, transportation, utilities ops. mgrs.	154	135	-19	-12

Source: Bureau of Labor Statistics, Monthly Labor Review, *November 1995*

Service Growth, Manufacturing Decline

By 2005, more than 74 percent of all jobs will be in service-producing industries.

The number of jobs in service-producing industries will expand by 20 percent between 1994 and 2005. According to the Bureau of Labor Statistics, the service industries projected to grow the fastest include health services, residential care, computer services, social services, and business services.

In contrast, goods-producing jobs are projected to decline by 4 percent between 1994 and 2005, accounting for fewer than 16 percent of all jobs by the year 2005. Manufacturing employment is projected to fall by 7 percent. The industries that will decline the most are those losing out to foreign competition and those in which automation is replacing human labor.

♦ These projections are based on current trends. Unforeseen technological break-throughs or major new government programs could shift growth from one industry to another in the next decade.

Employment by Industry, 1994 and 2005

(number and percent distribution of persons aged 16 or older employed by major industry division, 1994 and 2005; percent change in employment and percentage point change in distribution, 1994-2005; numbers in thousands)

	1994	2005	percent change 1994-2005
Total number	127,014	144,708	13.9%
Nonfarm wage and salary employment	113,340	130,185	14.9
Goods-producing	23,914	22,930	-4.1
Mining	601	439	-27.0
Construction	5,010	5,500	9.8
Manufacturing	18,304	16,991	-7.2
Durable	10,431	9,290	-10.9
Nondurable	7,873	7,700	-2.2
Service-producing	89,425	107,256	19.9
Transportation, communications, utilities	6,006	6,431	7.1
Wholesale trade	6,140	6,559	6.8
Retail trade	20,438	23,094	13.0
Finance, insurance, and real estate	6,933	7,373	6.3
Services	30,792	42,810	39.0
Government	19,117	20,990	9.8
Agriculture	3,623	3,399	-6.2
Private household wage and salary	966	800	-17.2
Nonagricultural self-employed, unpaid family workers	9,085	10,324	13.6

	1994	2005	percentage point change 1994-2005
Total percent	100.0%	100.0%	–
Nonfarm wage and salary employment	89.2	90.0	0.8
Goods-producing	18.8	15.8	-3.0
Mining	0.5	0.3	-0.2
Construction	3.9	3.8	-0.1
Manufacturing	14.4	11.7	-2.7
Durable	8.2	6.4	-1.8
Nondurable	6.2	5.3	-0.9
Service-producing	70.4	74.1	3.7
Transportation, communications, utilities	4.7	4.4	-0.3
Wholesale trade	4.8	4.5	-0.3
Retail trade	16.1	16.0	-0.1

(continued)

(continued from previous page)

	1994	2005	percentage point change 1994-2005
Finance, insurance, and real estate	5.5%	5.1%	-0.4
Services	24.2	29.6	5.4
Government	15.1	14.5	-0.6
Agriculture	2.9	2.3	-0.6
Private household wage and salary	0.8	0.6	-0.2
Nonagricultural self-employed, unpaid family workers	7.2	7.1	-0.1

Note: Total employment here is lower than in other tables because it does not include workers in some agricultural services or in nonclassified establishments.
Source: Bureau of Labor Statistics, Monthly Labor Review, *November 1995; calculations by New Strategist*

Fastest-Growing Industries, 1994 to 2005

(number of persons aged 16 or older employed in the 15 industries projected to grow the fastest, 1994-2005; numerical and average annual percent change in employment, 1994-2005; ranked by average annual percent change; numbers in thousands)

	1994	2005	change 1994-2005	average annual percent change 1994-2005
Health services	1,032	1,900	868	5.7%
Residential care	602	1,100	498	5.6
Computer and data processing services	950	1,611	661	4.9
Individual and miscellaneous social services	779	1,314	536	4.9
Micellaneous business services	1,741	2,932	1,191	4.9
Personnel supply services	2,254	3,564	1,310	4.3
Child daycare services	502	800	298	4.3
Services to buildings	855	1,350	496	4.2
Miscellaneous equipment rental and leasing	216	325	110	3.8
Management and public relations	716	1,049	333	3.5
Nursing and personal care facilities	1,649	2,400	751	3.5
Amusement and recreation services	1,005	1,434	429	3.3
Job training and related services	298	425	127	3.3
Museums, botanical, zoological gardens	79	112	33	3.2
Water and sanitation	213	300	87	3.2

Source: Bureau of Labor Statistics, Monthly Labor Review, *November 1995*

Fastest-Declining Industries, 1994 to 2005

(number of persons aged 16 or older employed in the 15 industries projected to decline the fastest, 1994-2005; numerical and average annual percent change in employment, 1994-2005; ranked by average annual percent loss; numbers in thousands)

	1994	2005	change 1994-2005	average annual percent change 1994-2005
Footwear, except rubber and plastic	61	29	-32	-6.7%
Watches, clocks, and parts	8	5	-4	-5.3
Coal mining	112	70	-43	-4.3
Household audio and video equipment	89	55	-34	-4.2
Tobacco products	42	26	-16	-4.2
Crude petroleum, natural gas, and gas liquids	168	105	-63	-4.2
Metal cans and shipping containers	42	27	-15	-3.9
Blast furnaces and basic steel products	239	155	-84	-3.9
Luggage, handbags, and leather products	53	37	-16	-3.3
Cutlery, hand tools, and hardware	129	90	-39	-3.2
Apparel	755	547	-208	-2.9
Search and navigation equipment	180	132	-48	-2.8
Iron and steel foundries	125	92	-33	-2.7
Electrical industrial apparatus	156	116	-40	-2.7
Beverages	178	132	-46	-2.7

Source: Bureau of Labor Statistics, Monthly Labor Review, *November 1995*

5

Living Arrangement Trends

♦ **Between 1995 and 2005, the number of couples with children should fall by 5 percent.**
In the next decade, the number of married couples with children is projected to decline by over 1 million as the children of boomers grow up and leave home.

♦ **Between 1995 and 2005, households headed by 45-to-54-year-olds are projected to grow by 42 percent—faster than any other age group.**
As the number of older householders expands, consumer spending should rise at a healthy clip because householders in their 40s and 50s spend more than all other age groups.

♦ **Fifty-seven percent of American households are home to only one or two people.**
Overall, 2.65 people lived in the average U.S. household in 1995.

♦ **Fifty-two percent of black children live only with their mother, while just 33 percent live with both parents.**
An increasing proportion of all children—black, white, and Hispanic—live only with their mothers, and a shrinking proportion live with two parents.

♦ **Fifty-three percent of the nation's 18-to-24-year-olds still live with their parents.**
Entry-level wages have fallen sharply over the past 15 years, forcing young adults to live with their parents until they can afford independence.

♦ **More than 5 million American households are headed by unmarried couples.**
Two out of three cohabiting couples are heterosexual partners, while about one-third are same-sex couples.

♦ **Men are more likely than women to be married—59 compared with 56 percent in 1995.**
Men are also more likely to be never-married than women—31 compared with 24 percent.

Married Couples with Children Will Decline

Between 1995 and 2005, the number of couples with children should fall by 5 percent.

After years of decline, the number of married couples with children rose in the first half of the 1990s as the baby-boom generation had children. The 3 percent gain in the number of couples with children was outpaced by growth in other household types, however. The number of female- and male-headed families increased by 12 percent, while the number of nonfamily households grew by 9 percent.

In the next decade, the number of married couples with children is projected to decline by over 1 million as the children of boomers grow up and leave home. The number of single-parent families headed by women is also projected to decline between 1995 and 2005. But the number of couples without children at home is projected to climb by 17 percent—or by nearly 5 million households—as boomers become empty-nesters.

◆ The number of people who live alone is projected to grow rapidly between 1995 and 2005. The proportion of households headed by people living alone will surpass the share headed by couples with children by 2005. Once boomers enter old age after 2011, single-person households could become the most common household type in the United States.

Households by Type, 1990 and 1995

(number and percent distribution of households by household type, 1990 and 1995; percent change 1990-1995; numbers in thousands)

| | 1995 | | 1990 | | percent change |
	number	percent	number	percent	1990-95
Total	98,990	100.0%	93,347	100.0%	6.0%
Family households	69,305	70.0	66,090	70.8	4.9
Married couples	53,858	54.4	52,317	56.0	2.9
With children <18	25,241	25.5	24,537	26.3	2.9
Without children <18	28,617	28.9	27,780	29.8	3.0
Female householder,					
no spouse present	12,220	12.3	10,890	11.7	12.2
With children <18	7,615	7.7	6,599	7.1	15.4
Without children <18	4,606	4.7	4,291	4.6	7.3
Male householder,					
no spouse present	3,226	3.3	2,884	3.1	11.9
With children <18	1,440	1.5	1,153	1.2	24.9
Without children <18	1,786	1.8	1,731	1.9	3.2
Nonfamily households	29,686	30.0	27,257	29.2	8.9
Female householder	16,496	16.7	15,651	16.8	5.4
Living alone	14,592	14.7	13,950	14.9	4.6
Male householder	13,190	13.3	11,606	12.4	13.6
Living alone	10,140	10.2	9,049	9.7	12.1

Source: Bureau of the Census, Internet web site, http://www.census.gov; *calculations by New Strategist*

Households by Type, 1995 to 2005

(number and percent distribution of households by household type, 1995 to 2005; percent change 1995-2005; numbers in thousands)

	1995		2000		2005		percent change 1995-2005
	number	*percent*	*number*	*percent*	*number*	*percent*	
Total	98,990	100.0%	103,246	100.0%	108,819	100.0%	9.9%
Family households	69,305	70.0	71,669	69.4	74,733	68.7	7.8
Married couples	53,858	54.4	55,496	53.8	57,371	52.7	6.5
With children <18	25,241	25.5	24,686	23.9	23,958	22.0	-5.1
Without children <18	28,617	28.9	30,810	29.8	33,413	30.7	16.8
Female householder,							
no spouse present	12,220	12.3	12,272	11.9	13,084	12.0	7.1
With children <18	7,615	7.7	6,737	6.5	6,944	6.4	-8.8
Without children <18	4,606	4.7	5,535	5.4	6,140	5.6	33.3
Male householder,							
no spouse present	3,226	3.3	3,901	3.8	4,278	3.9	32.6
With children <18	1,440	1.5	1,694	1.6	1,797	1.7	24.8
Without children <18	1,786	1.8	2,207	2.1	2,481	2.3	38.9
Nonfamily households	29,686	30.0	31,577	30.6	34,085	31.3	14.8
Female householder	16,496	16.7	17,095	16.6	18,301	16.8	10.9
Living alone	14,592	14.7	15,035	14.6	16,093	14.8	10.3
Male householder	13,190	13.3	14,482	14.0	15,784	14.5	19.7
Living alone	10,140	10.2	11,195	10.8	12,244	11.3	20.7

Source: Bureau of the Census, Internet web site, http://www.census.gov; *calculations by New Strategist*

Households Headed by 55-to-64-Year-Olds to Grow Fastest

Householders aged 55 to 64 are projected to increase 42 percent between 1995 and 2005.

Between 1990 and 1995, households headed by 45-to-54-year-olds grew by 22 percent, much faster than the 6 percent gain for all households. Behind this rapid growth was the aging of the baby-boom generation into its late 40s and early 50s. As boomers enter their late 50s during the next ten years, households headed by 55-to-64-year-olds will grow more than any other, with a gain of over 5 million.

During the first half of the 1990s, the number of households headed by 25-to-34-year-olds fell by 5 percent as the small baby-bust generation (or Generation X) entered this age group. Between 1995 and 2005, the number of householders in this age group should continue to drop, falling by nearly 3 million.

◆ As the number of older householders expands, consumer spending should rise at a healthy clip. Householders in their 40s and 50s spend far more money than those younger or older.

◆ The number of households headed by the elderly will grow slowly during the next ten years because the small generation born during the Depression is in its 60s and 70s.

Households by Age of Householder, 1990 to 1995

(number of households by age of householder, 1990 to 1995; percent change 1990-95; numbers in thousands)

	1995	1990	percent change 1990-95
Total	98,990	93,347	6.0%
Under age 25	5,444	5,121	6.3
Aged 25 to 34	19,452	20,472	-5.0
Aged 35 to 44	22,914	20,554	11.5
Aged 45 to 54	17,590	14,415	22.0
Aged 55 to 64	12,224	12,529	-2.4
Aged 65 or older	21,365	20,156	6.0

Source: Bureau of the Census, Household and Family Characteristics: March 1995, *Current Population Reports, P20-488, 1996; and Internet web site,* http://www.census.gov; *calculations by New Strategist*

Households by Age of Householder, 1995 to 2005

(number of households by age of householder, 1995 to 2005; percent change 1995-2005; numbers thousands)

	1995	2000	2005	percent change 1995-2005
Total	98,990	103,246	108,819	9.9%
Under age 25	5,444	4,966	5,399	-0.8
Aged 25 to 34	19,452	17,045	16,547	-14.9
Aged 35 to 44	22,914	23,914	22,560	-1.5
Aged 45 to 54	17,590	21,210	23,924	36.0
Aged 55 to 64	12,224	14,002	17,331	41.8
Aged 65 or older	21,365	22,109	23,059	7.9

Source: Bureau of the Census, Household and Family Characteristics: March 1995, *Current Population Reports, P20-488, 1996; and* Projections of the Number of Households and Families in the United States: 1995 to 2010, *Current Population Reports, P25-1129, 1996; calculations by New Strategist*

Married Couples Peak in 45-to-54 Age Group

Sixty-three percent of households headed by 45-to-54-year-olds are married couples.

A majority of households headed by people aged 25 to 64 are married couples. Only in the youngest and oldest age groups do couples account for fewer than half of households.

Among young adults, 21 percent of households are female-headed families, while 43 percent are nonfamily households—most of them men and women who live with nonrelatives. Among householders aged 65 or older, 35 percent are women who live alone.

The married-couple share of households is above 60 percent in the 35-to-64 age group. Female-headed families are a substantial 15 percent of households in the 25-to-44 age group, due to the propensity of boomers and younger adults to divorce. Nonfamily households fall to a low of 20 percent in the 35-to-44 age group. Householders aged 35 to 44 are less likely to live alone than those in any other age group.

◆ With the baby-boom generation entering the age group most likely to be married, family values will remain a hot topic for years to come.

Households by Type and Age of Householder, 1995

(number and percent distribution of households by household type and age of householder, 1995; numbers in thousands)

	total	under 25	25 to 34	35 to 44	45 to 54	55 to 64	65 or older
Total number	98,990	5,444	19,452	22,914	17,590	12,224	21,365
Family households	69,305	3,079	14,077	18,273	13,746	8,894	11,237
Married couples	53,858	1,632	10,316	13,919	11,153	7,552	9,286
Female householder, no spouse present	12,220	1,124	2,965	3,502	2,037	1,056	1,536
Male householder, no spouse present	3,226	323	796	852	556	285	414
Nonfamily households	29,686	2,365	5,376	4,641	3,845	3,330	10,128
Female householder	16,496	1,107	2,031	1,713	1,896	2,008	7,741
Living alone	14,592	573	1,440	1,400	1,756	1,852	7,534
Male householder	13,190	1,258	3,345	2,928	1,949	1,322	2,388
Living alone	10,140	623	2,213	2,263	1,650	1,137	2,253
Total percent	100.0%	100.0%	100.0%	100.0%	100.0%	100.0%	100.0%
Family households	70.0	56.6	72.4	79.7	78.1	72.8	52.6
Married couples	54.4	30.0	53.0	60.7	63.4	61.8	43.5
Female householder, no spouse present	12.3	20.6	15.2	15.3	11.6	8.6	7.2
Male householder, no spouse present	3.3	5.9	4.1	3.7	3.2	2.3	1.9
Nonfamily households	30.0	43.4	27.6	20.3	21.9	27.2	47.4
Female householder	16.7	20.3	10.4	7.5	10.8	16.4	36.2
Living alone	14.7	10.5	7.4	6.1	10.0	15.2	35.3
Male householder	13.3	23.1	17.2	12.8	11.1	10.8	11.2
Living alone	10.2	11.4	11.4	9.9	9.4	9.3	10.5

Source: Bureau of the Census, Internet web site, http://www.census.gov; *and unpublished tables from the 1995 Current Population Survey; calculations by New Strategist*

Stark Differences Between Black, White, and Hispanic Households

Married couples represent over half of white households, but just one-third of households headed by blacks.

One in five black households is a single-parent family headed by a woman. Only 6 percent of white households are female-headed single-parent families. The proportion among Hispanics is 13.5 percent.

For whites, married couples without children at home outnumber those with children. But among Hispanics, couples with children far outnumber those without. Nuclear families account for a larger share of Hispanic than white households because Hispanics are, on average, younger than whites and are more likely to be in their child-rearing years.

Hispanics are far less likely to live in nonfamily households than either whites or blacks. Only 8 percent of Hispanic women live alone, far below the 15 percent share among whites and blacks.

◆ Many black families are headed by women because black men have difficulty getting jobs that pay enough to support a family. The same trend is now affecting white men and could boost the proportion of white families headed by women in the future.

Households by Type, Race, and Hispanic Origin of Householder, 1995

(number and percent distribution of households by household type, race, and Hispanic origin of householder, 1995; numbers in thousands)

	total		white		black		Hispanic	
	number	*percent*	*number*	*percent*	*number*	*percent*	*number*	*percent*
Total	98,990	100.0%	83,737	100.0%	11,655	100.0%	7,735	100.0%
Family households	69,305	70.0	58,437	69.8	8,093	69.4	6,200	80.2
Married couples, total	53,858	54.4	47,899	57.2	3,842	33.0	4,235	54.8
With children <18	25,241	25.5	22,005	26.3	1,926	16.5	2,743	35.5
Without children <18	28,617	28.9	25,894	30.9	1,916	16.4	1,492	19.3
Female householder,								
no spouse present	12,220	12.3	8,031	9.6	3,716	31.9	1,485	19.2
With children <18	7,615	7.7	4,841	5.8	2,489	21.4	1,048	13.5
Without children <18	4,606	4.7	3,191	3.8	1,227	10.5	437	5.6
Male householder,								
no spouse present	3,226	3.3	2,507	3.0	536	4.6	479	6.2
With children <18	1,440	1.5	1,105	1.3	267	2.3	192	2.5
Without children <18	1,786	1.8	1,401	1.7	268	2.3	287	3.7
Nonfamily								
households	29,686	30.0	25,300	30.2	3,562	30.6	1,535	19.8
Female householder	16,496	16.7	14,207	17.0	1,909	16.4	745	9.6
Living alone	14,592	14.7	12,547	15.0	1,728	14.8	615	8.0
Male householder	13,190	13.3	11,093	13.2	1,653	14.2	790	10.2
Living alone	10,140	10.2	8,453	10.1	1,381	11.8	541	7.0

Note: Numbers will not add to total because Hispanics may be of any race and not all races are shown.
Source: Bureau of the Census, Household and Family Characteristics: March 1995, Current Population Reports, P20-488, 1996; calculations by New Strategist

Hispanic Households Younger Than Others

More than one-third of Hispanic households are headed by young adults, compared with just one-fifth of white households.

Among Hispanic households, fully 63 percent are headed by people under age 45, compared with only 47 percent of white households. In general, the Hispanic population is far more youthful than the white population, which accounts for these differences. Among black households, 55 percent are headed by people under age 45.

The differences between white and Hispanic households are just as extreme at the other end of the age spectrum. While 22 percent of white households are headed by people aged 65 or older, fewer than 12 percent of Hispanic households are headed by the elderly. Among blacks, the elderly head 16 percent of households.

♦ The generation gap between white and Hispanic households may lead to increased ethnic tension over the distribution of the nation's economic resources in the years ahead.

Households by Age, Race, and Hispanic Origin of Householder, 1995

(number and percent distribution of households by age, race, and Hispanic origin of householder, 1995; numbers in thousands)

	total		white		black		Hispanic	
	number	*percent*	*number*	*percent*	*number*	*percent*	*number*	*percent*
Total	98,990	100.0%	83,737	100.0%	11,655	100.0%	7,735	100.0%
Under age 25	5,444	5.5	4,364	5.2	833	7.1	673	8.7
Aged 25 to 34	19,452	19.7	15,845	18.9	2,675	23.0	2,237	28.9
Aged 35 to 44	22,914	23.1	18,977	22.7	2,951	25.3	1,949	25.2
Aged 45 to 54	17,590	17.8	14,796	17.7	2,046	17.6	1,232	15.9
Aged 55 to 64	12,224	12.3	10,574	12.6	1,325	11.4	755	9.8
Aged 65 to 74	11,803	11.9	10,479	12.5	1,086	9.3	607	7.8
Aged 75 or older	9,562	9.7	8,700	10.4	739	6.3	282	3.6

Note: Numbers will not add to total because Hispanics may be of any race and not all races are shown.
Source: Bureau of the Census, Household and Family Characteristics: March 1995, *Current Population Reports, P20-488, 1996; calculations by New Strategist*

Most Households Are Small

Fifty-seven percent of American households are home to only one or two people.

Two-person households are most common, accounting for 32 percent of the nation's 99 million households. Single-person households are one-fourth of the total. Three- and four-person households together account for another one-third of households. Only 10 percent of households have five or more people. Overall, the average household in the U.S. was home to 2.65 people in 1995.

Households headed by married couples are the largest, with an average of 3.27 people. Forty percent of married-couple households are home to two people, 21 percent have three, and 24 percent have four. Nonfamily households headed by women are the smallest, with an average of just 1.15 people. Eighty-nine percent of these households are people who live alone.

◆ Household size, which has been shrinking for years, should remain stable while the baby-boom generation is raising children. But as boomers become widowed in the decades ahead, household size could shrink again as the number of single-person households climbs.

Households by Size and Household Type, 1995

(number and percent distribution of households by household size and type of household, 1995; numbers in thousands)

| | total | family households | | | nonfamily households | |
		married couples	female hh, no spouse present	male hh, no spouse present	female householder	male householder
Total number	98,990	53,858	12,220	3,226	16,496	13,190
1 person	24,732	-	-	-	14,592	10,140
2 persons	31,834	21,366	5,065	1,444	1,677	2,282
3 persons	16,827	11,485	3,809	918	149	465
4 persons	15,321	12,741	1,837	478	56	209
5 persons	6,616	5,433	904	193	7	79
6 persons	2,279	1,823	337	100	12	8
7 or more persons	1,382	1,010	269	92	3	7
Percent distribution of households by size						
Total	100.0%	100.0%	100.0%	100.0%	100.0%	100.0%
1 person	25.0	-	-	-	88.5	76.9
2 persons	32.2	39.7	41.4	44.8	10.2	17.3
3 persons	17.0	21.3	31.2	28.5	0.9	3.5
4 persons	15.5	23.7	15.0	14.8	0.3	1.6
5 persons	6.7	10.1	7.4	6.0	0.0	0.6
6 persons	2.3	3.4	2.8	3.1	0.1	0.1
7 or more persons	1.4	1.9	2.2	2.9	0.0	0.1
Average household size (persons)	2.65	3.27	3.19	3.19	1.15	1.36
Percent with children <18	34.6%	46.9%	62.3%	44.6%	-	-

Source: Bureau of the Census, Household and Family Characteristics: March 1995, *Current Population Reports, P20-488, 1996; calculations by New Strategist*

Most Women Who Live Alone Are Elderly

Fifty-two percent of women who live alone are aged 65 or older.

Among the nation's single-person households, 59 percent are headed by women and 52 percent are headed by people aged 55 or older. Only 20 percent are headed by adults under age 35, while 29 percent are headed by people aged 35 to 54.

There are sharp differences in the ages of men and women who live alone. Most men who live alone are under age 55, while most women who live alone are aged 65 or older. Among men who live alone, the largest share is in the 35-to-44 age group (23 percent). Among women who live alone, the largest share is aged 75 or older (30 percent). Most men live alone before marriage or after divorce. Most women live alone following the death of a spouse.

♦ People who live alone account for 22 percent of all U.S. households, one of the most important segments of the household market. But because single-person households headed by men are at a different lifestage than those headed by women, they have very different needs.

Persons Living Alone by Sex and Age, 1995

(number and percent distribution of persons aged 15 or older living alone by sex and age, 1995; numbers in thousands)

	number	percent
Total	24,900	100.0%
Under age 25	1,072	4.3
Aged 25 to 34	3,736	15.0
Aged 35 to 44	3,803	15.3
Aged 45 to 54	3,506	14.1
Aged 55 to 64	2,941	11.8
Aged 65 to 74	4,377	17.6
Aged 75 or older	5,464	21.9
Total women	14,612	100.0
Under age 25	498	3.4
Aged 25 to 34	1,487	10.2
Aged 35 to 44	1,485	10.2
Aged 45 to 54	1,756	12.0
Aged 55 to 64	1,852	12.7
Aged 65 to 74	3,137	21.5
Aged 75 or older	4,397	30.1
Total men	10,288	100.0
Under age 25	574	5.6
Aged 25 to 34	2,249	21.9
Aged 35 to 44	2,318	22.5
Aged 45 to 54	1,750	17.0
Aged 55 to 64	1,089	10.6
Aged 65 to 74	1,240	12.1
Aged 75 or older	1,067	10.4

Source: Bureau of the Census, unpublished data from the 1996 Current Population Survey; calculations by New Strategist

Most Black Children Live with Mother Only

Fifty-two percent of black children live only with their mother, while just 33 percent live with both parents.

Among whites, 76 percent of children live with both parents, while just 18 percent live with their mothers only. Among Hispanic children, 63 percent live with both parents, while 28 percent live only with their mothers.

Few children live only with their father. Four percent of black and Hispanic children and 3 percent of white children live with their father only. Among blacks, a larger share of children (9 percent) live with other relatives—often their grandmothers—than with their fathers. Among whites and Hispanics, few children live with other relatives—only 2 percent of white and 3 percent of Hispanic children.

♦ While the living arrangements of black children are different from those of white or Hispanic children, the trends are the same for all three groups. An increasing proportion of children live only with their mothers, and a shrinking proportion live with two parents.

Living Arrangements of Children
by Race and Hispanic Origin, 1995

(number and percent distribution of children under age 18 by living arrangement, race, and Hispanic origin of child, 1995; numbers in thousands)

	number	percent
Total children	70,254	100.0%
Two parents	48,276	68.7
One parent	18,938	27.0
Mother only	16,477	23.5
Father only	2,461	3.5
Other relatives	2,352	3.3
Nonrelatives only	688	1.0
White children	55,327	100.0
Two parents	41,946	75.8
One parent	11,719	21.2
Mother only	9,827	17.8
Father only	1,892	3.4
Other relatives	1,212	2.2
Nonrelatives only	450	0.8
Black children	11,301	100.0
Two parents	3,746	33.1
One parent	6,339	56.1
Mother only	5,881	52.0
Father only	458	4.1
Other relatives	1,012	9.0
Nonrelatives only	204	1.8
Hispanic children	9,843	100.0
Two parents	6,191	62.9
One parent	3,215	32.7
Mother only	2,798	28.4
Father only	417	4.2
Other relatives	318	3.2
Nonrelatives only	120	1.2

Note: Numbers will not add to total because Hispanics may be of any race and not all races are shown.
Source: Bureau of the Census, Marital Status and Living Arrangements: March 1995, *Current Population Reports, P20-491, 1996; calculations by New Strategist*

Most Young Adults Live at Home

Fifty-three percent of the nation's 18-to-24-year-olds still live with their parents.

Young men are far more likely to live at home than are young women.

Fifty-eight percent of men and 47 percent of women aged 18 to 24 live with their parents. For both men and women, the proportion who live at home has been rising for more than a decade.

Only 30 percent of 18-to-24-year-olds head their own households (family householder, spouse, or nonfamily householder). Women aged 18 to 24 are more likely to head their own households than are men, 37 compared with 23 percent. This is because women marry at a younger age than men, with many 18-to-24-year-old women married to men aged 25 or older.

Among 25-to-34-year-olds, a majority head their own households. But more than one in eight still lives at home. The proportion of 25-to-34-year-olds who head their own households has fallen by over 9 percentage points since 1980.

♦ Young adults are more likely to live at home than they once were out of necessity. Entry-level wages have fallen sharply over the past 15 years, forcing young adults to live with their parents until they can afford independence.

Living Arrangements of Young Adults, 1995

(number and percent distribution of persons aged 18 to 34 by age, living arrangement, and sex, 1995; numbers in thousands)

	total		men		women	
	number	*percent*	*number*	*percent*	*number*	*percent*
Total, aged 18 to 24	25,158	100.0%	12,545	100.0%	12,613	100.0%
Child of householder	13,224	52.6	7,328	58.4	5,896	46.7
Family householder or spouse	5,252	20.9	1,684	13.4	3,568	28.3
Nonfamily householder	2,346	9.3	1,246	9.9	1,100	8.7
Other, not living with relative	2,544	10.1	1,372	10.9	1,172	9.3
Total, aged 25 to 34	41,389	100.0	20,589	100.0	20,800	100.0
Child of householder	4,925	11.9	3,166	15.4	1,759	8.5
Family householder or spouse	25,890	62.6	10,974	53.3	14,916	71.7
Nonfamily householder	5,376	13.0	3,345	16.2	2,031	9.8
Other, not living with relative	3,172	7.7	1,979	9.6	1,193	5.7

Source: Bureau of the Census, Marital Status and Living Arrangements: March 1995, *Current Population Reports, P20-491, 1996*

Most Older Women Live Alone

Fifty-four percent of women aged 75 or older live by themselves.

Among men in this age group, only 23 percent live alone. Most men aged 75 or older are married, while most older women are widows. These differences are due to the fact that women marry slightly older men, and men die at a younger age than women.

Among people aged 65 to 74, both men and women are likely to live with a spouse. Only 32 percent of women and 14 percent of men in this age group live alone. Fully 81 percent of men and 61 percent of women aged 65 to 74 live with a spouse.

♦ The different lifestyles of older men and women divide this market into two distinct segments: older women who live alone and older couples. These two segments will continue to dominate the elderly market into the foreseeable future.

Living Arrangements of the Elderly, 1995

(number and percent distribution of persons aged 65 or older by age, living arrangement, and sex, 1995; numbers in thousands)

	total		men		women	
	number	*percent*	*number*	*percent*	*number*	*percent*
Total, aged 65 or older	31,267	100.0%	13,005	100.0%	18,264	100.0%
Alone	9,862	31.5	2,255	17.3	7,607	41.7
Family householder or spouse	18,810	60.2	9,964	76.6	8,846	48.4
Other, with relatives	2,030	6.5	521	4.0	1,509	8.3
Other, with nonrelatives	567	1.8	265	2.0	302	1.7
Total, aged 65 to 74	18,214	100.0	8,097	100.0	10,117	100.0
Alone	4,381	24.1	1,134	14.0	3,247	32.1
Family householder or spouse	12,684	69.6	6,528	80.6	6,156	60.8
Other, with relatives	804	4.4	239	3.0	565	5.6
Other, with nonrelatives	345	1.9	196	2.4	149	1.5
Total, aged 75 or older	13,053	100.0	4,908	100.0	8,147	100.0
Alone	5,481	42.0	1,121	22.8	4,360	53.5
Family householder or spouse	6,126	46.9	3,436	70.0	2,690	33.0
Other, with relatives	1,226	9.4	282	5.7	944	11.6
Other, with nonrelatives	222	1.7	69	1.4	153	1.9

Source: Bureau of the Census, Marital Status and Living Arrangements: March 1995, *Current Population Reports, P20-491, 1996; calculations by New Strategist*

Most Married Couples under Age 45
Have Children at Home

Married couples most likely to have children at home are those aged 35 to 39.

Eighty-five percent of married couples headed by a 35-to-39-year-old have children under age 18 at home. Over half of couples in this age group have at least two children under age 18 at home. Although large families are becoming less common, couples aged 35 to 39 are more likely to have three children (25 percent) than just one child (21 percent) at home.

By the 45-to-54 age group, a minority of couples still have children under age 18 at home. But most still live with children. Sixty-six percent of couples aged 45 to 54 have children of any age at home—many of them aged 18 or older. Only 42 percent live with children under age 18.

Among couples with children under age 18 at home, the proportion with children of different ages is evenly split: 47 percent have children under age 6, 49 percent have children aged 6 to 11, and 44 percent have children aged 12 to 17.

♦ As the children of boomers enter their teens during the next decade, the number of couples with children aged 12 to 17 will expand, while the number with children under age 6 will shrink.

♦ Because young adults are living at home longer, the number of married couples with adult children at home should rise as the children of boomers enter their late teens and early 20s.

Married Couples by Age of Householder and Number of Children, 1995

(number and percent distribution of married couples by age of householder and number of children under age 18 at home, 1995; numbers in thousands)

	none		one		two		three or more	
	number	*percent*	*number*	*percent*	*number*	*percent*	*number*	*percent*
Total couples	28,617	53.1%	9,564	17.8%	10,358	19.2%	5,319	9.9%
Under age 25	733	44.9	563	34.5	273	16.7	63	3.9
Aged 25 to 29	1,418	35.8	1,130	28.5	983	24.8	427	10.8
Aged 30 to 34	1,370	21.5	1,526	24.0	2,235	35.2	1,227	19.3
Aged 35 to 39	1,063	14.9	1,504	21.1	2,798	39.2	1,766	24.8
Aged 40 to 44	1,473	21.7	1,718	25.3	2,375	35.0	1,223	18.0
Aged 45 to 54	6,441	57.8	2,621	23.5	1,538	13.8	553	5.0
Aged 55 to 64	6,951	92.0	410	5.4	135	1.8	57	0.8
Aged 65 or older	9,169	98.7	92	1.0	23	0.2	3	0.0

Source: Bureau of the Census, Household and Family Characteristics: March 1995, *Current Population Reports, P20-488, 1996; calculations by New Strategist*

Married Couples with Children by Age of Children, 1995

(number and percent distribution of total married couples and couples with children at home, by age of householder and age of children, 1995; numbers in thousands)

	total couples	with children				
		of any age	under age 18	aged 12 to 17	aged 6 to 11	under age 6
Total number	53,858	31,233	25,241	11,185	12,333	11,950
Under age 20	79	33	33	2	2	30
Aged 20 to 24	1,553	866	866	12	86	828
Aged 25 to 29	3,959	2,541	2,541	113	904	2,224
Aged 30 to 34	6,357	5,001	4,987	859	2,663	3,692
Aged 35 to 39	7,131	6,133	6,068	2,471	3,918	3,089
Aged 40 to 44	6,788	5,724	5,315	3,498	2,867	1,458
Aged 45 to 54	11,153	7,361	4,712	3,654	1,692	580
Aged 55 to 64	7,552	2,388	602	491	163	41
Aged 65 or older	9,286	1,186	118	85	39	8
Total percent	100.0%	58.0%	46.9%	20.8%	22.9%	22.2%
Under age 20	100.0	41.8	41.8	2.5	2.5	38.0
Aged 20 to 24	100.0	55.8	55.8	0.8	5.5	53.3
Aged 25 to 29	100.0	64.2	64.2	2.9	22.8	56.2
Aged 30 to 34	100.0	78.7	78.4	13.5	41.9	58.1
Aged 35 to 39	100.0	86.0	85.1	34.7	54.9	43.3
Aged 40 to 44	100.0	84.3	78.3	51.5	42.2	21.5
Aged 45 to 54	100.0	66.0	42.2	32.8	15.2	5.2
Aged 55 to 64	100.0	31.6	8.0	6.5	2.2	0.5
Aged 65 or older	100.0	12.8	1.3	0.9	0.4	0.1

Source: Bureau of the Census, Internet web site, http://www.census.gov; calculations by New Strategist

Most Single Parents Are Women

Of the nation's 9 million single-parent families, 85 percent are headed by women.

On average, the nation's single-parent families are much younger than married couples. Seventy-two percent of the women who head single-parent families are under age 40. Among men heading single-parent families, a smaller 61 percent are under age 40. The reason for the age difference between male and female single-parents is that many women become single parents after having a child out of wedlock during their teens or early 20s. In contrast, men who become single parents are likely to do so following a divorce in their late 20s or early 30s.

♦ As the children of baby boomers grow up and leave home, the number of single-parent families should stabilize or even decline.

Single-Parent Families by Age, 1995

(number and percent distribution of female- and male-headed families with children under age 18 at home, by sex and age of householder, 1995; numbers in thousands)

	number	percent
Total	9,055	100.0%
Under age 25	1,069	11.8
Aged 25 to 29	1,818	15.8
Aged 30 to 34	2,378	20.6
Aged 35 to 39	2,402	20.8
Aged 40 to 44	1,642	14.2
Aged 45 to 54	1,141	9.9
Aged 55 or older	188	1.6
Female-headed families	7,615	100.0
Under age 25	963	12.6
Aged 25 to 29	1,130	14.8
Aged 30 to 34	1,639	21.5
Aged 35 to 39	1,779	23.4
Aged 40 to 44	1,204	15.8
Aged 45 to 54	798	10.5
Aged 55 or older	101	1.3
Male-headed families	1,694	100.0
Under age 25	141	8.3
Aged 25 to 29	255	15.1
Aged 30 to 34	327	19.3
Aged 35 to 39	351	20.7
Aged 40 to 44	280	16.5
Aged 45 to 54	263	15.5
Aged 55 or older	78	4.6

Source: Bureau of the Census, Household and Family Characteristics: March 1995; *Current Population Reports, P20-488, 1996; calculations by New Strategist*

Unmarried Couples Are Diverse

More than 5 million American households are headed by unmarried couples.

Unmarried couples include young adults as well as middle-aged and older Americans. Only 22 percent of cohabiting couples are under age 25. Thirty-nine percent of couples are headed by people aged 25 to 34, 20 percent by people aged 35 to 44, and 19 percent by people aged 45 or older.

Two out of three cohabiting couples are heterosexual partners, while about one-third are homosexual couples. Among same-sex couples, 53 percent are men and 47 percent are women.

♦ Baby boomers were the first to make cohabitation common. As boomers age, the number of cohabitors aged 45 and older will soar.

♦ The number of same-sex cohabitors is likely to rise with the growing tolerance of homosexuality in the U.S.

Characteristics of Cohabiting Couples, 1995

(number and percent distribution of households with two unrelated adults, by sex of partner and age of householder, 1995; numbers in thousands)

	total		male householder		female householder	
	number	*percent*	*number*	*percent*	*number*	*percent*
Total	5,428	100.0%	3,015	100.0%	2,412	100.0%
Partner of opposite sex	3,668	67.6	2,076	68.9	1,593	66.0
Under age 25	742	13.7	343	11.4	399	16.5
Aged 25 to 34	1,420	26.2	814	27.0	606	25.1
Aged 35 to 44	768	14.1	505	16.7	263	10.9
Aged 45 to 64	558	10.3	307	10.2	251	10.4
Aged 65 or older	180	3.3	106	3.5	74	3.1
Partner of same sex	1,760	32.4	940	31.2	820	34.0
Under age 25	472	8.7	230	7.6	242	10.0
Aged 25 to 34	679	12.5	392	13.0	287	11.9
Aged 35 to 44	313	5.8	175	5.8	139	5.8
Aged 45 to 64	205	3.8	127	4.2	78	3.2
Aged 65 or older	90	1.7	16	0.5	74	3.1

Source: Bureau of the Census, Marital Status and Living Arrangements: March 1995; *Current Population Reports, P20-491, 1996; calculations by New Strategist*

Most Americans Are Married

Men are more likely to be married than women—59 compared with 56 percent in 1995.

Men are also more likely than women to never have been married—31 percent of men compared with 24 percent of women. Despite reports about never-married women in their 30s having trouble finding husbands, the reverse is more likely to be the case. Never-married men outnumber never-married women up to age 65.

The proportion of young adults who have not yet married has been growing for decades as men and women postpone marriage. The median age at first marriage is at an all-time high of 26.9 years for men and 24.5 years for women. By age 30, most men are married, with the proportion peaking at 82 percent for those aged 55 to 64. Among women, the proportion married peaks at 74 percent for those aged 40 to 54.

Men are likely to be married for the rest of their lives, while women are likely to be widowed in old age. Overall, 11 percent of women are currently widowed, compared with just 2 percent of men. Women are more likely to be widowed than men because they tend to marry men who are older, and because men's life expectancy is lower than women's. Most women aged 75 or older are widows, while the proportion of men who are widowers never rises above 41 percent.

♦ With an increasing proportion of young adults going to college, the median age at first marriage is likely to remain high as men and women postpone marriage until established in a career.

Marital Status of Men by Age, 1995

(number and percent distribution of men aged 15 or older by age and marital status, 1995; numbers in thousands)

	total men	never married	married	divorced	widowed
Total number	97,704	30,286	57,750	7,383	2,284
Aged 15 to 19	9,218	9,099	100	17	2
Aged 20 to 24	9,023	7,285	1,638	100	-
Aged 25 to 29	9,689	4,944	4,337	401	6
Aged 30 to 34	10,900	3,075	6,887	927	11
Aged 35 to 39	11,041	2,241	7,561	1,204	35
Aged 40 to 44	9,931	1,390	7,260	1,234	46
Aged 45 to 54	15,022	1,214	11,848	1,807	153
Aged 55 to 64	9,878	494	8,097	1,011	275
Aged 65 to 74	8,097	342	6,549	513	693
Aged 75 to 84	4,066	160	3,042	144	720
Aged 85 or older	840	41	432	24	342
Total percent	100.0%	31.0%	59.1%	7.6%	2.3%
Aged 15 to 19	100.0	98.7	1.1	0.2	0.0
Aged 20 to 24	100.0	80.7	18.2	1.1	-
Aged 25 to 29	100.0	51.0	44.8	4.1	0.1
Aged 30 to 34	100.0	28.2	63.2	8.5	0.1
Aged 35 to 39	100.0	20.3	68.5	10.9	0.3
Aged 40 to 44	100.0	14.0	73.1	12.4	0.5
Aged 45 to 54	100.0	8.1	78.9	12.0	1.0
Aged 55 to 64	100.0	5.0	82.0	10.2	2.8
Aged 65 to 74	100.0	4.2	80.9	6.3	8.6
Aged 75 to 84	100.0	3.9	74.8	3.5	17.7
Aged 85 or older	100.0	4.9	51.4	2.9	40.7

Note: (-) means sample is too small to make a reliable estimate.
Source: Bureau of the Census, Marital Status and Living Arrangements: March 1995, *Current Population Reports, P20-491, 1996*

Marital Status of Women by Age, 1995

(number and percent distribution of women aged 15 or older by age and marital status, 1995; numbers in thousands)

	total women	never married	married	divorced	widowed
Total number	105,028	24,693	58,984	10,270	11,082
Aged 15 to 19	8,934	8,582	330	17	4
Aged 20 to 24	9,119	6,087	2,769	247	17
Aged 25 to 20	9,712	3,429	5,576	689	17
Aged 30 to 34	11,088	2,111	7,758	1,150	69
Aged 35 to 39	11,200	1,408	8,103	1,569	120
Aged 40 to 44	10,163	881	7,519	1,604	159
Aged 45 to 54	15,672	959	11,617	2,441	655
Aged 55 to 64	10,878	467	7,543	1,463	1,405
Aged 65 to 74	10,117	408	5,571	786	3,352
Aged 75 to 84	6,122	255	1,961	264	3,641
Aged 85 or older	2,025	105	235	41	1,643
Total percent	100.0%	23.5%	56.2%	9.8%	10.6%
Aged 15 to 19	100.0	96.1	3.7	0.2	0.0
Aged 20 to 24	100.0	66.8	30.4	2.7	0.2
Aged 25 to 20	100.0	35.3	57.4	7.1	0.2
Aged 30 to 34	100.0	19.0	70.0	10.4	0.6
Aged 35 to 39	100.0	12.6	72.3	14.0	1.1
Aged 40 to 44	100.0	8.7	74.0	15.8	1.6
Aged 45 to 54	100.0	6.1	74.1	15.6	4.2
Aged 55 to 64	100.0	4.3	69.3	13.4	12.9
Aged 65 to 74	100.0	4.0	55.1	7.8	33.1
Aged 75 to 84	100.0	4.2	32.0	4.3	59.5
Aged 85 or older	100.0	5.2	11.6	2.0	81.1

Source: Bureau of the Census, Marital Status and Living Arrangements: March 1995, *Current Population Reports, P20-491*

Most Blacks Are Not Married

Only 40 percent of blacks are currently married, compared with 60 percent of whites and 55 percent of Hispanics.

Most whites and Hispanics are married by the time they reach their late 20s. But for blacks, marriage does not claim a majority until the 35-to-39 age group. Blacks are less likely to be married than whites or Hispanics because they postpone marriage until a much later age. Among whites aged 25 to 29 in 1995, only 40 percent had never married. But 61 percent of their black counterparts were still single. In the 30-to-34 age group, only 21 percent of whites but 43 percent of blacks had never married.

Blacks are more likely to be divorced than whites or Hispanics, particularly in the 40-to-54 age group. They are also more likely to be widowed in middle-age than are whites or Hispanics. Sixteen percent of blacks aged 55 to 64 are widowed, compared with only 7 percent of whites and 10 percent of Hispanics in this age group.

♦ Blacks are less likely to marry than whites because many black men have difficulty finding jobs that pay enough to support a family. With the incomes of men in all racial and ethnic groups falling, marriage may become less common for whites and Hispanics in the years ahead as well.

Marital Status by Race, Hispanic Origin, and Age, 1995

(total number of persons aged 15 or older and percent distribution by race, Hispanic origin, age, and marital status, 1995; numbers in thousands)

	total	never married	married	divorced	widowed
White	170,051	24.7%	60.0%	8.7%	6.7%
Aged 15 to 19	14,380	97.2	2.6	0.2	-
Aged 20 to 24	14,557	71.5	26.3	2.1	0.1
Aged 25 to 29	15,651	39.8	54.1	6.0	0.1
Aged 30 to 34	18,088	20.5	69.4	9.7	0.3
Aged 35 to 39	18,387	14.0	72.9	12.5	0.7
Aged 40 to 44	16,812	9.6	76.1	13.5	0.8
Aged 45 to 54	26,154	6.1	78.1	13.5	2.3
Aged 55 to 64	18,035	4.0	77.2	11.7	7.1
Aged 65 ot 74	16,201	3.9	68.0	6.8	21.3
Aged 75 to 84	9,212	3.8	50.3	3.9	42.0
Aged 85 or older	2,573	4.9	23.7	2.3	69.0
Black	23,922	43.0	40.0	9.9	7.1
Aged 15 to 19	2,861	99.1	0.5	0.3	-
Aged 20 to 24	2,605	86.9	11.9	1.2	0.1
Aged 25 to 29	2,643	61.4	33.7	5.0	-
Aged 30 to 34	2,804	42.8	47.7	8.9	0.7
Aged 35 to 39	2,786	32.7	52.0	14.4	1.0
Aged 40 to 44	2,404	23.3	54.4	19.8	2.4
Aged 45 to 54	3,195	15.7	60.8	18.2	5.2
Aged 55 to 64	2,069	10.8	59.5	13.4	16.3
Aged 65 ot 74	1,542	6.4	51.0	11.4	31.2
Aged 75 to 84	774	6.7	34.1	5.2	54.1
Aged 85 or older	241	6.3	17.4	2.5	73.7

(continued)

(continued from previous page)

	total	never married	married	divorced	widowed
Hispanic	18,988	33.6%	55.2%	7.3%	3.9%
Aged 15 to 19	2,339	94.6	5.2	0.1	0.1
Aged 20 to 24	2,479	63.1	35.1	1.7	0.1
Aged 25 to 29	2,600	39.6	55.5	4.7	0.1
Aged 30 to 34	2,616	24.4	67.5	7.6	0.5
Aged 35 to 39	2,168	18.2	69.2	11.5	1.1
Aged 40 to 44	1,693	11.3	74.3	13.0	1.3
Aged 45 to 54	2,271	8.4	76.3	11.9	3.3
Aged 55 to 64	1,395	6.0	73.5	11.0	9.5
Aged 65 ot 74	959	5.7	60.2	10.3	23.7
Aged 75 to 84	359	5.6	40.9	7.2	46.3
Aged 85 or older	110	3.5	29.8	2.3	64.4

Note: (-) means sample is too small to make a reliable estimate.
Source: Bureau of the Census, Marital Status and Living Arrangements: March 1995, *Current Population Reports, P20-491, 1996*

6

Population Trends

♦ **Older boomers will inflate the number of fiftysomethings between 1997 and 2005.**
Rapid growth in this population—the nation's biggest spenders—will force businesses to rethink the older market.

♦ **The minority share of the American population will rise to 30 percent by 2005.**
The number of Asians is projected to climb by more than 31 percent between 1997 and 2005, while Hispanics will grow by 26 percent, blacks by 10 percent, and non-Hispanic whites by just 2 percent.

♦ **The mountain states should grow faster than any other area of the U.S. between 1997 and 2005.**
The mountain states should grow by a rapid 17 percent between 1997 and 2005, while the Pacific states are projected to grow by 9 percent—slightly faster than the national average of 7 percent.

♦ **Las Vegas is the fastest-growing large metropolitan area.**
Three out of four Americans lived in one of the nation's metropolitan areas in 1990. In 1950, barely half of Americans were metropolitan residents.

♦ **Mobility rates have fallen sharply over the past few decades.**
As the enormous baby-boom generation enters its 50s during the next decade, the overall mobility rate will continue to decline because moving is infrequent among the middle-aged.

♦ **Crime is down, but many people are still victims.**
As the children of baby boomers enter their teens—the age of peak criminal victimization—expect Americans to get even tougher on criminals, especially juvenile offenders.

More Women Than Men

American women outnumbered men by 6 million in 1997.

Although there are more women than men in the population, women do not begin to outnumber men until the 30-to-34 age group. By ages 85 and older, there are only 39 men for every 100 women, or 61 percent fewer men than women. Men slightly outnumber women at younger ages because boys outnumber girls at birth. Women outnumber men at older ages because men have higher death rates than women throughout life. Research has shown that men's higher death rates are due primarily to biological factors rather than to lifestyle differences.

In 1997, the largest single five-year age group was 35-to-39-year-olds, at 22.6 million. Most of the people in this age group are the youngest members of the baby-boom generation, born between 1960 and 1964. The baby-boom generation, aged 33 to 51 in 1997, is moving up through the age distribution, changing America as it does.

♦ Because death rates are higher for men than for women, women will continue to outnumber men at older ages into the foreseeable future.

Population by Age and Sex, 1997

(number of persons by age and sex, and sex ratio by age, 1997; numbers in thousands)

	total	male	female	sex ratio
Total	267,645	130,712	136,933	95
Under age 5	19,229	9,839	9,389	105
Aged 5 to 9	19,854	10,163	9,691	105
Aged 10 to 14	19,205	9,835	9,370	105
Aged 15 to 19	19,013	9,745	9,268	105
Aged 20 to 24	17,287	8,773	8,515	103
Aged 25 to 29	18,848	9,430	9,419	100
Aged 30 to 34	20,775	10,344	10,431	99
Aged 35 to 39	22,607	11,260	11,347	99
Aged 40 to 44	21,323	10,548	10,775	98
Aged 45 to 49	18,442	9,044	9,398	96
Aged 50 to 54	15,149	7,366	7,784	95
Aged 55 to 59	11,754	5,642	6,111	92
Aged 60 to 64	10,062	4,747	5,315	89
Aged 65 to 69	9,758	4,454	5,305	84
Aged 70 to 74	8,753	3,812	4,941	77
Aged 75 to 79	7,072	2,914	4,157	70
Aged 80 to 84	4,652	1,707	2,945	58
Aged 85 or older	3,862	1,089	2,773	39
Aged 18 to 24	24,689	12,550	12,140	103
Aged 18 or older	197,747	94,907	102,840	92
Aged 65 or older	34,097	13,976	20,121	69
Median age	34.9	33.8	36.0	-

Note: The sex ratio is the number of males per 100 females.
Source: Bureau of the Census, Population Projections of the United States by Age, Sex, Race, and Hispanic Origin: 1995 to 2050, *Current Population Reports, P25-1130, 1996; calculations by New Strategist*

Biggest Gainer Will Be the 55-to-59 Age Group

Older boomers will inflate the number of fiftysomethings between 1997 and 2005.

The United States population is projected to grow by 7 percent between 1997 and 2005, according to the Census Bureau. But some age groups will expand rapidly while others shrink.

The fastest-growing age group will be 55-to-59-year-olds, projected to increase by 43 percent between 1997 and 2005 as the oldest boomers enter their late 50s. In contrast, the number of people in their 30s will fall by more than 12 percent as the small baby-bust generation (or Generation X) matures.

The children of baby boomers will boost the number of teens and young adults in the population after years of decline. The number of people aged 20 to 24 should expand by 16 percent between 1997 and 2005.

♦ Rapid growth in the fiftysomething population—the nation's biggest spenders—will force businesses to rethink the older market. Baby boomers will never become "seniors," but will instead create a vibrant "mid-youth" market that cannot be ignored.

♦ With an increase in the teen population, expect the public's attention to focus on teen issues. Baby boomers will be particularly concerned with protecting their children from the most destructive elements of teen culture—crime, drugs, smoking, and teen pregnancy.

Population by Age, 1997 to 2005

(number of persons by age, 1997 to 2005; percent change, 1997-2005; numbers in thousands)

	1997	2000	2005	percent change 1997-2005
Total	267,645	274,634	285,981	6.9%
Under age 5	19,229	18,987	19,127	-0.5
Aged 5 to 9	19,854	19,920	19,338	-2.6
Aged 10 to 14	19,205	20,057	20,809	8.4
Aged 15 to 19	19,013	19,820	20,997	10.4
Aged 20 to 24	17,287	18,257	19,960	15.5
Aged 25 to 29	18,848	17,722	18,057	-4.2
Aged 30 to 34	20,775	19,511	18,249	-12.2
Aged 35 to 39	22,607	22,180	19,802	-12.4
Aged 40 to 44	21,323	22,479	22,363	4.9
Aged 45 to 49	18,442	19,806	21,988	19.2
Aged 50 to 54	15,149	17,224	19,518	28.8
Aged 55 to 59	11,754	13,307	16,798	42.9
Aged 60 to 64	10,062	10,654	12,807	27.3
Aged 65 to 69	9,758	9,410	10,037	2.9
Aged 70 to 74	8,753	8,726	8,332	-4.8
Aged 75 to 79	7,072	7,415	7,393	4.5
Aged 80 to 84	4,652	4,900	5,505	18.3
Aged 85 or older	3,862	4,259	4,899	26.9
Aged 18 to 24	24,689	26,258	28,268	14.5
Aged 18 or older	197,747	203,852	214,017	8.2
Aged 65 or older	34,097	34,709	36,166	6.1

Source: Bureau of the Census, Population Projections of the United States by Age, Sex, Race, and Hispanic Origin: 1995 to 2050*; Current Population Reports, P25-1130, 1996; calculations by New Strategist*

Diversity on the Rise

The minority share of the American population will rise to 30 percent by 2005.

The non-Hispanic white share of the U.S. population will fall below 70 percent by 2005, down from 73 percent today.

Between 1997 and 2005, the fastest-growing minority will be non-Hispanic Asians, according to the Census Bureau. The number of Asians is projected to climb by more than 31 percent between 1997 and 2005. The number of Hispanics will grow by 26 percent, while non-Hispanic blacks will increase by 10 percent. The number of non-Hispanic whites will grow by just 2 percent between 1997 and 2005.

Hispanics will become the largest minority in the U.S. by 2005. Their numbers will rise to 36 million, surpassing the 35 million non-Hispanic blacks projected for that year. In 2005, 13 percent of Americans will be Hispanic, 12 percent will be non-Hispanic black, 4 percent will be non-Hispanic Asian, and fewer than 1 percent will be non-Hispanic Native Americans.

◆ Our multicultural society is here to stay. Businesses must reflect this diversity in their leadership, work force, products, and services or lose customers to those that more closely mirror America.

Population by Race and Hispanic Origin, 1997 to 2005

(number and percent distribution of persons by race and Hispanic origin, 1997 to 2005; percent change in number and percentage point change in share, 1997-2005; numbers in thousands)

	1997	2000	2005	percent change 1997-2005
Total number	267,645	274,634	285,981	6.9%
White, non-Hispanic	195,091	197,061	199,802	2.4
Black, non-Hispanic	32,396	33,568	35,485	9.5
Asian, non-Hispanic	9,497	10,584	12,454	31.1
Native American, non-Hispanic	1,980	2,054	2,183	10.3
Hispanic	28,680	31,366	36,057	25.7
				percentage point change, 1997-2005
Total percent	100.0%	100.0%	100.0%	-
White, non-Hispanic	72.9	71.8	69.9	-3.0
Black, non-Hispanic	12.1	12.2	12.4	0.3
Asian, non-Hispanic	3.5	3.9	4.4	0.8
Native American, non-Hispanic	0.7	0.7	0.8	0.0
Hispanic	10.7	11.4	12.6	1.9

Source: Bureau of the Census, Population Projections of the United States by Age, Sex, Race, and Hispanic Origin: 1995 to 2050; *Current Population Reports P25-1130, 1996; calculations by New Strategist*

Number of White, Black, and Hispanic Fiftysomethings to Soar

The middle-aging of the baby-boom generation will inflate the number of people in their 50s in all racial and ethnic groups.

The number of non-Hispanic whites will grow by just 2 percent from 1997 to 2005, according to projections by the Census Bureau. But the number of whites aged 55 to 59 will grow by 41 percent because of the middle-aging of the baby-boom generation. The number of non-Hispanic blacks will grow by 10 percent overall during those same years, while the number aged 50 to 54 will grow by 48 percent. For both non-Hispanic whites and non-Hispanic blacks, the fiftysomething age group will grow faster than any other.

For Hispanics and non-Hispanic Asians, rapid growth in fiftysomethings will be overshadowed by even faster growth among the older population. The number of Hispanics aged 55 to 59 will grow by 59 percent between 1997 and 2005, but the number aged 80 to 84 will grow by 63 percent. The number of non-Hispanic Asians aged 55 to 59 will grow by 68 percent between 1997 and 2005, but the number aged 85 or older will grow by fully 95 percent.

◆ By 2005, only 61 percent of Americans under age 18 will be non-Hispanic whites, compared with 82 percent of people aged 65 or older. The difference in the racial and ethnic composition of the nation's youth and elderly could lead to greater political conflict in determining the distribution of the nation's economic resources.

Non-Hispanic Asians by Age, 1997 to 2005

(number of non-Hispanic Asians by age, 1997 to 2005; percent change 1997-2005; numbers in thousands)

	1997	2000	2005	percent change 1997-2005
Total	9,497	10,584	12,454	31.1%
Under age 5	806	867	973	20.7
Aged 5 to 9	755	859	960	27.2
Aged 10 to 14	760	834	1,043	37.2
Aged 15 to 19	725	835	955	31.7
Aged 20 to 24	689	756	944	37.0
Aged 25 to 29	817	836	900	10.2
Aged 30 to 34	851	907	987	16.0
Aged 35 to 39	852	921	1,004	17.8
Aged 40 to 44	782	873	994	27.1
Aged 45 to 49	655	742	893	36.3
Aged 50 to 54	481	602	751	56.1
Aged 55 to 59	360	428	604	67.8
Aged 60 to 64	294	342	442	50.3
Aged 65 to 69	249	278	347	39.4
Aged 70 to 74	193	222	268	38.9
Aged 75 to 79	122	152	195	59.8
Aged 80 to 84	66	79	117	77.3
Aged 85 or older	40	51	78	95.0
Aged 18 to 24	957	1,080	1,312	37.1
Aged 18 or older	6,719	7,514	8,891	32.3
Aged 65 or older	669	783	1,004	50.1

Source: Bureau of the Census, Population Projections of the United States by Age, Sex, Race, and Hispanic Origin: 1995 to 2050; Current Population Reports, P25-1130, 1996; *calculations by New Strategist*

Non-Hispanic Blacks by Age, 1997 to 2005

(number of non-Hispanic blacks by age, 1997 to 2005; percent change 1997-2005; numbers in thousands)

	1997	2000	2005	percent change 1997-2005
Total	32,396	33,568	35,485	9.5%
Under age 5	2,910	2,929	3,016	3.6
Aged 5 to 9	2,971	2,966	2,967	-0.1
Aged 10 to 14	2,789	2,997	3,103	11.3
Aged 15 to 19	2,806	2,872	3,140	11.9
Aged 20 to 24	2,444	2,592	2,762	13.0
Aged 25 to 29	2,462	2,405	2,472	0.4
Aged 30 to 34	2,603	2,458	2,411	-7.4
Aged 35 to 39	2,709	2,706	2,478	-8.5
Aged 40 to 44	2,454	2,641	2,675	9.0
Aged 45 to 49	1,986	2,199	2,530	27.4
Aged 50 to 54	1,435	1,723	2,124	48.0
Aged 55 to 59	1,157	1,267	1,650	42.6
Aged 60 to 64	967	1,034	1,200	24.1
Aged 65 to 69	893	894	974	9.1
Aged 70 to 74	688	714	720	4.7
Aged 75 to 79	522	536	566	8.4
Aged 80 to 84	316	327	353	11.7
Aged 85 or older	285	310	344	20.7
Aged 18 to 24	3,539	3,752	3,975	12.3
Aged 18 or older	22,016	22,963	24,472	11.2
Aged 65 or older	2,704	2,781	2,957	9.4

Source: Bureau of the Census, Population Projections of the United States by Age, Sex, Race, and Hispanic Origin: 1995 to 2050; *Current Population Reports, P25-1130, 1996; calculations by New Strategist*

Hispanics by Age, 1997 to 2005

(number of Hispanics by age, 1997 to 2005; percent change 1997-2005; numbers in thousands)

	1997	2000	2005	percent change 1997-2005
Total	28,680	31,366	36,057	25.7%
Under age 5	3,131	3,203	3,580	14.3
Aged 5 to 9	2,985	3,298	3,366	12.8
Aged 10 to 14	2,575	2,906	3,558	38.2
Aged 15 to 19	2,479	2,732	3,221	29.9
Aged 20 to 24	2,370	2,574	3,012	27.1
Aged 25 to 29	2,519	2,510	2,734	8.5
Aged 30 to 34	2,627	2,671	2,681	2.1
Aged 35 to 39	2,355	2,618	2,751	16.8
Aged 40 to 44	1,925	2,218	2,670	38.7
Aged 45 to 49	1,468	1,727	2,200	49.9
Aged 50 to 54	1,098	1,322	1,727	57.3
Aged 55 to 59	827	962	1,312	58.6
Aged 60 to 64	674	755	948	40.7
Aged 65 to 69	578	618	734	27.0
Aged 70 to 74	442	502	574	29.9
Aged 75 to 79	297	362	453	52.5
Aged 80 to 84	181	206	295	63.0
Aged 85 or older	151	183	242	60.3
Aged 18 to 24	3,341	3,679	4,270	27.8
Aged 18 or older	18,481	20,332	23,590	27.6
Aged 65 or older	1,648	1,872	2,298	39.4

Source: Bureau of the Census, Population Projections of the United States by Age, Sex, Race, and Hispanic Origin: 1995 to 2050; *Current Population Reports, P25-1130, 1996; calculations by New Strategist*

Non-Hispanic Native Americans by Age, 1997 to 2005

(number of non-Hispanic Native Americans by age, 1997 to 2005; percent change 1997-2005; numbers in thousands)

	1997	2000	2005	percent change 1997-2005
Total	1,980	2,054	2,183	10.3%
Under age 5	176	180	192	9.1
Aged 5 to 9	190	182	186	-2.1
Aged 10 to 14	202	212	202	0.0
Aged 15 to 19	184	197	211	14.7
Aged 20 to 24	154	164	190	23.4
Aged 25 to 29	156	156	163	4.5
Aged 30 to 34	151	147	153	1.3
Aged 35 to 39	154	152	143	-7.1
Aged 40 to 44	142	149	149	4.9
Aged 45 to 49	118	127	140	18.6
Aged 50 to 54	92	104	119	29.3
Aged 55 to 59	69	77	95	37.7
Aged 60 to 64	55	59	70	27.3
Aged 65 to 69	44	46	52	18.2
Aged 70 to 74	35	36	40	14.3
Aged 75 to 79	26	28	30	15.4
Aged 80 to 84	16	18	22	37.5
Aged 85 or older	17	21	27	58.8
Aged 18 to 24	220	238	268	21.8
Aged 18 or older	1,294	1,358	1,470	13.6
Aged 65 or older	137	149	170	24.1

Source: Bureau of the Census, Population Projections of the United States by Age, Sex, Race, and Hispanic Origin: 1995 to 2050*; Current Population Reports, P25-1130, 1996; calculations by New Strategist*

Non-Hispanic Whites by Age, 1997 to 2005

(number of non-Hispanic whites by age, 1997 to 2005; percent change 1997-2005; numbers in thousands)

	1997	2000	2005	percent change 1997-2005
Total	195,091	197,061	199,802	2.4%
Under age 5	12,205	11,807	11,367	-6.9
Aged 5 to 9	12,953	12,615	11,859	-8.4
Aged 10 to 14	12,880	13,109	12,903	0.2
Aged 15 to 19	12,819	13,184	13,469	5.1
Aged 20 to 24	11,631	12,171	13,052	12.2
Aged 25 to 29	12,894	11,816	11,789	-8.6
Aged 30 to 34	14,543	13,328	12,017	-17.4
Aged 35 to 39	16,536	15,783	13,426	-18.8
Aged 40 to 44	16,020	16,599	15,874	-0.9
Aged 45 to 49	14,215	15,012	16,225	14.1
Aged 50 to 54	12,044	13,473	14,798	22.9
Aged 55 to 59	9,341	10,574	13,137	40.6
Aged 60 to 64	8,072	8,465	10,148	25.7
Aged 65 to 69	7,995	7,574	7,929	-0.8
Aged 70 to 74	7,396	7,251	6,731	-9.0
Aged 75 to 79	6,105	6,336	6,150	0.7
Aged 80 to 84	4,073	4,271	4,718	15.8
Aged 85 or older	3,370	3,694	4,209	24.9
Aged 18 to 24	16,632	17,510	18,443	10.9
Aged 18 or older	149,236	151,685	155,594	4.3
Aged 65 or older	28,938	29,126	29,737	2.8

Source: Bureau of the Census, Population Projections of the United States by Age, Sex, Race, and Hispanic Origin: 1995 to 2050; *Current Population Reports, P25-1130, 1996; calculations by New Strategist*

West to Grow Fastest

The mountain states should grow faster than any other area of the U.S. between 1997 and 2005.

While the U.S. population overall is projected to grow by 7 percent between 1997 and 2005, the population of the West should grow by 11 percent. The mountain states should grow by a rapid 17 percent, while the Pacific states are projected to grow 9 percent—slightly faster than the national average.

The Middle Atlantic division, which includes Pennsylvania, New Jersey, and New York, will be the slowest-growing area of the U.S. during the next few years. Between 1997 and 2005, the population of the Middle Atlantic division is projected to rise by just 1.6 percent. Overall, the Northeast should grow by 2 percent, the Midwest by 4 percent, and the South by 9 percent between 1997 and 2005.

◆ By 2005, the West will surpass the Midwest in population. Together, the South and West will be home to 59 percent of Americans in that year, up from 57 percent today—increasing the political and economic power of the Sunbelt states.

Population by Region and Division, 1997 to 2005

(number of persons by region and division, 1997 to 2005; percent change, 1997-2005; numbers in thousands)

	1997	2000	2005	percent change 1997-2005
Total	267,645	274,634	285,981	6.9%
Northeast	51,747	52,107	52,767	2.0
New England	13,428	13,581	13,843	3.1
Middle Atlantic	38,318	38,526	38,923	1.6
Midwest	62,526	63,502	64,825	3.7
East North Central	43,872	44,419	45,151	2.9
West North Central	18,654	19,082	19,673	5.5
South	94,242	97,613	102,788	9.1
South Atlantic	48,299	50,147	52,921	9.6
East South Central	16,420	16,918	17,604	7.2
West South Central	29,523	30,548	32,263	9.3
West	59,131	61,413	65,603	10.9
Mountain	16,511	17,725	19,249	16.6
Pacific	42,619	43,687	46,354	8.8

Source: Bureau of the Census, Projections of the Total Population of States: 1995 to 2025; PPL-47, 1996; calculations by New Strategist

Minority Populations Are Largest in South and West

Nearly one in five Southerners is non-Hispanic black, while one in five Westerners is Hispanic.

Minorities are unevenly distributed across the country, with the South and West home to the largest share. In the South, 30 percent of residents are minorities, while in the West the share is an even larger 36 percent.

In the Northeast, nearly one in four residents is a minority. The Midwest is the least diverse region, with 85 percent of its population being non-Hispanic white. The non-Hispanic white share of the population is projected to decline in every region between 1997 and 2005. In the West, only 58 percent of residents will be non-Hispanic whites in 2005.

Over half of non-Hispanic blacks live in the South, while over half of non-Hispanic Asians live in the West. Nearly half of Native Americans are also in the West, as are 45 percent of Hispanics. These proportions are not projected to change much between 1997 and 2005.

◆ The uneven distribution of minorities creates regional tensions as some states and metropolitan areas cope with racial and ethnic diversity on a daily basis, while others only rarely address diversity issues.

Population by Region, Race, and Hispanic Origin, 1995

(number and percent distribution of persons by region, race, and Hispanic origin, 1995; numbers in thousands)

| | | non-Hispanic | | | | |
	total	white	black	Asian	Native American	Hispanic
Number						
United States	262,755	193,523	31,591	8,779	1,930	26,932
Northeast	51,465	39,870	5,439	1,641	109	4,406
Midwest	61,803	52,338	6,094	943	339	2,089
South	91,887	64,488	17,169	1,441	565	8,224
West	57,596	36,827	2,888	4,752	917	12,212
Percent distribution by region						
United States	100.0%	73.7%	12.0%	3.3%	0.7%	10.2%
Northeast	100.0	77.5	10.6	3.2	0.2	8.6
Midwest	100.0	84.7	9.9	1.5	0.5	3.4
South	100.0	70.2	18.7	1.6	0.6	9.0
West	100.0	63.9	5.0	8.3	1.6	21.2
Percent distribution by race and Hispanic origin						
United States	100.0%	100.0%	100.0%	100.0%	100.0%	100.0%
Northeast	19.6	20.6	17.2	18.7	5.6	16.4
Midwest	23.5	27.0	19.3	10.7	17.6	7.8
South	35.0	33.3	54.3	16.4	29.3	30.5
West	21.9	19.0	9.1	54.1	47.5	45.3

Source: Bureau of the Census, Population Projections for States by Age, Sex, Race, and Hispanic Origin: 1995 to 2025, *PPL-47, 1996; calculations by New Strategist*

Population by Region, Race, and Hispanic Origin, 2000

(number and percent distribution of persons by region, race, and Hispanic origin, 2000; numbers in thousands)

	total	non-Hispanic white	black	Asian	Native American	Hispanic
Number						
United States	274,637	197,062	33,569	10,585	2,055	31,366
Northeast	52,107	39,327	5,634	2,017	113	5,016
Midwest	63,500	53,096	6,430	1,164	372	2,438
South	97,613	67,060	18,553	1,771	599	9,610
West	61,412	37,558	2,952	5,631	971	14,300
Percent distribution by region						
United States	100.0%	71.8%	12.2%	3.9%	0.7%	11.4%
Northeast	100.0	75.5	10.8	3.9	0.2	9.6
Midwest	100.0	83.6	10.1	1.8	0.6	3.8
South	100.0	68.7	19.0	1.8	0.6	9.8
West	100.0	61.2	4.8	9.2	1.6	23.3
Percent distribution by race and Hispanic origin						
United States	100.0%	100.0%	100.0%	100.0%	100.0%	100.0%
Northeast	19.0	20.0	16.8	19.1	5.5	16.0
Midwest	23.1	26.9	19.2	11.0	18.1	7.8
South	35.5	34.0	55.3	16.7	29.1	30.6
West	22.4	19.1	8.8	53.2	47.3	45.6

Source: Bureau of the Census, Population Projections for States by Age, Sex, Race, and Hispanic Origin: 1995 to 2025, *PPL-47, 1996; calculations by New Strategist*

Population by Region, Race, and Hispanic Origin, 2005

(number and percent distribution of persons by region, race, and Hispanic origin, 2005; numbers in thousands)

	total	non-Hispanic white	black	Asian	Native American	Hispanic
Number						
United States	285,962	199,802	35,485	12,454	2,184	36,057
Northeast	52,768	38,769	5,840	2,396	117	5,644
Midwest	64,825	53,521	6,734	1,369	404	2,797
South	102,787	69,168	19,855	2,083	632	11,049
West	65,603	38,344	3,057	6,604	1,030	16,568
Percent distribution by region						
United States	100.0%	69.9%	12.4%	4.4%	0.8%	12.6%
Northeast	100.0	73.5	11.1	4.5	0.2	10.7
Midwest	100.0	82.6	10.4	2.1	0.6	4.3
South	100.0	67.3	19.3	2.0	0.6	10.7
West	100.0	58.4	4.7	10.1	1.6	25.3
Percent distribution by race and Hispanic origin						
United States	100.0%	100.0%	100.0%	100.0%	100.0%	100.0%
Northeast	18.5	19.4	16.5	19.2	5.4	15.7
Midwest	22.7	26.8	19.0	11.0	18.5	7.8
South	35.9	34.6	56.0	16.7	28.9	30.6
West	22.9	19.2	8.6	53.0	47.2	45.9

Source: Bureau of the Census, Population Projections for States by Age, Sex, Race, and Hispanic Origin: 1995 to 2025, *PPL-47, 1996; calculations by New Strategist*

Nevada to Grow Fastest

Nevada's population is projected to grow by 24 percent between 1997 and 2005.

Other mountain states are also projected to grow rapidly in the next few years. The population of Idaho should grow by 19.5 percent between 1997 and 2005, Utah and Arizona by 17 percent, Colorado and Wyoming by 14 percent, and Montana by 11 percent. Overall, the mountain states should be the fastest-growing area of the United States during the next few years.

Many states are projected to grow slowly from 1997 to 2005, but only Washington, D.C., is projected to lose population. The states that should grow by less than 2 percent between 1997 and 2005 include Connecticut, Michigan, New York, Ohio, Pennsylvania, Rhode Island, and West Virginia. The nation's most populous state, California, should grow by 8 percent—just slightly higher than the 7 percent national rate.

♦ Political and economic power will continue to shift from the slow-growing Northeast and Midwest to the fast-growing South and West.

State Populations, 1997 to 2005

(number of persons by state, 1997 to 2005; percent change, 1997-2005; numbers in thousands)

	1997	2000	2005	percent change 1997-2005
Total U.S.	267,645	274,634	285,981	6.9%
Alabama	4,334	4,451	4,631	6.9
Alaska	624	653	700	12.2
Arizona	4,458	4,798	5,230	17.3
Arkansas	2,545	2,631	2,750	8.1
California	31,925	32,521	34,441	7.9
Colorado	3,925	4,168	4,468	13.8
Connecticut	3,280	3,284	3,317	1.1
Delaware	739	768	800	8.3
District of Columbia	538	523	529	-1.7
Florida	14,599	15,233	16,279	11.5
Georgia	7,481	7,875	8,413	12.5
Hawaii	1,214	1,257	1,342	10.5
Idaho	1,239	1,347	1,480	19.5
Illinois	11,923	12,051	12,266	2.9
Indiana	5,906	6,045	6,215	5.2
Iowa	2,866	2,900	2,941	2.6
Kansas	2,608	2,668	2,761	5.9
Kentucky	3,916	3,995	4,098	4.6
Louisiana	4,375	4,425	4,535	3.7
Maine	1,249	1,259	1,285	2.9
Maryland	5,143	5,275	5,467	6.3
Massachusetts	6,126	6,199	6,310	3.0
Michigan	9,609	9,679	9,763	1.6
Minnesota	4,702	4,830	5,005	6.4
Mississippi	2,746	2,816	2,908	5.9
Missouri	5,414	5,540	5,718	5.6
Montana	903	950	1,006	11.4
Nebraska	1,665	1,705	1,761	5.8
Nevada	1,675	1,871	2,070	23.6
New Hampshire	1,182	1,224	1,281	8.4
New Jersey	8,045	8,178	8,392	4.3
New Mexico	1,757	1,860	2,016	14.7
New York	18,140	18,146	18,250	0.6

(continued)

(continued from previous page)

	1997	2000	2005	percent change 1997-2005
North Carolina	7,437	7,777	8,227	10.6%
North Dakota	650	662	677	4.2
Ohio	11,227	11,319	11,428	1.8
Oklahoma	3,315	3,373	3,491	5.3
Oregon	3,248	3,397	3,613	11.2
Pennsylvania	12,133	12,202	12,281	1.2
Rhode Island	993	998	1,012	1.9
South Carolina	3,750	3,858	4,033	7.5
South Dakota	749	777	810	8.1
Tennessee	5,423	5,657	5,966	10.0
Texas	19,288	20,119	21,487	11.4
Utah	2,056	2,207	2,411	17.3
Vermont	599	617	638	6.5
Virginia	6,779	6,997	7,324	8.0
Washington	5,609	5,858	6,258	11.6
West Virginia	1,834	1,841	1,849	0.8
Wisconsin	5,209	5,326	5,479	5.2
Wyoming	498	525	568	14.1

Source: Bureau of the Census, Population Projections for States by Age, Sex, Race, and Hispanic Origin: 1995 to 2025, *PPL-47, 1996; calculations by New Strategist*

Every State Has a Different Racial and Ethnic Mix

Each of the nation's 50 states has a unique mix of people, but all are affected by the same trends.

Non-Hispanic blacks are much more dispersed among the states than are non-Hispanic Asians or Hispanics. Sixteen states had a non-Hispanic black population of more than 1 million in 1995. Only five states had more than 1 million Hispanics, and just one state had more than 1 million non-Hispanic Asians. Fifty-three percent of Hispanics live in just two states—California and Texas.

Every state is becoming increasingly diverse, some much faster than others. Non-Hispanic whites accounted for only 53 percent of the residents of California in 1995. By 2000, California will be a minority majority state, with only 48 percent of residents being non-Hispanic white. In contrast, 98 percent of the residents of Maine were non-Hispanic white in 1995. This proportion will fall only slightly, to 97.5 percent, by 2005.

♦ Because some states are far ahead of others in the transition to a multicultural society, expect to see political conflict at the federal level as pioneering states ask for more resources and changes in regulations to help them cope with diversity. States with small minority populations may wonder what all the fuss is about.

Population by State, Race, and Hispanic Origin, 1995

(number of persons by state, race, and Hispanic origin, 1995; numbers in thousands)

	total	non-Hispanic white	non-Hispanic black	non-Hispanic Asian	non-Hispanic Native American	Hispanic
U.S.	262,755	193,523	31,591	8,779	1,930	26,932
Alabama	4,252	3,094	1,083	27	16	32
Alaska	606	441	24	26	90	25
Arizona	4,218	2,936	127	70	217	868
Arkansas	2,484	2,036	392	15	14	27
California	31,589	16,630	2,184	3,380	189	9,206
Colorado	3,746	2,989	150	75	25	507
Connecticut	3,277	2,685	275	63	6	248
Delaware	715	553	129	12	2	19
District of Columbia	553	156	346	13	1	37
Florida	14,164	10,010	1,964	199	36	1,955
Georgia	7,202	4,926	2,004	108	14	150
Hawaii	1,188	354	26	704	4	100
Idaho	1,164	1,063	4	11	14	72
Illinois	11,831	8,615	1,770	338	18	1,090
Indiana	5,803	5,161	465	46	12	119
Iowa	2,843	2,704	54	32	7	46
Kansas	2,566	2,241	152	39	20	114
Kentucky	3,859	3,532	272	22	6	27
Louisiana	4,344	2,800	1,372	49	18	105
Maine	1,241	1,216	5	8	6	6
Maryland	5,042	3,357	1,326	175	12	172
Massachusetts	6,075	5,222	303	184	11	355
Michigan	9,551	7,774	1,363	128	53	233
Minnesota	4,607	4,254	123	104	53	73
Mississippi	2,695	1,687	965	16	8	19
Missouri	5,324	4,593	585	52	20	74
Montana	871	796	3	5	51	16
Nebraska	1,637	1,496	62	17	12	50
Nevada	1,530	1,159	102	55	22	192
New Hampshire	1,148	1,115	7	11	2	13
New Jersey	7,946	5,636	1,043	357	14	896
New Mexico	1,684	839	31	17	140	657
New York	18,134	12,082	2,635	825	51	2,541

(continued)

(continued from previous page)

| | total | non-Hispanic | | | | Hispanic |
		white	black	Asian	Native American	
North Carolina	7,195	5,350	1,587	71	87	100
North Dakota	638	599	3	4	28	4
Ohio	11,153	9,622	1,238	111	20	162
Oklahoma	3,276	2,624	251	40	257	104
Oregon	3,140	2,810	52	88	40	150
Pennsylvania	12,071	10,474	1,133	171	14	279
Rhode Island	990	868	38	20	4	60
South Carolina	3,673	2,503	1,099	27	8	36
South Dakota	729	662	3	4	53	7
Tennessee	5,254	4,308	849	42	10	45
Texas	18,722	10,891	2,189	412	57	5,173
Utah	1,953	1,758	14	44	27	110
Vermont	584	572	2	4	2	4
Virginia	6,618	4,909	1,281	204	15	209
Washington	5,432	4,616	169	274	89	284
West Virginia	1,827	1,750	57	9	2	9
Wisconsin	5,121	4,617	277	71	42	114
Wyoming	479	436	3	3	10	27

Source: Bureau of the Census, Population Projections for States by Age, Sex, Race, and Hispanic Origin: 1995 to 2025, *PPL-47, 1996*

Percent Distribution of State Populations by Race and Hispanic Origin, 1995

(percent distribution of persons by state, race, and Hispanic origin, 1995)

| | total | non-Hispanic | | | | Hispanic |
		white	black	Asian	Native American	
United States	100.0%	73.7%	12.0%	3.3%	0.7%	10.2%
Alabama	100.0	72.8	25.5	0.6	0.4	0.8
Alaska	100.0	72.8	4.0	4.3	14.9	4.1
Arizona	100.0	69.6	3.0	1.7	5.1	20.6
Arkansas	100.0	82.0	15.8	0.6	0.6	1.1
California	100.0	52.6	6.9	10.7	0.6	29.1
Colorado	100.0	79.8	4.0	2.0	0.7	13.5
Connecticut	100.0	81.9	8.4	1.9	0.2	7.6
Delaware	100.0	77.3	18.0	1.7	0.3	2.7
District of Columbia	100.0	28.2	62.6	2.4	0.2	6.7
Florida	100.0	70.7	13.9	1.4	0.3	13.8
Georgia	100.0	68.4	27.8	1.5	0.2	2.1
Hawaii	100.0	29.8	2.2	59.3	0.3	8.4
Idaho	100.0	91.3	0.3	0.9	1.2	6.2
Illinois	100.0	72.8	15.0	2.9	0.2	9.2
Indiana	100.0	88.9	8.0	0.8	0.2	2.1
Iowa	100.0	95.1	1.9	1.1	0.2	1.6
Kansas	100.0	87.3	5.9	1.5	0.8	4.4
Kentucky	100.0	91.5	7.0	0.6	0.2	0.7
Louisiana	100.0	64.5	31.6	1.1	0.4	2.4
Maine	100.0	98.0	0.4	0.6	0.5	0.5
Maryland	100.0	66.6	26.3	3.5	0.2	3.4
Massachusetts	100.0	86.0	5.0	3.0	0.2	5.8
Michigan	100.0	81.4	14.3	1.3	0.6	2.4
Minnesota	100.0	92.3	2.7	2.3	1.2	1.6
Mississippi	100.0	62.6	35.8	0.6	0.3	0.7
Missouri	100.0	86.3	11.0	1.0	0.4	1.4
Montana	100.0	91.4	0.3	0.6	5.9	1.8
Nebraska	100.0	91.4	3.8	1.0	0.7	3.1
Nevada	100.0	75.8	6.7	3.6	1.4	12.5
New Hampshire	100.0	97.1	0.6	1.0	0.2	1.1
New Jersey	100.0	70.9	13.1	4.5	0.2	11.3
New Mexico	100.0	49.8	1.8	1.0	8.3	39.0
New York	100.0	66.6	14.5	4.5	0.3	14.0

(continued)

(continued from previous page)

| | total | non-Hispanic | | | | Hispanic |
		white	black	Asian	Native American	
North Carolina	100.0%	74.4%	22.1%	1.0%	1.2%	1.4%
North Dakota	100.0	93.9	0.5	0.6	4.4	0.6
Ohio	100.0	86.3	11.1	1.0	0.2	1.5
Oklahoma	100.0	80.1	7.7	1.2	7.8	3.2
Oregon	100.0	89.5	1.7	2.8	1.3	4.8
Pennsylvania	100.0	86.8	9.4	1.4	0.1	2.3
Rhode Island	100.0	87.7	3.8	2.0	0.4	6.1
South Carolina	100.0	68.1	29.9	0.7	0.2	1.0
South Dakota	100.0	90.8	0.4	0.5	7.3	1.0
Tennessee	100.0	82.0	16.2	0.8	0.2	0.9
Texas	100.0	58.2	11.7	2.2	0.3	27.6
Utah	100.0	90.0	0.7	2.3	1.4	5.6
Vermont	100.0	97.9	0.3	0.7	0.3	0.7
Virginia	100.0	74.2	19.4	3.1	0.2	3.2
Washington	100.0	85.0	3.1	5.0	1.6	5.2
West Virginia	100.0	95.8	3.1	0.5	0.1	0.5
Wisconsin	100.0	90.2	5.4	1.4	0.8	2.2
Wyoming	100.0	91.0	0.6	0.6	2.1	5.6

Source: Bureau of the Census, Population Projections for States by Age, Sex, Race, and Hispanic Origin: 1995 to 2025, *PPL-47, 1996; calculations by New Strategist*

Population by State, Race, and Hispanic Origin, 2000

(number of persons by state, race, and Hispanic origin, 2000; numbers in thousands)

	total	*white*	*black*	*Asian*	*Native American*	*Hispanic*
		non-Hispanic				
U.S.	274,637	197,062	33,569	10,585	2,055	31,366
Alabama	4,451	3,231	1,133	32	18	37
Alaska	654	461	27	44	91	31
Arizona	4,798	3,254	150	91	232	1,071
Arkansas	2,629	2,155	407	19	15	33
California	32,523	15,562	2,138	4,006	170	10,647
Colorado	4,168	3,268	178	98	30	594
Connecticut	3,285	2,622	293	76	6	288
Delaware	767	582	143	15	2	25
District of Columbia	520	152	315	13	-	40
Florida	15,232	10,405	2,159	239	39	2,390
Georgia	7,874	5,270	2,262	138	15	189
Hawaii	1,256	363	27	755	4	107
Idaho	1,346	1,211	6	15	18	96
Illinois	12,050	8,553	1,813	399	18	1,267
Indiana	6,044	5,338	494	58	14	140
Iowa	2,900	2,737	60	41	8	54
Kansas	2,669	2,293	167	48	23	138
Kentucky	3,993	3,643	285	27	6	32
Louisiana	4,425	2,792	1,438	58	18	119
Maine	1,258	1,230	5	9	6	8
Maryland	5,274	3,371	1,462	213	14	214
Massachusetts	6,200	5,182	332	239	10	437
Michigan	9,680	7,790	1,417	157	55	261
Minnesota	4,830	4,387	152	135	61	95
Mississippi	2,813	1,755	1,010	19	8	21
Missouri	5,540	4,745	622	61	22	90
Montana	950	861	3	7	59	20
Nebraska	1,706	1,540	70	21	14	61
Nevada	1,873	1,366	128	77	25	277
New Hampshire	1,224	1,184	7	14	2	17
New Jersey	8,176	5,558	1,104	456	14	1,044
New Mexico	1,861	912	34	22	157	736
New York	18,147	11,640	2,668	7	53	2,805

(continued)

(continued from previous page)

| | total | non-Hispanic | | | | Hispanic |
		white	black	Asian	Native American	
North Carolina	7,779	5,748	1,726	92	92	121
North Dakota	660	611	5	6	32	6
Ohio	11,317	9,672	1,306	136	20	183
Oklahoma	3,373	2,653	276	47	273	124
Oregon	3,399	2,990	59	110	45	195
Pennsylvania	12,201	10,460	1,181	210	16	334
Rhode Island	997	851	40	26	4	76
South Carolina	3,857	2,624	1,152	31	8	42
South Dakota	776	698	5	5	60	8
Tennessee	5,656	4,607	925	55	12	57
Texas	20,120	11,273	2,406	506	60	5,875
Utah	2,208	1,961	18	58	33	138
Vermont	616	600	2	6	2	6
Virginia	6,997	5,061	1,394	257	16	269
Washington	5,857	4,881	179	342	95	360
West Virginia	1,840	1,758	58	11	2	11
Wisconsin	5,328	4,732	318	97	45	136
Wyoming	524	469	4	4	12	35

Source: Bureau of the Census, Population Projections for States by Age, Sex, Race, and Hispanic Origin: 1995 to 2025, *PPL-47, 1996*

Percent Distribution of State Populations
by Race and Hispanic Origin, 2000

(percent distribution of persons by state, race, and Hispanic origin, 2000; numbers in thousands)

	total	non-Hispanic white	non-Hispanic black	non-Hispanic Asian	non-Hispanic Native American	Hispanic
U.S.	100.0%	71.8%	12.2%	3.9%	0.7%	11.4%
Alabama	100.0	72.6	25.5	0.7	0.4	0.8
Alaska	100.0	70.5	4.1	6.7	13.9	4.7
Arizona	100.0	67.8	3.1	1.9	4.8	22.3
Arkansas	100.0	82.0	15.5	0.7	0.6	1.3
California	100.0	47.8	6.6	12.3	0.5	32.7
Colorado	100.0	78.4	4.3	2.4	0.7	14.3
Connecticut	100.0	79.8	8.9	2.3	0.2	8.8
Delaware	100.0	75.9	18.6	2.0	0.3	3.3
District of Columbia	100.0	29.2	60.6	2.5	-	7.7
Florida	100.0	68.3	14.2	1.6	0.3	15.7
Georgia	100.0	66.9	28.7	1.8	0.2	2.4
Hawaii	100.0	28.9	2.1	60.1	0.3	8.5
Idaho	100.0	90.0	0.4	1.1	1.3	7.1
Illinois	100.0	71.0	15.0	3.3	0.1	10.5
Indiana	100.0	88.3	8.2	1.0	0.2	2.3
Iowa	100.0	94.4	2.1	1.4	0.3	1.9
Kansas	100.0	85.9	6.3	1.8	0.9	5.2
Kentucky	100.0	91.2	7.1	0.7	0.2	0.8
Louisiana	100.0	63.1	32.5	1.3	0.4	2.7
Maine	100.0	97.8	0.4	0.7	0.5	0.6
Maryland	100.0	63.9	27.7	4.0	0.3	4.1
Massachusetts	100.0	83.6	5.4	3.9	0.2	7.0
Michigan	100.0	80.5	14.6	1.6	0.6	2.7
Minnesota	100.0	90.8	3.1	2.8	1.3	2.0
Mississippi	100.0	62.4	35.9	0.7	0.3	0.7
Missouri	100.0	85.6	11.2	1.1	0.4	1.6
Montana	100.0	90.6	0.3	0.7	6.2	2.1
Nebraska	100.0	90.3	4.1	1.2	0.8	3.6
Nevada	100.0	72.9	6.8	4.1	1.3	14.8
New Hampshire	100.0	96.7	0.6	1.1	0.2	1.4
New Jersey	100.0	68.0	13.5	5.6	0.2	12.8
New Mexico	100.0	49.0	1.8	1.2	8.4	39.5
New York	100.0	64.1	14.7	0.0	0.3	15.5

(continued)

(continued from previous page)

| | total | non-Hispanic | | | | Hispanic |
		white	black	Asian	Native American	
North Carolina	100.0%	73.9%	22.2%	1.2%	1.2%	1.6%
North Dakota	100.0	92.6	0.8	0.9	4.8	0.9
Ohio	100.0	85.5	11.5	1.2	0.2	1.6
Oklahoma	100.0	78.7	8.2	1.4	8.1	3.7
Oregon	100.0	88.0	1.7	3.2	1.3	5.7
Pennsylvania	100.0	85.7	9.7	1.7	0.1	2.7
Rhode Island	100.0	85.4	4.0	2.6	0.4	7.6
South Carolina	100.0	68.0	29.9	0.8	0.2	1.1
South Dakota	100.0	89.9	0.6	0.6	7.7	1.0
Tennessee	100.0	81.5	16.4	1.0	0.2	1.0
Texas	100.0	56.0	12.0	2.5	0.3	29.2
Utah	100.0	88.8	0.8	2.6	1.5	6.3
Vermont	100.0	97.4	0.3	1.0	0.3	1.0
Virginia	100.0	72.3	19.9	3.7	0.2	3.8
Washington	100.0	83.3	3.1	5.8	1.6	6.1
West Virginia	100.0	95.5	3.2	0.6	0.1	0.6
Wisconsin	100.0	88.8	6.0	1.8	0.8	2.6
Wyoming	100.0	89.5	0.8	0.8	2.3	6.7

Source: Bureau of the Census, Population Projections for States by Age, Sex, Race, and Hispanic Origin: 1995 to 2025, *PPL-47, 1996; calculations by New Strategist*

Population by State, Race, and Hispanic Origin, 2005

(number of persons by state, race, and Hispanic origin, 2005; numbers in thousands)

	total	non-Hispanic white	non-Hispanic black	non-Hispanic Asian	non-Hispanic Native American	Hispanic
U.S.	285,982	199,802	35,485	12,454	2,184	36,057
Alabama	4,632	3,355	1,179	38	18	42
Alaska	700	476	29	67	91	37
Arizona	5,232	3,441	168	109	245	1,269
Arkansas	2,747	2,249	421	21	16	40
California	34,441	15,123	2,158	4,731	161	12,268
Colorado	4,467	3,434	200	117	34	682
Connecticut	3,316	2,574	313	91	6	332
Delaware	798	596	154	17	2	29
District of Columbia	528	156	310	16	-	46
Florida	16,279	10,764	2,349	279	42	2,845
Georgia	8,414	5,515	2,495	162	16	226
Hawaii	1,341	372	28	818	4	119
Idaho	1,480	1,314	7	17	21	121
Illinois	12,265	8,487	1,853	457	18	1,450
Indiana	6,217	5,453	520	68	14	162
Iowa	2,942	2,755	67	50	9	61
Kansas	2,763	2,337	180	55	25	166
Kentucky	4,097	3,727	295	31	6	38
Louisiana	4,536	2,803	1,509	68	18	138
Maine	1,283	1,251	5	11	6	10
Maryland	5,465	3,368	1,577	248	14	258
Massachusetts	6,312	5,123	361	294	10	524
Michigan	9,763	7,767	1,466	184	57	289
Minnesota	5,006	4,480	178	166	68	114
Mississippi	2,906	1,804	1,047	23	8	24
Missouri	5,717	4,863	656	69	24	105
Montana	1,008	904	4	9	65	26
Nebraska	1,765	1,572	78	27	16	72
Nevada	2,071	1,456	146	93	26	350
New Hampshire	1,280	1,233	8	17	2	20
New Jersey	8,394	5,462	1,165	556	15	1,196
New Mexico	2,014	958	36	25	174	821
New York	18,250	11,271	2,714	1,140	54	3,071

(continued)

(continued from previous page)

	total	non-Hispanic				Hispanic
		white	black	Asian	Native American	
North Carolina	8,228	6,040	1,844	109	96	139
North Dakota	676	620	5	6	37	8
Ohio	11,428	9,669	1,370	161	22	206
Oklahoma	3,489	2,700	303	54	289	143
Oregon	3,614	3,133	66	129	49	237
Pennsylvania	12,284	10,398	1,228	249	18	391
Rhode Island	1,012	838	44	33	5	92
South Carolina	4,032	2,738	1,200	36	8	50
South Dakota	807	721	5	6	66	9
Tennessee	5,966	4,828	993	64	14	67
Texas	21,487	11,587	2,620	593	63	6,624
Utah	2,412	2,117	21	71	39	164
Vermont	638	619	4	7	2	6
Virginia	7,322	5,175	1,500	309	16	322
Washington	6,256	5,115	191	410	103	437
West Virginia	1,849	1,761	58	13	2	15
Wisconsin	5,481	4,799	356	122	48	156
Wyoming	568	501	5	6	14	42

Source: Bureau of the Census, Population Projections for States by Age, Sex, Race, and Hispanic Origin: 1995 to 2025, *PPL-47, 1996*

Percent Distribution of State Populations
by Race and Hispanic Origin, 2005

(percent distribution of persons by state, race, and Hispanic origin, 2005; numbers in thousands)

	total	non-Hispanic white	black	Asian	Native American	Hispanic
U.S.	100.0%	69.9%	12.4%	4.4%	0.8%	12.6%
Alabama	100.0	72.4	25.5	0.8	0.4	0.9
Alaska	100.0	68.0	4.1	9.6	13.0	5.3
Arizona	100.0	65.8	3.2	2.1	4.7	24.3
Arkansas	100.0	81.9	15.3	0.8	0.6	1.5
California	100.0	43.9	6.3	13.7	0.5	35.6
Colorado	100.0	76.9	4.5	2.6	0.8	15.3
Connecticut	100.0	77.6	9.4	2.7	0.2	10.0
Delaware	100.0	74.7	19.3	2.1	0.3	3.6
District of Columbia	100.0	29.5	58.7	3.0	-	8.7
Florida	100.0	66.1	14.4	1.7	0.3	17.5
Georgia	100.0	65.5	29.7	1.9	0.2	2.7
Hawaii	100.0	27.7	2.1	61.0	0.3	8.9
Idaho	100.0	88.8	0.5	1.1	1.4	8.2
Illinois	100.0	69.2	15.1	3.7	0.1	11.8
Indiana	100.0	87.7	8.4	1.1	0.2	2.6
Iowa	100.0	93.6	2.3	1.7	0.3	2.1
Kansas	100.0	84.6	6.5	2.0	0.9	6.0
Kentucky	100.0	91.0	7.2	0.8	0.1	0.9
Louisiana	100.0	61.8	33.3	1.5	0.4	3.0
Maine	100.0	97.5	0.4	0.9	0.5	0.8
Maryland	100.0	61.6	28.9	4.5	0.3	4.7
Massachusetts	100.0	81.2	5.7	4.7	0.2	8.3
Michigan	100.0	79.6	15.0	1.9	0.6	3.0
Minnesota	100.0	89.5	3.6	3.3	1.4	2.3
Mississippi	100.0	62.1	36.0	0.8	0.3	0.8
Missouri	100.0	85.1	11.5	1.2	0.4	1.8
Montana	100.0	89.7	0.4	0.9	6.4	2.6
Nebraska	100.0	89.1	4.4	1.5	0.9	4.1
Nevada	100.0	70.3	7.0	4.5	1.3	16.9
New Hampshire	100.0	96.3	0.6	1.3	0.2	1.6
New Jersey	100.0	65.1	13.9	6.6	0.2	14.2
New Mexico	100.0	47.6	1.8	1.2	8.6	40.8
New York	100.0	61.8	14.9	6.2	0.3	16.8

(continued)

(continued from previous page)

| | total | non-Hispanic | | | | Hispanic |
		white	black	Asian	Native American	
North Carolina	100.0%	73.4%	22.4%	1.3%	1.2%	1.7%
North Dakota	100.0	91.7	0.7	0.9	5.5	1.2
Ohio	100.0	84.6	12.0	1.4	0.2	1.8
Oklahoma	100.0	77.4	8.7	1.5	8.3	4.1
Oregon	100.0	86.7	1.8	3.6	1.4	6.6
Pennsylvania	100.0	84.6	10.0	2.0	0.1	3.2
Rhode Island	100.0	82.8	4.3	3.3	0.5	9.1
South Carolina	100.0	67.9	29.8	0.9	0.2	1.2
South Dakota	100.0	89.3	0.6	0.7	8.2	1.1
Tennessee	100.0	80.9	16.6	1.1	0.2	1.1
Texas	100.0	53.9	12.2	2.8	0.3	30.8
Utah	100.0	87.8	0.9	2.9	1.6	6.8
Vermont	100.0	97.0	0.6	1.1	0.3	0.9
Virginia	100.0	70.7	20.5	4.2	0.2	4.4
Washington	100.0	81.8	3.1	6.6	1.6	7.0
West Virginia	100.0	95.2	3.1	0.7	0.1	0.8
Wisconsin	100.0	87.6	6.5	2.2	0.9	2.8
Wyoming	100.0	88.2	0.9	1.1	2.5	7.4

Source: Bureau of the Census, Population Projections for States by Age, Sex, Race, and Hispanic Origin: 1995 to 2025, *PPL-47, 1996; calculations by New Strategist*

A Metropolitan Nation

Las Vegas is the fastest-growing large metropolitan area.

Three out of four Americans lived in one of the nation's metropolitan areas in 1990. In 1950, barely half of Americans were metropolitan residents. Within metropolitan areas, the distribution of the population has changed dramatically as well. The suburbs are now home to 46 percent of Americans, up from just 23 percent in 1950. About one-third of Americans live in the nation's central cities, a figure that has barely changed over the past 40 years. The proportion of Americans living in the nation's nonmetropolitan areas has fallen sharply, from 44 percent in 1950 to just 23 percent in 1990.

New York is by far the nation's largest metropolitan area, with almost 20 million residents. It will be several more years before Los Angeles, with a population of 15 million, catches up to New York. Among the nation's 50 largest metropolitan areas, the fastest-growing is Las Vegas, up 26 percent between 1990 and 1994. Only one of the largest metropolitan areas—Hartford, Connecticut—lost population between 1990 and 1994.

◆ Metropolitan areas in the South and West will continue to grow faster than those in the Northeast or Midwest as Americans flock to warm climates and plentiful jobs.

◆ Metropolitan areas in the mountain states, such as Las Vegas, Salt Lake City, and Phoenix, will grow rapidly along with their states—which are projected to be the biggest gainers in population between 1997 and 2005.

Population by Metropolitan Status, 1950 to 1990

(percent of persons by metropolitan status, 1950 to 1990; metropolitan areas as defined at each census)

	1990	1980	1970	1960	1950
Metropolitan areas	77.5%	74.8%	69.0%	63.3%	56.1%
Central cities	31.3	30.0	31.4	32.3	32.8
Suburbs	46.2	44.8	37.6	30.9	23.3
Nonmetropolitan	22.5	25.2	31.0	36.7	43.9

Note: The suburbs are the portion of a metropolitan area that is outside the central city.

(percent of persons by metropolitan status and size of metropolitan area, 1950 to 1990; metropolitan areas as defined at each census)

	1990	1980	1970	1960	1950
Metropolitan	77.5%	74.8%	69.0%	63.3%	56.1%
More than 5 million	21.1	20.4	15.2	15.8	12.2
1 million to 5 million	28.9	25.2	25.5	19.5	17.2
250,000 to 1 million	18.7	19.4	19.9	18.9	18.1
Less than 250,000	8.6	9.9	8.4	9.1	8.6
Nonmetropolitan	22.5	25.2	31.0	36.7	43.9

Source: Bureau of the Census, Metropolitan Areas and Cities, 1990 Census Profile, No. 3, 1991; calculations by New Strategist

Populations of the Top 50 Metropolitan Areas, 1990 and 1994

(number of persons in the 50 largest metropolitan areas, April 1,1990 and July 1, 1994, and percent change, 1990-94; ranked by size in 1994; numbers in thousands; metropolitan areas as defined by the Office of Management and Budget, June 30, 1995)

	1994	1990	percent change 1990-94
New York-No. New Jersey-Long Island, NY-NJ-CT-PA	19,796	19,550	1.3%
Los Angeles-Riverside-Orange County, CA	15,302	14,532	5.3
Chicago-Gary-Kenosha, IL-IN-WI	8,527	8,240	3.5
Washington-Baltimore, DC-MD-VA-WV	7,051	6,726	4.8
San Francisco-Oakland-San Jose, CA	6,513	6,250	4.2
Philadelphia-Wilmington-Atlantic City, PA-NJ-DE-MD	5,959	5,893	1.1
Boston-Worcester-Lawrence, MA-NH-ME-CT	5,497	5,455	0.8
Detroit-Ann Arbor-Flint, MI	5,256	5,187	1.3
Dallas-Fort Worth, TX	4,362	4,037	8.0
Houston-Galveston-Brazoria, TX	4,099	3,731	9.9
Miami-Fort Lauderdale, FL	3,408	3,193	6.7
Atlanta, GA	3,331	2,960	12.6
Seattle-Tacoma-Bremerton, WA	3,226	2,970	8.6
Cleveland-Akron, OH	2,899	2,860	1.4
Minneapolis-St. Paul, MN-WI	2,688	2,539	5.9
San Diego, CA	2,632	2,498	5.4
St. Louis, MO-IL	2,536	2,492	1.8
Phoenix-Mesa, AZ	2,473	2,238	10.5
Pittsburgh, PA	2,402	2,395	0.3
Denver-Boulder-Greeley, CO	2,190	1,980	10.6
Tampa-St. Petersburg-Clearwater, FL	2,157	2,068	4.3
Portland-Salem, OR-WA	1,982	1,793	10.5
Cincinnati-Hamilton, OH-KY-IN	1,894	1,818	4.2
Kansas City, MO-KS	1,647	1,583	4.1
Milwaukee-Racine, WI	1,637	1,607	1.9
Sacramento-Yolo, CA	1,588	1,481	7.2
Norfolk-Virginia Beach-Newport News, VA-NC	1,529	1,445	5.8
Indianapolis, IN	1,462	1,380	5.9
San Antonio, TX	1,437	1,325	8.5
Columbus, OH	1,423	1,345	5.8
Orlando, FL	1,361	1,225	11.1
New Orleans, LA	1,309	1,285	1.8
Charlotte-Gastonia-Rock Hill, NC-SC	1,260	1,162	8.4

(continued)

(continued from previous page)

	1994	1990	percent change 1990-94
Buffalo-Niagara Falls, NY	1,189	1,189	-0.0%
Salt Lake City-Ogden, UT	1,178	1,072	9.9
Hartford, CT	1,151	1,158	-0.6
Greensboro-Winston-Salem-High Point, NC	1,107	1,050	5.4
Rochester, NY	1,091	1,062	2.7
Las Vegas, NV-AZ	1,076	853	26.2
Nashville, TN	1,070	985	8.6
Memphis, TN-AR-MS	1,056	1,007	4.8
Oklahoma City, OK	1,007	959	5.0
Grand Rapids-Muskegon-Holland, MI	985	938	5.0
Louisville, KY-IN	981	949	3.4
Jacksonville, FL	972	907	7.2
Raleigh-Durham-Chapel Hill, NC	965	858	12.4
Austin-San Marcos, TX	964	846	13.9
Dayton-Springfield, OH	956	951	0.5
West Palm Beach-Boca Raton, FL	955	864	10.6
Richmond-Petersburg, VA	917	866	5.9

Source: Bureau of the Census, Statistical Abstract of the United States: 1996

Americans Are Moving Less

Mobility rates have fallen sharply over the past few decades.

Between March 1993 and March 1994, only 16.7 percent of Americans moved to a different house. This figure is far below the 21.2 percent of Americans who moved between 1950 and 1951. Most movers remain in their local area, which indicates that most moves are related to housing needs rather than job relocation. Only 6 percent of people moved to a different county between 1993 and 1994, and only 3 percent moved to a different state. Many long-distance moves are job related.

Overall, nearly 43 million Americans moved between 1993 and 1994, 36 percent more than in 1950-51 because of population growth. Those most likely to move are young adults, many of them seeking jobs. Many college students, for example, move from their college community to a job site after graduation.

One-third of renters move each year, compared with just 9 percent of homeowners. Only 13 percent of people who are not in the labor force move each year, compared with 39 percent of those in the armed forces.

♦ As the enormous baby-boom generation enters its 50s during the next decade, the overall mobility rate will continue to decline because moving is infrequent among the middle-aged.

Mobility of the Population, 1950 to 1994

(total number of persons aged 1 or older, and number and percent moving by type of move; selected years 1950-94; numbers in thousands)

	total	total movers	living in the U.S. at the beginning of the year					not living in U.S. at beginning of year
			different house, same county total	different house, same county	different county total	same state	different state	
Number								
1993-94	255,774	42,835	41,590	26,638	14,952	8,226	6,726	1,245
1992-93	250,210	42,048	40,743	26,212	14,532	7,735	6,797	1,305
1991-92	247,380	42,800	41,545	26,587	14,957	7,853	7,105	1,255
1990-91	244,884	41,539	40,154	25,151	15,003	7,881	7,122	1,385
1989-90	242,208	43,381	41,821	25,726	16,094	8,061	8,033	1,560
1985-86	232,998	43,237	42,037	26,401	15,636	8,665	6,971	1,200
1980-81	221,641	38,200	36,887	23,097	13,789	7,614	6,175	1,313
1970-71	201,506	37,705	36,161	23,018	13,143	6,197	6,946	1,544
1960-61	177,354	36,533	35,535	24,289	11,246	5,493	5,753	998
1950-51	148,400	31,464	31,158	20,694	10,464	5,276	5,188	306
Percent								
1993-94	100.0%	16.7%	16.3%	10.4%	5.8%	3.2%	2.6%	0.5%
1992-93	100.0	16.8	16.3	10.5	5.8	3.1	2.7	0.5
1991-92	100.0	17.3	16.8	10.7	6.0	3.2	2.9	0.5
1990-91	100.0	17.0	16.4	10.3	6.1	3.2	2.9	0.6
1989-90	100.0	17.9	17.3	10.6	6.6	3.3	3.3	0.6
1985-86	100.0	18.6	18.0	11.3	6.7	3.7	3.0	0.5
1980-81	100.0	17.2	16.6	10.4	6.2	3.4	2.8	0.6
1970-71	100.0	18.7	17.9	11.4	6.5	3.1	3.4	0.8
1960-61	100.0	20.6	20.0	13.7	6.3	3.1	3.2	0.6
1950-51	100.0	21.2	21.0	13.9	7.1	3.6	3.5	0.2

Source: Bureau of the Census, Geographical Mobility: March 1993 to March 1994, *Current Population Reports, P20-485, 1995*

Characteristics of Movers, 1994

(percent of persons aged 1 or older moving between March 1993 and March 1994, by age, housing tenure, employment status, and type of move)

| | total | total movers | different house in the U.S. | | | | | movers from abroad |
| | | | total | local move (same county) | long distance (different county) | | | |
					total	same state	different state	
Total	100.0%	16.7%	16.3%	10.4%	5.8%	3.2%	2.6%	0.5%
Aged 1 to 4	100.0	22.0	21.5	14.6	6.9	3.6	3.3	0.5
Aged 5 to 9	100.0	17.3	16.9	11.2	5.7	3.1	2.6	0.4
Aged 10 to 14	100.0	13.2	12.9	8.7	4.2	2.4	1.8	0.4
Aged 15 to 19	100.0	17.6	16.9	10.8	6.0	3.2	2.9	0.7
Aged 20 to 24	100.0	35.6	34.4	22.0	12.4	7.4	5.0	1.2
Aged 25 to 29	100.0	30.7	29.7	19.1	10.7	6.0	4.7	0.9
Aged 30 to 34	100.0	22.9	22.2	14.4	7.9	4.6	3.2	0.6
Aged 35 to 44	100.0	15.1	14.7	9.2	5.5	3.0	2.5	0.4
Aged 45 to 54	100.0	10.5	10.1	6.2	3.9	1.9	1.9	0.4
Aged 55 to 64	100.0	6.8	6.6	3.9	2.7	1.4	1.3	0.2
Aged 65 to 74	100.0	6.0	5.9	3.3	2.6	1.2	1.3	0.1
Aged 75 to 84	100.0	4.9	4.8	2.9	1.9	0.9	1.0	0.1
Aged 85 or older	100.0	5.8	5.6	3.4	2.2	1.0	1.2	0.1
Housing tenure								
Owner	100.0	8.9	8.7	5.2	3.5	1.9	1.6	0.2
Renter	100.0	32.6	31.5	20.9	10.6	5.8	4.8	1.1
Employment status								
Civilian labor force	100.0	18.4	18.0	11.4	6.6	3.8	2.7	0.4
Employed	100.0	17.7	17.3	11.1	6.2	3.6	2.6	0.4
Unemployed	100.0	27.5	26.7	15.2	11.4	6.1	5.3	0.9
Armed forces	100.0	38.9	34.3	17.7	16.5	2.3	14.2	4.7
Not in labor force	100.0	12.8	12.2	7.7	4.5	2.3	2.3	0.6

Source: Bureau of the Census, Geographical Mobility: March 1993 to March 1994, *Current Population Reports, P20-485, 1995*

Immigration Boosts Nation's Growth

More than 5 million immigrants came to the United States between 1991 and 1995.

The United States gained more immigrants during the 1980s than in any ten years since the first decade of the century. More than 7 million immigrants were granted permanent resident status in the United States during the 1980s, surpassed only by the 8.8 million immigrants who came to the U.S. between 1901 and 1910.

A new record may be set in the 1990s. The number of immigrants coming to the U.S. in the first half of the decade is 60 percent of the amount needed to surpass the record number. Since immigrants are a much smaller share of our population today than they were at the beginning of the 20th century, however, their impact on American society is far less.

◆ A slowing of immigration would sharply reduce U.S. population growth because immigration accounts for a large share of the nation's population gain each year.

◆ Since most immigrants are of working age, many people worry that immigrants take jobs away from Americans—particularly minorities. With millions more immigrants coming to the U.S. in the 1990s, this issue is likely to be hotly debated by citizens and politicians alike.

Immigration to the U.S., 1901 to 1995

(number of immigrants granted permanent residence in the U.S. by decade, 1901-1995; and by single year, 1981-95)

year	immigrants
1995	720,461
1994	804,416
1993	904,292
1992	973,977
1991	1,827,167
1990	1,536,483
1989	1,090,924
1988	643,025
1987	601,516
1986	601,708
1985	570,009
1984	543,903
1983	559,763
1982	594,131
1981	596,600
1991-95	5,230,313
1981-90	7,338,062
1971-80	4,493,314
1961-70	3,321,677
1951-60	2,515,479
1941-50	1,035,039
1931-40	528,431
1921-30	4,107,209
1911-20	5,735,811
1901-10	8,795,386

Note: Immigrants are persons granted legal permanent residence in the United States. They either arrive in the U.S. with immigrant visas issued abroad or they adjust their status in the United States from temporary to permanent residence.
Source: Immigration and Naturalization Service, 1994 Statistical Yearbook of the Immigration and Naturalization Service, 1996; *and Internet web site,* http://www.usdoj.gov/ins

Immigrants Head to California

The impact of immigration varies dramatically across the country. Some states are overwhelmed with immigrants, while others rarely see them.

Among the more than 800,000 immigrants admitted to the United States in 1994, over one-third planned to live in the West, 30 percent in the Northeast, 23 percent in the South, and only 12 percent in the Midwest.

Among immigrants from Mexico, 59 percent planned to live in the West. Sixty percent of immigrants from the Philippines also intended to live in the West. Fifty percent of immigrants from China and 47 percent of those from Vietnam headed West. Most immigrants who settle in the West live in California.

Thirty percent of immigrants from Vietnam planned to live in the South. Forty-four percent of immigrants from Poland intended to live in the Midwest. And 73 percent of immigrants from the Dominican Republic planned to make their homes in the Northeast.

♦ An influx of non-English-speaking immigrants who need jobs, schools and health care creates severe problems for some states. There are no easy political answers to their problems, since only a few states are severely affected while others are untouched.

Immigrants by Country of Birth and Region of Residence, 1994

(total number of immigrants admitted to the U.S. from the eight leading countries of birth and percent distribution by intended region of residence, 1994)

	total	percent	Northeast	Midwest	South	West
Total	804,416	100.0%	30.1%	11.5%	22.9%	33.6%
Mexico	111,398	100.0	2.2	9.8	28.4	59.4
Former Soviet Union	63,420	100.0	43.7	13.6	9.8	32.8
China	53,985	100.0	34.2	10.4	15.4	39.7
Philippines	53,535	100.0	14.8	8.1	12.6	60.4
Vietnam	41,345	100.0	10.8	11.4	30.8	46.9
Dominican Republic	51,189	100.0	73.3	0.6	6.2	0.4
India	34,921	100.0	34.0	19.0	22.9	24.0
Poland	28,048	100.0	47.4	44.2	4.7	3.8

Note: Total includes immigrants from other countries not shown separately.
Source: Bureau of the Census, Statistical Abstract of the United States: 1996; calculations by New Strategist

Foreign-Born Americans Are Diverse

Nearly 23 million Americans—or 9 percent of the population—are foreign-born.

The largest share of the foreign-born are from Mexico (28 percent). No other country accounts for more than 5 percent of the nation's foreign-born population. Only 68 percent of the foreign-born are white, compared with 84 percent of native-born Americans. Fully 46 percent of the foreign-born are Hispanic, compared with just 7 percent of native-born Americans.

The foreign-born are more likely to be high school dropouts than are native-born Americans, and they are also more likely to be college graduates. This diversity in education stems from the diversity of the foreign-born. Some are immigrants with very little education, while others are highly educated professionals. Thirty-six percent of the foreign-born are high school dropouts, compared with only 17 percent of native-born Americans. Twenty-three percent of the foreign-born have at least a bachelor's degree, compared with 22 percent of native-born Americans.

The unemployment rate of the foreign-born is not much greater than that of the native-born population. But poverty is more widespread. Twenty-three percent of the foreign-born are poor, compared with 14 percent of native-born Americans.

♦ The number of foreign-born Americans will continue to expand rapidly as long as immigration remains high.

Foreign-Born Population by Country of Birth, 1994

(number and percent distribution of foreign-born persons by country of birth, for the 14 largest foreign-born populations in the United States ranked by size, 1994; numbers in thousands)

	number	percent
Total persons	259,752	-
Total native born	237,184	-
Total foreign born	22,568	100.0%
Mexico	6,264	27.8
Philippines	1,033	4.6
Cuba	805	3.6
El Salvador	718	3.2
Canada	679	3.0
Germany	625	2.8
China	565	2.5
Dominican Republic	556	2.5
Korea	533	2.4
Vietnam	496	2.2
India	493	2.2
Italy	483	2.1
England	454	2.0
Russia	454	2.0

Source: Bureau of the Census, The Foreign-Born Population: 1994, *Current Population Reports, P20-486, 1995; and Internet web site,* http://www.census.gov; *calculations by New Strategist*

Characteristics of the Foreign-Born Population, 1994

(number and percent distribution of the native- and foreign-born populations by selected characteristics, 1994; numbers in thousands)

	native-born		foreign-born	
	number	*percent*	*number*	*percent*
Total	237,184	100.0%	22,568	100.0%
Under age 5	20,160	8.5	298	1.3
Aged 5 to 17	47,118	19.9	2,190	9.7
Aged 18 to 24	22,839	9.6	2,636	11.7
Aged 25 to 29	17,034	7.2	2,592	11.5
Aged 30 to 34	19,643	8.3	2,677	11.9
Aged 35 to 44	37,006	15.6	4,522	20.0
Aged 45 to 64	45,245	19.1	5,014	22.2
Aged 65 or older	28,139	11.9	2,640	11.7
Sex				
Male	115,782	48.8	11,132	49.3
Female	121,402	51.2	11,436	50.7
Race				
White	199,793	84.2	15,428	68.4
Black	31,443	13.3	1,596	7.1
Asian	2,813	1.2	4,630	20.5
Hispanic origin				
Non-Hispanic	220,808	93.1	12,298	54.5
Hispanic	16,376	6.9	10,270	45.5
Educational attainment				
Total, aged 25 or older	147,067	100.0	17,445	100.0
Not a high school graduate	25,166	17.1	6,274	36.0
High school graudate, some college	89,382	60.8	7,147	41.0
Bachelor's degree	21,660	14.7	2,596	14.9
Graduate or professional degree	10,859	7.4	1,428	8.2
Labor force status				
Total, aged 16 or older	176,607	100.0	20,559	100.0
In labor force	116,281	65.8	12,883	62.7
Employed	108,402	61.4	11,706	56.9
Unemployed	7,880	4.5	1,176	5.7
Not in labor force	59,411	33.6	7,635	37.1
Income and poverty				
Median personal income	$15,876	-	$12,179	-
In poverty	34,086	14.4	5,179	22.9

Source: Bureau of the Census, Statistical Abstract of the United States: 1996

Who Are the Crime Victims?

Crime is down, but many people are still victims.

Police are reporting a decline in crime across the nation, and so is the average American, according to the National Crime Victimization Survey of the Bureau of Justice Statistics. This household survey asks a representative sample of Americans whether anyone in their household has been a crime victim in the past year. Overall, 39.6 million personal and property crimes were reported by respondents in the 1995 survey, down from 42.4 million in 1994.

While crime is down overall, some people are more likely to be crime victims than others. Detailed data for 1994 show that 53.1 of every 1,000 Americans aged 12 or older were victims of crime in 1994. Those most likely to be victims of crime are males (61.7), teenagers (125.9), blacks (65.4), Hispanics (63.3), and those with household incomes below $7,500 (88.3).

♦ As the children of baby boomers enter their teens—the age of peak criminal victimization—expect Americans to get even tougher on criminals, especially juvenile offenders.

Crime Victims, 1994

(rate of criminal victimization per 1,000 persons aged 12 or older, by selected characteristics of victims and type of crime, 1994)

	total	*violent crime*	*personal theft*
Total	53.1	50.8	2.3
Sex			
Male	61.7	59.6	2.0
Female	45.1	42.5	2.5
Age			
Aged 12 to 15	117.4	114.8	2.6
Aged 16 to 19	125.9	121.7	4.2
Aged 20 to 24	102.5	99.2	3.3
Aged 25 to 34	63.2	60.9	2.3
Aged 35 to 49	41.4	39.5	1.9
Aged 50 to 64	16.8	15.1	1.7
Aged 65 or older	7.2	5.1	2.1
Race			
White	51.5	49.4	2.1
Black	65.4	61.8	3.6
Other	49.1	47.6	1.6
Hispanic origin			
Non-Hispanic	51.9	49.8	2.1
Hispanic	63.3	59.8	3.5
Household income			
Under $7,500	88.3	83.6	4.7
$7,500 to $14,999	60.8	58.6	2.2
$15,000 to $24,999	51.7	49.9	1.8
$25,000 to $34,999	51.3	49.3	2.0
$35,000 to $49,999	49.3	46.8	2.6
$50,000 to $74,999	47.6	46.1	1.5
$75,000 or more	42.7	40.0	2.7

Source: Bureau of the Census, Statistical Abstract of the United States: 1996

7

Spending Trends

◆ **Average household spending fell from $33,271 in 1985 to $32,277 in 1995.**
Most of the cuts were for discretionary items such as restaurant meals, alcohol, furniture, and major appliances.

◆ **Some categories, however, saw substantial spending increases.**
As local governments tried to make up for funding cuts, households were forced to spend 50 percent more on property taxes and 28 percent more on water and public services.

◆ **Households headed by 45-to-54-year-olds spend the most.**
They spend 31 percent more than the average household—$42,181 in 1995.

◆ **Not surprisingly, households that spend the most have the highest incomes.**
The 25 percent of households with incomes of $50,000 or more account for fully 44 percent of all household spending.

◆ **Low-income households are above-average spenders on some items, however.**
Households with incomes below $30,000 spend more than average on rent, children's clothes, drugs, and some gifts.

◆ **Married couples with children spend much more than average.**
They account for over one-third of all spending, although they are just 27 percent of all households.

◆ **Overall, whites spend more than blacks and Hispanics, although it varies by category.**
Blacks spend more than average on electricity, fuel oil, and processed vegetables. Hispanics spend above average on rent, cleaning supplies, and baby clothes.

◆ **Both income and spending are highest in the West and lowest in the South.**
Because climate has a lot to do with spending, regional spending patterns are not expected to change much in the years ahead.

Household Spending Slides

Household spending fell by 3 percent between 1985 and 1995, after adjusting for inflation.

As consumers tighten their belts, spending has fallen. The average household spent $32,277 in 1995, down from $33,271 ten years earlier in 1985. Spending fell far more in some categories than in others, according to the Bureau of Labor Statistics' Consumer Expenditure Survey. This survey collects data on the spending of American households on nearly 1,000 products and services.

Americans had no choice but to limit their spending on discretionary items when the recession of the early 1990s cut their incomes. Spending on food away from home fell by nearly 17 percent between 1985 and 1995, after adjusting for inflation. Spending on other discretionary items fell even more. Spending on alcoholic beverages fell by 36 percent between 1985 and 1995, spending on furniture was down by 19 percent, major appliance spending was down by 18 percent, and spending on new cars and trucks fell by 30 percent.

Spending rose in many categories over which consumers had little control. Spending on property taxes rose by 50 percent as local governments tried to make up for cuts in spending at the federal and state levels. Spending on water and public services rose by 28 percent. Out-of-pocket spending on health insurance rose by 62 percent.

♦ While the decline in spending may halt in the latter half of the 1990s, spending is not likely to rise substantially because Americans are getting serious about saving for retirement.

Household Spending Trends, 1985 to 1995

(average annual spending of consumer units by category, 1985 to 1995; percent change, 1990-95 and 1985-95; in 1995 dollars)

	1995	1990	1985	percent change 1990-95	percent change 1985-95
Number of consumer units*	103,024	96,968	91,564	6.2%	12.5%
Average income before taxes	$36,948	$37,183	$35,590	-0.6	3.8
Average annual spending	32,277	33,092	33,271	-2.5	-3.0
FOOD	**$4,505**	**$5,009**	**$4,925**	**-10.1%**	**-8.5%**
Food at home	**2,803**	**2,898**	**2,885**	**-3.3**	**-2.8**
Cereals & bakery products	441	429	401	2.8	10.0
Cereals & cereal products	165	150	126	9.7	30.9
Bakery products	276	280	275	-1.4	0.4
Meats, poultry, fish, & eggs	752	779	820	-3.5	-8.3
Beef	228	254	275	-10.3	-17.0
Pork	156	154	173	1.4	-9.7
Other meats	104	115	122	-9.9	-14.6
Poultry	138	126	118	9.6	17.4
Fish & seafood	97	96	92	1.5	5.4
Eggs	30	35	42	-14.2	-29.4
Dairy products	297	344	377	-13.7	-21.2
Fresh milk & cream	123	163	186	-24.7	-33.7
Other dairy products	174	181	191	-3.7	-9.0
Fruits & vegetables	457	476	456	-3.9	0.2
Fresh fruits	144	148	136	-2.8	5.9
Fresh vegetables	137	138	133	-0.4	2.9
Processed fruits	96	108	110	-11.5	-13.1
Processed vegetables	80	82	76	-2.0	4.6
Other food at home	856	870	789	-1.6	8.5
Sugar & other sweets	112	110	109	2.2	2.7
Fats & oils	82	79	82	3.4	-0.2
Miscellaneous foods	377	392	331	-3.8	13.7
Nonalcoholic beverages	240	248	265	-3.4	-9.4
Food prepared by householder, out-of-town trips	45	41	41	10.3	9.6
Food away from home	**1,702**	**2,112**	**2,041**	**-19.4**	**-16.6**
ALCOHOLIC BEVERAGES	**277**	**342**	**433**	**-18.9**	**-36.1**
HOUSING	**10,465**	**10,148**	**10,038**	**3.1**	**4.3**
Shelter	**5,932**	**5,639**	**5,429**	**5.2**	**9.3**

(continued)

(continued from previous page)

| | 1995 | 1990 | 1985 | percent change | |
				1990-95	1985-95
Owned dwellings	$3,754	$3,443	$3,202	9.0%	17.2%
Mortgage interest & charges	2,107	2,119	1,957	-0.5	7.6
Property taxes	932	696	620	33.9	50.2
Maintenance, repairs, insurance, other expenses	716	630	625	13.7	14.6
Rented dwellings	1,786	1,787	1,671	-0.1	6.9
Other lodging	392	407	555	-3.7	-29.4
Utilities, fuels, & public services	**2,193**	**2,204**	**2,334**	**-0.5**	**-6.1**
Natural gas	268	287	390	-6.6	-31.2
Electricity	870	884	916	-1.6	-5.1
Fuel oil & other fuels	87	117	181	-25.4	-52.0
Telephone	708	690	644	2.6	9.9
Water & other public services	260	225	203	15.5	28.4
Household operations	**508**	**520**	**490**	**-2.3**	**3.7**
Personal services	258	255	217	1.0	19.1
Other household expenses	250	265	273	-5.5	-8.5
Housekeeping supplies	**430**	**473**	**460**	**-9.2**	**-6.6**
Laundry & cleaning supplies	110	132	132	-16.5	-16.5
Other household products	194	199	187	-2.7	3.8
Postage & stationery	125	142	142	-12.1	-11.7
Household furnishings & equip.	**1,403**	**1,312**	**1,326**	**7.0**	**5.8**
Household textiles	100	115	136	-13.4	-26.5
Furniture	327	361	404	-9.5	-19.0
Floor coverings	177	107	99	65.0	78.5
Major appliances	155	171	188	-9.6	-17.7
Small appliances, misc. housewares	85	87	85	-2.8	0.0
Miscellaneous household equipment	557	469	414	18.8	34.7
APPAREL AND SERVICES	**1,704**	**1,887**	**2,011**	**-9.7**	**-15.3**
Men & boys	**425**	**458**	**516**	**-7.3**	**-17.6**
Men, 16 & over	329	378	429	-12.9	-23.3
Boys, 2 to 15	96	82	86	17.6	11.1
Women & girls	**660**	**785**	**822**	**-15.9**	**-19.7**
Women, 16 & over	559	683	707	-18.2	-20.9
Girls, 2 to 15	101	101	115	-0.4	-12.0
Children under 2	**81**	**82**	**79**	**-0.8**	**2.1**
Footwear	**278**	**262**	**261**	**6.0**	**6.7**
Other apparel products & services	**259**	**301**	**333**	**-13.9**	**-22.2**
TRANSPORTATION	**6,016**	**5,970**	**6,497**	**0.8**	**-7.4**
Vehicle purchases (net outlay)	**2,639**	**2,482**	**2,894**	**6.3**	**-8.8**
Cars & trucks, new	1,194	1,351	1,695	-11.6	-29.6

(continued)

(continued from previous page)

	1995	1990	1985	percent change 1990-95	percent change 1985-95
Cars & trucks, used	$1,411	$1,105	$1,142	27.6%	23.6%
Other vehicles	34	26	57	32.5	-40.0
Gasoline & motor oil	**1,006**	**1,221**	**1,466**	**-17.6**	**-31.4**
Other vehicle expenses	**2,016**	**1,915**	**1,758**	**5.3**	**14.7**
Vehicle finance charges	261	350	357	-25.4	-26.9
Maintenance & repairs	653	687	670	-4.9	-2.5
Vehicle insurance	713	656	528	8.6	35.0
Vehicle renting, leasing, licensing, other charges	390	222	203	76.0	92.5
Public transportation	**355**	**352**	**380**	**0.8**	**-6.5**
HEALTH CARE	**1,732**	**1,726**	**1,569**	**0.4**	**10.4**
Health insurance	860	677	531	26.9	61.9
Medical services	511	655	703	-22.0	-27.3
Drugs	280	294	252	-4.7	11.1
Medical supplies	80	99	85	-19.3	-5.9
ENTERTAINMENT	**1,612**	**1,658**	**1,657**	**-2.8**	**-2.7**
Fees & admissions	433	433	453	0.1	-4.5
Television, radios, sound equipment	542	529	525	2.4	3.1
Pets, toys, & playground equipment	322	322	302	0.1	6.7
Other supplies, equip., & services	315	374	377	-15.8	-16.4
PERSONAL CARE PRODUCTS AND SERVICES	**403**	**424**	**429**	**-5.0**	**-6.1**
READING	**163**	**178**	**200**	**-8.6**	**-18.4**
EDUCATION	**471**	**473**	**455**	**-0.5**	**3.6**
TOBACCO PRODUCTS AND SMOKING SUPPLIES	**269**	**319**	**310**	**-15.8**	**-13.3**
MISCELLANEOUS	**766**	**982**	**749**	**-22.0**	**2.2**
CASH CONTRIBUTIONS	**925**	**951**	**1,140**	**-2.8**	**-18.9**
PERSONAL INSURANCE AND PENSIONS	**2,967**	**3,022**	**2,855**	**-1.8**	**3.9**
Life & other personal insurance	374	402	394	-7.0	-5.0
Pensions & Social Security	2,593	2,621	2,462	-1.1	5.3

* The Consumer Expenditure Survey uses consumer units rather than households as the sampling unit. See Glossary for definition of consumer unit.
Source: Bureau of Labor Statistics, unpublished data from various Consumer Expenditure Surveys; calculations by New Strategist

The Middle-Aged Are the Biggest Spenders

Spending peaks among householders aged 45 to 54.

Households headed by people aged 45 to 54 spent an average of $42,181 in 1995—31 percent more than the average household. In second place are householders aged 35 to 44, who spent an average of $38,425 in 1995, according to the Bureau of Labor Statistics' Consumer Expenditure Survey. Householders aged 35 to 54 spend more than younger or older householders not only because they have higher incomes, but also because their households are likely to include children.

After chasing the youth market for years, it may surprise many businesses to discover that young adults are not the nation's big spenders. Households headed by people under age 25 spend less than any other age group, just $18,429 in 1995. This figure was even below the spending of householders aged 75 or older, $18,573 in 1995. The oldest householders spend more than young adults on a surprising number of items, including housekeeping supplies, floor coverings, major appliances, postage and stationery, reading materials, and gifts.

The Indexed Spending table shows spending by age of householder in comparison to what the average household spends. An index of 100 means the age group spends an average amount on an item. An index of above 100 means households in the age group spend more than average on an item, while an index less than 100 reveals below-average spending. A look at the table shows that spending is below average on most items for households headed by people under age 25. Spending is close to the average on most items for households headed by 25-to-34-year-olds. Spending is above average in most categories for householders aged 35 to 64, then falls below average again in most categories for householders aged 65 or older.

There are some exceptions, however. Householders under age 25 spend 67 percent more than the average household on rent (with an index of 167). They spend 17 percent more than the average household on baby clothing, and 42 percent more than the average on education because many are in college. The oldest householders spend 60 percent more than the average household on fuel oil, 98 percent more on drugs, and 81 percent more on health insurance. Householders aged 45 to 54 spend 25 percent less (with an index of 75) than the average household on rent, since most own their homes. They spend 55 percent less than average on personal services— much of this category consists of day care expenses, which these households no longer have. Householders aged 45 to 54 spend 65 percent more than the average household on such things as "other vehicles" (including airplanes and boats), and more than three times what the average household spends on gifts of education (their children's college bills).

The Market Share table shows how much of total spending by category is accounted for by three broad age groups of householders. The middle-aged market—households headed by people aged 35 to 54—accounted for fully 51 percent of all household spending in 1995. Middle-aged householders dominate spending on most items, ranging from furniture to entertainment. Only 22 percent of all household spending is accounted for by young adults, householders under age 35. Young adults dominate only a few spending categories, such as their nearly 50 percent share of spending on personal services (day care expenses) and baby clothes. The remaining 27 percent of spending is controlled by older consumers, householders aged 55 or older. Older householders dominate spending only in a few categories such as health insurance and drugs.

◆ While household spending should rise as the huge baby-boom generation entirely fills the big-spending 35-to-54 age group, the increase could be dampened by greater savings.

Spending by Age of Householder, 1995

(average annual spending of consumer units by category and age of householder, 1995)

	total	under 25	25 to 34	35 to 44	45 to 54	55 to 64	aged 65 or older		
							total	65 to 74	75 or older
Number of cu's (in 000s)*	103,024	7,067	19,500	23,441	18,633	12,626	21,759	11,924	9,835
Aver. no. of persons per cu	2.5	1.9	2.8	3.2	2.8	2.2	1.7	1.9	1.5
Aver. before-tax income	$36,948	$17,264	$35,685	$45,168	$52,052	$38,306	$22,180	$25,589	$18,025
Aver. annual spending	32,277	18,429	31,488	38,425	42,181	32,604	22,265	25,302	18,573
FOOD	**$4,505**	**$2,690**	**$4,470**	**$5,367**	**$5,469**	**$4,539**	**$3,388**	**$3,895**	**$2,767**
Food at home	**2,803**	**1,407**	**2,759**	**3,345**	**3,223**	**2,832**	**2,367**	**2,610**	**2,069**
Cereals and bakery products	441	227	422	539	501	425	385	419	344
Cereals and cereal products	165	95	172	208	183	151	130	141	117
Bakery products	276	133	251	331	318	274	255	277	227
Meats, poultry, fish, and eggs	752	331	724	900	899	807	610	699	500
Beef	228	108	217	273	274	253	175	205	140
Pork	156	61	159	181	184	169	127	136	116
Other meats	104	52	99	129	114	111	86	91	79
Poultry	138	66	132	170	169	127	113	137	84
Fish and seafood	97	27	90	111	125	114	81	101	56
Eggs	30	16	28	36	32	33	28	29	26
Dairy products	297	155	301	352	338	293	248	274	217
Fresh milk and cream	123	66	135	147	134	121	98	110	84
Other dairy products	174	89	167	206	204	171	150	164	133

(continued)

(continued on next page)

	total	under 25	25 to 34	35 to 44	45 to 54	55 to 64	aged 65 or older		
							total	65 to 74	75 or older
Fruits and vegetables	$457	$213	$433	$509	$513	$496	$437	$459	$409
Fresh fruits	144	61	137	157	157	153	151	160	139
Fresh vegetables	137	57	122	148	166	157	132	142	120
Processed fruits	96	55	96	110	100	102	87	86	89
Processed vegetables	80	40	78	94	90	84	67	71	61
Other food at home	856	482	878	1,044	973	811	687	759	599
Sugar and other sweets	112	50	113	129	124	113	104	103	104
Fats and oils	82	34	80	97	87	86	79	89	66
Miscellaneous foods	377	227	402	477	422	325	287	316	252
Nonalcoholic beverages	240	155	246	289	283	230	182	201	159
Food prepared by householder, out-of-town trips	45	17	37	52	57	58	36	50	18
Food away from home	**1,702**	**1,283**	**1,711**	**2,022**	**2,246**	**1,707**	**1,021**	**1,285**	**698**
ALCOHOLIC BEVERAGES	**277**	**277**	**299**	**314**	**348**	**253**	**171**	**206**	**129**
HOUSING	**10,465**	**5,908**	**10,541**	**12,631**	**12,894**	**10,291**	**7,590**	**7,927**	**7,184**
Shelter	**5,932**	**3,625**	**6,162**	**7,552**	**7,560**	**5,358**	**3,668**	**4,018**	**3,243**
Owned dwellings	3,754	485	3,104	5,066	5,576	3,799	2,401	2,819	1,895
Mortgage interest and charges	2,107	306	2,211	3,385	3,201	1,719	511	732	242
Property taxes	932	86	546	986	1,414	1,117	973	1,071	855
Maintenance, repairs, insurance, other expenses	716	93	347	695	961	963	917	1,015	798
Rented dwellings	1,786	2,985	2,873	2,102	1,334	986	931	783	1,111
Other lodging	392	155	185	384	650	572	335	416	238

(continued)

(continued on next page)

	total	under 25	25 to 34	35 to 44	45 to 54	55 to 64	aged 65 or older		
							total	65 to 74	75 or older
Utilities, fuels, public services	**$2,193**	**$1,159**	**$1,989**	**$2,388**	**$2,628**	**$2,442**	**$1,982**	**$2,152**	**$1,777**
Natural gas	268	95	222	279	314	322	284	295	271
Electricity	870	436	762	962	1,034	984	801	888	697
Fuel oil and other fuels	87	17	49	86	92	105	129	120	139
Telephone	708	541	745	778	859	723	517	578	443
Water and other public services	260	69	211	284	329	308	251	271	226
Household operations	**508**	**199**	**701**	**604**	**445**	**374**	**466**	**343**	**615**
Personal services	258	155	559	378	115	65	127	26	249
Other household expenses	250	44	141	226	330	309	339	317	366
Housekeeping supplies	**430**	**135**	**360**	**490**	**501**	**514**	**423**	**481**	**351**
Laundry and cleaning supplies	110	38	114	131	121	129	90	112	62
Other household products	194	44	152	216	239	243	195	224	160
Postage and stationery	125	52	95	143	141	141	138	145	130
Household furnishings & equip.	**1,403**	**790**	**1,329**	**1,597**	**1,760**	**1,603**	**1,051**	**934**	**1,197**
Household textiles	100	24	83	112	158	126	67	93	36
Furniture	327	271	391	434	397	279	143	172	107
Floor coverings	177	38	85	142	165	167	366	85	712
Major appliances	155	93	137	171	189	176	132	159	98
Small appliances, misc. housewares	85	63	71	85	101	143	58	70	44
Misc. household equipment	557	301	561	653	750	712	284	353	200

(continued)

(continued on next page)

	total	under 25	25 to 34	35 to 44	45 to 54	55 to 64	aged 65 or older		
							total	65 to 74	75 or older
APPAREL & SERVICES	$1,704	$1,206	$1,904	$2,079	$2,090	$1,833	$876	$1,117	$582
Men and boys	425	279	511	536	519	431	191	252	116
Men, 16 and over	329	242	360	372	437	369	171	222	108
Boys, 2 to 15	96	37	152	164	82	62	20	30	9
Women and girls	660	383	611	774	868	830	407	513	277
Women, 16 and over	559	358	481	590	764	765	378	470	264
Girls, 2 to 15	101	25	130	184	104	65	29	43	13
Children under 2	81	95	154	106	59	45	18	20	17
Footwear	278	230	334	380	311	207	145	176	107
Other apparel products, svcs.	259	219	294	284	333	320	115	156	66
TRANSPORTATION	6,016	4,033	6,188	7,488	8,017	5,726	3,377	4,484	2,035
Vehicle purchases (net outlay)	2,639	1,913	2,846	3,643	3,516	2,108	1,166	1,712	503
Cars and trucks, new	1,194	555	1,273	1,730	1,332	1,118	680	980	316
Cars and trucks, used	1,411	1,322	1,531	1,873	2,129	953	485	731	187
Other vehicles	34	36	42	41	56	37	1	1	0.0
Gasoline and motor oil	1,006	701	1,014	1,182	1,324	1,063	604	749	429
Other vehicle expenses	2,016	1,236	2,029	2,289	2,725	2,142	1,285	1,599	904
Vehicle finance charges	261	179	347	322	361	223	78	113	36
Maintenance and repairs	653	379	579	720	923	709	474	587	336
Vehicle insurance	713	455	668	781	930	792	531	621	422
Vehicle renting, leasing, licensing, other charges	390	222	435	465	510	419	201	277	110

(continued)

(continued on next page)

	total	under 25	25 to 34	35 to 44	45 to 54	55 to 64	aged 65 or older		
							total	65 to 74	75 or older
Public transportation	$355	$184	$299	$374	$452	$413	$323	$424	$199
HEALTH CARE	1,732	465	1,096	1,609	1,850	1,909	2,647	2,617	2,683
Health insurance	860	209	517	726	817	896	1,541	1,528	1,557
Medical services	511	157	380	596	664	587	479	471	487
Drugs	280	65	139	205	254	344	544	536	555
Medical supplies	80	34	60	81	115	83	83	82	84
ENTERTAINMENT	1,612	1,081	1,682	1,951	2,138	1,577	929	1,156	652
Fees and admissions	433	225	394	531	585	418	307	377	223
Television, radios, sound equip.	542	456	580	657	664	492	335	397	260
Pets, toys, playground equip.	322	156	368	444	398	316	145	182	100
Other supplies, equip., services	315	244	340	319	491	350	141	200	70
PERSONAL CARE PRODUCTS AND SERVICES	403	243	387	450	517	407	326	380	260
READING	163	71	134	173	199	188	161	180	138
EDUCATION	471	667	335	436	1,028	366	155	237	55
TOBACCO PRODUCTS AND SMOKING SUPPLIES	269	245	270	310	347	314	139	183	85
MISCELLANEOUS	766	347	687	815	1,018	948	603	629	571
CASH CONTRIBUTIONS	925	114	455	908	1,463	1,043	1,101	1,165	1,023

(continued)

(continued on next page)

	total	under 25	25 to 34	35 to 44	45 to 54	55 to 64	aged 65 or older		
							total	65 to 74	75 or older
PERSONAL INSURANCE AND PENSIONS	**$2,967**	**$1,081**	**$3,040**	**$3,894**	**$4,803**	**$3,211**	**$802**	**$1,127**	**$409**
Life and other personal insurance	374	69	251	440	563	555	245	304	172
Pensions and Social Security	2,593	1,012	2,788	3,453	4,240	2,656	558	823	236
GIFTS**	**987**	**426**	**694**	**895**	**1,719**	**1,361**	**693**	**801**	**562**
Food	**88**	**20**	**43**	**59**	**200**	**127**	**63**	**56**	**71**
Housing	**250**	**165**	**221**	**232**	**403**	**289**	**172**	**207**	**129**
Housekeeping supplies	38	22	28	41	53	46	31	34	27
Household textiles	10	0.0	9	10	17	12	8	11	4
Appliances and misc. housewares	27	12	21	20	35	60	21	31	9
Major appliances	5	0	1	3	8	9	5	8	1
Small appl., misc. housewares	23	12	20	16	27	50	16	22	8
Misc. household equipment	66	36	48	72	89	77	60	82	33
Other housing	109	94	115	88	208	93	53	49	57
Apparel and services	**258**	**124**	**241**	**264**	**321**	**457**	**144**	**180**	**101**
Males 2 and over	70	52	60	76	79	120	41	48	32
Females 2 and over	94	27	67	82	110	240	55	67	41
Children under 2	39	22	48	53	46	39	17	18	16
Other apparel products, services	55	23	66	53	85	58	31	46	13
Jewelry and watches	27	17	26	25	44	23	19	32	4
All other apparel pdts., svcs.	29	6	40	28	41	35	12	14	9
Transportation	**48**	**14**	**24**	**45**	**73**	**76**	**46**	**48**	**44**
Health care	**22**	**1**	**7**	**17**	**42**	**23**	**31**	**10**	**56**

(continued)

(continued on next page)

| | total | under 25 | 25 to 34 | 35 to 44 | 45 to 54 | 55 to 64 | aged 65 or older | | |
							total	65 to 74	75 or older
Entertainment	**$86**	**$46**	**$67**	**$93**	**$110**	**$134**	**$62**	**$78**	**$42**
Toys, games, hobbies, and tricycles	29	10	25	25	38	57	20	30	9
Other entertainment	57	36	42	68	72	77	42	48	33
Education	**120**	**16**	**16**	**65**	**407**	**131**	**55**	**84**	**20**
All other gifts	**114**	**39**	**76**	**121**	**162**	**123**	**120**	**138**	**98**

* The Consumer Expenditure Survey uses consumer units rather than households as the sampling unit. See Glossary for definition of consumer unit.
** Gift spending is also included in the preceding categories.
Source: Bureau of Labor Statistics, unpublished tables from the 1995 Consumer Expenditure Survey

Indexed Spending by Age of Householder, 1995

(indexed average annual spending of consumer units by category and age of householder, 1995)

	total	under 25	25 to 34	35 to 44	45 to 54	55 to 64	aged 65 or older		
							total	65 to 74	75 or older
Number of cu's (in 000s)*	103,024	7,067	19,500	23,441	18,633	12,626	21,759	11,924	9,835
Indexed aver. annual spending	100	57	98	119	131	101	69	78	58
FOOD	**100**	**60**	**99**	**119**	**121**	**101**	**75**	**86**	**61**
Food at home	**100**	**50**	**98**	**119**	**115**	**101**	**84**	**93**	**74**
Cereals and bakery products	100	51	96	122	114	96	87	95	78
Cereals and cereal products	100	58	104	126	111	92	79	85	71
Bakery products	100	48	91	120	115	99	92	100	82
Meats, poultry, fish, and eggs	100	44	96	120	120	107	81	93	66
Beef	100	47	95	120	120	111	77	90	61
Pork	100	39	102	116	118	108	81	87	74
Other meats	100	50	95	124	110	107	83	88	76
Poultry	100	48	96	123	122	92	82	99	61
Fish and seafood	100	28	93	114	129	118	84	104	58
Eggs	100	53	93	120	107	110	93	97	87
Dairy products	100	52	101	119	114	99	84	92	73
Fresh milk and cream	100	54	110	120	109	98	80	89	68
Other dairy products	100	51	96	118	117	98	86	94	76

(continued)

(continued from previous page)

	total	under 25	25 to 34	35 to 44	45 to 54	55 to 64	aged 65 or older		
							total	65 to 74	75 or older
Fruits and vegetables	100	47	95	111	112	109	96	100	89
Fresh fruits	100	42	95	109	109	106	105	111	97
Fresh vegetables	100	42	89	108	121	115	96	104	88
Processed fruits	100	57	100	115	104	106	91	90	93
Processed vegetables	100	50	98	118	113	105	84	89	76
Other food at home	100	56	103	122	114	95	80	89	70
Sugar and other sweets	100	45	101	115	111	101	93	92	93
Fats and oils	100	41	98	118	106	105	96	109	80
Miscellaneous foods	100	60	107	127	112	86	76	84	67
Nonalcoholic beverages	100	65	102	120	118	96	76	84	66
Food prepared by householder, out-of-town trips	100	38	82	116	127	129	80	111	40
Food away from home	**100**	**75**	**101**	**119**	**132**	**100**	**60**	**75**	**41**
ALCOHOLIC BEVERAGES	**100**	**100**	**108**	**113**	**126**	**91**	**62**	**74**	**47**
HOUSING	**100**	**56**	**101**	**121**	**123**	**98**	**73**	**76**	**69**
Shelter	**100**	**61**	**104**	**127**	**127**	**90**	**62**	**68**	**55**
Owned dwellings	100	13	83	135	149	101	64	75	50
Mortgage interest and charges	100	15	105	161	152	82	24	35	11
Property taxes	100	9	59	106	152	120	104	115	92
Maintenance, repair, insurance, other expenses	100	13	48	97	134	134	128	142	111
Rented dwellings	100	167	161	118	75	55	52	44	62
Other lodging	100	40	47	98	166	146	85	106	61

(continued)

(continued from previous page)

	total	under 25	25 to 34	35 to 44	45 to 54	55 to 64	aged 65 or older		
							total	65 to 74	75 or older
Utilities, fuels, & public services	**100**	**53**	**91**	**109**	**120**	**111**	**90**	**98**	**81**
Natural gas	100	35	83	104	117	120	106	110	101
Electricity	100	50	88	111	119	113	92	102	80
Fuel oil and other fuels	100	20	56	99	106	121	148	138	160
Telephone	100	76	105	110	121	102	73	82	63
Water and other public services	100	27	81	109	127	118	97	104	87
Household operations	**100**	**39**	**138**	**119**	**88**	**74**	**92**	**68**	**121**
Personal services	100	60	217	147	45	25	49	10	97
Other household expenses	100	18	56	90	132	124	136	127	146
Housekeeping supplies	**100**	**31**	**84**	**114**	**117**	**120**	**98**	**112**	**82**
Laundry and cleaning supplies	100	35	104	119	110	117	82	102	56
Other household products	100	23	78	111	123	125	101	115	82
Postage and stationery	100	42	76	114	113	113	110	116	104
Household furnishings & equip.	**100**	**56**	**95**	**114**	**125**	**114**	**75**	**67**	**85**
Household textiles	100	24	83	112	158	126	67	93	36
Furniture	100	83	120	133	121	85	44	53	33
Floor coverings	100	21	48	80	93	94	207	48	402
Major appliances	100	60	88	110	122	114	85	103	63
Small appliances, misc. housewares	100	74	84	100	119	168	68	82	52
Misc. household equipment	100	54	101	117	135	128	51	63	36

(continued)

(continued from previous page)

	total	under 25	25 to 34	35 to 44	45 to 54	55 to 64	aged 65 or older		
							total	65 to 74	75 or older
APPAREL	**100**	**71**	**112**	**122**	**123**	**108**	**51**	**66**	**34**
Men and boys	**100**	**66**	**120**	**126**	**122**	**101**	**45**	**59**	**27**
Men, 16 and over	100	74	109	113	133	112	52	67	33
Boys, 2 to 15	100	39	158	171	85	65	21	31	9
Women and girls	**100**	**58**	**93**	**117**	**132**	**126**	**62**	**78**	**42**
Women, 16 and over	100	64	86	106	137	137	68	84	47
Girls, 2 to 15	100	25	129	182	103	64	29	43	13
Children under 2	**100**	**117**	**190**	**131**	**73**	**56**	**22**	**25**	**21**
Footwear	**100**	**83**	**120**	**137**	**112**	**74**	**52**	**63**	**38**
Other apparel products, svcs.	**100**	**85**	**114**	**110**	**129**	**124**	**44**	**60**	**25**
TRANSPORTATION	**100**	**67**	**103**	**124**	**133**	**95**	**56**	**75**	**34**
Vehicle purchases (net outlay)	**100**	**72**	**108**	**138**	**133**	**80**	**44**	**65**	**19**
Cars and trucks, new	100	46	107	145	112	94	57	82	26
Cars and trucks, used	100	94	109	133	151	68	34	52	13
Other vehicles	100	106	124	121	165	109	3	3	0
Gasoline and motor oil	**100**	**70**	**101**	**117**	**132**	**106**	**60**	**74**	**43**
Other vehicle expenses	**100**	**61**	**101**	**114**	**135**	**106**	**64**	**79**	**45**
Vehicle finance charges	100	69	133	123	138	85	30	43	14
Maintenance and repairs	100	58	89	110	141	109	73	90	51
Vehicle insurance	100	64	94	110	130	111	74	87	59
Vehicle renting, leasing, licensing, other charges	100	57	112	119	131	107	52	71	28

(continued)

(continued from previous page)

| | total | under 25 | 25 to 34 | 35 to 44 | 45 to 54 | 55 to 64 | aged 65 or older | | |
							total	65 to 74	75 or older
Public transportation	**100**	**52**	**84**	**105**	**127**	**116**	**91**	**119**	**56**
HEALTH CARE	**100**	**27**	**63**	**93**	**107**	**110**	**153**	**151**	**155**
Health insurance	100	24	60	84	95	104	179	178	181
Medical services	100	31	74	117	130	115	94	92	95
Drugs	100	23	50	73	91	123	194	191	198
Medical supplies	100	43	75	101	144	104	104	102	105
ENTERTAINMENT	**100**	**67**	**104**	**121**	**133**	**98**	**58**	**72**	**40**
Fees and admissions	100	52	91	123	135	97	71	87	52
Television, radios, sound equip.	100	84	107	121	123	91	62	73	48
Pets, toys, playground equip.	100	48	114	138	124	98	45	57	31
Other supplies, equip., services	100	77	108	101	156	111	45	63	22
PERSONAL CARE PRODUCTS. AND SERVICES	**100**	**60**	**96**	**112**	**128**	**101**	**81**	**94**	**65**
READING	**100**	**44**	**82**	**106**	**122**	**115**	**99**	**110**	**85**
EDUCATION	**100**	**142**	**71**	**93**	**218**	**78**	**33**	**50**	**12**
TOBACCO PRODUCTS AND SMOKING SUPPLIES	**100**	**91**	**100**	**115**	**129**	**117**	**52**	**68**	**32**
MISSCELLANEOUS	**100**	**45**	**90**	**106**	**133**	**124**	**79**	**82**	**75**
CASH CONTRIBUTIONS	**100**	**12**	**49**	**98**	**158**	**113**	**119**	**126**	**111**

(continued)

(continued from previous page)

	total	under 25	25 to 34	35 to 44	45 to 54	55 to 64	aged 65 or older		
							total	65 to 74	75 or older
PERSONAL INSURANCE AND PENSIONS	**100**	**36**	**102**	**131**	**162**	**108**	**27**	**38**	**14**
Life and other personal insurance	100	18	67	118	151	148	66	81	46
Pensions and Social Security	100	39	108	133	164	102	22	32	9
GIFTS	**100**	**43**	**70**	**91**	**174**	**138**	**70**	**81**	**57**
Food	**100**	**23**	**49**	**67**	**227**	**144**	**72**	**64**	**81**
Housing	**100**	**66**	**88**	**93**	**161**	**116**	**69**	**83**	**52**
Housekeeping supplies	100	58	74	108	139	121	82	89	71
Household textiles	100	0	90	100	170	120	80	110	40
Appliances and misc. housewares	100	44	78	74	130	222	78	115	33
Major appliances	100	0	20	60	160	180	100	160	20
Small appl., misc. housewares	100	52	87	70	117	217	70	96	35
Misc. household equipment	100	55	73	109	135	117	91	124	50
Other housing	100	86	106	81	191	85	49	45	52
Apparel and services	**100**	**48**	**93**	**102**	**124**	**177**	**56**	**70**	**39**
Males 2 and over	100	74	86	109	113	171	59	69	46
Females 2 and over	100	29	71	87	117	255	59	71	44
Children under 2	100	56	123	136	118	100	44	46	41
Other apparel products, services	100	42	120	96	155	105	56	84	24
Jewelry and watches	100	63	96	93	163	85	70	119	15
All other apparel pdts., svcs.	100	21	138	97	141	121	41	48	31
Transportation	**100**	**29**	**50**	**94**	**152**	**158**	**96**	**100**	**92**
Health care	**100**	**5**	**32**	**77**	**191**	**105**	**141**	**45**	**255**

(continued)

(continued from previous page)

	total	under 25	25 to 34	35 to 44	45 to 54	55 to 64	total	65 to 74	75 or older
							aged 65 or older		
Entertainment	**100**	**53**	**78**	**108**	**128**	**156**	**72**	**91**	**49**
Toys, games, hobbies, tricycles	100	34	86	86	131	197	69	103	31
Other entertainment	100	63	74	119	126	135	74	84	58
Education	**100**	**13**	**13**	**54**	**339**	**109**	**46**	**70**	**17**
All other gifts	**100**	**34**	**67**	**106**	**142**	**108**	**105**	**121**	**86**

*The Consumer Expenditure Survey uses consumer units rather than households as the sampling unit. See Glossary for definition of consumer unit.
Note: An index of 100 is the average for all households. An index of 132 means households in the age group spend 32 percent more than the average household. An index of 68 means households in the age group spend 32 percent less than the average household.
Source: New Strategist calculations based on unpublished tables from the Bureau of Labor Statistics' 1995 Consumer Expenditure Survey

Market Shares by Age of Householder, 1995

(share of total annual spending accounted for by consumer unit age groups, 1995)

	total	under age 35	35 to 54	55 or older
Total consumer units *	100%	26%	41%	33%
Share of total annual spending	100	22	51	27
FOOD	100%	23%	49%	28%
Food at home	**100**	**22**	**48**	**30**
Cereals and bakery products	100	22	48	30
Cereals and cereal products	100	24	49	28
Bakery products	100	21	48	32
Meats, poultry, fish, and eggs	100	21	49	30
Beef	100	21	49	30
Pork	100	22	48	30
Other meats	100	21	48	31
Poultry	100	21	50	29
Fish and seafood	100	19	49	32
Eggs	100	21	47	33
Dairy products	100	23	48	30
Fresh milk and cream	100	24	47	29
Other dairy products	100	22	48	30
Fruits and vegetables	100	21	46	33
Fresh fruits	100	21	45	35
Fresh vegetables	100	20	46	34
Processed fruits	100	23	45	32
Processed vegetables	100	22	47	31
Other food at home	100	23	48	29
Sugar and other sweets	100	22	46	32
Fats and oils	100	21	46	33
Miscellaneous foods	100	24	49	27
Nonalcoholic beverages	100	24	49	28
Food prepared by householder, out-of-town trips	100	18	49	33
Food away from home	100	24	51	25
ALCOHOLIC BEVERAGES	**100**	**27**	**49**	**24**
HOUSING	**100**	**23**	**50**	**27**
Shelter	**100**	**24**	**52**	**24**
Owned dwellings	100	17	58	26

(continued)

(continued from previous page)

	total	under age 35	35 to 54	55 or older
Mortgage interest and charges	100%	21%	64%	15%
Property taxes	100	12	52	37
Maintenance, repair, insurance, other expenses	100	10	46	44
Rented dwellings	100	42	40	18
Other lodging	100	12	52	36
Utilities, fuels, and public services	**100**	**21**	**46**	**33**
Natural gas	100	18	45	37
Electricity	100	20	47	33
Fuel oil and other fuels	100	12	42	46
Telephone	100	25	47	28
Water and other public services	100	17	48	35
Household operations	**100**	**29**	**43**	**28**
Personal services	100	45	41	13
Other household expenses	100	12	44	44
Housekeeping supplies	**100**	**18**	**47**	**35**
Laundry and cleaning supplies	100	22	47	32
Other household products	100	16	48	37
Postage and stationery	100	17	46	37
Household furnishings and equipment	**100**	**22**	**49**	**30**
Household textiles	100	17	54	30
Furniture	100	28	52	20
Floor coverings	100	11	35	55
Major appliances	100	21	47	32
Small appliances, misc. housewares	100	21	44	35
Miscellaneous household equipment	100	23	51	26
APPAREL & SERVICES	**100**	**26**	**50**	**24**
Men and boys	**100**	**27**	**51**	**22**
Men, 16 and over	100	26	50	25
Boys, 2 to 15	100	33	54	12
Women and girls	**100**	**22**	**50**	**28**
Women, 16 and over	100	21	49	31
Girls, 2 to 15	100	26	60	14
Children under 2	**100**	**44**	**43**	**12**
Footwear	**100**	**28**	**51**	**20**
Other apparel products and services	**100**	**27**	**48**	**25**
TRANSPORTATION	**100**	**24**	**52**	**24**
Vehicle purchases (net outlay)	**100**	**25**	**56**	**19**
Cars and trucks, new	100	23	53	24

(continued)

(continued from previous page)

	total	under age 35	35 to 54	55 or older
Cars and trucks, used	100%	27%	57%	16%
Other vehicles	100	31	57	14
Gasoline and motor oil	**100**	**24**	**51**	**26**
Other vehicle expenses	**100**	**23**	**50**	**26**
Vehicle finance charges	100	30	53	17
Maintenance and repairs	100	21	51	29
Vehicle insurance	100	22	49	29
Vehicle rental, lease, license, other charges	100	25	51	24
Public transportation	**100**	**19**	**47**	**33**
HEALTH CARE	**100**	**14**	**40**	**46**
Health insurance	100	13	36	51
Medical services	100	16	50	34
Drugs	100	11	33	56
Medical supplies	100	17	49	35
ENTERTAINMENT	**100**	**24**	**52**	**24**
Fees and admissions	100	21	52	27
Television, radios, sound equipment	100	26	50	24
Pets, toys, and playground equipment	100	25	54	22
Other supplies, equip., and services	100	26	51	23
PERSONAL CARE PRODUCTS AND SERVICES.	**100**	**22**	**49**	**29**
READING	**100**	**19**	**46**	**35**
EDUCATION	**100**	**23**	**61**	**16**
TOBACCO PRODUCTS AND SMOKING SUPPLIES	**100**	**25**	**50**	**25**
MISCELLANEOUS	**100**	**20**	**48**	**32**
CASH CONTRIBUTIONS	**100**	**10**	**51**	**39**
PERSONAL INSURANCE AND PENSIONS	**100**	**22**	**59**	**19**
Life and other personal insurance	100	14	54	32
Pensions and Social Security	100	23	60	17
GIFTS	**100**	**16**	**52**	**32**
Food	**100**	**11**	**56**	**33**
Housing	**100**	**21**	**50**	**29**
Housekeeping supplies	100	18	50	32
Household textiles	100	17	53	32

(continued)

(continued from previous page)

	total	under age 35	35 to 54	55 or older
Appliances and misc. housewares	100%	18%	40%	44%
Major appliances	100	4	43	43
Small appliances and misc. housewares	100	20	37	41
Miscellaneous household equipment	100	18	49	33
Other housing	100	26	53	21
Apparel and services	**100**	**21**	**46**	**33**
Males 2 and over	100	21	45	33
Females 2 and over	100	15	41	44
Children under 2	100	27	52	21
Other apparel products and services	100	26	50	25
Jewelry and watches	100	23	51	25
All other apparel products and services	100	28	48	24
Transportation	**100**	**11**	**49**	**40**
Health care	**100**	**6**	**52**	**43**
Entertainment	**100**	**18**	**48**	**34**
Toys, games, hobbies, and tricycles	100	19	43	39
Other entertainment	100	18	50	32
Education	**100**	**3**	**74**	**23**
All other gifts	**100**	**15**	**50**	**35**

* The Consumer Expenditure Survey uses consumer units rather than households as the sampling unit. See Glossary for definition of consumer unit.
Note: Numbers may not add to 100 because of rounding.
Source: New Strategist calculations based on unpublished tables from the Bureau of Labor Statistics' 1995 Consumer Expenditure Survey

Spending Rises with Income

Households with incomes of $70,000 or more spent an average of $69,303 in 1995, more than twice as much as the average household.

The households that spend the most are also the largest, with an average of 3.1 people according to the Bureau of Labor Statistics' Consumer Expenditure Survey. High-income households spend more than average on nearly every category of goods and services, with few exceptions.

The Indexed Spending table shows spending by householder income group in comparison to what the average household spends. An index of 100 means households in the income group spend an average amount on an item. An index above 100 means households in the income group spend more than average on an item, while an index below 100 signifies below-average spending. A look at the table reveals that spending is well below average on most items for households with incomes below $30,000. Spending is close to average on most items for households with incomes of $30,000 to $40,000. Spending is above average on most items for households with incomes of $40,000 or more. For households with incomes of $70,000 or more, spending is two to three times above average on many items.

There are some notable exceptions, however. Households with incomes below $30,000 spend an average or slightly above-average amount on rent, children's clothes, drugs, and a variety of gifts (with indexes of 100 or more). Households with incomes of $70,000 or more spend 42 percent less than average on rent (with an index of 58). They spend 5 percent less than average on tobacco. The most affluent households spend at least three times more than the average household on a variety of items such as mortgage interest, education, insurance, and gifts of education.

The Market Share table shows how much of total household spending by category is accounted for by three broad income groups: Households with annual incomes below $30,000, between $30,000 to $50,000, and $50,000 or more. Fully 52 percent of the nation's households have annual incomes of less than $30,000, but these households accounted for just 32 percent of all household spending in 1995. The 23 percent of households with incomes between $30,000 and $50,000 accounted for 24 percent of spending. The remaining 25 percent of households with incomes of $50,000 or more accounted for fully 44 percent of all household spending in 1995.

The share of spending accounted for by high-income households is above 50 percent on a variety of categories such as "other lodging," which includes hotel and motel expenses; new cars and trucks; fees and admissions to entertainment events; cash contributions; and personal insurance. The share of spending accounted for by low-income households is 50 percent or greater for only one item: drugs. Many low-income households are headed by elderly retirees, which accounts for their above-average spending on drugs.

◆ Spending patterns by income group will remain stable during the next ten years because the demographic characteristics of those with low or high incomes will not change much. Low-income households will continue to be dominated by young adults and the elderly. High-income households will continue to be dominated by middle-aged, two-earner couples.

Spending by Household Income, 1995

(average annual spending of consumer units by category and household income, 1995; complete income reporters only)

	total	under $10,000	$10,000 to $19,999	$20,000 to $29,999	$30,000 to $39,999	$40,000 to $49,999	$50,000 to $69,999	$70,000 or more
Number of cu's (in 000s)*	83,364	14,474	16,449	12,643	10,648	8,191	10,378	10,582
Average number of persons per cu	2.5	1.8	2.2	2.5	2.7	2.8	3.1	3.1
Average before-tax income	$36,948	$5,672	$14,731	$24,603	$34,606	$44,408	$58,363	$104,589
Average annual spending	33,610	14,338	20,652	26,732	33,324	38,496	48,844	69,303
FOOD	**$4,691**	**$2,421**	**$3,451**	**$4,066**	**$4,710**	**$5,498**	**$6,229**	**$8,027**
Food at home	**2,886**	**1,786**	**2,453**	**2,611**	**2,907**	**3,359**	**3,598**	**4,140**
Cereals and bakery products	455	282	377	406	479	525	563	661
Cereals and cereal products	169	109	148	159	174	203	201	225
Bakery products	285	173	228	247	305	322	362	437
Meats, poultry, fish, and eggs	758	506	716	697	769	861	876	994
Beef	232	150	203	207	268	266	281	296
Pork	158	113	158	156	154	183	170	179
Other meats	105	73	103	86	104	117	127	143
Poultry	136	82	128	124	140	161	144	201
Fish and seafood	95	63	92	93	70	103	121	136
Eggs	32	24	33	30	33	31	33	38
Dairy products	311	183	258	283	320	365	395	452
Fresh milk and cream	129	89	117	125	135	151	154	156
Other dairy products	182	94	142	158	185	214	241	296

(continued)

(continued from previous page)

	total	under $10,000	$10,000 to $19,999	$20,000 to $29,999	$30,000 to $39,999	$40,000 to $49,999	$50,000 to $69,999	$70,000 or more
Fruits and vegetables	$467	$303	$408	$427	$463	$519	$563	$679
Fresh fruits	148	100	126	139	136	157	176	229
Fresh vegetables	141	85	118	133	145	156	168	209
Processed fruits	97	64	86	82	100	107	118	140
Processed vegetables	81	53	77	73	81	98	101	101
Other food at home	894	512	694	799	877	1,089	1,201	1,353
Sugar and other sweets	119	67	97	110	112	156	146	185
Fats and oils	84	55	78	75	86	103	97	106
Miscellaneous foods	394	224	294	345	388	489	547	601
Nonalcoholic beverages	250	148	205	233	242	286	336	359
Food prepared by housholder, out-of-town trips	46	17	20	36	49	54	74	103
Food away from home	**1,805**	**635**	**998**	**1,455**	**1,803**	**2,139**	**2,631**	**3,887**
ALCOHOLIC BEVERAGES	**302**	**102**	**187**	**219**	**242**	**378**	**459**	**677**
HOUSING	**10,577**	**5,524**	**7,056**	**8,419**	**10,470**	**11,240**	**14,456**	**21,211**
Shelter	**5,913**	**3,106**	**3,947**	**4,558**	**5,870**	**6,317**	**7,793**	**12,310**
Owned dwellings	3,750	1,044	1,722	2,291	3,431	4,179	6,020	10,111
Mortgage interest and charges	2,121	353	585	1,077	1,963	2,398	3,777	6,492
Property taxes	909	382	564	610	824	916	1,319	2,204
Maintenance, repairs, insurance, other expenses	720	308	573	603	643	865	924	1,415
Rented dwellings	1,787	1,955	2,029	2,069	2,127	1,745	1,278	1,031
Other lodging	376	108	195	199	312	394	495	1,168

(continued)

	total	under $10,000	$10,000 to $19,999	$20,000 to $29,999	$30,000 to $39,999	$40,000 to $49,999	$50,000 to $69,999	$70,000 or more
Utilities, fuels, and public services	**$2,180**	**$1,435**	**$1,817**	**$2,044**	**$2,257**	**$2,343**	**$2,706**	**$3,207**
Natural gas	269	188	230	239	256	298	315	418
Electricity	854	565	726	820	891	889	1,053	1,232
Fuel oil and other fuels	86	56	76	94	80	92	106	110
Telephone	710	488	581	669	758	759	876	1,012
Water and other public services	262	140	205	221	271	305	355	434
Household operations	**518**	**200**	**282**	**325**	**539**	**522**	**651**	**1,396**
Personal services	264	103	118	166	344	350	367	578
Other household expenses	254	97	164	159	195	172	284	818
Housekeeping supplies	**465**	**200**	**309**	**412**	**479**	**543**	**569**	**927**
Laundry and cleaning supplies	118	57	96	115	120	131	140	195
Other household products	208	88	130	181	198	223	254	461
Postage and stationery	140	55	83	116	160	188	175	270
Household furnishings and equipment	**1,501**	**584**	**701**	**1,078**	**1,326**	**1,514**	**2,737**	**3,371**
Household textiles	108	53	47	69	85	160	171	242
Furniture	320	120	173	236	324	364	420	787
Floor coverings	212	140	44	140	59	83	757	328
Major appliances	156	82	115	151	182	158	229	226
Small appliances, misc. housewares	91	39	49	70	117	79	122	202
Miscellaneous household equipment	615	150	274	413	560	670	1,037	1,587

(continued)

(continued from previous page)

	total	under $10,000	$10,000 to $19,999	$20,000 to $29,999	$30,000 to $39,999	$40,000 to $49,999	$50,000 to $69,999	$70,000 or more
APPAREL, SERVICES	**$1,771**	**$726**	**$1,047**	**$1,469**	**$1,658**	**$2,075**	**$2,436**	**$3,808**
Men and boys	**437**	**141**	**227**	**343**	**408**	**457**	**679**	**1,016**
Men, 16 and over	339	90	181	264	339	359	479	830
Boys, 2 to 15	98	52	46	79	69	99	200	186
Women and girls	**694**	**246**	**370**	**605**	**638**	**955**	**925**	**1,503**
Women, 16 and over	591	205	307	491	521	841	781	1,330
Girls, 2 to 15	103	41	64	114	117	114	144	173
Children under 2	**84**	**54**	**50**	**65**	**107**	**94**	**105**	**147**
Footwear	**287**	**163**	**230**	**271**	**236**	**335**	**334**	**519**
Other apparel products and services	**268**	**121**	**169**	**185**	**270**	**235**	**393**	**623**
TRANSPORTATION	**6,123**	**1,999**	**3,650**	**5,281**	**6,411**	**7,505**	**9,619**	**11,812**
Vehicle purchases (net outlay)	**2,678**	**667**	**1,548**	**2,486**	**2,809**	**3,472**	**4,277**	**5,100**
Cars and trucks, new	1,189	242	706	749	1,076	1,416	2,004	2,898
Cars and trucks, used	1,456	416	836	1,711	1,725	1,978	2,186	2,150
Other vehicles	33	9	6	26	7	78	87	52
Gasoline and motor oil	**1,014**	**457**	**679**	**901**	**1,147**	**1,238**	**1,506**	**1,646**
Other vehicle expenses	**2,064**	**731**	**1,230**	**1,665**	**2,131**	**2,472**	**3,326**	**4,028**
Vehicle finance charges	267	63	113	225	322	400	444	506
Maintenance and repairs	675	297	441	571	692	811	1,095	1,136
Vehicle insurance	726	250	505	611	774	883	1,102	1,320
Vehicle renting, leasing, licensing, other charges	396	121	171	257	344	378	685	1,066

(continued)

(continued from previous page)

	total	under $10,000	$10,000 to $19,999	$20,000 to $29,999	$30,000 to $39,999	$40,000 to $49,999	$50,000 to $69,999	$70,000 or more
Public transportation	**$367**	**$144**	**$193**	**$229**	**$324**	**$324**	**$511**	**$1,039**
HEALTH CARE	**1,747**	**1,085**	**1,545**	**1,725**	**1,666**	**1,960**	**2,137**	**2,518**
Health insurance	864	541	833	884	876	997	979	1,107
Medical services	502	265	323	447	468	574	743	908
Drugs	293	243	320	320	242	289	295	337
Medical supplies	87	36	69	74	80	101	121	165
ENTERTAINMENT	**1,687**	**684**	**898**	**1,216**	**1,763**	**1,922**	**2,508**	**3,776**
Fees and admissions	447	124	211	236	422	461	702	1,274
Television, radios, sound equipment	561	315	383	445	587	656	818	958
Pets, toys, and playground equipment	349	132	171	290	367	413	542	721
Other supplies, equip., and services	331	113	133	245	387	393	445	823
PERSONAL CARE PRODUCTS AND SERVICES	**430**	**187**	**285**	**363**	**450**	**541**	**600**	**769**
READING	**170**	**68**	**104**	**142**	**179**	**191**	**244**	**351**
EDUCATION	**478**	**334**	**175**	**196**	**376**	**438**	**655**	**1,440**
TOBACCO PRODUCTS AND SMOKING SUPPLIES	**272**	**202**	**235**	**309**	**324**	**275**	**339**	**258**
MISCELLANEOUS	**808**	**430**	**522**	**689**	**1,008**	**987**	**1,080**	**1,304**
CASH CONTRIBUTIONS	**1,035**	**281**	**618**	**730**	**816**	**1,046**	**1,808**	**2,529**

(continued)

(continued from previous page)

	total	under $10,000	$10,000 to $19,999	$20,000 to $29,999	$30,000 to $39,999	$40,000 to $49,999	$50,000 to $69,999	$70,000 or more
PERSONAL INSURANCE AND PENSIONS	**$3,521**	**$294**	**$879**	**$1,910**	**$3,249**	**$4,439**	**$6,276**	**$10,824**
Life and other personal insurance	382	116	176	262	351	437	598	989
Pensions and Social Security	3,138	178	703	1,648	2,898	4,002	5,678	9,836
GIFTS**	**1,037**	**375**	**586**	**693**	**933**	**1,094**	**1,344**	**2,772**
Food	**90**	**18**	**40**	**69**	**87**	**82**	**110**	**274**
Housing	**266**	**128**	**157**	**167**	**240**	**282**	**348**	**664**
Housekeeping supplies	41	13	17	37	37	50	49	113
Household textiles	11	1	8	6	13	15	17	21
Appliances and misc. housewares	29	15	16	17	44	19	31	72
Major appliances	5	0	5	8	5	3	5	9
Small appliances and misc. housewares	24	15	11	8	40	16	26	63
Miscellaneous household equipment	75	19	48	43	49	112	138	159
Other housing	110	80	70	65	97	86	113	299
Apparel and services	**263**	**91**	**182**	**200**	**280**	**270**	**318**	**606**
Males 2 and over	72	22	39	63	88	74	88	163
Females 2 and over	94	28	59	64	86	90	122	252
Children under 2	40	24	24	27	52	36	58	77
Other apparel products and services	57	18	62	46	54	70	50	115
Jewelry and watches	29	7	38	17	41	28	23	53
All other apparel products and services	28	10	23	28	12	42	26	62
Transportation	**50**	**18**	**25**	**41**	**50**	**41**	**67**	**132**
Health care	**26**	**34**	**8**	**20**	**18**	**28**	**37**	**46**

(continued)

(continued from previous page)

	total	under $10,000	$10,000 to $19,999	$20,000 to $29,999	$30,000 to $39,999	$40,000 to $49,999	$50,000 to $69,999	$70,000 or more
Entertainment	**$93**	**$27**	**$64**	**$59**	**$92**	**$114**	**$142**	**$207**
Toys, games, hobbies, and tricycles	30	9	23	23	33	38	48	56
Other entertainment	63	18	41	36	59	76	94	151
Education	124	14	28	51	41	130	134	579
All other gifts	125	45	82	86	126	146	189	263

* The Consumer Expenditure Survey uses consumer units rather than households as the sampling unit. See Glossary for definition of consumer unit. For definition of complete income reporters, see Glossary.
** Gift spending is also included in the preceding categories.
Source: Bureau of Labor Statistics, unpublished tables from the 1995 Consumer Expenditure Survey

Indexed Spending by Household Income, 1995

(indexed average annual spending of consumer units by category and household income, 1995; complete income reporters only)

	total	under $10,000	$10,000 to $19,999	$20,000 to $29,999	$30,000 to $39,999	$40,000 to $49,999	$50,000 to $69,999	$70,000 or more
Number of cu's (in 000s)*	83,364	14,474	16,449	12,643	10,648	8,191	10,378	10,582
Indexed average annual spending	100	43	61	80	99	115	145	206
FOOD	**100**	**52**	**74**	**87**	**100**	**117**	**133**	**171**
Food at home	**100**	**62**	**85**	**90**	**101**	**116**	**125**	**143**
Cereals and bakery products	100	62	83	89	105	115	124	145
Cereals and cereal products	100	65	88	94	103	120	119	133
Bakery products	100	61	80	87	107	113	127	153
Meats, poultry, fish, and eggs	100	67	95	92	101	114	116	131
Beef	100	65	87	89	116	115	121	128
Pork	100	72	100	99	97	116	108	113
Other meats	100	70	99	82	99	111	121	136
Poultry	100	60	94	91	103	118	106	148
Fish and seafood	100	66	97	98	74	108	127	143
Eggs	100	75	103	94	103	97	103	119
Dairy products	100	59	83	91	103	117	127	145
Fresh milk and cream	100	69	91	97	105	117	119	121
Other dairy products	100	52	78	87	102	118	132	163

(continued)

	total	under $10,000	$10,000 to $19,999	$20,000 to $29,999	$30,000 to $39,999	$40,000 to $49,999	$50,000 to $69,999	$70,000 or more
Fruits and vegetables	100	65	87	91	99	111	121	145
Fresh fruits	100	67	85	94	92	106	119	155
Fresh vegetables	100	60	84	94	103	111	119	148
Processed fruits	100	66	89	85	103	110	122	144
Processed vegetables	100	66	95	90	100	121	125	125
Other food at home	100	57	78	89	98	122	134	151
Sugar and other sweets	100	56	81	92	94	131	123	155
Fats and oils	100	66	93	89	102	123	115	126
Miscellaneous foods	100	57	75	88	98	124	139	153
Nonalcoholic beverages	100	59	82	93	97	114	134	144
Food prepared by housholder, out-of-town trips	100	37	44	78	107	117	161	224
Food away from home	**100**	**35**	**55**	**81**	**100**	**119**	**146**	**215**
ALCOHOLIC BEVERAGES	**100**	**34**	**62**	**73**	**80**	**125**	**152**	**224**
HOUSING	**100**	**52**	**67**	**80**	**99**	**106**	**137**	**201**
Shelter	**100**	**53**	**67**	**77**	**99**	**107**	**132**	**208**
Owned dwellings	100	28	46	61	91	111	161	270
Mortgage interest and charges	100	17	28	51	93	113	178	306
Property taxes	100	42	62	67	91	101	145	242
Maintenance, repairs, insurance, other expenses	100	43	80	84	89	120	128	197
Rented dwellings	100	109	114	116	119	98	72	58
Other lodging	100	29	52	53	83	105	132	311

(continued)

(continued from previous page)

	total	under $10,000	$10,000 to $19,999	$20,000 to $29,999	$30,000 to $39,999	$40,000 to $49,999	$50,000 to $69,999	$70,000 or more
Utilities, fuels, and public services	**100**	**66**	**83**	**94**	**104**	**107**	**124**	**147**
Natural gas	100	70	86	89	95	111	117	155
Electricity	100	66	85	96	104	104	123	144
Fuel oil and other fuels	100	65	88	109	93	107	123	128
Telephone	100	69	82	94	107	107	123	143
Water and other public services	100	53	78	84	103	116	135	166
Household operations	**100**	**39**	**54**	**63**	**104**	**101**	**126**	**269**
Personal services	100	39	45	63	130	133	139	219
Other household expenses	100	38	64	63	77	68	112	322
Housekeeping supplies	**100**	**43**	**66**	**89**	**103**	**117**	**122**	**199**
Laundry and cleaning supplies	100	49	81	97	102	111	119	165
Other household products	100	42	62	87	95	107	122	222
Postage and stationery	100	39	59	83	114	134	125	193
Household furnishings and equipment	**100**	**39**	**47**	**72**	**88**	**101**	**182**	**225**
Household textiles	100	49	44	64	79	148	158	224
Furniture	100	38	54	74	101	114	131	246
Floor coverings	100	66	21	66	28	39	357	155
Major appliances	100	53	74	97	117	101	147	145
Small appliances, misc. housewares	100	43	54	77	129	87	134	222
Miscellaneous household equipment	100	24	44	67	91	109	169	258

(continued)

	total	under $10,000	$10,000 to $19,999	$20,000 to $29,999	$30,000 to $39,999	$40,000 to $49,999	$50,000 to $69,999	$70,000 or more
APPAREL AND SERVICES	**100**	**41**	**59**	**83**	**94**	**117**	**138**	**215**
Men and boys	**100**	**32**	**52**	**78**	**93**	**105**	**155**	**232**
Men, 16 and over	100	27	53	78	100	106	141	245
Boys, 2 to 15	100	53	47	81	70	101	204	190
Women and girls	**100**	**35**	**53**	**87**	**92**	**138**	**133**	**217**
Women, 16 and over	100	35	52	83	88	142	132	225
Girls, 2 to 15	100	40	62	111	114	111	140	168
Children under 2	**100**	**65**	**60**	**77**	**127**	**112**	**125**	**175**
Footwear	**100**	**57**	**80**	**94**	**82**	**117**	**116**	**181**
Other apparel products and services	**100**	**45**	**63**	**69**	**101**	**88**	**147**	**232**
TRANSPORTATION	**100**	**33**	**60**	**86**	**105**	**123**	**157**	**193**
Vehicle purchases (net outlay)	**100**	**25**	**58**	**93**	**105**	**130**	**160**	**190**
Cars and trucks, new	100	20	59	63	90	119	169	244
Cars and trucks, used	100	29	57	118	118	136	150	148
Other vehicles	100	29	19	79	21	236	264	158
Gasoline and motor oil	**100**	**45**	**67**	**89**	**113**	**122**	**149**	**162**
Other vehicle expenses	**100**	**35**	**60**	**81**	**103**	**120**	**161**	**195**
Vehicle finance charges	100	24	42	84	121	150	166	190
Maintenance and repairs	100	44	65	85	103	120	162	168
Vehicle insurance	100	34	70	84	107	122	152	182
Vehicle renting, leasing, licensing, other charges	100	31	43	65	87	95	173	269

(continued)

(continued from previous page)

	total	under $10,000	$10,000 to $19,999	$20,000 to $29,999	$30,000 to $39,999	$40,000 to $49,999	$50,000 to $69,999	$70,000 or more
Public transportation	**100**	**39**	**53**	**62**	**88**	**88**	**139**	**283**
HEALTH CARE	**100**	**62**	**88**	**99**	**95**	**112**	**122**	**144**
Health insurance	100	63	96	102	101	115	113	128
Medical services	100	53	64	89	93	114	148	181
Drugs	100	83	109	109	83	99	101	115
Medical supplies	100	42	80	85	92	116	139	190
ENTERTAINMENT	**100**	**41**	**53**	**72**	**105**	**114**	**149**	**224**
Fees and admissions	100	28	47	53	94	103	157	285
Television, radios, sound equipment	100	56	68	79	105	117	146	171
Pets, toys, and playground equipment	100	38	49	83	105	118	155	207
Other supplies, equip., and services	100	34	40	74	117	119	134	249
PERSONAL CARE PRODUCTS AND SERVICES	**100**	**43**	**66**	**84**	**105**	**126**	**140**	**179**
READING	**100**	**40**	**61**	**84**	**105**	**112**	**144**	**206**
EDUCATION	**100**	**70**	**37**	**41**	**79**	**92**	**137**	**301**
TOBACCO PRODUCTS AND SMOKING SUPPLIES	**100**	**74**	**86**	**114**	**119**	**101**	**125**	**95**
MISCELLANEOUS	**100**	**53**	**65**	**85**	**125**	**122**	**134**	**161**
CASH CONTRIBUTIONS	**100**	**27**	**60**	**71**	**79**	**101**	**175**	**244**

(continued)

	total	under $10,000	$10,000 to $19,999	$20,000 to $29,999	$30,000 to $39,999	$40,000 to $49,999	$50,000 to $69,999	$70,000 or more
PERSONAL INSURANCE AND PENSIONS	**100**	**8**	**25**	**54**	**92**	**126**	**178**	**307**
Life and other personal insurance	100	30	46	69	92	114	157	259
Pensions and Social Security	100	6	22	53	92	128	181	313
GIFTS	**100**	**36**	**57**	**67**	**90**	**105**	**130**	**267**
Food	**100**	**20**	**44**	**77**	**97**	**91**	**122**	**304**
Housing	**100**	**48**	**59**	**63**	**90**	**106**	**131**	**250**
Housekeeping supplies	100	31	40	90	90	122	120	276
Household textiles	100	12	69	55	118	136	155	191
Appliances and misc. housewares	100	53	56	59	152	66	107	248
Major appliances	100	0	98	160	100	60	100	180
Small appliances and misc. housewares	100	62	48	33	167	67	108	263
Miscellaneous household equipment	100	25	64	57	65	149	184	212
Other housing	100	73	63	59	88	78	103	272
Apparel and services	**100**	**35**	**69**	**76**	**106**	**103**	**121**	**230**
Males 2 and over	100	30	54	88	122	103	122	226
Females 2 and over	100	30	63	68	91	96	130	268
Children under 2	100	60	59	68	130	90	145	193
Other apparel products and services	100	32	108	81	95	123	88	202
Jewelry and watches	100	24	132	59	141	97	79	183
All other apparel products and services	100	37	81	100	43	150	93	221
Transportation	**100**	**36**	**51**	**82**	**100**	**82**	**134**	**264**
Health care	**100**	**131**	**29**	**77**	**69**	**108**	**142**	**177**

(continued)

(continued from previous page)

	total	under $10,000	$10,000 to $19,999	$20,000 to $29,999	$30,000 to $39,999	$40,000 to $49,999	$50,000 to $69,999	$70,000 or more
Entertainment	**100**	**29**	**68**	**63**	**99**	**123**	**153**	**223**
Toys, games, hobbies, and tricycles	100	30	76	77	110	127	160	187
Other entertainment	100	29	65	57	94	121	149	240
Education	**100**	**11**	**23**	**41**	**33**	**105**	**108**	**467**
All other gifts	**100**	**36**	**66**	**69**	**101**	**117**	**151**	**210**

* The Consumer Expenditure Survey uses consumer units rather than households as the sampling unit. See Glossary for definition of consumer unit.
Note: An index of 100 is the average for all households. An index of 132 means households in the income group spend 32 percent more than the average household. An index of 68 means households in the income group spend 32 percent less than the average household.
Source: Calculations by New Strategist based on unpublished tables from the Bureau of Labor Statistics' 1995 Consumer Expenditure Survey

Market Shares by Household Income, 1995

(share of total household spending accounted for by income groups, 1995)

	total households	under $30,000	$30,000 to $49,999	$50,000 or more
Total consumer units*	100%	52%	23%	25%
Share of total spending	100	32	24	44
FOOD	100%	37%	24%	38%
Food at home	100	41	24	34
Cereals and bakery products	100	41	25	34
Cereals and cereal products	100	43	25	32
Bakery products	100	39	25	35
Meats, poultry, fish, and eggs	100	44	24	31
Beef	100	42	26	31
Pork	100	47	24	28
Other meats	100	44	24	32
Poultry	100	43	25	32
Fish and seafood	100	45	20	34
Eggs	100	48	23	28
Dairy products	100	40	25	34
Fresh milk and cream	100	45	25	30
Other dairy products	100	37	25	37
Fruits and vegetables	100	42	24	33
Fresh fruits	100	43	22	34
Fresh vegetables	100	41	24	34
Processed fruits	100	42	24	33
Processed vegetables	100	44	25	31
Other food at home	100	39	24	36
Sugar and other sweets	100	40	25	35
Fats and oils	100	43	25	30
Miscellaneous foods	100	38	25	37
Nonalcoholic beverages	100	41	24	35
Food prepared by housholder, out-of-town trips	100	27	25	48
Food away from home	100	29	24	45
ALCOHOLIC BEVERAGES	100	29	23	47
HOUSING	100	34	23	42
Shelter	100	34	23	43
Owned dwellings	100	23	23	54

(continued)

(continued from previous page)

	total households	under $30,000	$30,000 to $49,999	$50,000 or more
Mortgage interest and charges	100%	16%	23%	61%
Property taxes	100	30	21	49
Maintenance, repairs, insurance, other expenses	100	36	23	41
Rented dwellings	100	59	25	16
Other lodging	100	23	21	56
Utilities, fuels, and public services	**100**	**42**	**24**	**34**
Natural gas	100	42	23	34
Electricity	100	43	24	34
Fuel oil and other fuels	100	45	22	32
Telephone	100	42	24	33
Water and other public services	100	37	25	38
Household operations	**100**	**27**	**23**	**50**
Personal services	100	25	30	45
Other household expenses	100	29	16	55
Housekeeping supplies	**100**	**34**	**25**	**41**
Laundry and cleaning supplies	100	39	24	36
Other household products	100	33	23	43
Postage and stationery	100	31	28	40
Household furnishings and equipment	**100**	**27**	**21**	**51**
Household textiles	100	27	25	48
Furniture	100	28	24	48
Floor coverings	100	26	7	64
Major appliances	100	38	25	37
Small appliances, misc. housewares	100	30	25	45
Miscellaneous household equipment	100	23	22	54
APPAREL AND SERVICES	**100**	**31**	**23**	**44**
Men and boys	**100**	**28**	**22**	**49**
Men, 16 and over	100	27	23	49
Boys, 2 to 15	100	31	19	49
Women and girls	**100**	**30**	**25**	**44**
Women, 16 and over	100	29	25	45
Girls, 2 to 15	100	36	25	39
Children under 2	**100**	**35**	**27**	**38**
Footwear	**100**	**40**	**22**	**37**
Other apparel products and services	**100**	**31**	**21**	**48**
TRANSPORTATION	**100**	**31**	**25**	**44**
Vehicle purchases (net outlay)	**100**	**30**	**26**	**44**
Cars and trucks, new	100	25	23	52

(continued)

(continued from previous page)

	total households	under $30,000	$30,000 to $49,999	$50,000 or more
Cars and trucks, used	100%	34%	28%	37%
Other vehicles	100	21	26	53
Gasoline and motor oil	**100**	**35**	**26**	**39**
Other vehicle expenses	**100**	**30**	**25**	**45**
Vehicle finance charges	100	25	30	45
Maintenance and repairs	100	33	25	42
Vehicle insurance	100	32	26	42
Vehicle renting, leasing, licensing, other charges	100	24	20	56
Public transportation	**100**	**27**	**20**	**53**
HEALTH CARE	**100**	**43**	**23**	**34**
Health insurance	100	45	24	30
Medical services	100	35	23	41
Drugs	100	53	20	27
Medical supplies	100	36	23	41
ENTERTAINMENT	**100**	**28**	**25**	**47**
Fees and admissions	100	22	22	56
Television, radios, sound equipment	100	35	25	40
Pets, toys, and playground equipment	100	29	25	46
Other supplies, equip., and services	100	25	27	48
PERSONAL CARE PRODUCTS AND SERVICES	**100**	**33**	**26**	**40**
READING	**100**	**32**	**24**	**44**
EDUCATION	**100**	**26**	**19**	**55**
TOBACCO PRODUCTS AND SMOKING SUPPLIES	**100**	**47**	**25**	**28**
MISCELLANEOUS	**100**	**35**	**28**	**37**
CASH CONTRIBUTIONS	**100**	**27**	**20**	**53**
PERSONAL INSURANCE AND PENSIONS	**100**	**15**	**24**	**61**
Life and other personal insurance	100	25	23	52
Pensions and Social Security	100	13	24	62
GIFTS	**100**	**28**	**22**	**50**
Food	**100**	**24**	**21**	**54**
Housing	**100**	**30**	**22**	**48**
Housekeeping supplies	100	27	24	50
Household textiles	100	24	28	43

(continued)

(continued from previous page)

	total households	under $30,000	$30,000 to $49,999	$50,000 or more
Appliances and misc. housewares	100%	29%	26%	45%
Major appliances	100	44	19	35
Small appliances and misc. housewares	100	25	28	47
Miscellaneous household equipment	100	26	23	50
Other housing	100	34	19	47
Apparel and services	**100**	**31**	**24**	**44**
Males 2 and over	100	29	26	44
Females 2 and over	100	28	21	50
Children under 2	100	32	25	42
Other apparel products and services	100	39	24	37
Jewelry and watches	100	39	28	33
All other apparel products and services	100	38	20	40
Transportation	**100**	**29**	**21**	**50**
Health care	**100**	**40**	**19**	**40**
Entertainment	**100**	**28**	**25**	**47**
Toys, games, hobbies, and tricycles	100	32	26	44
Other entertainment	100	26	24	49
Education	**100**	**13**	**15**	**73**
All other gifts	**100**	**30**	**24**	**46**

* The Consumer Expenditure Survey uses consumer units rather than households as the sampling unit. See Glossary for definition of consumer unit.
Note: Numbers may not sum to 100 because of rounding.
Source: Calculations by New Strategist based on unpublished tables from the Bureau of Labor Statistics' 1995 Consumer Expenditure Survey

Spending Highest for Couples with Kids

Married couples with children spend 66 percent more than the average household—nearly $45,000 in 1995.

Married couples with children spend much more than average because they have the highest incomes and the largest households. Married couples without children at home spend 39 percent more than average. Most are empty nesters with grown children living elsewhere or are young couples who have not had children yet. Single-person households spend the least among the household types shown in these tables, slightly more than $22,000 in 1995.

The Indexed Spending table shows spending by household type in comparison to what the average household spends. An index of 100 means the household type spends an average amount on an item. An index above 100 means the household type spends more than average on an item, while an index below 100 signifies below-average spending. A look at the table reveals spending well below average for single-parent and single-person households, although single-parent households spend close to the average on most foods. Single-parent households spend 81 percent more than the average household (with an index of 181) on personal services, much of which is day care expenses.

Married couples without children at home spend more than average on many items. But these households spend much less than average on rent, personal services, and children's clothing.

The Market Share table shows how much of total household spending is accounted for by each household type. Over one-third of all spending is accounted for by married couples with children, although they are just 27 percent of all households. Married couples without children at home spend slightly more than their share of all households. Both single-parent and single-person households account for a smaller share of spending than their share of households.

Within categories, market shares vary sharply by household type. Married couples with children account for more than half of all spending on some items, such as personal services (day care), and children's clothing. Married couples without children at home account for more than 50 percent of all spending on floor coverings. Single-parent households account for less than 10 percent of spending in all categories except rent, personal services, and children's clothing. Single-person householders, many of whom are elderly women, account for a disproportionate share of spending on such things as rent and gifts of jewelry and watches.

♦ The spending of married couples with children is likely to rise faster than that of other households in the next few years as baby-boom couples enter their peak earning years and as their children become teen consumers.

Spending by Household Type, 1995

(average annual spending of consumer units by category and type of consumer unit, 1995)

	total	total married couples	husband and wife only	husband/ wife with children	single parent, children <18	single person
Number of cu's (in 000s)*	103,024	53,999	22,034	27,928	6,702	42,323
Average number of persons per cu	2.5	3.2	2.0	3.9	2.9	1.6
Average before-tax income	$36,948	$49,526	$44,765	$53,715	$19,595	$24,036
Average annual spending	32,277	41,139	36,052	44,989	22,626	22,351
FOOD	**$4,505**	**$5,725**	**$4,722**	**$6,368**	**$3,586**	**$3,017**
Food at home	**2,803**	**3,558**	**2,772**	**4,041**	**2,529**	**1,830**
Cereals and bakery products	441	562	430	649	406	284
Cereals and cereal products	165	209	151	249	172	105
Bakery products	276	352	279	400	234	180
Meats, poultry, fish, and eggs	752	947	717	1,078	752	490
Beef	228	287	214	322	241	145
Pork	156	192	148	218	164	106
Other meats	104	131	93	159	105	66
Poultry	138	173	126	201	134	91
Fish and seafood	97	126	109	135	79	61
Eggs	30	37	28	42	29	21
Dairy products	297	377	285	437	273	193
Fresh milk and cream	123	154	107	185	128	80
Other dairy products	174	222	179	252	146	112
Fruits and vegetables	457	577	490	621	372	307
Fresh fruits	144	182	161	189	115	98
Fresh vegetables	137	173	153	179	90	96
Processed fruits	96	122	93	142	90	62
Processed vegetables	80	101	82	112	77	51
Other food at home	856	1,096	849	1,256	726	555
Sugar and other sweets	112	145	118	163	95	71
Fats and oils	82	104	85	114	72	54
Miscellaneous foods	377	482	348	574	338	240
Nonalcoholic beverages	240	300	230	343	202	166
Food prepared by householder, out-of-town trips	45	64	68	62	20	24
Food away from home	**1,702**	**2,166**	**1,950**	**2,327**	**1,057**	**1,187**
ALCOHOLIC BEVERAGES	**277**	**318**	**338**	**303**	**95**	**251**

(continued)

(continued from previous page)

	total	total married couples	husband and wife only	husband/ wife with children	single parent, children <18	single person
HOUSING	**$10,465**	**$12,940**	**$11,512**	**$13,997**	**$8,171**	**$7,643**
Shelter	**5,932**	**7,145**	**6,176**	**7,863**	**4,710**	**4,577**
Owned dwellings	3,754	5,356	4,637	5,963	1,788	2,022
Mortgage interest and charges	2,107	3,137	2,190	3,857	1,176	941
Property taxes	932	1,307	1,419	1,263	404	537
Maintenance, repair,						
insurance, other expenses	716	913	1,029	843	208	545
Rented dwellings	1,786	1,224	909	1,376	2,808	2,341
Other lodging	392	565	630	524	114	215
Utilities, fuels, and public services	**2,193**	**2,629**	**2,396**	**2,751**	**1,880**	**1,685**
Natural gas	268	319	304	328	238	208
Electricity	870	1,065	956	1,128	761	637
Fuel oil and other fuels	87	105	112	99	42	70
Telephone	708	805	723	845	658	592
Water and other public services	260	334	301	351	180	178
Household operations	**508**	**680**	**451**	**888**	**589**	**276**
Personal services	258	360	93	586	468	94
Other household expenses	250	320	358	302	121	182
Housekeeping supplies	**430**	**569**	**548**	**584**	**270**	**266**
Laundry and cleaning supplies	110	143	115	160	93	68
Other household products	194	264	262	263	110	112
Postage and stationery	125	162	171	160	67	85
Household furnishings & equip.	**1,403**	**1,916**	**1,941**	**1,911**	**722**	**839**
Household textiles	100	129	144	115	54	70
Furniture	327	452	367	520	236	183
Floor coverings	177	259	437	145	24	91
Major appliances	155	206	194	207	92	99
Small appliances, misc. housewares	85	106	109	106	51	63
Miscellaneous household equipment	557	763	689	818	265	333
APPAREL & SERVICES	**1,704**	**2,100**	**1,588**	**2,477**	**1,655**	**1,188**
Men and boys	**425**	**532**	**380**	**647**	**441**	**282**
Men, 16 and over	329	419	360	462	121	243
Boys, 2 to 15	96	113	20	184	321	39
Women and girls	**660**	**807**	**666**	**914**	**624**	**471**
Women, 16 and over	559	671	635	697	376	437
Girls, 2 to 15	101	136	31	217	248	34
Children under 2	**81**	**112**	**41**	**159**	**120**	**33**

(continued)

(continued from previous page)

	total	total married couples	husband and wife only	husband/ wife with children	single parent, children <18	single person
Footwear	$278	$334	$199	$431	$286	$202
Other apparel products and services	259	315	301	326	184	199
TRANSPORTATION	6,016	7,941	6,535	8,936	3,919	3,887
Vehicle purchases (net outlay)	2,639	3,516	2,584	4,169	1,913	1,635
Cars and trucks, new	1,194	1,620	1,417	1,776	617	742
Cars and trucks, used	1,411	1,855	1,128	2,343	1,274	867
Other vehicles	34	42	40	50	22	26
Gasoline and motor oil	1,006	1,315	1,096	1,463	642	669
Other vehicle expenses	2,016	2,652	2,337	2,899	1,151	1,337
Vehicle finance charges	261	361	286	408	167	148
Maintenance and repairs	653	831	759	888	406	461
Vehicle insurance	713	915	797	1,002	450	496
Vehicle renting, leasing, licensing, other charges	390	546	494	601	128	232
Public transportation	355	458	518	404	213	246
HEALTH CARE	1,732	2,244	2,438	2,102	803	1,225
Health insurance	860	1,117	1,314	959	385	609
Medical services	511	675	567	777	237	347
Drugs	280	349	460	257	129	214
Medical supplies	80	103	96	109	53	56
ENTERTAINMENT	1,612	2,077	1,830	2,319	1,082	1,099
Fees and admissions	433	593	543	658	195	266
Television, radios, sound equipment	542	640	517	728	457	429
Pets, toys, and playground equipment	322	421	348	485	286	199
Other supplies, equip, and services	315	422	422	447	144	205
PERSONAL CARE PRODUCTS AND SERVICES	403	498	451	530	305	294
READING	163	205	211	206	77	122
EDUCATION	471	631	391	847	264	299
TOBACCO PRODUCTS AND SMOKING SUPPLIES	269	296	242	312	234	239
MISCELLANEOUS	766	817	798	822	514	741
CASH CONTRIBUTIONS	925	1,191	1,457	1,033	550	646

(continued)

(continued from previous page)

	total	total married couples	husband and wife only	husband/ wife with children	single parent, children <18	single person
PERSONAL INSURANCE AND PENSIONS	**$2,967**	**$4,159**	**$3,541**	**$4,738**	**$1,372**	**$1,699**
Life and other personal insurance	374	551	505	598	194	176
Pensions and Social Security	2,593	3,607	3,035	4,140	1,177	1,523
GIFTS**	**987**	**1,202**	**1,359**	**1,120**	**462**	**788**
Food	**88**	**121**	**132**	**114**	**27**	**54**
Housing	**250**	**315**	**325**	**313**	**159**	**178**
Housekeeping supplies	38	50	56	48	25	23
Household textiles	10	13	14	10	12	7
Appliances and misc. housewares	27	35	42	31	11	20
Major appliances	5	6	8	4	3	4
Small appliances and misc. housewares	23	29	35	28	8	16
Miscellaneous household equipment	66	79	90	72	15	56
Other housing	109	139	123	151	95	72
Apparel and services	**258**	**282**	**320**	**261**	**161**	**241**
Males 2 and over	70	70	81	68	52	72
Females 2 and over	94	108	151	79	49	80
Children under 2	39	54	41	62	42	20
Other apparel products and services	55	49	47	52	17	69
Jewelry and watches	27	19	27	13	8	39
All other apparel products, services	29	30	21	39	10	29
Transportation	**48**	**61**	**71**	**48**	**14**	**36**
Health care	**22**	**21**	**28**	**16**	**12**	**26**
Entertainment	**86**	**103**	**122**	**92**	**31**	**73**
Toys, games, hobbies, and tricycles	29	36	46	28	13	24
Other entertainment	57	67	75	64	18	50
Education	**120**	**181**	**214**	**175**	**21**	**58**
All other gifts	**114**	**118**	**146**	**103**	**38**	**121**

* *The Consumer Expenditure Survey uses consumer units rather than households as the sampling unit. See Glossary for definition of consumer unit.*
** *Gift spending is also included in the preceding categories.*
Source: Bureau of Labor Statistics, unpublished tables from the 1995 Consumer Expenditure Survey

Indexed Spending by Household Type, 1995

(indexed average annual spending of households by category and type of household, 1995)

	total	total married couples	husband and wife only	husband/ wife with children	single parent, children <18	single person
Number of cu's (in 000s)*	103,024	53,999	22,034	27,928	6,702	42,323
Indexed average annual spending	**100**	**127**	**139**	**166**	**61**	**74**
FOOD	**100**	**127**	**105**	**141**	**80**	**67**
Food at home	**100**	**127**	**99**	**144**	**90**	**65**
Cereals and bakery products	100	127	98	147	92	64
Cereals and cereal products	100	127	92	151	104	64
Bakery products	100	128	101	145	85	65
Meats, poultry, fish, and eggs	100	126	95	143	100	65
Beef	100	126	94	141	106	64
Pork	100	123	95	140	105	68
Other meats	100	126	89	153	101	63
Poultry	100	125	91	146	97	66
Fish and seafood	100	130	112	139	81	63
Eggs	100	123	93	140	97	70
Dairy products	100	127	96	147	92	65
Fresh milk and cream	100	125	87	150	104	65
Other dairy products	100	128	103	145	84	64
Fruits and vegetables	100	126	107	136	81	67
Fresh fruits	100	126	112	131	80	68
Fresh vegetables	100	126	112	131	66	70
Processed fruits	100	127	97	148	94	65
Processed vegetables	100	126	102	140	96	64
Other food at home	100	128	99	147	85	65
Sugar and other sweets	100	129	105	146	85	63
Fats and oils	100	127	104	139	88	66
Miscellaneous foods	100	128	92	152	90	64
Nonalcoholic beverages	100	125	96	143	84	69
Food prepared by householder, out-of-town trips	100	142	151	138	44	53
Food away from home	**100**	**127**	**115**	**137**	**62**	**70**
ALCOHOLIC BEVERAGES	**100**	**115**	**122**	**109**	**34**	**91**

(continued)

(continued from previous page)

	total	total married couples	husband and wife only	husband/ wife with children	single parent, children <18	single person
HOUSING	100	124	110	134	78	73
Shelter	100	120	104	133	79	77
Owned dwellings	100	143	124	159	48	54
Mortgage interest and charges	100	149	104	183	56	45
Property taxes	100	140	152	136	43	58
Maintenance, repairs,						
insurance, other expenses	100	128	144	118	29	76
Rented dwellings	100	69	51	77	157	131
Other lodging	100	144	161	134	29	55
Utilities, fuels, and public services	100	120	109	125	86	77
Natural gas	100	119	113	122	89	78
Electricity	100	122	110	130	87	73
Fuel oil and other fuels	100	121	129	114	48	80
Telephone	100	114	102	119	93	84
Water and other public services	100	128	116	135	69	68
Household operations	100	134	89	175	116	54
Personal services	100	140	36	227	181	36
Other household expenses	100	128	143	121	48	73
Housekeeping supplies	100	132	127	136	63	62
Laundry and cleaning supplies	100	130	105	145	85	62
Other household products	100	136	135	136	57	58
Postage and stationery	100	130	137	128	54	68
Household furnishings & equip.	100	137	138	136	51	60
Household textiles	100	129	144	115	54	70
Furniture	100	138	112	159	72	56
Floor coverings	100	146	247	82	14	51
Major appliances	100	133	125	134	59	64
Small appliances, misc. housewares	100	125	128	125	60	74
Miscellaneous household equipment	100	137	124	147	48	60
APPAREL & SERVICES	100	123	93	145	97	70
Men and boys	100	125	89	152	104	66
Men, 16 and over	100	127	109	140	37	74
Boys, 2 to 15	100	118	21	192	334	41
Women and girls	100	122	101	138	95	71
Women, 16 and over	100	120	114	125	67	78
Girls, 2 to 15	100	135	31	215	246	34
Children under 2	100	138	51	196	148	41

(continued)

(continued from previous page)

	total	total married couples	husband and wife only	husband/ wife with children	single parent, children <18	single person
Footwear	100	120	72	155	103	73
Other apparel products and services	100	122	116	126	71	77
TRANSPORTATION	100	132	109	149	65	65
Vehicle purchases (net outlay)	100	133	98	158	72	62
Cars and trucks, new	100	136	119	149	52	62
Cars and trucks, used	100	131	80	166	90	61
Other vehicles	100	124	118	147	65	76
Gasoline and motor oil	100	131	109	145	64	67
Other vehicle expenses	100	132	116	144	57	66
Vehicle finance charges	100	138	110	156	64	57
Maintenance and repairs	100	127	116	136	62	71
Vehicle insurance	100	128	112	141	63	70
Vehicle renting, leasing, licensing, other charges	100	140	127	154	33	59
Public transportation	100	129	146	114	60	69
HEALTH CARE	100	130	141	121	46	71
Health insurance	100	130	153	112	45	71
Medical services	100	132	111	152	46	68
Drugs	100	125	164	92	46	76
Medical supplies	100	129	120	136	66	70
ENTERTAINMENT	100	129	114	144	67	68
Fees and admissions	100	137	125	152	45	61
Television, radios, sound equipment	100	118	95	134	84	79
Pets, toys, and playground equipment	100	131	108	151	89	62
Other supplies, equip., and services	100	134	134	142	46	65
PERSONAL CARE PRODUCTS AND SERVICES	100	124	112	132	76	73
READING	100	126	129	126	47	75
EDUCATION	100	134	83	180	56	63
TOBACCO PRODUCTS AND SMOKING SUPPLIES	100	110	90	116	87	89
MISCELLANEOUS	100	107	104	107	67	97
CASH CONTRIBUTIONS	100	129	158	112	59	70

(continued)

(continued from previous page)

PERSONAL INSURANCE	total	total married couples	husband and wife only	husband/ wife with children	single parent, children <18	single person
AND PENSIONS	**100**	**140**	**119**	**160**	**46**	**57**
Life and other personal insurance	100	147	135	160	52	47
Pensions and Social Security	100	139	117	160	45	59
GIFTS	**100**	**122**	**138**	**113**	**47**	**80**
Food	**100**	**138**	**150**	**130**	**31**	**61**
Housing	**100**	**126**	**130**	**125**	**64**	**71**
Housekeeping supplies	100	132	147	126	66	61
Household textiles	100	130	140	100	120	70
Appliances and misc. housewares	100	130	156	115	41	74
Major appliances	100	120	160	80	60	80
Small appliances and misc. housewares	100	126	152	122	35	70
Miscellaneous household equipment	100	120	136	109	23	85
Other housing	100	128	113	139	87	66
Apparel and services	**100**	**109**	**124**	**101**	**62**	**93**
Males 2 and over	100	100	116	97	74	103
Females 2 and over	100	115	161	84	52	85
Children under 2	100	138	105	159	108	51
Other apparel products and services	100	89	85	95	31	125
Jewelry and watches	100	70	100	48	30	144
All other apparel products, services	100	103	72	134	34	100
Transportation	**100**	**127**	**148**	**100**	**29**	**75**
Health care	**100**	**95**	**127**	**73**	**55**	**118**
Entertainment	**100**	**120**	**142**	**107**	**36**	**85**
Toys, games, hobbies, and tricycles	100	124	159	97	45	83
Other entertainment	100	118	132	112	32	88
Education	**100**	**151**	**178**	**146**	**18**	**48**
All other gifts	**100**	**104**	**128**	**90**	**33**	**106**

* The Consumer Expenditure Survey uses consumer units rather than households as the sampling unit. See Glossary for definition of consumer unit.
Note: An index of 100 is the average for all households. An index of 132 means the household type spends 32 percent more than the average household. An index of 68 means the household type spends 32 percent less than the average household.
Source: New Strategist calculations based on unpublished data from the Bureau of Labor Statistics' 1995 Consumer Expenditure Survey

Market Shares by Household Type, 1995

(share of total household spending accounted for by household types, 1995)

	total	total married couples	husband and wife only	husband/ wife with children	single parent, children <18	single person
Total consumer units*	100%	52%	21%	27%	7%	41%
Share of total spending	100	67	24	38	5	28
FOOD	100%	67%	22%	38%	5%	28%
Food at home	100	67	21	39	6	27
Cereals and bakery products	100	67	21	40	6	26
Cereals and cereal products	100	66	20	41	7	26
Bakery products	100	67	22	39	6	27
Meats, poultry, fish, and eggs	100	66	20	39	7	27
Beef	100	66	20	38	7	26
Pork	100	65	20	38	7	28
Other meats	100	66	19	41	7	26
Poultry	100	66	20	39	6	27
Fish and seafood	100	68	24	38	5	26
Eggs	100	65	20	38	6	29
Dairy products	100	67	21	40	6	27
Fresh milk and cream	100	66	19	41	7	27
Other dairy products	100	67	22	39	5	26
Fruits and vegetables	100	66	23	37	5	28
Fresh fruits	100	66	24	36	5	28
Fresh vegetables	100	66	24	35	4	29
Processed fruits	100	67	21	40	6	27
Processed vegetables	100	66	22	38	6	26
Other food at home	100	67	21	40	6	27
Sugar and other sweets	100	68	23	39	6	26
Fats and oils	100	66	22	38	6	27
Miscellaneous foods	100	67	20	41	6	26
Nonalcoholic beverages	100	66	20	39	5	28
Food prepared by householder, out-of-town trips	100	75	32	37	3	22
Food away from home	100	67	25	37	4	29
ALCOHOLIC BEVERAGES	100	60	26	30	2	37

(continued)

(continued from previous page)

	total	total married couples	husband and wife only	husband/ wife with children	single parent, children <18	single person
HOUSING	100%	65%	24%	36%	5%	30%
Shelter	100	63	22	36	5	32
Owned dwellings	100	75	26	43	3	22
Mortgage interest and charges	100	78	22	50	4	18
Property taxes	100	74	33	37	3	24
Maintenance, repairs,						
insurance, other expenses	100	67	31	32	2	31
Rented dwellings	100	36	11	21	10	54
Other lodging	100	76	34	36	2	23
Utilities, fuels, and public services	100	63	23	34	6	32
Natural gas	100	62	24	33	6	32
Electricity	100	64	24	35	6	30
Fuel oil and other fuels	100	63	28	31	3	33
Telephone	100	60	22	32	6	34
Water and other public services	100	67	25	37	5	28
Household operations	100	70	19	47	8	22
Personal services	100	73	8	62	12	15
Other household expenses	100	67	31	33	3	30
Housekeeping supplies	100	69	27	37	4	25
Laundry and cleaning supplies	100	68	22	39	5	25
Other household products	100	71	29	37	4	24
Postage and stationery	100	68	29	35	3	28
Household furnishings & equip.	100	72	30	37	3	25
Household textiles	100	68	31	31	4	29
Furniture	100	72	24	43	5	23
Floor coverings	100	77	53	22	1	21
Major appliances	100	70	27	36	4	26
Small appliances, misc. housewares	100	65	27	34	4	30
Miscellaneous household equipment	100	72	26	40	3	25
APPAREL & SERVICES	100	65	20	39	6	29
Men and boys	100	66	19	41	7	27
Men, 16 and over	100	67	23	38	2	30
Boys, 2 to 15	100	62	4	52	22	17
Women and girls	100	64	22	38	6	29
Women, 16 and over	100	63	24	34	4	32
Girls, 2 to 15	100	71	7	58	16	14
Children under 2	100	72	11	53	10	17

(continued)

(continued from previous page)

	total	total married couples	husband and wife only	husband/ wife with children	single parent, children <18	single person
Footwear	100%	63%	15%	42%	7%	30%
Other apparel products and services	100	64	25	34	5	32
TRANSPORTATION	100	69	23	40	4	27
Vehicle purchases (net outlay)	100	70	21	43	5	25
Cars and trucks, new	100	71	25	40	3	26
Cars and trucks, used	100	69	17	45	6	25
Other vehicles	100	65	25	40	4	31
Gasoline and motor oil	100	69	23	39	4	27
Other vehicle expenses	100	69	25	39	4	27
Vehicle finance charges	100	72	23	42	4	23
Maintenance and repairs	100	67	25	37	4	29
Vehicle insurance	100	67	24	38	4	29
Vehicle renting, leasing, licensince, other charges	100	73	27	42	2	24
Public transportation	100	68	31	31	4	28
HEALTH CARE	100	68	30	33	3	29
Health insurance	100	68	33	30	3	29
Medical services	100	69	24	41	3	28
Drugs	100	65	35	25	3	31
Medical supplies	100	67	26	37	4	29
ENTERTAINMENT	100	68	24	39	4	28
Fees and admissions	100	72	27	41	3	25
Television, radios, sound equipment	100	62	20	36	5	33
Pets, toys, and playground equipment	100	69	23	41	6	25
Other supplies, equip., and services	100	70	29	38	3	27
PERSONAL CARE PRODUCTS AND SERVICES	100	65	24	36	5	30
READING	100	66	28	34	3	31
EDUCATION	100	70	18	49	4	26
TOBACCO PRODUCTS AND SMOKING SUPPLIES	100	58	19	31	6	36
MISSCELLANEOUS	100	56	22	29	4	40
CASH CONTRIBUTIONS	100	67	34	30	4	29

(continued)

(continued from previous page)

	total	total married couples	husband and wife only	husband/ wife with children	single parent, children <18	single person
PERSONAL INSURANCE						
AND PENSIONS	100%	73%	26%	43%	3%	24%
Life and other personal insurance	100	77	29	43	3	19
Pensions and Social Security	100	73	25	43	3	24
GIFTS	100	64	29	31	3	33
Food	100	72	32	35	2	25
Housing	100	66	28	34	4	29
Housekeeping supplies	100	69	32	34	4	25
Household textiles	100	68	30	27	8	29
Appliances and misc. housewares	100	68	33	31	3	30
Major appliances	100	63	34	22	4	33
Small appliances and misc. housewares	100	66	33	33	2	29
Miscellaneous household equipment	100	63	29	30	1	35
Other housing	100	67	24	38	6	27
Apparel and services	100	57	27	27	4	38
Males 2 and over	100	52	25	26	5	42
Females 2 and over	100	60	34	23	3	35
Children under 2	100	73	22	43	7	21
Other apparel products and services	100	47	18	26	2	52
Jewelry and watches	100	37	21	13	2	59
All other apparel products, services	100	54	15	36	2	41
Transportation	100	67	32	27	2	31
Health care	100	50	27	20	4	49
Entertainment	100	63	30	29	2	35
Toys, games, hobbies, and tricycles	100	65	34	26	3	34
Other entertainment	100	62	28	30	2	36
Education	100	79	38	40	1	20
All other gifts	100	54	27	24	2	44

* *The Consumer Expenditure Survey uses consumer units rather than households as the sampling unit. See Glossary for definition of consumer unit.*
Note: Numbers will not sum to 100 because not all household types are shown.
Source: New Strategist calculations based on unpublished data from the Bureau of Labor Statistics' 1995 Consumer Expenditure Survey

Blacks and Hispanics Spend Less than Whites

Because spending rises with income, black and Hispanic households spend less than non-Hispanic whites.

Spending patterns by race and ethnicity are more complex than total spending levels would suggest. In some categories of goods and services, blacks and Hispanics spend more than whites and non-Hispanics.

Overall, white households spent an average of $33,114 in 1995, compared with the $27,166 spent by blacks. Non-Hispanic households spent an average of $32,739, while Hispanic households spent $26,794. But an examination of the Indexed Spending table shows that both blacks and Hispanics spend more than the average household on a number of items.

The Indexed Spending table shows the household spending of each racial and ethnic group relative to what the average household spends. An index of 100 means the racial or ethnic group spends an average amount on an item. An index above 100 means the racial or ethnic group spends more than average on an item, while an index below 100 signifies below-average spending. A look at the table reveals below-average spending for black and Hispanic households on most items and average spending for white and non-Hispanic households.

There are some important exceptions, however. Black households spend 17 percent more than average on electricity and twice as much on fuel oil and other fuels. They spend 9 percent more than the average household on processed vegetables. Black households also spend 31 percent more than average on tobacco products and smoking supplies.

Hispanic households spend more than average on most foods, probably because their households are above average in size—3.4 people compared with 2.5 people in the average household. Hispanic households spend 74 percent more than the average household on rented dwellings, 45 percent more on laundry and cleaning supplies, 95 percent more on baby clothes, and 20 percent more on footwear. They also spend 95 percent more on gifts of baby clothes.

Because black and Hispanic households account for a minority of all households, and because their spending is below average as well, they account for a small share of the overall household market in most product and service categories.

♦ The spending of black households will remain well below average for the forseeable future because of differences in household composition. Black households have far lower incomes and spending than white households because so many are headed by single parents rather than married couples.

♦ The spending of Hispanic households will remain below average for years to come because so many Hispanic households are headed by recent immigrants with low incomes.

Spending by Race and Hispanic Origin of Householder, 1995

(average annual spending of consumer units by category and race and Hispanic origin of householder, 1995)

		race		Hispanic origin	
	total	white & other	black	non-Hispanic	Hispanic
Number of cu's (in 000s)*	103,024	88,554	14,470	95,018	8,006
Average number of persons per cu	2.5	2.5	2.6	2.5	3.4
Average before-tax income	$36,948	$38,032	$29,993	$37,822	$27,242
Average annual spending	32,277	33,114	27,166	32,739	26,794
FOOD	$4,505	$4,589	$3,998	$4,490	$4,678
Food at home	2,803	2,822	2,688	2,753	3,370
Cereals and bakery products	441	443	430	440	454
Cereals and cereal products	165	166	159	162	203
Bakery products	276	277	271	278	251
Meats, poultry, fish, and eggs	752	759	711	722	1,097
Beef	228	226	239	218	331
Pork	156	156	153	150	229
Other meats	104	103	106	102	121
Poultry	138	142	113	132	205
Fish and seafood	97	101	75	93	148
Eggs	30	31	25	27	62
Dairy products	297	298	290	292	347
Fresh milk and cream	123	123	124	118	179
Other dairy products	174	175	166	174	168
Fruits and vegetables	457	464	410	445	593
Fresh fruits	144	148	122	139	202
Fresh vegetables	137	141	114	133	185
Processed fruits	96	97	86	94	117
Processed vegetables	80	78	87	79	89
Other food at home	856	858	846	854	879
Sugar and other sweets	112	113	109	114	96
Fats and oils	82	81	91	80	113
Miscellaneous foods	377	377	375	376	386
Nonalcoholic beverages	240	242	233	239	258
Food prepared by householder, out-of-town trips	45	46	39	46	27
Food away from home	1,702	1,767	1,310	1,736	1,309
ALCOHOLIC BEVERAGES	277	291	195	284	197

(continued from previous page)

	total	race		Hispanic origin	
		white & other	black	non-Hispanic	Hispanic
HOUSING	**$10,465**	**$11,002**	**$7,185**	**$10,570**	**$9,223**
Shelter	**5,932**	**6,349**	**3,376**	**5,962**	**5,572**
Owned dwellings	3,754	3,969	2,441	3,872	2,354
Mortgage interest and charges	2,107	2,272	1,098	2,156	1,521
Property taxes	932	976	659	971	466
Maintenance, repairs,					
insurance, other expenses	716	721	685	745	367
Rented dwellings	1,786	1,969	661	1,675	3,102
Other lodging	392	411	274	415	115
Utilities, fuels, public services	**2,193**	**2,200**	**2,148**	**2,212**	**1,958**
Natural gas	268	295	102	272	223
Electricity	870	845	1,021	885	693
Fuel oil and other fuels	87	71	182	92	19
Telephone	708	721	633	701	796
Water and other public services	260	268	210	262	226
Household operations	**508**	**541**	**309**	**525**	**316**
Personal services	258	272	174	262	211
Other household expenses	250	269	135	263	104
Housekeeping supplies	**430**	**440**	**368**	**433**	**387**
Laundry and cleaning supplies	110	111	105	106	160
Other household products	194	199	165	197	158
Postage and stationery	125	130	98	130	70
Household furnishings & equip.	**1,403**	**1,471**	**985**	**1,438**	**991**
Household textiles	100	108	55	104	59
Furniture	327	343	231	332	278
Floor coverings	177	198	50	182	122
Major appliances	155	152	175	158	118
Small appliances, misc. housewares	85	86	82	88	50
Miscellaneous household equipment	557	585	393	574	364
APPAREL & SERVICES	**1,704**	**1,797**	**1,139**	**1,702**	**1,719**
Men and boys	**425**	**451**	**272**	**426**	**422**
Men, 16 and over	329	354	178	331	309
Boys, 2 to 15	96	96	94	94	113
Women and girls	**660**	**694**	**457**	**674**	**507**
Women, 16 and over	559	592	361	573	398
Girls, 2 to 15	101	102	96	101	109
Children under 2	**81**	**85**	**55**	**74**	**158**

(continued)

(continued from previous page)

	total	race		Hispanic origin	
		white & other	black	non-Hispanic	Hispanic
Footwear	$278	$294	$182	$273	$334
Other apparel products & services	259	273	172	256	298
TRANSPORTATION	**6,016**	**6,014**	**6,030**	**6,090**	**5,145**
Vehicle purchases (net outlay)	**2,639**	**2,587**	**2,959**	**2,651**	**2,497**
Cars and trucks, new	1,194	1,202	1,142	1,222	861
Cars and trucks, used	1,411	1,351	1,780	1,392	1,636
Other vehicles	34	34	37	37	-
Gasoline and motor oil	**1,006**	**977**	**1,183**	**1,016**	**891**
Other vehicle expenses	**2,016**	**2,062**	**1,736**	**2,065**	**1,438**
Vehicle finance charges	261	247	342	268	172
Maintenance and repairs	653	667	565	668	477
Vehicle insurance	713	723	647	728	528
Vehicle renting, leasing, licensing, other charges	390	424	181	400	261
Public transportation	**355**	**388**	**152**	**358**	**319**
HEALTH CARE	**1,732**	**1,679**	**2,056**	**1,790**	**1,055**
Health insurance	860	825	1,078	893	477
Medical services	511	509	526	521	394
Drugs	280	265	369	292	139
Medical supplies	80	80	83	83	45
ENTERTAINMENT	**1,612**	**1,643**	**1,421**	**1,659**	**1,060**
Fees and admissions	433	460	269	450	231
Television, radios, sound equipment	542	562	415	549	459
Pets, toys, playground equipment	322	314	372	335	174
Other supplies, equip., and services	315	307	365	325	195
PERSONAL CARE PRODUCTS AND SERVICES	**403**	**417**	**323**	**407**	**369**
READING	**163**	**168**	**130**	**170**	**74**
EDUCATION	**471**	**500**	**297**	**487**	**293**
TOBACCO PRODUCTS AND SMOKING SUPPLIES	**269**	**255**	**353**	**280**	**142**
MISCELLANEOUS	**766**	**743**	**907**	**787**	**526**
CASH CONTRIBUTIONS	**925**	**952**	**760**	**972**	**378**

(continued)

(continued from previous page)

	total	race		Hispanic origin	
		white & other	black	non-Hispanic	Hispanic
PERSONAL INSURANCE AND PENSIONS	$2,967	$3,064	$2,371	$3,054	$1,936
Life and other personal insurance	374	372	384	390	190
Pensions and Social Security	2,593	2,692	1,987	2,664	1,746
GIFTS**	987	1,032	711	1,029	493
Food	88	95	45	93	28
Housing	250	259	192	264	88
Housekeeping supplies	38	40	27	39	18
Household textiles	10	11	6	11	6
Appliances and misc housewares	27	29	17	29	6
Major appliances	5	5	4	5	1
Small appl. and misc. housewares	23	24	13	24	4
Miscellaneous household equipment	66	69	45	70	21
Other housing	109	110	97	114	38
Apparel and services	258	279	131	259	246
Males 2 and over	70	74	43	72	41
Females 2 and over	94	103	39	94	86
Children under 2	39	41	32	36	76
Other apparel products and services	55	62	17	56	43
Jewelry and watches	27	30	6	28	8
All other apparel products, services	29	32	11	28	34
Transportation	48	47	50	50	23
Health care	22	19	40	24	3
Entertainment	86	90	67	91	37
Toys, games, hobbies, and tricycles	29	30	25	30	22
Other entertainment	57	60	42	61	15
Education	120	125	89	129	15
All other gifts	114	117	97	120	52

* The Consumer Expenditure Survey uses consumer units rather than households as the sampling unit. See Glossary for definition of consumer unit.
** Gift spending is also included in the preceding categories.
Note: Hispanics may be of any race.
Source: Bureau of Labor Statistics, unpublished tables from the 1995 Consumer Expenditure Survey

Indexed Spending by Race and Hispanic Origin of Householder, 1995

(indexed average annual spending of households by category and race and Hispanic origin of householder, 1995)

	total	race		Hispanic origin	
		white & other	black	non-Hispanic	Hispanic
Number of cu's (in 000s)*	103,024	88,554	14,470	95,018	8,006
Indexed average annual spending	100	103	84	101	83
FOOD	**100**	**102**	**89**	**100**	**104**
Food at home	**100**	**101**	**96**	**98**	**120**
Cereals and bakery products	100	100	100	103	
Cereals and cereal products	100	101	96	98	123
Bakery products	100	100	98	101	91
Meats, poultry, fish, and eggs	100	101	95	96	146
Beef	100	99	105	96	145
Pork	100	100	98	96	147
Other meats	100	99	102	98	116
Poultry	100	103	82	96	149
Fish and seafood	100	104	77	96	153
Eggs	100	103	83	90	207
Dairy products	100	100	98	98	117
Fresh milk and cream	100	100	101	96	146
Other dairy products	100	101	95	100	97
Fruits and vegetables	100	102	90	97	130
Fresh fruits	100	103	85	97	140
Fresh vegetables	100	103	83	97	135
Processed fruits	100	101	90	98	122
Processed vegetables	100	98	109	99	111
Other food at home	100	100	99	100	103
Sugar and other sweets	100	101	97	102	86
Fats and oils	100	99	111	98	138
Miscellaneous foods	100	100	99	100	102
Nonalcoholic beverages	100	101	97	100	108
Food prepared by householder, out-of-town trips	100	102	87	102	60
Food away from home	**100**	**104**	**77**	**102**	**77**
ALCOHOLIC BEVERAGES	**100**	**105**	**70**	**103**	**71**

(continued)

(continued from previous page)

	total	race		Hispanic origin	
		white & other	black	non-Hispanic	Hispanic
HOUSING	100	105	69	101	88
Shelter	100	107	57	101	94
Owned dwellings	100	106	65	103	63
Mortgage interest and charges	100	108	52	102	72
Property taxes	100	105	71	104	50
Maintenance, repairs, insurance, other expenses	100	101	96	104	51
Rented dwellings	100	110	37	94	174
Other lodging	100	105	70	106	29
Utilities, fuels, and public services	100	100	98	101	89
Natural gas	100	110	38	101	83
Electricity	100	97	117	102	80
Fuel oil and other fuels	100	82	209	106	22
Telephone	100	102	89	99	112
Water and other public services	100	103	81	101	87
Household operations	100	106	61	103	62
Personal services	100	105	67	102	82
Other household expenses	100	108	54	105	42
Housekeeping supplies	100	102	86	101	90
Laundry and cleaning supplies	100	101	95	96	145
Other household products	100	103	85	102	81
Postage and stationery	100	104	78	104	56
Household furnishings & equip.	100	105	70	102	71
Household textiles	100	108	55	104	59
Furniture	100	105	71	102	85
Floor coverings	100	112	28	103	69
Major appliances	100	98	113	102	76
Small appliances, misc. housewares	100	101	96	104	59
Miscellaneous household equipment	100	105	71	103	65
APPAREL & SERVICES.	100	105	67	100	101
Men and boys	100	106	64	100	99
Men, 16 and over	100	108	54	101	94
Boys, 2 to 15	100	100	98	98	118
Women and girls	100	105	69	102	77
Women, 16 and over	100	106	65	103	71
Girls, 2 to 15	100	101	95	100	108
Children under 2	100	105	68	91	195

(continued)

(continued from previous page)

	total	race		Hispanic origin	
		white & other	*black*	*non-Hispanic*	*Hispanic*
Footwear	**100**	106	65	98	120
Other apparel products, services	**100**	105	66	99	115
TRANSPORTATION	**100**	**100**	**100**	101	86
Vehicle purchases (net outlay)	**100**	98	112	100	95
Cars and trucks, new	100	101	96	102	72
Cars and trucks, used	100	96	126	99	116
Other vehicles	100	100	109	109	0
Gasoline and motor oil	**100**	97	118	101	89
Other vehicle expenses	**100**	102	86	102	71
Vehicle finance charges	100	95	131	103	66
Maintenance and repairs	100	102	87	102	73
Vehicle insurance	100	101	91	102	74
Vehicle renting, leasing, licensing, other charges	100	109	46	103	67
Public transportation	**100**	109	43	101	90
HEALTH CARE	**100**	97	119	103	61
Health insurance	100	96	125	104	55
Medical services	100	100	103	102	77
Drugs	100	95	132	104	50
Medical supplies	100	100	104	104	56
ENTERTAINMENT	**100**	102	88	103	66
Fees and admissions	100	106	62	104	53
Television, radios, sound equipment	100	104	77	101	85
Pets, toys, playground equipment	100	98	116	104	54
Other supplies, equip., services	100	97	116	103	62
PERSONAL CARE PRODUCTS AND SERVICES	**100**	103	80	101	92
READING	**100**	103	80	104	45
EDUCATION	**100**	106	63	103	62
TOBACCO PRODUCTS AND SMOKING SUPPLIES	**100**	95	131	104	53
MISSCELLANEOUS	**100**	97	118	103	69
CASH CONTRIBUTIONS	**100**	103	82	105	41

(continued)

(continued from previous page)

	total	race		Hispanic origin	
		white & other	black	non-Hispanic	Hispanic
PERSONAL INSURANCE					
AND PENSIONS	100	103	80	103	65
Life and other personal insurance	100	99	103	104	51
Pensions and Social Security	100	104	77	103	67
GIFTS	100	105	72	104	50
Food	100	108	51	106	32
Housing	100	104	77	106	35
Housekeeping supplies	100	105	71	103	47
Household textiles	100	110	60	110	60
Appliances and misc. housewares	100	107	63	107	22
Major appliances	100	100	80	100	20
Small appl. and misc. housewares	100	104	57	104	17
Miscellaneous household equipment	100	105	68	106	32
Other housing	100	101	89	105	35
Apparel and services	100	108	51	100	95
Males 2 and over	100	106	61	103	59
Females 2 and over	100	110	41	100	91
Children under 2	100	105	82	92	195
Other apparel products and services	100	113	31	102	78
Jewelry and watches	100	111	22	104	30
All other apparel products, services	100	110	38	97	117
Transportation	100	98	104	104	48
Health care	100	86	182	109	14
Entertainment	100	105	78	106	43
Toys, games, hobbies, and tricycles	100	103	86	103	76
Other entertainment	100	105	74	107	26
Education	100	104	74	108	13
All other gifts	100	103	85	105	46

* The Consumer Expenditure Survey uses consumer units rather than households as the sampling unit. See Glossary for definition of consumer unit.
Note: An index of 100 is the average for all households. An index of 132 means households in the race/ethnicity group spend 32 percent more than the average household. An index of 68 means households in the race/ethnicity group spend 32 percent less than the average household.
Source: Calculations by New Strategist based on unpublished tables from the Bureau of Labor Statistics' 1995 Consumer Expenditure Survey

Market Shares by Race and Hispanic Origin of Householder, 1995

(share of total household spending accounted for by households in racial or ethnic group, 1995)

	total	race		Hispanic origin	
		white & other	black	non-Hispanic	Hispanic
Total consumer units*	100%	86%	14%	92%	8%
Share of annual spending	100	88	12	94	6
FOOD	100%	88%	12%	92%	8%
Food at home	100	87	13	91	9
Cereals and bakery products	100	86	14	92	8
Cereals and cereal products	100	86	14	91	10
Bakery products	100	86	14	93	7
Meats, poultry, fish, and eggs	100	87	13	89	11
Beef	100	85	15	88	11
Pork	100	86	14	89	11
Other meats	100	85	14	90	9
Poultry	100	88	12	88	12
Fish and seafood	100	89	11	88	12
Eggs	100	89	12	83	16
Dairy products	100	86	14	91	9
Fresh milk and cream	100	86	14	88	11
Other dairy products	100	86	13	92	8
Fruits and vegetables	100	87	13	90	10
Fresh fruits	100	88	12	89	11
Fresh vegetables	100	88	12	90	10
Processed fruits	100	87	13	90	9
Processed vegetables	100	84	15	91	9
Other food at home	100	86	14	92	8
Sugar and other sweets	100	87	14	94	7
Fats and oils	100	85	16	90	11
Miscellaneous foods	100	86	14	92	8
Nonalcoholic beverages	100	87	14	92	8
Food prepared by householder, out-of-town trips	100	88	12	94	5
Food away from home	100	89	11	94	6
ALCOHOLIC BEVERAGES	100	90	10	95	6

(continued)

(continued from previous page)

	total	race		Hispanic origin	
		white & other	black	non-Hispanic	Hispanic
HOUSING	100%	90%	10%	93%	7$
Shelter	100	92	8	93	7
Owned dwellings	100	91	9	95	5
Mortgage interest and charges	100	93	7	94	6
Property taxes	100	90	10	96	4
Maintenance, repairs, insurance, other expenses	100	87	13	96	4
Rented dwellings	100	95	5	86	13
Other lodging	100	90	10	98	2
Utilities, fuels, public services	100	86	14	93	7
Natural gas	100	95	5	94	6
Electricity	100	83	16	94	6
Fuel oil and other fuels	100	70	29	98	2
Telephone	100	88	13	91	9
Water and other public services	100	89	11	93	7
Household operations	100	92	9	95	5
Personal services	100	91	9	94	6
Other household expenses	100	92	8	97	3
Housekeeping supplies	100	88	12	93	7
Laundry and cleaning supplies	100	87	13	89	11
Other household products	100	88	12	94	6
Postage and stationery	100	89	11	96	4
Household furnishings & equip.	100	90	10	95	5
Household textiles	100	93	8	96	5
Furniture	100	90	10	94	7
Floor coverings	100	96	4	95	5
Major appliances	100	84	16	94	6
Small appliances, misc. housewares	100	87	14	95	5
Miscellaneous household equipment	100	90	10	95	5
APPAREL & SERVICES	100	91	9	92	8
Men and boys	100	91	9	92	8
Men, 16 and over	100	92	8	93	7
Boys, 2 to 15	100	86	14	90	9
Women and girls	100	90	10	94	6
Women, 16 and over	100	91	9	95	6
Girls, 2 to 15	100	87	13	92	8
Children under 2	100	90	10	84	15

(continued)

(continued from previous page)

	total	race		Hispanic origin	
		white & other	black	non-Hispanic	Hispanic
Footwear	100%	91%	9%	91%	9%
Other apparel products & services	100	91	9	91	9
TRANSPORTATION	100	86	14	93	7
Vehicle purchases (net outlay)	100	84	16	93	7
Cars and trucks, new	100	87	13	94	6
Cars and trucks, used	100	82	18	91	9
Other vehicles	100	86	15	100	0
Gasoline and motor oil	100	83	17	93	7
Other vehicle expenses	100	88	12	94	6
Vehicle finance charges	100	81	18	95	5
Maintenance and repairs	100	88	12	94	6
Vehicle insurance	100	87	13	94	6
Vehicle renting, leasing, licensing, other charges	100	93	7	95	5
Public transportation	100	94	6	93	7
HEALTH CARE	100	83	17	95	5
Health insurance	100	82	18	96	4
Medical services	100	86	14	94	6
Drugs	100	81	19	96	4
Medical supplies	100	86	15	96	4
ENTERTAINMENT	100	88	12	95	5
Fees and admissions	100	91	9	96	4
Television, radios, sound equipment	100	89	11	93	7
Pets, toys, playground equipment	100	84	16	96	4
Other supplies, equip., and services	100	84	16	95	5
PERSONAL CARE PRODUCTS AND SSERVICES	100	89	11	93	7
READING	100	89	11	96	4
EDUCATION	100	91	9	95	5
TOBACCO PRODUCTS AND SMOKING SUPPLIES	100	81	18	96	4
MISCELLANEOUS	100	83	17	95	5
CASH CONTRIBUTIONS	100	88	12	97	3

(continued)

(continued from previous page)

	total	race		Hispanic origin	
		white & other	black	non-Hispanic	Hispanic
PERSONAL INSURANCE					
AND PENSIONS	100%	89%	11%	95%	5%
Life and other personal insurance	100	85	14	96	4
Pensions and Social Security	100	89	11	95	5
GIFTS	**100**	**90**	**10**	**96**	**4**
Food	**100**	**93**	**7**	**97**	**2**
Housing	**100**	**89**	**11**	**97**	**3**
Housekeeping supplies	100	90	10	95	4
Household textiles	100	95	8	101	5
Appliances and misc housewares	100	92	9	99	2
Major appliances	100	86	11	92	2
Small appl. and misc. housewares	100	90	8	96	1
Miscellaneous household equipment	100	90	10	98	2
Other housing	100	87	12	96	3
Apparel and services	**100**	**93**	**7**	**93**	**7**
Males 2 and over	100	91	9	95	5
Females 2 and over	100	94	6	92	7
Children under 2	100	90	12	85	15
Other apparel products and services	100	97	4	94	6
Jewelry and watches	100	96	3	96	2
All other apparel products, services	100	95	5	89	9
Transportation	**100**	**84**	**15**	**96**	**4**
Health care	**100**	**74**	**26**	**101**	**1**
Entertainment	**100**	**90**	**11**	**98**	**3**
Toys, games, hobbies, and tricycles	100	89	12	95	6
Other entertainment	100	90	10	99	2
Education	**100**	**90**	**10**	**99**	**1**
All other gifts	**100**	**88**	**12**	**97**	**4**

* The Consumer Expenditure Survey uses consumer units rather than households as the sampling unit. See Glossary for definition of consumer unit.
Note: Numbers may not add to 100 because of rounding. Hispanics may be of any race.
Source: Calculations by New Strategist based on unpublished tables from the Bureau of Labor Statistics' 1995 Consumer Expenditure Survey

Spending Highest in the West and Northeast

Households in the Midwest and South spend less than average.

Spending closely tracks income. Both income and spending are highest in the West, where average household income was $39,884 in 1995 and average household spending was $35,222. Income and spending are lowest in the South, where average household income was $33,843 and average household spending was $30,289. On specific product and service categories, however, spending varies by region.

The Indexed Spending table compares the spending of households by region with average household spending. An index of 100 means households in the region spend an average amount on an item. An index above 100 means households in the region spend more than average on an item, while an index below 100 signifies below-average spending.

Households in the Northeast and West spend more than average on "owned dwellings" (with an index of 115 in the Northeast and 125 in the West), because housing costs are higher in those regions. While households in the South spend less than average on most items, they spend more than average on pork, processed vegetables, electricity, and new cars and trucks. Households in the Midwest spend more than average on natural gas, floor coverings, and used cars and trucks.

The Market Share table shows how much of total household spending by category is accounted for by households in each region. In most categories, spending closely matches each region's share of total households. The South, which is home to 34 percent of the nation's households, accounts for 32 percent of all household spending. With 21 percent of all households in the West, the region accounts for 23 percent of all household spending. There are some exceptions, however. Households in the South, for example, account for a disproportionate share of spending on tobacco, while those in the West spend relatively little on this item.

♦ Because regional spending patterns are partly determined by climate, spending by region is not likely to change much in the years ahead.

Household Spending by Region, 1995

(average annual spending of consumer units by category and region, 1995)

	total	Northeast	Midwest	South	West
Number of cu's (in 000s)*	**103,024**	**20,611**	**25,855**	**35,083**	**21,475**
Average number of persons per cu	2.5	2.5	2.5	2.5	2.7
Average before-tax income	$36,948	$39,547	$36,480	$33,843	$39,884
Average annual spending	32,277	33,014	31,937	30,289	35,222
FOOD	**$4,505**	**$4,870**	**$4,348**	**$4,272**	**$4,726**
Food at home	**2,803**	**3,122**	**2,626**	**2,626**	**2,998**
Cereals and bakery products	441	528	411	404	454
Cereals and cereal products	165	195	152	153	171
Bakery products	276	333	259	251	282
Meats, poultry, fish, and eggs	752	866	669	746	754
Beef	228	232	221	233	223
Pork	156	156	137	172	153
Other meats	104	131	101	93	97
Poultry	138	182	116	131	132
Fish and seafood	97	129	70	88	116
Eggs	30	36	24	29	34
Dairy products	297	328	279	270	331
Fresh milk and cream	123	132	118	116	132
Other dairy products	174	196	161	154	199
Fruits and vegetables	457	552	412	419	480
Fresh fruits	144	175	136	126	154
Fresh vegetables	137	176	114	127	145
Processed fruits	96	120	87	83	104
Processed vegetables	80	81	75	84	77
Other food at home	856	847	855	787	979
Sugar and other sweets	112	114	113	100	129
Fats and oils	82	87	76	79	91
Miscellaneous foods	377	353	379	345	447
Nonalcoholic beverages	240	250	244	226	250
Food prepared by householder, out-of-town trips	45	42	44	37	62
Food away from home	**1,702**	**1,748**	**1,722**	**1,646**	**1,728**
ALCOHOLIC BEVERAGES	**277**	**327**	**261**	**242**	**307**
HOUSING	**10,465**	**11,485**	**9,754**	**9,287**	**12,265**
Shelter	**5,932**	**6,993**	**5,198**	**4,859**	**7,550**
Owned dwellings	3,754	4,311	3,521	3,026	4,691

(continued)

	total	Northeast	Midwest	South	West
Mortgage interest and charges	$2,107	$2,212	$1,903	$1,634	$3,026
Property taxes	932	1,439	955	693	807
Maintenance, repairs, insurance, other expenses	716	659	663	700	859
Rented dwellings	1,786	2,164	1,316	1,524	2,416
Other lodging	392	518	361	309	443
Utilities, fuels, and public services	**2,193**	**2,297**	**2,184**	**2,266**	**1,982**
Natural gas	268	332	395	159	234
Electricity	870	810	783	1,065	713
Fuel oil and other fuels	87	223	77	47	33
Telephone	708	718	706	715	692
Water and other public services	260	214	224	281	311
Household operations	**508**	**482**	**451**	**544**	**545**
Personal services	258	238	270	261	258
Other household expenses	250	244	180	283	286
Housekeeping supplies	**430**	**467**	**418**	**393**	**467**
Laundry and cleaning supplies	110	115	117	102	111
Other household products	194	210	184	187	201
Postage and stationery	125	142	117	104	155
Household furnishings & equip.	**1,403**	**1,245**	**1,504**	**1,225**	**1,721**
Household textiles	100	122	109	100	70
Furniture	327	304	313	327	368
Floor coverings	177	54	221	50	450
Major appliances	155	132	167	166	145
Small appliances, misc. housewares	85	84	91	82	85
Miscellaneous household equipment	557	548	603	501	604
APPAREL & SERVICES	**1,704**	**1,751**	**1,721**	**1,667**	**1,697**
Men and boys	**425**	**421**	**418**	**414**	**457**
Men, 16 and over	329	332	323	319	352
Boys, 2 to 15	96	89	96	95	104
Women and girls	**660**	**695**	**713**	**622**	**628**
Women, 16 and over	559	605	605	515	532
Girls, 2 to 15	101	90	108	107	95
Children under 2	**81**	**87**	**75**	**81**	**80**
Footwear	**278**	**278**	**277**	**289**	**262**
Other apparel products, services	**259**	**270**	**237**	**261**	**271**
TRANSPORTATION	**6,016**	**5,468**	**6,378**	**6,039**	**6,069**
Vehicle purchases (net outlay)	**2,639**	**2,145**	**2,954**	**2,856**	**2,380**
Cars and trucks, new	1,194	1,111	1,212	1,327	1,036

(continued)

(continued from previous page)

	total	Northeast	Midwest	South	West
Cars and trucks, used	$1,411	$975	$1,696	$1,505	$1,332
Other vehicles	34	59	47	25	12
Gasoline and motor oil	**1,006**	**877**	**1,043**	**1,031**	**1,045**
Other vehicle expenses	**2,016**	**1,960**	**2,078**	**1,881**	**2,214**
Vehicle finance charges	261	182	278	305	244
Maintenance and repairs	653	584	643	632	764
Vehicle insurance	713	767	689	682	739
Vehicle renting, leasing, licensing, other charges	390	427	468	262	467
Public transportation	**355**	**486**	**302**	**271**	**429**
HEALTH CARE	**1,732**	**1,757**	**1,759**	**1,790**	**1,584**
Health insurance	860	890	890	907	720
Medical services	511	541	479	483	567
Drugs	280	243	300	327	214
Medical supplies	80	82	90	72	82
ENTERTAINMENT	**1,612**	**1,544**	**1,602**	**1,459**	**1,939**
Fees and admissions	433	429	419	373	552
Television, radios, sound equipment	542	520	572	514	570
Pets, toys, playground equipment	322	306	317	308	367
Other supplies, equip., and services	315	289	295	264	449
PERSONAL CARE PRODUCTS AND SERVICES	**403**	**438**	**373**	**386**	**435**
READING	**163**	**186**	**170**	**135**	**177**
EDUCATION	**471**	**576**	**492**	**436**	**403**
TOBACCO PRODUCTS AND SMOKING SUPPLIES	**269**	**260**	**299**	**283**	**217**
MISCELLANEOUS	**766**	**708**	**794**	**722**	**860**
CASH CONTRIBUTIONS	**925**	**724**	**962**	**902**	**1,113**
PERSONAL INSURANCE AND PENSIONS	**2,967**	**2,920**	**3,022**	**2,670**	**3,432**
Life and other personal insurance	374	353	403	392	330
Pensions and Social Security	2,593	2,567	2,619	2,277	3,102
GIFTS**	**987**	**1,072**	**1,084**	**879**	**962**
Food	**88**	**126**	**100**	**68**	**69**
Housing	**250**	**292**	**263**	**224**	**235**
Housekeeping supplies	38	46	44	22	47
Household textiles	10	19	11	8	4

(continued)

(continued from previous page)

	total	Northeast	Midwest	South	West
Appliances and misc housewares	$27	$28	$33	$25	$23
Major appliances	5	4	8	3	4
Small appl. and misc. housewares	23	24	25	22	19
Miscellaneous household equipment	66	70	82	58	56
Other housing	109	129	94	110	104
Apparel and services	**258**	**268**	**277**	**234**	**265**
Males 2 and over	70	79	81	62	59
Females 2 and over	94	96	118	72	98
Children under 2	39	45	36	43	32
Other apparel products and services	55	48	43	57	75
Jewelry and watches	27	33	18	19	44
All other apparel products, services	29	15	25	39	31
Transportation	**48**	**34**	**49**	**45**	**64**
Health care	**22**	**15**	**30**	**22**	**20**
Entertainment	**86**	**78**	**85**	**89**	**93**
Toys, games, hobbies, and tricycles	29	27	31	27	33
Other entertainment	57	51	54	62	59
Education	**120**	**142**	**146**	**110**	**85**
All other gifts	**114**	**118**	**134**	**86**	**132**

* The Consumer Expenditure Survey uses consumer units rather than households as the sampling unit. See Glossary for definition of consumer unit.
** Gift spending is also included in the preceding categories.
Source: Bureau of Labor Statistics, unpublished tables from the 1995 Consumer Expenditure Survey

Indexed Spending by Region, 1995

(indexed average annual spending of consumer units by category and region, 1995)

	total	Northeast	Midwest	South	West
Number of cu's (in 000s)*	102,210	20,542	25,919	34,728	21,428
Indexed average annual spending	100	102	99	94	109
FOOD	100	108	97	95	105
Food at home	100	111	94	94	107
Cereals and bakery products	100	120	93	92	103
Cereals and cereal products	100	118	92	93	104
Bakery products	100	121	94	91	102
Meats, poultry, fish, and eggs	100	115	89	99	100
Beef	100	102	97	102	98
Pork	100	100	88	110	98
Other meats	100	126	97	89	93
Poultry	100	132	84	95	96
Fish and seafood	100	133	72	91	120
Eggs	100	120	80	97	113
Dairy products	100	110	94	91	111
Fresh milk and cream	100	107	96	94	107
Other dairy products	100	113	93	89	114
Fruits and vegetables	100	121	90	92	105
Fresh fruits	100	122	94	88	107
Fresh vegetables	100	128	83	93	106
Processed fruits	100	125	91	86	108
Processed vegetables	100	101	94	105	96
Other food at home	100	99	100	92	114
Sugar and other sweets	100	102	101	89	115
Fats and oils	100	106	93	96	111
Miscellaneous foods	100	94	101	92	119
Nonalcoholic beverages	100	104	102	94	104
Food prepared by householder, out-of-town trips	100	93	98	82	138
Food away from home	100	103	101	97	102
ALCOHOLIC BEVERAGES	100	118	94	87	111
HOUSING	100	110	93	89	117
Shelter	100	118	88	82	127
Owned dwellings	100	115	94	81	125

(continued)

(continued from previous page)

	total	Northeast	Midwest	South	West
Mortgage interest and charges	100	105	90	78	144
Property taxes	100	154	102	74	87
Maintenance, repairs, insurance, other expenses	100	92	93	98	120
Rented dwellings	100	121	74	85	135
Other lodging	100	132	92	79	113
Utilities, fuels, and public services	**100**	**105**	**100**	**103**	**90**
Natural gas	100	124	147	59	87
Electricity	100	93	90	122	82
Fuel oil and other fuels	100	256	89	54	38
Telephone	100	101	100	101	98
Water and other public services	100	82	86	108	120
Household operations	**100**	**95**	**89**	**107**	**107**
Personal services	100	92	105	101	100
Other household expenses	100	98	72	113	114
Housekeeping supplies	**100**	**109**	**97**	**91**	**109**
Laundry and cleaning supplies	100	105	106	93	101
Other household products	100	108	95	96	104
Postage and stationery	100	114	94	83	124
Household furnishings & equip.	**100**	**89**	**107**	**87**	**123**
Household textiles	100	122	109	100	70
Furniture	100	93	96	100	113
Floor coverings	100	31	125	28	254
Major appliances	100	85	108	107	94
Small appliances, misc. housewares	100	99	107	96	100
Miscellaneous household equipment	100	98	108	90	108
APPAREL & SERVICES	**100**	**103**	**101**	**98**	**100**
Men and boys	**100**	**99**	**98**	**97**	**108**
Men, 16 and over	100	101	98	97	107
Boys, 2 to 15	100	93	100	99	108
Women and girls	**100**	**105**	**108**	**94**	**95**
Women, 16 and over	100	108	108	92	95
Girls, 2 to 15	100	89	107	106	94
Children under 2	**100**	**107**	**93**	**100**	**99**
Footwear	**100**	**100**	**100**	**104**	**94**
Other apparel products, services	**100**	**104**	**92**	**101**	**105**
TRANSPORTATION	**100**	**91**	**106**	**100**	**101**
Vehicle purchases (net outlay)	**100**	**81**	**112**	**108**	**90**
Cars and trucks, new	100	93	102	111	87

(continued)

(continued from previous page)

	total	Northeast	Midwest	South	West
Cars and trucks, used	100	69	120	107	94
Other vehicles	100	174	138	74	35
Gasoline and motor oil	**100**	**87**	**104**	**102**	**104**
Other vehicle expenses	**100**	**97**	**103**	**93**	**110**
Vehicle finance charges	100	70	107	117	93
Maintenance and repairs	100	89	98	97	117
Vehicle insurance	100	108	97	96	104
Vehicle renting, leasing, licensing, other charges	100	109	120	67	120
Public transportation	**100**	**137**	**85**	**76**	**121**
HEALTH CARE	**100**	**101**	**102**	**103**	**91**
Health insurance	100	103	103	105	84
Medical services	100	106	94	95	111
Drugs	100	87	107	117	76
Medical supplies	100	102	113	90	102
ENTERTAINMENT	**100**	**96**	**99**	**91**	**120**
Fees and admissions	100	99	97	86	127
Television, radios, sound equipment	100	96	106	95	105
Pets, toys, playground equipment	100	95	98	96	114
Other supplies, equip., and services	100	92	94	84	143
PERSONAL CARE PRODUCTS AND SERVICES	**100**	**109**	**93**	**96**	**108**
READING	**100**	**114**	**104**	**83**	**109**
EDUCATION	**100**	**122**	**104**	**93**	**86**
TOBACCO PRODUCTS AND SMOKING SUPPLIES	**100**	**97**	**111**	**105**	**81**
MISCELLANEOUS	**100**	**92**	**104**	**94**	**112**
CASH CONTRIBUTIONS	**100**	**78**	**104**	**98**	**120**
PERSONAL INSURANCE AND PENSIONS	**100**	**98**	**102**	**90**	**116**
Life and other personal insurance	100	94	108	105	88
Pensions and Social Security	100	99	101	88	120
GIFTS	**100**	**109**	**110**	**89**	**97**
Food	**100**	**143**	**114**	**77**	**78**
Housing	**100**	**117**	**105**	**90**	**94**
Housekeeping supplies	100	121	116	58	124
Household textiles	100	190	110	80	40

(continued)

(continued from previous page)

	total	Northeast	Midwest	South	West
Appliances and misc. housewares	100	104	122	93	85
Major appliances	100	80	160	60	80
Small appl. and misc. housewares	100	104	109	96	83
Miscellaneous household equipmen	100	106	124	88	85
Other housing	100	118	86	101	95
Apparel and services	**100**	**104**	**107**	**91**	**103**
Males 2 and over	100	113	116	89	84
Females 2 and over	100	102	126	77	104
Children under 2	100	115	92	110	82
Other apparel products and service	100	87	78	104	136
Jewelry and watches	100	122	67	70	163
All other apparel products, services	100	52	86	134	107
Transportation	**100**	**71**	**102**	**94**	**133**
Health care	**100**	**68**	**136**	**100**	**91**
Entertainment	**100**	**91**	**99**	**103**	**108**
Toys, games, hobbies, and tricycles	100	93	107	93	114
Other entertainment	100	89	95	109	104
Education	**100**	**118**	**122**	**92**	**71**
All other gifts	**100**	**104**	**118**	**75**	**116**

* The Consumer Expenditure Survey uses consumer units rather than households as the sampling unit. See Glossary for definition of consumer unit.
Note: An index of 100 is the average for all households. An index of 132 means households in the region spend 32 percent more than the average household. An index of 68 means households in the region spend 32 percent less than the average household.
Source: Calculations by New Strategist based on unpublished tables from the Bureau of Labor Statistics' 1995 Consumer Expenditure Survey

Market Shares by Region, 1995

(share of total household spending accounted for by region, 1995)

	total	Northeast	Midwest	South	West
Total consumer units*	**100%**	**20%**	**25%**	**34%**	**21%**
Share of total spending	**100**	**20**	**25**	**32**	**23**
FOOD	**100%**	**22%**	**24%**	**32%**	**22%**
Food at home	**100**	**22**	**24**	**32**	**22**
Cereals and bakery products	100	24	23	31	21
Cereals and cereal products	100	24	23	32	22
Bakery products	100	24	24	31	21
Meats, poultry, fish, and eggs	100	23	22	34	21
Beef	100	20	24	35	20
Pork	100	20	22	38	20
Other meats	100	25	24	30	19
Poultry	100	26	21	32	20
Fish and seafood	100	27	18	31	25
Eggs	100	24	20	33	24
Dairy products	100	22	24	31	23
Fresh milk and cream	100	21	24	32	22
Other dairy products	100	23	23	30	24
Fruits and vegetables	100	24	23	31	22
Fresh fruits	100	24	24	30	22
Fresh vegetables	100	26	21	32	22
Processed fruits	100	25	23	29	23
Processed vegetables	100	20	24	36	20
Other food at home	100	20	25	31	24
Sugar and other sweets	100	20	25	30	24
Fats and oils	100	21	23	33	23
Miscellaneous foods	100	19	25	31	25
Nonalcoholic beverages	100	21	26	32	22
Food prepared by householder, out-of-town trips	100	19	25	28	29
Food away from home	**100**	**21**	**25**	**33**	**21**
ALCOHOLIC BEVERAGES	**100**	**24**	**24**	**30**	**23**
HOUSING	**100**	**22**	**23**	**30**	**24**
Shelter	**100**	**24**	**22**	**28**	**27**
Owned dwellings	100	23	24	27	26

(continued)

(continued from previous page)

	total	Northeast	Midwest	South	West
Mortgage interest and charges	100%	21%	23%	26%	30%
Property taxes	100	31	26	25	18
Maintenance, repairs, insurance, other expenses	100	18	23	33	25
Rented dwellings	100	24	18	29	28
Other lodging	100	26	23	27	24
Utilities, fuels, and public services	**100**	**21**	**25**	**35**	**19**
Natural gas	100	25	37	20	18
Electricity	100	19	23	42	17
Fuel oil and other fuels	100	51	22	18	8
Telephone	100	20	25	34	20
Water and other public services	100	16	22	37	25
Household operations	**100**	**19**	**22**	**36**	**22**
Personal services	100	18	26	34	21
Other household expenses	100	20	18	39	24
Housekeeping supplies	**100**	**22**	**24**	**31**	**23**
Laundry and cleaning supplies	100	21	27	32	21
Other household products	100	22	24	33	22
Postage and stationery	100	23	23	28	26
Household furnishings & equip.	**100**	**18**	**27**	**30**	**26**
Household textiles	100	24	27	34	15
Furniture	100	19	24	34	23
Floor coverings	100	6	31	10	53
Major appliances	100	17	27	36	19
Small appliances, misc. housewares	100	20	27	33	21
Miscellaneous household equipment	100	20	27	31	23
APPAREL & SERVICES	**100**	**21**	**25**	**33**	**21**
Men and boys	**100**	**20**	**25**	**33**	**22**
Men, 16 and over	100	20	25	33	22
Boys, 2 to 15	100	19	25	34	23
Women and girls	**100**	**21**	**27**	**32**	**20**
Women, 16 and over	100	22	27	31	20
Girls, 2 to 15	100	18	27	36	20
Children under 2	**100**	**21**	**23**	**34**	**21**
Footwear	**100**	**20**	**25**	**35**	**20**
Other apparel products, services	**100**	**21**	**23**	**34**	**22**
TRANSPORTATION	**100**	**18**	**27**	**34**	**21**
Vehicle purchases (net outlay)	**100**	**16**	**28**	**37**	**19**
Cars and trucks, new	100	19	25	38	18

(continued)

(continued from previous page)

	total	Northeast	Midwest	South	West
Cars and trucks, used	100%	14%	30%	36%	20%
Other vehicles	100	35	35	25	7
Gasoline and motor oil	**100**	**17**	**26**	**35**	**22**
Other vehicle expenses	**100**	**19**	**26**	**32**	**23**
Vehicle finance charges	100	14	27	40	19
Maintenance and repairs	100	18	25	33	24
Vehicle insurance	100	22	24	33	22
Vehicle renting, leasing, licensing, other charges	100	22	30	23	25
Public transportation	**100**	**27**	**21**	**26**	**25**
HEALTH CARE	**100**	**20**	**25**	**35**	**19**
Health insurance	100	21	26	36	17
Medical services	100	21	24	32	23
Drugs	100	17	27	40	16
Medical supplies	100	21	28	31	21
ENTERTAINMENT	**100**	**19**	**25**	**31**	**25**
Fees and admissions	100	20	24	29	27
Television, radios, sound equipment	100	19	26	32	22
Pets, toys, playground equipment	100	19	25	33	24
Other supplies, equip., and services	100	18	24	29	30
PERSONAL CARE PRODUCTS AND SERVICES.	**100**	**22**	**23**	**33**	**22**
READING	**100**	**23**	**26**	**28**	**23**
EDUCATION	**100**	**24**	**26**	**32**	**18**
TOBACCO PRODUCTS AND SMOKING SUPPLIES	**100**	**19**	**28**	**36**	**17**
MISCELLANEOUS	**100**	**18**	**26**	**32**	**23**
CASH CONTRIBUTIONS	**100**	**16**	**26**	**33**	**25**
PERSONAL INSURANCE AND PENSIONS	**100**	**20**	**26**	**31**	**24**
Life and other personal insurance	100	19	27	36	18
Pensions and Social Security	100	20	25	30	25
GIFTS	**100**	**22**	**28**	**30**	**20**
Food	**100**	**29**	**29**	**26**	**16**
Housing	**100**	**23**	**26**	**31**	**20**
Housekeeping supplies	100	24	29	20	26
Household textiles	100	38	28	27	8

(continued)

(continued from previous page)

	total	Northeast	Midwest	South	West
Appliances and misc. housewares	100%	21%	31%	32%	18%
Major appliances	100	16	40	20	17
Small appl. and misc. housewares	100	21	27	33	17
Miscellaneous household equipment	100	21	31	30	18
Other housing	100	24	22	34	20
Apparel and services	**100**	**21**	**27**	**31**	**21**
Males 2 and over	100	23	29	30	18
Females 2 and over	100	20	32	26	22
Children under 2	100	23	23	38	17
Other apparel products and services	100	17	20	35	28
Jewelry and watches	100	24	17	24	34
All other apparel products, services	100	10	22	46	22
Transportation	**100**	**14**	**26**	**32**	**28**
Health care	**100**	**14**	**34**	**34**	**19**
Entertainment	**100**	**18**	**25**	**35**	**23**
Toys, games, hobbies, and tricycles	100	19	27	32	24
Other entertainment	100	18	24	37	22
Education	**100**	**24**	**31**	**31**	**15**
All other gifts	**100**	**21**	**29**	**26**	**24**

* The Consumer Expenditure Survey uses consumer units rather than households as the sampling unit. See Glossary for definition of consumer unit.
Note: Numbers may not add to 100 due to rounding.
Source: Calculations by New Strategist based on unpublished tables from the Bureau of Labor Statistics' 1995 Consumer Expenditure Survey

8

Wealth Trends

◆ **The average household's median net worth rose 7 percent between 1992 and 1995.**
The gain boosted net worth to a median of $56,400 in 1995, up from $52,800 in 1992.

◆ **Financial assets accounted for 34 percent of total households assets in 1995.**
Nine out of ten households own financial assets, which peak at $32,000 among householders aged 55 to 64.

◆ **Ownership of nonfinancial assets rises with age and income.**
Ninety-four percent of households headed by 55-to-64-year-olds own nonfinancial assets, the value of which peaks in the 45-to-64 age group.

◆ **The median value of Americans' primary residence was $90,000 in 1995.**
The primary residence accounts for 65 percent of the average household's nonfinancial assets.

◆ **Two-thirds of American households have debts.**
Median debt totals $22,500 and credit card debt is most common, held by 48 percent of households.

◆ **Gains and losses in homeownership rates between 1982 and 1996 varied by type of household.**
The greatest increase was for men who live alone—up 7 percentage points, while male-headed families experienced the biggest decline—down 3.8 percentage points.

◆ **The median size of American homes has been growing for decades.**
One in five homes is at least 2,000 square feet and fewer than 10 percent are smaller than 1,000 square feet.

◆ **Among all civilian, nonagricultural workers, 40 percent are vested in a pension plan.**
Among employees who work for organizations offering pension plans, fully 76 percent participate and 86 percent of participants are vested in a plan.

Household Net Worth Is Growing

Between 1992 and 1995, the median net worth of the average household rose by 7 percent after adjusting for inflation.

The increase in net worth was welcome news after the decline between 1989 and 1992. The 7 percent gain boosted net worth to a median of $56,400 in 1995, up from $52,800 in 1992.

The youngest age groups saw the biggest gains in net worth. The net worth of householders under age 35 rose by 13 percent between 1992 and 1995, after adjusting for inflation. Despite this increase, the youngest householders have little net worth, a median of just $11,400 in 1995. Net worth peaks at $111,000 among householders aged 55 to 64, then falls slightly with age as people spend down their retirement savings.

Net worth is greatest for households with incomes of $100,000 or more, a median of $486,000 in 1995. This was down slightly from a net worth of over $500,000 in 1992, however.

Net worth also rises with education, but the link to education is not as strong as the link to age or income. This is because older Americans have the highest net worth, yet they are the least-educated generation. As well-educated baby boomers age, the link between education and net worth will become much stronger.

The median net worth of non-Hispanic whites stood at $73,900 in 1995, compared with just $16,500 for non-whites and Hispanics. One reason for this gap is the far lower homeownership rate among blacks and Hispanics.

◆ As boomers save for retirement, net worth should grow for years to come.

Net Worth of Households, 1992 and 1995

(median net worth of households by selected characteristics of householders, 1992 and 1995, and percent change, 1992-95; in 1995 dollars; numbers in thousands)

	1995	1992	percent change 1992-95
Total households	$56.4	$52.8	6.8%
Income			
Under $10,000	4.8	3.3	45.5
$10,000 to $24,999	30.0	28.2	6.4
$25,000 to $49,999	54.9	54.8	0.2
$50,000 to $99,999	121.1	121.2	-0.1
$100,000 or more	485.9	506.1	-4.0
Age of householder			
Under age 35	11.4	10.1	12.9
Aged 35 to 44	48.5	46.0	5.4
Aged 45 to 54	90.5	83.4	8.5
Aged 55 to 64	110.8	122.5	-9.6
Aged 65 to 74	104.1	105.8	-1.6
Aged 75 or older	95.0	92.8	2.4
Education of householder			
No high school diploma	26.3	21.6	21.8
High school diploma	50.0	41.4	20.8
Some college	43.2	62.6	-31.0
College degree	104.1	103.1	1.0
Race or ethnicity of householder			
Non-Hispanic white	73.9	71.7	3.1
Non-white or Hispanic	16.5	16.9	-2.4
Current work status of householder			
Professional, managerial	89.3	78.8	13.3
Technical, sales, clerical	43.3	48.0	-9.8
Precision production	43.5	38.4	13.3
Machine operators and laborers	37.3	23.5	58.7
Service occupations	15.8	15.7	0.6
Self-employed	152.9	155.6	-1.7
Retired	81.6	76.3	6.9
Other not working	4.5	5.5	-18.2
Housing tenure			
Owner	102.3	106.1	-3.6
Renter or other	4.5	3.6	25.0

Source: Federal Reserve Board, Family Finances in the U.S.: Recent Evidence from the Survey of Consumer Finances, *Federal Reserve Bulletin, January 1997; calculations by New Strategist*

Most Households Own Financial Assets

The median value of the financial assets owned by the average household stood at $13,000 in 1995.

The financial assets of Americans are growing as people pour money into the stock market. Financial assets accounted for 34 percent of total household assets in 1995, up from 28 percent in 1989. During those years, direct and indirect stock ownership grew as a share of total financial assets, rising from 26 percent in 1989 to 40 percent in 1995.

Nine out of ten households own financial assets, with little variation by age. The value of the financial assets owned by households does vary by age, however, peaking at $32,000 among householders aged 55 to 64. The value then declines as people spend their wealth in retirement.

The proportion of households with financial assets does not vary much by income, but the value of those assets is much greater for affluent households. Households with incomes of $100,000 or more have a median of $214,500 in financial assets, with the largest share in retirement accounts.

♦ With millions of Americans anxious to boost their retirement savings, the financial assets of households should expand substantially in the years ahead.

Households with Financial Assets, 1995

(percentage of households owning financial assets, by selected characteristics of households and type of asset, 1995)

	any financial asset	transaction accounts	CDs	savings bonds	bonds	stocks	mutual funds	retirement accounts	life insurance	other managed	other financial
Total households	90.8%	87.1%	14.1%	22.9%	3.0%	15.3%	12.0%	43.0%	31.4%	3.8%	11.0%
Income											
Under $10,000	68.1	61.1	7.2	5.9	–	2.5	1.8	5.9	15.8	–	8.9
$10,000 to $24,999	87.6	82.3	16.0	11.8	–	9.2	4.9	24.2	25.2	3.2	8.6
$25,000 to $49,999	97.8	94.7	13.7	27.4	3.2	14.3	12.4	52.6	33.1	4.2	13.2
$50,000 to $99,999	99.5	98.6	15.6	39.9	4.8	26.0	20.9	69.8	42.5	5.3	11.3
$100,000 or more	100.0	100.0	21.1	36.3	14.5	45.2	38.0	84.6	54.1	8.0	15.2
Age of householder											
Under age 35	87.0	80.8	7.1	21.1	0.5	11.1	8.8	39.2	22.3	1.6	13.5
Aged 35 to 44	92.0	87.4	8.2	31.0	1.6	14.5	10.5	51.5	28.9	3.4	10.5
Aged 45 to 54	92.4	88.9	12.5	25.1	4.6	17.5	16.0	54.3	37.5	2.9	13.0
Aged 55 to 64	90.5	88.2	16.2	19.6	2.9	14.9	15.2	47.2	37.5	7.1	9.0
Aged 65 to 74	92.0	91.1	23.9	17.0	5.1	18.0	13.7	35.0	37.0	5.6	10.4
Aged 75 or older	93.8	93.0	34.1	15.3	7.0	21.3	10.4	16.5	35.1	5.7	5.3

(continued)

(continued from previous page)

	any financial asset	transaction accounts	CDs	savings bonds	bonds	stocks	mutual funds	retirement accounts	life insurance	other managed	other financial
Race and ethnicity of householder											
Non-Hispanic white	94.7%	92.4%	16.5%	26.2%	3.7%	18.2%	14.5%	47.0%	33.5%	4.7%	11.7%
Non-white or Hispanic	77.4	69.1	5.9	11.3	0.6	5.5	3.5	29.2	24.4	1.0	8.5
Current work status of householder											
Professional, managerial	98.9	97.4	16.1	36.8	4.6	26.1	21.3	70.3	39.1	5.7	11.6
Technical, sales, clerical	96.2	93.0	9.4	24.5	3.1	15.7	11.7	55.8	29.8	3.6	14.0
Precision production	93.5	88.9	7.3	26.2	-	12.4	9.7	48.5	29.0	2.5	9.9
Machine operators and laborers	91.5	84.3	8.2	24.0	1.1	9.0	6.9	47.3	30.1	1.2	10.9
Service occupations	83.3	76.6	55.5	14.0	-	4.0	5.2	24.3	26.1	2.9	10.2
Self-employed	94.3	91.3	18.6	26.0	5.4	18.8	18.2	47.8	41.5	3.1	15.6
Retired	88.2	86.4	23.1	15.1	3.9	16.9	11.0	24.2	31.2	5.4	7.6
Other not working	66.4	59.6	7.8	12.8	0.1	5.1	4.6	16.0	13.3	2.7	11.7
Housing tenure											
Owner	96.3	94.8	17.1	28.4	4.1	19.3	15.6	52.2	38.1	4.9	9.3
Renter or other	80.8	73.0	8.6	12.8	0.9	8.1	5.4	26.2	19.2	1.8	14.1

Note: (-) means sample is too small to make a reliable estimate.
Source: Federal Reserve Board, Family Finances in the U.S.: Recent Evidence from the Survey of Consumer Finances, Federal Reserve Bulletin, January 1997

Median Value of Financial Assets, 1995

(median value of financial assets for owners, by selected characteristics of households and type of asset, 1995; numbers in thousands)

	any financial asset	transaction accounts	CDs	savings bonds	bonds	stocks	mutual funds	retirement accounts	life insurance	other managed	other financial
Total households	$13.0	$2.1	$10.0	$1.0	$26.2	$8.0	$19.0	$15.6	$5.0	$30.0	$3.0
Income											
Under $10,000	1.2	0.7	7.0	0.4	–	2.0	25.0	3.5	1.5	–	2.0
$10,000 to $24,999	5.4	1.4	10.0	0.8	–	5.7	8.0	6.0	3.0	19.7	2.0
$25,000 to $49,999	12.1	2.0	10.0	0.7	29.0	6.9	12.5	10.0	5.0	25.0	2.5
$50,000 to $99,999	40.7	4.5	13.0	1.2	9.4	5.7	15.0	23.0	7.0	35.0	3.0
$100,000 or more	214.5	15.8	15.6	1.5	58.0	30.0	48.0	85.0	12.0	62.5	23.0
Age of householder											
Under age 35	5.3	1.2	6.0	0.5	2.0	3.7	5.0	5.2	3.4	3.8	1.0
Aged 35 to 44	11.6	2.0	6.0	1.0	11.0	4.0	10.0	12.0	5.0	10.8	2.0
Aged 45 to 54	24.8	2.7	12.0	1.0	17.0	10.0	17.5	25.0	6.5	43.0	5.0
Aged 55 to 64	32.3	3.0	14.0	1.1	10.0	17.0	55.0	32.8	6.0	42.0	9.0
Aged 65 to 74	19.1	3.0	17.0	1.5	58.0	15.0	50.0	28.5	5.0	26.0	9.0
Aged 75 or older	20.9	5.0	11.0	4.0	40.0	25.0	50.0	17.5	5.0	100.0	35.0
Race and ethnicity of householder											
Non-Hispanic white	16.9	2.5	10.0	1.0	26.2	8.6	20.0	17.5	5.0	30.0	4.0
Non-white or Hispanic	5.2	1.5	10.0	0.5	27.0	5.0	7.8	9.6	5.0	1.8	1.5

(continued)

(continued from previous page)

	any financial asset	transaction accounts	CDs	savings bonds	bonds	stocks	mutual funds	retirement accounts	life insurance	other managed	other financial
Current work status of householder											
Professional, managerial	$32.1	$3.3	$10.0	$1.0	$17.0	$9.3	$15.5	$23.0	$7.0	$21.0	$3.0
Technical, sales, clerical	12.7	2.0	10.0	0.8	13.0	5.0	11.0	11.4	5.0	10.3	1.8
Precision production	8.7	1.5	4.0	1.0	-	4.8	10.0	10.0	5.0	10.0	2.3
Machine operators and laborers	6.7	1.2	5.3	0.6	3.8	1.3	6.0	7.6	6.0	30.0	1.1
Service occupations	3.4	1.2	8.0	0.8	-	5.7	20.0	8.8	3.0	5.0	4.5
Self-employed	24.0	4.4	15.0	1.0	50.0	17.5	25.0	28.0	6.0	39.0	4.0
Retired	17.4	3.1	14.0	2.0	40.0	20.0	48.0	24.0	4.5	52.0	7.0
Other not working	3.4	0.7	10.0	0.4	225.0	2.4	37.0	10.0	3.5	26.0	5.0
Housing tenure											
Owner	22.3	3.0	10.0	1.0	36.3	10.0	20.0	20.0	6.0	30.0	5.0
Renter or other	4.0	1.2	8.0	0.8	7.0	4.0	10.0	5.6	3.0	20.0	1.7

Note: (-) means sample is too small to make a reliable estimate.
Source: Federal Reserve Board, Family Finances in the U.S.: Recent Evidence from the Survey of Consumer Finances, Federal Reserve Bulletin, January 1997

Most Important Nonfinancial Asset Is a Home

The primary residence accounts for 65 percent of the average household's nonfinancial assets.

The median value of Americans' primary residence was $90,000 in 1995. Although a greater percentage of households own a vehicle (84 percent) than own a home (65 percent), the median value of vehicles was just $10,000.

Not surprisingly, ownership of nonfinancial assets rises with income, as does the the median value of those assets. Ownership of nonfinancial assets also rises with age, peaking at 94 percent in the 55-to-64 age group. The median value of non-financial assets peaks in the 45-to-64 age group.

Whites and non-Hispanics are much more likely to own nonfinancial assets than are nonwhites or Hispanics. The asset most likely to be owned by all racial and ethnic groups is a vehicle, owned by 71 percent of non-whites or Hispanics and by 88 percent of non-Hispanic whites. The median value of the nonfinancial assets owned by non-whites and Hispanics is far lower than that for non-Hispanic whites, $42,100 versus $93,000. Behind this difference is home ownership. Sixty-nine percent of non-Hispanic whites own a home, compared with just 48 percent of non-whites and Hispanics.

♦ Because nonfinancial assets account for the largest share of household wealth, and because homes account for the largest share of nonfinancial assets, trends in homeownership and home values have a major impact on Americans' wealth.

Households with Nonfinancial Assets, 1995

(percentage of households owning nonfinancial assets, by selected characteristics of households and type of asset, 1995)

	any nonfinancial asset	vehicles	primary residence	investment real estate	business	other nonfinancial
Total households	91.1%	84.2%	64.7%	17.5%	11.0%	9.0%
Income						
Under $10,000	69.8	57.7	37.6	6.9	4.8	3.8
$10,000 to $24,999	89.4	82.7	55.4	11.5	6.2	6.2
$25,000 to $49,999	96.6	92.2	68.4	16.5	9.8	9.6
$50,000 to $99,999	99.1	93.3	84.4	24.9	17.5	11.5
$100,000 or more	99.4	90.2	91.1	52.3	32.1	22.6
Age of householder						
Under age 35	87.6	83.9	37.9	7.2	9.3	7.6
Aged 35 to 44	90.9	85.1	64.6	14.4	13.9	10.2
Aged 45 to 54	93.7	88.2	75.4	23.9	14.8	10.7
Aged 55 to 64	94.0	88.7	82.1	26.9	11.7	9.8
Aged 65 to 74	92.5	82.0	79.0	26.5	7.9	8.9
Aged 75 or older	90.2	72.8	73.0	16.6	3.8	5.4
Race and ethnicity of householder						
Non-Hispanic white	94.9	88.1	69.4	19.7	12.6	10.5
Non-white or Hispanic	78.1	71.1	48.2	10.2	5.4	3.5
Current work status of householder						
Professional, managerial	96.7	90.8	71.1	24.6	11.8	14.5
Technical, sales, clerical	92.9	88.0	63.4	10.5	6.4	10.6
Precision production	97.2	93.4	66.9	16.2	7.3	9.0
Machine operators & laborers	93.8	91.9	61.2	14.0	5.1	6.5
Service occupations	86.9	83.8	50.5	8.6	3.5	2.0
Self-employed	96.1	85.7	73.9	32.1	58.0	16.1
Retired	88.3	76.6	70.3	18.6	2.9	5.6
Other not working	67.9	60.6	34.8	8.0	3.7	5.9
Housing tenure						
Owner	100.0	90.8	100.0	22.3	13.4	10.3
Renter or other	74.8	72.2	-	8.7	6.4	6.5

Note: (-) means sample is too small to make a reliable estimate.
Source: Federal Reserve Board, Family Finances in the U.S.: Recent Evidence from the Survey of Consumer Finances, *Federal Reserve Bulletin, January 1997*

Median Value of Nonfinancial Assets, 1995

(median value of nonfinancial assets for owners, by selected characteristics of households and type of asset, 1995; numbers in thousands)

	any nonfinancial asset	vehicles	primary residence	investment real estate	business	other nonfinancial
Total households	$83.0	$10.0	$90.0	$50.0	$41.0	$10.0
Income						
Under $10,000	13.1	3.6	40.0	16.2	50.6	2.5
$10,000 to $24,999	44.5	6.1	65.0	30.0	30.0	8.0
$25,000 to $49,999	81.5	11.1	80.0	40.0	26.3	6.0
$50,000 to $99,999	145.2	16.2	120.0	57.3	30.0	14.0
$100,000 or more	319.3	22.8	200.0	130.0	300.0	20.0
Age of householder						
Under age 35	21.5	9.0	80.0	33.5	20.0	5.0
Aged 35 to 44	95.6	10.7	95.0	45.0	35.0	9.0
Aged 45 to 54	111.7	12.4	100.0	55.0	60.0	12.0
Aged 55 to 64	107.0	11.9	85.0	82.5	75.0	10.0
Aged 65 to 74	93.5	8.0	80.0	55.0	100.0	16.0
Aged 75 or older	79.0	5.3	80.0	20.0	30.0	15.0
Race and ethnicity of householder						
Non-Hispanic white	93.0	10.8	92.0	50.0	45.0	10.0
Non-white or Hispanic	42.1	7.7	70.0	33.5	26.3	8.0
Current work status of householder						
Professional, managerial	133.5	12.4	130.0	57.3	15.0	10.0
Technical, sales, clerical	83.1	10.4	90.0	40.0	17.5	10.0
Precision production	72.9	12.2	78.0	37.5	30.0	5.0
Machine operators and laborers	57.9	10.8	68.0	36.0	24.0	8.0
Service occupations	35.8	7.2	69.0	17.5	80.2	10.0
Self-employed	175.6	12.0	120.0	100.0	71.0	8.0
Retired	78.0	7.3	76.0	45.0	90.0	10.0
Other not working	17.4	6.2	80.0	59.0	12.0	7.0
Housing tenure						
Owner	115.4	11.9	90.0	53.0	50.0	10.0
Renter or other	7.5	6.4	-	35.0	26.0	5.0

Note: (-) means sample is too small to make a reliable estimate.
Source: Federal Reserve Board, Family Finances in the U.S.: Recent Evidence from the Survey of Consumer Finances, *Federal Reserve Bulletin, January 1997*

Forty-Eight Percent of American Households Have Credit Card Debt

The median amount of credit card debt stood at $1,500 in 1995.

Two-thirds of American households have debts, totalling a median of $22,500 in 1995. Credit card debt is most common, with a near majority of households (48 percent) holding this form of debt. The biggest debts are for mortgages and home equity loans, with a median value of $51,000.

The percentage of American households with debt rises with income. In contrast, debt levels decline with age after peaking in the 35-to-54 age group. The expenses of buying a home and raising children explain why 87 percent of 35-to-54-year-olds are in debt. The proportion is a smaller 75 percent among 55-to-64-year-olds, then falls to 54 percent among 65-to-74-year-olds. Only among householders aged 75 or older are a minority in debt.

The proportion of households with debt does not vary much by race or ethnicity. But the median value of debt is much greater for non-Hispanic whites ($27,000) than it is for non-whites or Hispanics ($12,200).

♦ Although the average American household is not deeply in debt, the total debt load carried by Americans overall is substantial because the enormous baby-boom generation is in the most debt-prone age group, 35 to 54.

Households with Debt, 1995

(percentage of households with debt, by selected characteristics of households and type of debt, 1995; numbers in thousands)

	any debt	mortgage & home equity	installment	other lines of credit	credit card	investment real estate	other debt
Total households	75.2%	41.1%	46.5%	1.9%	47.8%	6.3%	9.0%
Income							
Under $10,000	48.5	8.9	25.9	-	25.4	1.6	6.6
$10,000 to $24,999	67.3	24.8	41.3	1.4	41.9	2.5	8.7
$25,000 to $49,999	83.9	47.3	54.3	2.0	56.7	5.8	8.5
$50,000 to $99,999	89.9	68.7	60.7	3.2	62.8	9.5	10.0
$100,000 or more	86.4	73.6	37.0	4.0	37.0	27.9	15.8
Age of householder							
Under age 35	83.8	32.9	62.2	2.6	55.4	2.6	7.8
Aged 35 to 44	87.2	54.1	60.7	2.2	55.8	6.5	11.1
Aged 45 to 54	86.5	61.9	54.0	2.3	57.3	10.4	14.1
Aged 55 to 64	75.2	45.8	36.0	1.4	43.4	12.5	7.5
Aged 65 to 74	54.2	24.8	16.7	1.3	31.3	5.0	5.5
Aged 75 or older	30.1	7.1	9.6	-	18.3	1.5	3.6
Race and ethnicity of householder							
Non-Hispanic white	75.8	43.5	46.4	2.1	47.5	6.9	9.1
Non-white or Hispanic	73.1	32.7	46.9	1.3	48.8	4.4	8.5
Current work status of householder							
Professional, managerial	90.3	63.4	56.2	3.7	56.8	10.5	10.9
Technical, sales, clerical	88.6	51.4	61.1	2.0	60.1	4.1	12.3
Precision production	88.3	53.3	64.5	2.3	64.8	5.4	9.1
Machine operators and laborers	86.0	44.1	61.3	0.9	56.9	6.8	9.5
Service occupations	82.6	34.6	50.3	-	53.1	2.2	9.0
Self-employed	81.9	51.3	45.6	3.6	44.9	15.4	10.0
Retired	45.9	19.0	18.4	0.3	26.6	3.6	4.8
Other not working	65.0	17.9	42.8	-	38.7	2.7	9.8
Housing tenure							
Owner	80.2	63.6	46.0	1.5	51.4	7.9	8.7
Renter or other	66.2	-	47.5	2.6	41.2	3.5	9.5

Note: (-) means sample is too small to make a reliable estimate.
Source: Federal Reserve Board, Family Finances in the U.S.: Recent Evidence from the Survey of Consumer Finances, *Federal Reserve Bulletin, January 1997*

Median Value of Debt, 1995

(median value of debt for households with debt, by selected characteristics of households and type of debt, 1995; numbers in thousands)

	any debt	mortgage & home equity	installment	other lines of credit	credit card	investment real estate	other debt
Total households	$22.5	$51.0	$6.1	$3.5	$1.5	$28.0	$2.0
Income							
Under $10,000	2.6	14.0	2.9	-	0.6	15.0	2.0
$10,000 to $24,999	9.2	26.0	3.9	3.0	1.2	18.3	1.2
$25,000 to $49,999	23.4	46.0	6.6	3.0	1.4	25.0	1.5
$50,000 to $99,999	65.0	68.0	9.0	2.2	2.2	34.0	2.5
$100,000 or more	112.2	103.4	8.5	19.5	3.0	36.8	7.0
Age of householder							
Under age 35	15.2	63.0	7.0	1.4	1.4	22.8	1.5
Aged 35 to 44	37.6	60.0	5.6	2.0	1.8	30.0	1.7
Aged 45 to 54	41.0	48.0	7.0	5.7	2.0	28.1	2.5
Aged 55 to 64	25.8	36.0	5.9	3.5	1.3	26.0	4.0
Aged 65 to 74	7.7	19.0	4.9	3.8	0.8	36.0	2.0
Aged 75 or older	2.0	15.9	3.9	-	0.4	8.0	3.0
Race and ethnicity of householder							
Non-Hispanic white	27.2	54.0	6.4	3.5	1.5	29.0	2.0
Non-white or Hispanic	12.2	36.5	5.0	0.8	1.2	25.0	1.5
Current work status of householder							
Professional, managerial	65.1	79.0	8.2	2.5	2.2	26.3	2.7
Technical, sales, clerical	30.1	52.6	8.0	0.6	1.7	25.0	1.6
Precision production	29.5	50.0	6.3	1.5	1.4	35.0	2.0
Machine operators and laborers	15.2	36.8	5.2	1.6	1.3	17.0	1.0
Service occupations	12.0	38.5	5.1	-	1.3	13.0	1.0
Self-employed	42.2	62.0	5.8	8.0	2.6	50.0	4.8
Retired	6.5	23.3	4.4	3.8	1.0	23.0	2.5
Other not working	7.5	45.0	5.0	-	0.8	20.0	1.7
Housing tenure							
Owner	46.0	51.0	6.9	5.0	1.5	27.0	2.5
Renter or other	4.9	-	5.0	1.5	1.3	28.0	1.5

Note: (-) means sample is too small to make a reliable estimate.
Source: Federal Reserve Board, Family Finances in the U.S.: Recent Evidence from the Survey of Consumer Finances, *Federal Reserve Bulletin, January 1997*

Homeownership Down for Some in the 1990s

Although the overall homeownership rate rose from 64.8 to 65.4 percent between 1982 and 1996, only the oldest age group made gains.

Householders aged 30 to 34 saw the greatest decline in homeownership, with their rate falling from 57 to 53 percent between 1982 and 1996. Only householders aged 65 or older experienced a gain in homeownership, with their rate rising from 74 to 76 percent during those years.

One reason for the declining homeownership rate among young adults is the increase in nontraditional households, such as single-parent families. But even among young married couples, homeownership rates fell. Homeownership rates are rising for older Americans because a more affluent elderly population is replacing the less affluent elderly.

Although most age groups saw a decline in homeownership between 1982 and 1996, rates rose for some types of households. The greatest increase was for men who live alone, rising from 38 to 45 percent between 1982 and 1996. The greatest decline in homeownership was for male-headed families, with a 3.8 percentage point decline between 1982 and 1996.

♦ The proportion of American households owning a home is likely to reach a record high as the baby-boom generation ages.

Homeownership by Age of Householder, 1982 and 1996

(percent of householders who own their home by household type and age of householder, 1982 and 1996; percentage point change 1982-96)

	1996	1982	percentage point change, 1982-96
TOTAL HOUSEHOLDS	65.4%	64.8%	0.6
Under age 25	18.0	19.3	-1.3
Aged 25 to 29	34.7	38.6	-3.9
Aged 30 to 34	53.0	57.1	-4.1
Aged 35 to 44	66.3	70.0	-3.7
Aged 45 to 54	75.2	77.4	-2.2
Aged 55 to 64	79.3	80.0	-0.7
Aged 65 or older	76.3	74.4	1.9
FAMILY HOUSEHOLDS			
Married-couple families	80.2	78.5	1.7
Under age 25	29.8	32.6	-2.8
Aged 25 to 29	53.0	53.9	-0.9
Aged 30 to 34	68.2	71.9	-3.7
Aged 35 to 44	79.6	82.0	-2.4
Aged 45 to 54	87.5	87.4	0.1
Aged 55 to 64	90.3	89.5	0.8
Aged 65 or older	91.3	86.6	4.7
Female householder, no spouse present	46.1	47.1	-1.0
Under age 25	15.4	8.9	6.5
Aged 25 to 29	16.3	17.3	-1.0
Aged 30 to 34	28.9	31.3	-2.4
Aged 35 to 44	42.8	48.3	-5.5
Aged 45 to 54	60.2	61.7	-1.5
Aged 55 to 64	69.2	68.7	0.5
Aged 65 or older	81.1	75.1	6.0
Male householder, no spouse present	55.5	59.3	-3.8
Under age 25	29.6	21.6	8.0
Aged 25 to 29	35.6	34.7	0.9
Aged 30 to 34	43.3	50.9	-7.6
Aged 35 to 44	56.7	62.3	-5.6
Aged 45 to 54	66.2	72.2	-6.0
Aged 55 to 64	74.5	77.7	-3.2
Aged 65 or older	85.6	75.3	10.3

(continued)

(continued from previous page)

	1996	1982	percentage point change, 1982-96
NONFAMILY HOUSEHOLDS			
Single-person households	51.4%	45.6%	5.8
Female householder	56.0	51.2	4.8
Under age 25	8.3	7.5	0.8
Aged 25 to 29	15.0	14.3	0.7
Aged 30 to 34	29.9	24.7	5.2
Aged 35 to 44	40.4	37.0	3.4
Aged 45 to 54	55.5	49.1	6.4
Aged 55 to 64	63.8	62.4	1.4
Aged 65 or older	67.2	62.2	5.0
Male householder	44.9	38.0	6.9
Under age 25	12.1	13.9	-1.8
Aged 25 to 29	21.6	23.7	-2.1
Aged 30 to 34	35.5	31.7	3.8
Aged 35 to 44	43.3	37.6	5.7
Aged 45 to 54	48.6	39.5	9.1
Aged 55 to 64	55.1	49.1	6.0
Aged 65 or older	65.2	58.6	6.6
Two+ person households	35.7	30.1	5.6
Male householder	35.5	28.3	7.2
Under age 35	21.0	19.9	1.1
Aged 35 to 44	47.4	43.0	4.4
Aged 45 to 54	58.8	46.8	12.0
Aged 55 to 64	64.9	50.0	14.9
Aged 65 or older	70.6	61.1	9.5
Female householder	35.9	30.1	5.8
Less than 35 years	15.4	12.7	2.7
Aged 35 to 44	52.9	37.9	15.0
Aged 45 to 54	62.1	60.2	1.9
Aged 55 to 64	68.0	72.6	-4.6
Aged 65 or older	70.8	77.2	-6.4

Source: Bureau of the Census, Internet web site, http://www.census.gov; *calculations by New Strategist*

American Homes Are Well-Equipped

American homes are spacious, with a median of 1,725 square feet.

The average American home has 5.5 rooms. Half have more than one bathroom. The median size of American homes has been growing for decades, and today one in five homes is at least 2,000 square feet. Fewer than 10 percent of homes are smaller than 1,000 square feet.

Among single-family and mobile homes, more than half sit on lots of one-quarter acre or greater. Median lot size is .43 acres.

American homes are not only spacious but also well-appointed. Three out of four have a porch, deck, balcony, or patio. Over half have a garage or carport. About one in three has a useable fireplace, and another one-third have two or more living/recreation rooms.

♦ The average home is likely to become even more impressive in the decade ahead as earnings peak and boomers trade in their small, starter homes for larger models.

Housing Characteristics, 1993

(number and percent distribution of occupied housing units by selected characteristics, 1993; numbers in thousands)

	number	percent
Total occupied units	94,724	100.0%
Number of rooms		
3 or fewer rooms	9,559	10.1
4 rooms	17,221	18.2
5 rooms	21,030	22.2
6 rooms	19,870	21.0
7 rooms	13,083	13.8
8 rooms	7,683	8.1
9 rooms	3,738	3.9
10 or more rooms	2,541	2.7
Median number of rooms	5.5	-
Bathrooms		
No bathroom	526	0.6
1 bathroom	43,944	46.4
1.5 bathrooms	14,740	15.6
2 or more bathrooms	35,515	37.5
Square footage*		
Less than 500	697	0.7
500 to 749	2,381	2.5
750 to 999	5,704	6.0
1,000 to 1,499	15,084	15.9
1,500 to 1,999	13,414	14.2
2,000 to 2,499	9,653	10.2
2,500 to 2,999	5,374	5.7
3,000 to 3,999	4,799	5.1
4,000 or more	2,688	2.8
Median square feet	1,725	-

(continued)

(continued from previous page)

	number	percent
Lot size*		
Less than one-eighth acre	6,608	7.0
One-eighth to one-quarter acre	11,976	12.6
One-quarter to one-half acre	9,830	10.4
One-half to one acre	6,958	7.3
One to four acres	10,519	11.1
Five to nine acres	1,633	1.7
Ten or more acres	3,621	3.8
Median acreage	0.43	-
Amenities		
Porch, deck, balcony, or patio	73,181	77.3
Usable fireplace	30,254	31.9
Separate dining room	43,791	46.2
Two or more living/recreation room	30,555	32.3
Garage or carport	55,351	58.4

* For single detached and mobile homes only.
Source: Bureau of the Census, American Housing Survey for the United States in 1993, *Current Housing Reports, H150/93, 1995; calculations by New Strategist*

Forty-One Percent of Households Own Stock

The proportion of American households owning stock is rising.

In 1989, only 32 percent of American households owned stock either directly or indirectly through retirement accounts. This proportion rose to 37 percent in 1992 and to 41 percent in 1995 as the stock market lured more Americans with the promise of higher returns than traditional savings accounts.

Not surprisingly, stock ownership rises directly with income, peaking at 84 percent among households with incomes of $100,000 or more. In contrast, stock ownership falls with age after peaking at 49 percent among householders aged 45 to 54. Only 28 percent of householders aged 75 or older own stock.

Among households owning stock, the median value was $13,500 in 1995, up from $10,400 in 1989 (in 1995 dollars). Stock values peak among the oldest householders, at $28,100 in 1995.

Stocks now account for 40 percent of the financial assets of American households, up from 26 percent in 1989. This proportion is highest among the most affluent households (48 percent) and among householders aged 55 to 64 (45 percent).

◆ The public's enthusiasm for the stock market is revealed by these statistics. If stock values retreat significantly, American households could shift their financial assets into other types of investments.

Stock Ownership of Households, 1995

(percent of households owning stock, median value of stock holdings by owners, and stock holdings as a share of total household financial assets, by selected characteristics of households, 1995)

	percent owning stock	median value for owners (in thousands)	stock value as a share of financial assets
Total households	41.1%	$13.5	40.4%
Income			
Under $10,000	6.0	4.0	21.1
$10,000 to $24,999	25.3	5.0	21.6
$25,000 to $49,999	47.7	8.0	33.0
$50,000 to $99,999	66.7	21.3	39.9
$100,000 or more	83.9	90.8	47.6
Age of householder			
Under age 35	38.5	5.4	32.4
Aged 35 to 44	46.7	9.0	41.4
Aged 45 to 54	49.3	24.0	44.2
Aged 55 to 64	41.4	20.0	45.3
Aged 65 to 74	34.0	25.0	34.3
Aged 75 or older	28.1	28.1	39.5

Source: Federal Reserve Board, Family Finances in the U.S.: Recent Evidence from the Survey of Consumer Finances, *Federal Reserve Bulletin, January 1997*

Pension Plan Participation Strong

Over 60 percent of employees work for organizations that offer pension plans.

Among all civilian, nonagricultural workers, 40 percent are vested in a pension plan—meaning they eventually will receive at least some pension income. This proportion is relatively low because many workers are employed by organizations that do not offer pension coverage.

Among employees who work for organizations offering pension plans, fully 76 percent participate in a plan. Among the participants, 86 percent are vested in the plan.

Men and women are about equally likely to work for an organization that offers a pension plan, but men are more likely than women to participate in a plan. Among all workers, 50 percent of men and 44 percent of women participate in pension plans. Among workers whose organization offers a plan, 80 percent of men and 71 percent of women participate.

Between the ages of 21 and 64, most workers are employed by an organization that offers some sort of pension plan. Participation in such plans rises with age to a peak of 89 percent among workers aged 51 to 60.

◆ The public's concern about retirement savings could spur more employers to offer pension plans in the years ahead. But increasingly, those plans will be defined contribution (where employees must contribute their own money) rather than defined benefit (where the employer guarantees a retirement benefit).

Pension Plan Participation by Sex and Age, 1993

(total number of civilian, nonagricultural workers aged 16 or older; percent with employers who sponsor a pension plan, participation rates of total workers and those with plans, and vesting rates of total workers and those with plans, by sex and age, 1993; numbers in thousands)

	total workers	sponsorship rate	participation rate (total workers)	sponsored participation rate	vesting rate (total workers)	participant vesting rate
Total	105,815	62.1%	47.1%	75.9%	40.3%	85.8%
Men	55,582	62.3	50.0	80.2	42.8	85.6
Women	50,233	61.8	44.0	71.2	37.6	85.3
Aged 16 to 20	6,634	32.2	3.5	11.0	1.6	45.6
Aged 21 to 30	26,359	56.6	33.8	59.8	25.8	76.2
Aged 31 to 40	31,047	65.8	52.7	80.1	45.0	85.3
Aged 41 to 50	23,459	70.6	61.5	87.1	54.5	88.7
Aged 51 to 60	13,164	66.8	59.3	88.8	53.3	89.9
Aged 61 to 64	2,781	62.4	51.3	82.3	47.7	92.9
Aged 65 or older	2,371	46.1	29.0	63.0	26.6	91.6

Note: Sponsorship rate is the percent of total workers who work for an employer where a plan was sponsored for any of the employees. Participation rate is the percent of total workers who participate in a pension plan. Sponsored participation rate is the percent of employees working for an employer where a retirement plan was sponsored who participated in the plan. Vesting rate is the percent of all workers who are vested in a pension plan. Participant vesting rate is the percent of workers who participate in an employer-sponsored plan and are vested in a plan.

Source: Employee Benefit Research Institute, Baby Boomers in Retirement: What Are Their Prospects? *Special Report and Issue Brief Number 151, July 1994*

For More Information

The federal government is a rich source of accurate and reliable data about almost every aspect of American life. Below are phone numbers and web site addresses to help you in your research:

Web site addresses

Bureau of the Census .... http://www.census.gov
Bureau of Labor Statistics .... http://stats.bls.gov
National Center for Education Statistics .... http://ed.gov/NCES
National Center for Health Statistics .... http://www.cdc.govnchswww/nchshome.htm.
New Strategist Publications .... http://www.newstrategist.com

Contact phone numbers, by topic

Absences from work, Staff 202-606-6378
Aging population of the U.S., Staff 301-457-2378
Ancestry, Manuel de la Puente 301-457-2403
Apportionment, Stan Rolark 301-457-2381
Census: 1990 tabulations, Staff 301-457-2422
Census: 2000 plans, Arthur Cresce/John Stuart 301-457-3947/3949
Child care, Martin O'Connell/Lynne Casper 301-457-2417
Children, Staff 301-457-2465
Citizenship, Manuel de la Puente 301-457-2403
Commuting, means of transportation, & place of work,
Phil Salopek/Celia Boertlein 301-457-2454
Consumer Expenditure Survey, Ron Dopkowski 301-457-3914
Contingent workers, Sharn Cohany 202-606-6378
County populations, Staff 301-457-2422
Crime, Kathleen Creighton 301-457-3925
Current Population Survey, Staff 301-457-4100
Demographic surveys (general information), Staff 301-457-3811
Disability, Jack McNeil/Bob Bennefield 301-763-8300/8213
Discouraged workers, Harvey Hamel 202-606-6378
Displaced workers, Steve Hipple 202-606-6378
Education surveys, Steve Tourkin 301-457-3791
Educational attainment, Staff 301-457-2464
Emigration, Edward Fernandez 301-457-2103

Employment & unemployment, Staff 301-763-8576

Equal Employment Opportunity data, Staff 301-763-8576

Fertility, Amara Bachu 301-457-2449

Flex-time and shift work, staff 202-606-6378

Foreign born, Kristin Hansen/Carol Faber 301-457-2454

Group quarters population, Denis Smith 301-457-2378

Health statistics, Staff 301-436-8500

Health surveys, Adrienne Quasney 301-457-3879

Hispanic & ethnic statistics, Manuel de la Puente 301-457-2403

Home-based work, William Deming 202-606-6378

Homeless, Annetta Clark-Smith 301-457-2378

Households & families, Staff 301-457-2465

Housing

• American Housing Survey, Edward Montford 301-763-8551

• Housing affordability, Peter Fronczek/Howard Savage 301-763-8165

• Residential finance, Howard Savage 301-763-8165

• Vacancy data, Alan Friedman/Robert Callis 301-763-8165

Immigration, Staff 301-457-2422

Income & poverty statistics, Staff 301-763-8576

Job tenure, Jay Meisenheimer 202-606-6378

Journey to work, Phil Salopek/Gloria Swieczkowski 301-457-2454

Language, Staff 301-457-2464

Longitudinal surveys, Sarah Higgins 301-457-3801

Marital status & living arrangements, Arlene Saluter 301-457-2465

Metropolitan area population, Staff 301-457-2422

Migration, Kristin Hansen/Carol Faber 301-457-2454

Minimum wage data, Steven Haugen 202-606-6378

Minority workers, Staff 202-606-6378

Multiple jobholders, John Stinson 202-606-6373, x263

National estimates & projections, Staff 301-457-2422

Occupational & industrial statistics, Staff 301-457-8576

Occupational mobility, Lawrence Leith 202-606-6378

Older workers, Diane Herz 202-606-6378

Part-time workers, Staff 202-606-6378

Place of birth, Kristin Hansen/Carol Faber 301-457-2454

Population information, Staff 301-457-2422/2435

Prisoner surveys, Kathleen Creighton 301-457-3925

Puerto Rico, Staff 301-457-4041

Race statistics, Staff 301-457-2422

Reapportionment & redistricting, Marshall Turner, Jr. 301-457-4015

School district data, Jane Ingold 301-457-2408

School enrollment, Staff 301-457-2464

Special tabulations, Rose Cowan/Jane Ingold 301-457-2408

State populations & projections, Staff 301-457-2422

Survey of Income & Program Participation, Staff 301-457-8576

Undercount, demographic analysis, Gregg Robinson 301-457-2103

Union membership, Staff 202-606-6378

Urban/rural population, staff 301-457-2381

Veterans' status, Staff 301-457-8574

Voters, characteristics, Lynne Casper 301-457-2445

Voting age population, Staff 301-457-2422

Weekly earnings, Staff 202-606-6378

Women, Staff 301-457-2378

Women in the labor force, Howard Hayghe 202-606-6378

Work experience, Staff 202-606-6378

Working poor, Monica Castillo 202-606-6378

Youth, students, and dropouts, Staff 202-606-6378

Glossary

adjusted for inflation Income or a change in income that has been adjusted for the rise in the cost of living, or the consumer price index (CPI-U-XI). The CPI-U-XI adjustment factors are as follows:

year	index
1995	152.4
1994	148.2
1993	144.5
1992	140.3
1991	136.2
1990	130.7
1989	124.0
1988	118.3
1987	113.6
1986	109.6
1985	107.6
1984	103.9
1983	99.6
1982	95.6
1981	90.1
1980	82.3

To figure the inflation rate between two years, divide the index in the later year by the index in the earlier year. Multiply the result by the income of the earlier year. For example, to adjust 1990 income for inflation through 1995, divide 152.4 by 130.7 to arrive at the ratio 1.166. Multiply that figure by income in 1990 to arrive at 1990 income expressed in 1995 dollars.

Asian In this book, the term "Asian" includes both Asians and Pacific Islanders.

baby boom Americans born between 1946 and 1964.

baby bust Americans born between 1965 and 1976, also known as Generation X.

central cities The largest city in a metropolitan area is called the central city. The balance of the metropolitan area outside the central city is regarded as the "suburbs."

complete income reporters (on spending tables only) Survey respondents who told government interviewers how much money they received from major sources of income, such as wages and salaries, self-employment income, and Social Security income.

consumer unit (on spending tables only) For convenience, the term consumer unit and households are used interchangeably in the spending chapter of this book, although consumer units are somewhat different from the Census Bureau's households. Consumer units are all related members of a household, or financially independent members of a household. A household may include more than one consumer unit.

dual-earner couple A married couple in which both the householder and the householder's spouse are in the labor force.

employed All civilians who did any work as a paid employee or farmer/self-employed worker, or who worked 15 hours or more as an unpaid farm worker or in a family-owned business, during the reference period. All those who have jobs but who are temporarily absent from their jobs due to illness, bad weather, vacation, labor management dispute, or personal reasons are considered employed.

expenditure The transaction cost including excise and sales taxes of goods and services acquired during the survey period. The full cost of each purchase is recorded even though full payment may not have been made at the date of purchase. Average expenditure figures may be artifically low for infrequently purchased items such as cars because figures are calculated using all consumer units within a demographic segment rather than just purchasers. Expenditure estimates include money spent on gifts for others.

family A group of two or more people (one of whom is the householder) related by birth, marriage, or adoption and living in the same household.

family household A household maintained by a householder who lives with one or more people related to him or her by blood, marriage, or adoption.

female/male householder A woman or man who maintains a household without a spouse present. May head family or nonfamily households.

full-time, year-round Indicates 50 or more weeks of full-time employment during the previous calendar year.

geographic region The four major regions and nine census divisions of the United States are the state groupings as shown below:

Northeast:
—New England: Connecticut, Maine, Massachusetts, New Hampshire, Rhode Island, and Vermont
—Middle Atlantic: New Jersey, New York, and Pennsylvania

Midwest:
—East North Central: Illinois, Indiana, Michigan, Ohio, and Wisconsin
—West North Central: Iowa, Kansas, Minnesota, Missouri, Nebraska, North Dakota, and South Dakota

South:
—South Atlantic: Delaware, District of Columbia, Florida, Georgia, Maryland, North Carolina, South Carolina, Virginia, and West Virginia
—East South Central: Alabama, Kentucky, Mississippi, and Tennessee
—West South Central: Arkansas, Louisiana, Oklahoma, and Texas

West:
—Mountain: Arizona, Colorado, Idaho, Montana, Nevada, New Mexico, Utah, and Wyoming
—Pacific: Alaska, California, Hawaii, Oregon, and Washington

Generation X *See* baby bust.

Hispanic Persons or householders who identify their origin as Mexican, Puerto Rican, Central or South American, or some other Hispanic origin. Persons of Hispanic origin may be of any race. In other words, there are black Hispanics, white Hispanics, and Asian Hispanics.

household All the persons who occupy a housing unit. A household includes the related family members and all the unrelated persons, if any, such as lodgers, foster children, wards, or employees who share the housing unit. A person living alone is counted as a household. A group of unrelated people who share a housing unit as roommates or unmarried partners is also counted as a household. Households do not include group quarters such as college dormitories, prisons, or nursing homes.

household, race/ethnicity of Households are categorized according to the race or ethnicity of the householder only.

householder The householder is the person (or one of the persons) in whose name the housing unit is owned or rented or, if there is no such person, any adult member. With married couples, the householder may be either the husband or wife. The householder is the reference person for the household.

householder, age of The age of the householder is used to categorize households into age groups such as those used in this book. Married couples, for example, are classified according to the age of either the husband or wife, depending on which one identified him or herself as the householder.

income Money received in the preceding calendar year by each person aged 15 or older from each of the following sources: (1) earnings from longest job (or self-employment); (2) earnings from jobs other than longest job; (3) unemployment compensation; (4) workers' compensation; (5) Social Security; (6) Supplemental Security income; (7) public assistance; (8) veterans' payments; (9) survivor benefits; (10) disability benefits; (11) retirement pensions; (12) interest; (13) dividends; (14) rents and royalties or estates and trusts; (15) educational assistance; (16) alimony; (17) child support; (18) financial assistance from outside the household, and other periodic income. Income is reported in several ways in this book. Household income is the combined income of all household members. Income of persons is all income accruing to a person from all sources. Earnings is the amount of money a person receives from his or her job.

industry Refers to the industry in which a person worked longest in the preceding calendar year.

labor force The labor force tables in this book are for the civilian labor force, which includes both the employed and the unemployed.

labor force participation rate The percent of the civilian noninstitutional population that is in the civilian labor force, which includes both the employed and the unemployed.

married couples with or without children under age 18 Refers to married couples with or without children under age 18 living in the same household. Couples without children under age 18 may be parents of grown children who live elsewhere, or they could be childless couples.

median The median is the amount that divides the population or households into two equal portions: one below and one above the median. Medians can be calculated for income, age, and many other characteristics.

median income The amount that divides the income distribution into two equal groups, half having incomes above the median, half having incomes below the median. The medians for households or families are based on all households or families. The median for persons are based on all persons aged 15 or older with income.

metropolitan area An area qualifies for recognition as a metropolitan area if: (1) it includes a city of at least 50,000 population, or (2) it includes a Census Bureau-defined urbanized area of at least 50,000 with a total metropolitan population of at least 100,000 (75,000 in New England). In addition to the county containing the main city or urbanized area, a metropolitan area may include other counties having strong commuting ties to the central county.

net worth **The amount of money left after subtracting a household's liabilities from its assets.**

nonfamily household A household maintained by a householder who lives alone or with people to whom he or she is not related.

nonfamily householder A householder who lives alone or with nonrelatives.

non-Hispanic People who do not identify themselves as Hispanic. Non-Hispanics may be of any race.

nonmetropolitan area Counties that are not classified as metropolitan areas.

occupation Occupational classification is based on the kind of work a person did at his or her job during the previous calendar year. If a person changed jobs during the year, the data refer to the occupation of the job held the longest during that year.

outside central city The portion of a metropolitan county or counties that falls outside of the central city or cities; generally regarded as the suburbs.

part-time or full-time employment Part-time is less than 35 hours of work per week in a majority of the weeks worked during the year. Full-time is 35 or more hours of work per week during a majority of the weeks worked.

percent change The change (either positive or negative) in a measure that is expressed as a proportion of the starting measure. When median income changes from $20,000 to $25,000, for example, this is a 25 percent increase.

percentage point change The change (either positive or negative) in a value which is already expressed as a percentage. When a labor force participation rate changes from 70 percent of 75 percent, for example, this is a 5 percentage point increase.

poverty level The official income threshold below which families and persons are classified as living in poverty. The threshold rises each year with inflation and varies depending on family size and age of householder. In 1995, the poverty threshold for a family of four was $15,569.

proportion or share The value of a part expressed as a percentage of the whole. If there are 4 million people aged 25 and 3 million of them are white, then the white proportion is 75 percent.

race Race is self-reported and appears in four categories in this book: white, black, Native American, and Asian. A household is assigned the race of the householder.

rounding Percentages are rounded to the nearest tenth of a percent; therefore, the percentages in a distribution do not always add exactly to 100.0 percent. The totals, however, are always shown as 100.0. Moreover, individual figures are rounded to the nearest thousand without being adjusted to group totals, which are independently rounded; percentages are based on the unrounded numbers.

suburbs See outside central city.

tenure, housing A housing unit is "owner occupied" if the owner lives in the unit, even if it is mortgaged or not fully paid for. A cooperative or condominium unit is "owner occupied" only if the owner lives in it. All other occupied units are classified as "renter occupied."

tenure, job The number of years a person has been working for his or her current employer.

Index

School enrollment. *See* Education

Sex. *See also* Men and Women
  age
    living alone, 222-223
  crime, victims of, 293
  earnings, 142-144
    by education, 139-141
  education
    attainment, 4-6
    college enrollment, 23-24, 26-27, 31-32
    degrees conferred, 33-38
    high school dropouts, 15-16
    of husband by education of wife, 39-40
  employment status, 162-163
    by age, 154-155
    by Hispanic origin, 161
    by race, 159-160
    by school enrollment status, 189-190
    self-employed, 185-186
    with a work disability, 191-192
  foreign-born, 291
  health
    AIDS, 81
    cigarette smoking, 65-66
    home health or hospice care, 78-79
    homicides, 83-84
    hospital care, 76-77
    insurance coverage, 63
    life expectancy, 87-88
    physician visits, 74-75
    status, self-assessed, 51
    work disabilities, 72-73
  income
    by age, 128-133, 137-138
    by employment status, 137-138
    by race and Hispanic origin, 134-136
  labor force
    alternative work arrangements, 187-188
    job tenure, 168-169
    occupation, 170-175
    participation, 156-157
    projections, 193-194
    work disabilities, 72-73
    workers entering and leaving, 195-196
  living alone, 222-223
  pension coverage, 404
  population

  by age, 244-245
  projections
    labor force, 193-194

Single-parent families by age, 233-234. *See also* Households

Spending
  by age, 300-319
  by household type, 340-353
  by income, 320-339
  by race and Hispanic origin, 354-367
  by region, 368-380
  trends, 296-299

Sports and fitness participation, 60-62

States. *See* Geography

Stock ownership. *See* Wealth

Whites. *See also* Race and Hispanic origin
  income by age, 102-103
  projections of population, 255

Wealth
  assets
    financial, 385-388
    nonfinancial, 389-391
  net worth, 382-383
  stock ownership, 401-402

Women. *See also* Sex
  earnings, 142-144
    by education, 141
  income, 125, 130
    by age, 133
    by race and Hispanic origin, 136
  labor force participation, 164-167
  marital status
    by age, 239
  occupation, 176-178
    by industry, 174-175

Young adults. *See* Age